TREASURE CHEST OF WELLNESS

Heal Your Trauma, Own Your Recovery, and Change Your Life

Matthew Kowalski, CADC-II, ICADC

Copyright © 2021 by Matthew Kowalski

All rights reserved

Printed in the United States of America

First published as a paperback, 2021

Book design by Matthew Kowalski and Kathryn Sterbenc

Graphic design and formatting by Daria Lacy

Book editing by Kathryn Sterbenc

Cover image © 2013 Matthew Kowalski, CALM DECLARATION

airbrushed acrylics on paper, 23 x 35 inches

See more Kowalski artwork at **www.MatthewKowalskiArt.com**

ISBN 978-0-9848914-3-6

Radical Relief Publications, Lupton, Michigan

www.MatthewKowalski.com

This publication may not be reproduced, stored in a retrieval system, or transmitted in whole or in part, in any form or by any means, electronic, mechanical, photocopying, recording, or otherwise, without the prior written permission of Radical Relief Publications.

For information about permission to reproduce selections from this book, write to **Matt@MatthewKowalski.com**.

Almost every essay in this book was read aloud in recovery discussion groups to evoke self-change thoughts and recovery ideals. In particular, the clients in the recovery discussion groups I led for six years at Fremont Hospital in Fremont, Calif., provided priceless feedback through countless readings. For that reason, I extend my deepest gratitude to my clients in the Chemical Dependency-Intensive Outpatient Program. You will always be part of my "Treasure Chest of Wellness."

Contents

Introduction 1
Abundance, Thriving and Success 10
Abuse: to Give and to Receive 14
Acceptance 18
Advocating and Demonstrating for Life, and Getting Consistent Results 21
Aggression 24
Ambivalence and Discernment 27
Anger Management 30
Assertiveness 36
Attachment 41
Attention Deficit Disorder /Attention Deficit Hyperactivity Disorder 45
Biological Vulnerability 51
Bipolar Disorder/Manic Depression 54
Body Image 57
Bookending 61
Boundaries and How to Set Them 64
Brain Chemistry, Neural Elasticity, and Chemical Cascades 69
Burnout 72
Closure with Unfinished Business 75
Conflict Resolution 79
Consequences 83
Control Issues 85
Co-Occurring Disorders and Triple Diagnoses 88
Coping Mechanisms 92
Critical Eye – Criticism 96
Cultural Sensitivity, Diversity, Inclusivity and Competency 100
Curiosity 106
Death and Dying 108
Discovery 112
Ego 115

Emotional Enmeshment 118
Enabling and Codependency 121
Family Psycho-Education 124
Family Reunification 128
Fatal Peril and Fight-or-Flight Syndrome 132
Generational Dysfunction 135
Grace and Surrender 139
Gratitude: It's an Attitude. 142
Grief and Loss 146
Habitual Reactive Response 150
Happiness and the Pursuit 154
Harm Reduction. 156
Healing with Humor 159
Healthy Relationships 162
Homelessness. 166
Internalized Oppression 169
Intimacy. 173
Jealousy 176
Jobs and Employment 180
Judgment – Yourself and Others 183
Keeping an Open Mind 187
Medications: Compliance, Side Effects, and Traversing the System 193
Mental-Health System: Navigating the Quagmire. 199
Mindfulness: An Awakened Mind Can Access Emotional Intelligence 202
Neutrality: Staying in the Middle 206
Objectifying Others and Being Objectified 208
Oppressor and Perpetrator: Healing from Causing Harm to Others 212
Original Diagnosis. 215
Overwhelming Debt and Spiritual Ecology. 217
Person-Oriented Recovery: Client-Centered Approach. 224
Personalizing and Internalizing 227
Pleasure and Information-Gathering 231
Posifying Your Resistance 234
Positive Affirmations and Gratitude Lists 239

- Post-Traumatic Stress Disorder (PTSD) 242
- 13 Steps for Managing Flashbacks 247
- Powerlessness and Unmanageability 249
- Rage Disorders – Intermittent Explosive Outbursts 253
- Relapse 256
- Relaxing 261
- Resilience 264
- Sanity 268
- Secrets and Self-Disclosure 271
- Self-Care 275
- Self-Empowerment 281
- Self-Esteem and Negative Self-Evaluation 286
- Self-Monitoring and Self-Regulation 290
- Service to Ourselves and Our Community 293
- Shame 297
- Situational Awareness 300
- Social and Sexual Anorexia 304
- The Spiritual Moment Is Now 309
- Stress – Negative and Positive 313
- Survival Strategies 318
- Survivor Guilt 321
- Thrill-Seeking Behaviors 325
- Transferrable Skill Sets 328
- Trust 332
- Turn-Around Thinking 335
- Victims and Survivors 338
- Warning Signs 343
- Wholesome Discipline 346
- Epilogue 348
- Acknowledgements 349

About the Author

Matthew Kowalski is a recovery coach, certified addiction counselor, Chemical Dependency – Intensive Outpatient Program leader, and motivational speaker who has worked with recovering addicts in both clinical and Twelve-Step settings since 1999. Matt has led thousands of recovery discussion groups during more than 20 years in clinical and recovery settings.

He also is an abstract artist who creates multi-media works in his own Radical Relief style. A professional multi-instrument musician, Matt played drums and guitar and sang with dozens of bands in San Francisco in the 1980s. He continues to play music and make art wherever he goes. He and his wife, Kathryn Sterbenc, reside in Northern Michigan, where they actively participate in building a healthier community. They work with people daily on having the difficult conversations needed to create a valued world, where we all have a voice and a choice.

Introduction

So you're new to recovery. Or you need a kick in the pants – or a reminder of how it works.

You can work to regain sanity and the peace you experienced in the past (if you had any). But for most of us, recovery means learning new and healthy behaviors for the first time in our lives.

With this book in your hands, you can begin right here and right now – or pick up where you left off.

Now is the only moment we have on the planet to attain enlightenment, health, well-being, or whatever language you use to describe that state of mind and soul. No matter where you came from, rich or poor, no matter how much you lost, this book is the perfect place for you to begin again.

As a sentient being, you inherently have more than enough to start recovery. In this book, we will cultivate aspirations and intentions with a pleasure- and information-gathering mindset. You might believe, "I have more pain than others, and I am too damaged to be helped." And yet here you are, courageously giving life a shot. Well done.

The journey of a lifetime begins with one step, and you have already taken it. Think of it this way: I am writing, and you are reading. We are doing the same thing at different times. If I have the courage to write and you have the courage to read, we are in motion.

Tragic things happen. Unfair situations in our lives make us feel unsafe and angry. Depression is real. In this book, you will discover that it does not matter what happened to you or what the storyline of your life is. What happened to you was not personal; the same things happen to thousands of us daily. Others are suffering just as you are right now. If we can learn that we share a common experience, then we can develop empathy and compassion for ourselves and others. Painful things happen, but our vessel of suffering can be developed into a valuable tool. You are not alone. Within you already lies all the answers and wisdom you need to succeed. You already know how to do many things similar to accomplishing recovery. Using this book as a tool, we will take those transferrable skill sets and use them for your healing.

Think of the recovery process as learning to ride a bike. Balance is developed by falling, over and over again. It teaches you to look ahead of where you are going and plan your journey. Progressing from a bicycle to a vehicle, you learn to drive safely and trust your skills. After a while, you will be able to drive in dangerous places with safety and make healthy choices. When you fall, you will know how to get back up and try again.

Now, let's get back on the bike!

Read on to learn how to move forward and choose the areas you want to work on. I always encourage research with an open mind. There are as many ways to recover as there are people recovering. This is your program; your only quest is to do no harm to yourself or others as you recover.

We will follow the rule of physics recovery: $E=mc^2$. You have to exert energy to get your brain to function with elasticity, firing and connecting.

Bear with me as I do a quick overview about how your brain can recover. New neurons are formed in everyone – elderly people, people with developmental disabilities, people whose development was arrested by environment or drugs. Basically, there is hope for most everyone.

Physical activity of any kind is needed to kick-start your muscles and release your own brain chemistry. It's a proven fact that running triggers a release of dopamine and serotonin — feel-good chemicals in your brain. Try gentle running, weightlifting, sex, housecleaning – do one thing or a combination to exercise for one hour, five days per week. Brain recovery begins with your muscles and progresses through creating a memory of the pleasure of working out. If you keep it up, your body wants more. Your muscles enjoy being used. Develop your muscle memory, and get your brain firing. You will get neuron production.

When you pursue the renewed growth and development of nerve tissue, your brain needs a workout. In this book, we will begin with simple learning tasks and work toward more complex ideas.

Your brain is in control of what it learns after your childhood years. It adapts to sustain itself and survive its environment. We learn to cater our learning and skills to match our environment. As Neuropsychologist Donald Hebb said, "Neurons that fire together wire together."

While learning new skills, the more ways you can get awareness, the more ways your body will release brain food — or chemical synapses. The following is a plan I devised, based on nearly 30 years of doing life wrong. Like Edison, I learned from making a million mistakes.

First, we will go over the concepts of learning to learn. If you learn to write a song properly, you can write many songs. Give a man a fish and he can eat once, but if you teach him to fish, he will eat for a lifetime.

Helping another suffering being is also a way to reinforce your own learning. A helps B in recovery, and A gets better simply from the effort.

Humans live in an unpredictable, hectic world. The teacher of life always shows up for us; we have no need to travel far to learn what we need in order to work on and improve our station in this life.

Bad choices are a poverty of the mind. Let's work on making better choices. You already have all the answers within you. I will be your sherpa, supporting and guiding you to the top of your Mount Everest, while you solve your own problems and engage in your opportunities for a lifetime of learning.

All of this is messy and complicated. Let's get our hands dirty and gather the supplies you have right now to begin your trek to recovery.

The Five Concepts

Despite its unassuming weight in your hands, this book provides you with almost 100 tools for your recovery toolkit. It doesn't matter what your issues are. It matters only that you walk into this opportunity with a beginner's mind.

You may wonder how you can stay open, flexible, teachable, honest and willing, while all your character defects and muscle memories are being triggered. How can you detach with love and not personalize your experience? How can you develop compassion and empathy for others and realize that troubles are not personal – that they happen to everyone all the time?

This is living life on life's terms. Sometimes others seem to be more skillful and have more dexterity at processing life. That's OK.

In this fast-paced world where we often feel we are under the gun and driven to a workaholic state of mind, how can we be mindful and change everything we think, say and do – all of our thoughts, words and deeds? How can we surrender a lifetime's experience of conditioned responses? Our gut says, "No! I can't do this," but we actually can move beyond our superficial pain body and our fear- and shame-based existence and into healthier choices.

As a person with a thousand thoughts moving a million miles per hour in my busy brain, I start with my breath. This precious moment for me consists of counting breaths. One, breathe in. Two, breathe out. Over and over, I slow my thoughts. I think of thoughts as clouds, impermanent and moving.

As I relax my breathing and stay in touch with my thoughts, they slow down. If I let my thoughts go by like clouds in the sky, they begin to break up, and I find that I have clear skies.

Another analogy of our lives can be likened to a jar of water with mud at the bottom. During the course of any day, the water of our lives gets shaken up and muddied. Our emotions get mixed up, and our thoughts become cloudy. We cannot perceive our peripheral distortions accurately.

My last metaphor here is that we are like rough, unpolished mirrors. This recovery work makes us shine and see ourselves and the reflection of the world more clearly.

Each time we begin our study, let's start with our breathing and then engage in one of the exercises of opportunity herein. The opportunity for mindfulness will enable us to choose to do all things in a different manner and create safety for ourselves and others around us.

I have about a three-minute attention span before my mind strays. As a person with Attention Deficit Hyperactivity Disorder, I must introduce any new skill I want to learn via as many senses as I can. I invite you to do this as we learn together. When we integrate knowledge through our eyes, ears, mouths, hands and brains while practicing, we internalize new information. This way, it passes through six or seven channels of our interpreting brains. We have invested emotionally and become like Velcro for new thoughts, looking for ways to use, share, implement and practice. Shift happens with this new recovery mission statement: "Life abhors a vacuum." Once you finally let go of all the reasons you can't change or heal, you start to welcome how you can learn and change what seemed impossible yesterday.

Whenever I am introduced to a new concept, I am inspired and think I really have it. Then I get distracted, and most of the training seems to evaporate right before my eyes. Life happens and I get busy again, and any hope of permanence slips away.

So for me, it is important to use the following methods to permanently capture and hold healthy, new concepts in my brain. I practice these over and over. With practice, one by one, day by day, month by month, you also will create a gallery of intentions to live your life differently.

Are you sick and tired of being sick and tired? Do you feel insane doing the same things over and over and expecting different results? Are you a moth to a flame, trying to receive comfort from the source of your pain? Well-worn clichés – do you want to use them or come up with something original? Keep a sense of urgency so you do not give up quickly and stomp on your seedlings of change, while simultaneously stammering, "This stuff doesn't work."

It does work. Don't give up before your miracle. Remember, neurons that fire together wire together, so let's get as many of our senses firing to as many parts of our brains as we can.

Let's begin. The following concepts do not need to be done in any particular order. They all enter your brain via one sense, then integrate with other senses, which gives you a real chance at cognizance and lasting imprints. Through inquiry, we get to closely investigate new thoughts as we practice knowledge and awareness of these new concepts.

Concept 1: Listen

They say it is the journey, not the destination, that is so important. As we pass through life, people, places and things bring discoveries and revelations about our destination. The universe is calling to us. Are we listening?

Most of our listening is about hearing what we think others should say. Mostly we want to hear about the fastest way to satisfy and be accepted for our immediate and convenient wants and needs. However, that seldom happens. The result is a lot of suffering on the planet. This creates an atmosphere of unheard people with unmet needs, unwilling to let go of bias and judgment when they hear another's needs or truth.

It is time to let go of our selective listening and remain neutral and groundless as we, maybe for the first time in our lives, listen without agenda.

To begin, listen to another's idea. The new idea will go in one area of cognition and fire the neural receptors to capture whatever you can retain. Don't judge the speaker or the source; respond to the speaker's message, not his personality.

Show interest in the topic. There's nothing worse than someone who groans or rolls her eyes while a speaker imparts new information. Wait until the speaker is finished before sharing any information you have. It's impolite and unskillful to think of what to say as a rebuttal before someone is done speaking. That's not listening; that's creating an argument.

Write questions down as you think of them, and use keywords. Ask for explanations of words you don't know. Stop and point out where you lost the message, or ask to have it explained again. Listen without adding your own ideas. Be open-minded to different cultures, genders, ages and other diversities.

The way we present ourselves is congruent with our environment. If there is a topic that escalates you or others emotionally, limit the talk to short amounts of time so you are not triggered or overstimulated. Be an empathetic listener, and help make the speaker feel safe and comfortable. Know that it is hard to impart information to a new crowd. Use your body language when listening – nodding, posture, facial expressions and open body movements.

There are no stupid questions; all are welcome. Through active listening, we can solve our own problems and remind others that they have all the answers within them. We open the doors to working together and collaborating as a team, with everyone's participation of equal value.

If you listen to people and let them say crazy things, it might be the first time they heard the craziness out loud, too. Let them know their feelings are acceptable and safe and that you have a few emotions that are crazy, too.

To move into self-change talk, we must be honest about what we really think with peers who will not judge us. Shift happens in this open environment, without defensive gesturing on anyone's part. Know what you're listening to and why you're listening. Relate the topic to your own life. This is where your brain really kicks in and gives you the attention you need to retain the subject and information. If your mind is open and willing, you can hold the space for thoughts and access a concept called "evoking self-change talk."

We must resist the urge to get onto the hamster wheel of "Huh-uh," "Why bother?" "Who cares?" "Miss me with that," and "Forget it." Your willingness for active listening opens a world of omniscience, or "seeing all views" of a situation. When you can listen to everyone's view, you have a choice of what to do with your precious life. You also can hold space for another's truth. If you believe that what you think is true, you also must know that *others* believe what *they* think is true.

Just for a minute, how can we hold both truths and not judge? No longer do you have to react to life. You can breathe slowly, and mindfully respond to your situation. You don't need to respond to your empirical learning with defensiveness.

With continued practice, you will develop just enough space between your thoughts and your reactions. This space is what we will try to stretch longer and longer, so you do not have to be held hostage by your reactions and then pay the consequences long after the incident is over.

This is where learning and peace of mind begin – with an open mind. If you begin listening with a positive attitude, you will probably end up with one. Give it a try.

Concept 2: Write

Write down what you hear.

This feeds new information into another cognitive part of the learning brain. My practice is to write down what everyone says that rings a bell for me. I even write down what I do not believe, just so I can see the difference with my own belief. As I write, I ask myself, "Why do I believe this? How does this polarize my thinking? What would I lose in stature, relations, jobs or family life if I let these debilitating thoughts go and lived with a new freedom? Do I have the courage to do this?"

Sometimes when you get the juices flowing, you can write down all the thoughts you are afraid to show others. "Oh, don't read that!" "That's personal!" "Oh my God, how dare you?" We are sometimes afraid of our own inner thoughts, so they stay inside our brains, which are a "closed system." Everything is safe inside our well-accessorized lanes. We do not want to rock the emotional boat. Write down positive and negative thoughts, and draw a line between them. Write down the pros and cons of these beliefs. Above all, don't believe everything you think.

When you write down your thoughts, you likely will see the ways you repeat your resentments. You might see that you are scared, racist, sexist, or unable to look at other truths because it will pop your "look-good bubble" view of the world. Suspend your belief system for a moment, and step into what you fear most: real freedom, real courage, limitless thinking and fearlessness.

It is helpful to share your written thoughts with an accountability partner and bookend weekly. Doing so will increase the likelihood of achieving your goals by 70 percent, if you work with a group of peers for, say, three months. Even if it were only a 50-percent success rate, isn't that good enough?

What will it take for you to write life contracts you will stick to? Write it down, and believe your words. You make a list when you shop for food and holiday gifts, so you don't look in every aisle and mission-creep away from why you were there in the first place. Write down what you want to learn and what you want to get out of something. Why are you doing this task? Write it down!

Concept 3: See

In the following paragraphs, you will find myriad questions designed to make you think about the way you use your eyes to see life, yourself and other people. These questions are concepts designed to be food for your brain and a catalyst for recovery and change.

How can you process what you see without the interference and disruption of your life? How can you see with new vision? How can you turn on the mechanism of faith with what you see and not bring the past into the present moment? How can you let go of your empirical visions and see through the eyes of a child with new, fresh insight, coupled with hope and compassion for others and yourself? How can you see things as they really are without adding your tractor-trailer load of baggage from your past? How can you work with your critical eye, which is connected to your ego?

Your eyes view what "you" see as truth. Your "reptile brain" processes and reacts in one thousandth of a second. It is responsible for protection. Our primal urge for safety and security is focused on "eat, work, sleep, procreate."

How can you safely let go of old thoughts? How can you use more of your brain and not simply react to life in protection mode, when that safety mechanism has gone awry? It no longer works with your new way of thinking. It is said that the eyes are the windows of the soul. Indeed they are. How can you choose to see things with a new pair of glasses and not the old, hacked-up, bandaged lenses of judgment, disbelief, lust, comparison, safety-seeking, victimhood, desperation and neediness?

Why do your eyes want things they cannot have? As a brand-driven society, we are collectively drawn by advertisements to shiny, new cars; a house that is too expensive; food that tastes so good but is not healthy; and air-brushed beauty that is held as a standard but never able to be reached. Most things are difficult, if not impossible, to obtain for the vast majority and often produce longings that manifest in frustration, self-deprecation and mistrust of the haves and have-nots.

Why are your eyes tricked into disbelief about your station in life? Why do you see others who seemingly have it all together? Why is your eye telling you the grass is greener over there? When did that "eye-sloth" mentality arrive in your life? Why can't you just see the beauty in everything as it is? Why is your view of the world tinted by fear when you walk down the street and see a person you assume is going to harm you — even if he is a child — because he looks different than you?

Do you know we have all been taught to see things a certain way from birth? How can we train our eyes to look at what is and accept life on life's terms? Acceptance is the answer to all our questions.

The anxiety you feel is the distance that separates you from your higher self and keeps you from relating to others in a genuine, honest fashion. Let's really take a look at this. As you see new material, no matter the source, encourage your brain to attract the goodness, not focus only on the bad. Don't let the troublesome things you see outshine the sun. There is a beautiful sky full of clear choices and just one dark cloud. Do not give that somber cloud all of your power.

Concept 4: Speak

Say aloud what you have heard, written and seen. By speaking, you internalize in yet another part of your brain. When you speak, you take the vulnerable chance or vulgar intention of exposing your thoughts where others will hear them. What motivates your intentions for others to hear you? How might that compromise another person's truth and integrity? Do you speak only to be right or oppose another? Are you impeccable with your words and intentions? Are you responding only from fear-based thinking? Are you trying to be a people-pleaser, so you do not have to risk being authentic?

We all learn through the process of making mistakes with our newly discovered ideas and intentions. Be sure you are not making each new concept a "Flavor of the Month" idea and then moving onto the next artificial sweetener. Create equity with others by baring your vulnerability and speaking your truth.

Learning new concepts can be similar to going to prison and learning new skills for devious intentions – using newfound knowledge to overpower others. You must be careful and realize there is a learning curve. You will make many mistakes before you master skills. You may not be of help to anyone when you begin the process. But it is imperative to let yourself make mistakes. Move beyond the superficial way you usually stay safe and "talk about the weather," which, by the way, is not holding a real conversation.

The world will change when you can speak your truths to others. Speaking is where the vehicle of transformation hits the asphalt of life, and you put into practice what you have learned. Can you maneuver in difficult conversations? Can you "drive in bad weather" — i.e., an emotionally charged topic? In the future, your truth will be tested by the way you communicate your beliefs.

Concept 5: Practice

Similar to Edison, I practice what I learn and make mistakes, like he did while getting his first light bulb to burn brightly. After a thousand tries, he finally got it right.

We, on the other hand, are learning concepts new to us that have been around for thousands of years. In fact, we are simply re-inventing the spiritual mythology of our lives. When sharing and imparting our newfound truths, we must be able to hear what others think. They may respond the same way we used to respond. We must have compassion when they are where we used to be. We must let that be OK.

There is wisdom, and then there is intelligence. There is a saying I've heard: "Inspiration comes and goes, but living your life as an aspiration lasts a lifetime." This kind of wisdom gives us that one nanosecond of calm disposition to respond in any situation, instead of thoughtlessly reacting and then regretting our response with years of resentment and angry thoughts. This new wisdom also helps us understand that we have changed, but not everyone and everything around us will or wants to change. We also understand that change is inevitable, whether we like it or not.

Sometimes it's lonely where we are going, so we need community and a coalition of like minds. We are not doing the work on ourselves for an instant reward. We know the result might not come to fruition for many years, but at least we will start the work here. Think of how Jesus, Buddha or Muhammad felt when they attained their timeless truths. Look at the world right now. It might seem that nothing has changed, but it's how you look at it.

As we explore each pertinent behavior, we must remember the backstory of "scraping a house to repaint it." We are removing old layers and adding new layers that will improve our stations in life.

We all have overflowing cups of abundance. Is it good abundance or bad abundance? Either way, we are either healthy or full of suffering. In this process of learning, we must let go and empty our dis-eased cup, so we can fill up with the good stuff.

How do we move beyond our polarized existence and into a life brimming with curiosity and discovery? Attaining new elasticity in our brain's neural pathways creates an opportunity for faith. Faith is belief in the unknown or in things unseen – whatever it is that we cannot see or that we refuse to believe right now. We must suspend our belief system and be completely open to change. How can we surrender everything we think, say and do? What do we do with all our thoughts, words and deeds in our dualistic world of right or wrong, good or bad?

The answer is that we surrender. Surrender does not mean that we lose face or are proven wrong. It means simply that we are willing look at something differently. It means we want to either join the other side or at least be willing to have a dialogue about a new concept. With an open mind, we are willing to be flexible, open, teachable and curious. For us, surrender really means joining, partnering, collaborating and creating safe equity with the thoughts of others on the same journey we are.

Here we are, with an open mind full of curiosity. We have a plan to dispose of wasteful thoughts, and we have a plan for holding firmly onto new concepts we want to explore.

At this point, we are holding onto our old belief system that has worked so far. We are considering new concepts that may change our life experience. We are also holding the conflicting truths of ambivalence and discernment in the paradox of our times. Let's begin.

Your recovery toolkit can be filled and emptied as needed in the course of your life. As you read through the chapter titles in this book and get a brief idea of what I have learned, you have the option to say, "If it does not apply, let it fly." In other words, take what you like and leave the rest.

You are on a journey of a lifetime. I hope that you will learn enough to be graceful in accepting life on life's terms. You are the proud owner of a clean slate and an unblemished, spotless future. Bring everything you need to this party of life, so you will always be happy and in acceptance. Others may enjoy the space you have cleansed around you, and they will join you in this safe place to thrive. But remember, you can change only yourself.

Each of these tools can give you a lifetime of work on your particular issues. Take your time and slowly process them with your spiritual community, neighbors, support groups or colleagues. When learning anything new during recovery, you get to feel the learning curve, and you need supervision to properly digest your new thoughts. You will be amazed that you have so many thoughts on a subject or, on the other hand, that you have so few. Keep at it, and you will learn that perseverance and persistence are keys to your success.

Choose issues and tools accessible to you within your capabilities and timeframe. Clear your energy, and develop your attention span as you go. Be gentle with your mental space. You were interested emotionally to do this work, and you have set aside space and time for it. Now you want to experience how it makes you feel.

Lastly, practice, practice, practice what you have absorbed in dealing with your own resistance to learning. Remember to cultivate empathy for those you practice with. Develop a habit of paying attention to what you want to learn or improve upon. Interest drives emotion. Emotion drives inspiration. And learning is driven by keeping a sense of urgency about your intentions.

It is only by applying ideals and thoughts to your life that you will ever benefit. So get out there, make some mistakes with family and friends — and learn. Be the change you want to see! It all starts with you.

Abundance, Thriving and Success

For many years, I have worked on the ideals and lessons laid out in this book. It is appropriate that the most significant concept I learned is the one that comes first. Yet, it was one of the last ideas to sink into my brain.

That idea that took me so long to learn is the knowledge and belief that I deserve; I belong; I get to participate in an abundant life. For me, these are the last positive-stress models I get to embrace completely for a full and fruitful life.

This is where the pedal hits the metal. This is where we push our disbelief out of the way and accept that abundance means abundance. It doesn't mean sometimes. It doesn't mean for someone else. It doesn't mean that we can't access it. Abundance for everyone is one of the immutable laws of the universe.

My entire life was built upon the dualistic model of good/bad, win/lose, right/wrong, compare/despair, and compete/defeat. I always experienced immediate gratification and bliss that faded after only a few moments. Someone else won or got the job or the partner or the house or the car. I lived in constant fear of losing my immediate gratification and the convenience of having status and possessions.

A society built upon the principle that only one person or group must win means the rest of us must lose. The integrity of the organism is tossed into a no-win, fear-based paradigm. When most are made to feel bad, look bad, not have, hate the other and hate ourselves, we all lose.

It is unsustainable to spend our entire lives trying to reach an unreachable goal and be always on the hunt for more possessions and accolades. With that mindset, we can never be happy now, with the abundance of this moment. This moment right here, right now, is filled with the abundance that we have to give and share with each other.

There is an unstoppable flow of indwelling goodness in each of us with no upper limit, such as smiles and kind gestures toward each other. Our ability to have gratitude for all of our life — good and bad — creates an unstoppable flow. Only then, when we shift our focus from misery to our own abundance, do we realize that others are suffering.

What is hard-wired in us to grasp at things with a desperate neediness? We are like the monkey who shoves his hand through a small opening in the top of a candy jar, grabs all he can in his little fist, but won't let go to get his hand unstuck. Why do we show up at our "party of life" without everything we need to be happy?

This moment right here, right now, is the only chance for happiness that we have on the planet. The past is gone, and the future is never certain. How do we come to a complete acceptance that bad things will happen sometimes, and they will make us feel uncomfortable? In what ways can we turn poison into medicine? How do we become real metaphysical alchemists of our times?

First of all, we can't believe everything we think.

We become slaves through constant subliminal advertising. We become obsessed with feelings of entitlement and wanting the privilege of having things. *I must have that car, partner, smartphone, etc.*

The power of abundance is that even when we suffer, we can still come to terms with our lives just as they are and with their pain and suffering. We still can choose to do the next right thing. That choice requires us to go beyond our counter-intuitive, gotta-wanna-getta-coulda-shoulda-woulda attitude and "not-enough" injuries to ourselves. Abundance is accepting the richness of our lives as real, tried, proven and thrilling. Not having something we want or losing the game is part of the other side of abundance. It is positive stress in healthy proportions that helps us to appreciate and respect the gratitude we feel for the rest of our existence.

We must learn to roll with our natural, in-bred resistance toward things we feel bring us suffering.

This endless ebb and flow of resilience, ability, gratitude, acceptance and the way we joyfully exert our life force creates the "safety" of our state of mind. Fleeting pleasures, the chasing game, the thrill of the hunt, and new possessions do not bring peace. If everyone chose to be happy right here and right now, to accept things straight up as they are and become happy in this moment, we would find that this attitude is the only real lasting abundance. Instead, we get our wires crossed and things get messed up when we react with expectation or entitlement to life on life's terms.

Our quest is making just enough space between reacting to life and choosing to respond to what happens. Acceptance is the answer to successfully handling our problems. Anxiety creates distance between us and our higher selves.

In what ways can we develop the kind of faith that believes there is enough? How can we develop our flabby, skinny, rarely used muscles of spiritual origin to believe in the unseen? To believe in the unknown? If we don't use those muscles, we lose them.

Remember that we know our abundance by what we do to help others who suffer more than us. The more grateful we become with what we have and the more we develop our ability to be satisfied here and now – that is the mark of our commitment to an abundant life. When we cleanse the air around us, we can see the lack in our society: always wanting more, never satisfied. To feel goodness, we must do good acts. To feel estimable, we must do estimable acts. Coming from abundance, we generate an unstoppable flow of passion for our work, family, art, spiritual and other communities, and government. We *are* the abundance, and we are the agents of change.

But, as I learned, I am the one person who must do the work to get results. I can't rely on others for my own abundance. If we do not make plans for our abundance, we default to the plans of others. This is the point where unhappiness begins.

We must be the change we want in our lives. In the end, the energy we give out is the energy fed back to us. We get to choose whether to regenerate the perpetual-motion abundance machine or bring it to a halt.

And what if something bad happens?

We cannot appreciate the good things in our lives without rough moments. When we accept, just for today, that pain and suffering are our abundance teachers, we will realize this is a timed event. The sooner we have parity with our pain, the sooner we will come into acceptance. When we try to move away from grief and loss, death and dying, we create an unwillingness to learn from pain and suffering. Yet when we move into discomfort and become skillful at the opportunity to have a balanced life, our new world will emerge. Our compassion and empathy will have multiplied, and our spiritual muscles will skillfully respond to life, not blindly react.

Think about abundance with this frame of mind: The U.S. comprises about 4 percent of the world population, but we use roughly 24 percent of all the resources and energy on the planet. If we do not change our mindset of continually being unsatisfied with what we have, we will never be happy, because everything will be depleted. What if all of the people in China or India wanted all the abundance we have on a personal level? Look at climate change now, and think about how our planet will sustain itself in that new acceptance of life on life's terms.

Let's be grateful for winning the lottery of life on this planet and be more reasonable about how to help others achieve a sustainable abundance.

Workbook Questions:

1. In what ways do you have gratitude for the good, healthy things that happen in your life?

2. What has negative emoting and stinking thinking given you in abundance? Does it stop you from accessing things readily available to you?

3. Why do you sometimes feel desperate and needy? Do you feel that abundance is for others, and you rarely have it in your life? With this "poverty of the mind" thinking, in what ways do you reinforce the idea that you will not have this goodness coming to you?

4. How do you process positive stress from receiving graceful and good things? Do you think the other boot will drop, and it will be taken away? Do you think it is a fleeting quality that comes and goes, and when you miss it, you are deemed unlucky or a loser?

5. In what ways do you feel like you have sinned or are otherwise unworthy to enjoy abundance?

6. If you could make a wish list of all the things you want to happen in your life, what would be on that list? Make a list of 10 things that would help you feel abundant.

7. Do you associate pain and suffering with joy and abundance? Why do you think this way?

8. What could you do to access abundance? Is it hard work? Is it spiritual work? Is it just relaxing and enjoying every precious breath? Is this real and lasting abundance? Why or why not?

9. Are you afraid if you give your energy to others, you will have less abundance in the end?

10. When others have wonderful things seemingly happening all the time, do you feel envious? Do you feel their abundance is your abundance? If not, why is their abundance separate from yours?

11. Do you feel other cultures do not deserve abundance? Other religions? Other countries? Explore this question.

12. How does the rest of the world live well and find happiness with one-10th of the resources Americans consume to be "happy"? Is there some entitlement and privilege that makes you think you are better and deserve the other six-10ths of the world's resources and wealth?

Abuse: to Give and to Receive

As a society of caring and responsible people, it is our duty to speak up when we see signs of abuse in anyone.

We may even save an abused person's life; cause them to develop survival mechanisms toward change, or even get the perpetrator help so he/she does not go to prison and destroy everything for everyone. Abuse in some form happens to each of us. It is most hidden with children; partners; elders, and persons with mental illness.

I'll draw on my personal experience. I could write a book solely about my experiences with abuse. So many people are caught up in polarized views about what abuse is and isn't. There are as many explanations about it as there are people who endure it.

A word of advice: When talking about any subject, please scrape the paint off your own house first. Let the old thoughts about what you experienced fall away. Know also that with patience and new knowledge, you develop your own awareness. You will devise your own plans for safety and boundaries, along with a support community.

Abuse is a learned trait that is taught and sometimes passed from generation to generation. For example, slavery is a toxic form of abuse and a mechanism of controlling someone else so that another has power. Holding unfair power over another is a form of abuse.

In my family line, my father was taught how to be abusive by his father, who was taught by his father.

I believe it is possible for a person — whether the perpetrator or survivor — to learn to make better choices.

The idea of vilifying one person over another perpetuates the fraudulent blame game. It takes two for many behaviors to have fruition. "Fool me once, shame on you. Fool me twice, shame on me." On some level, adults with the power to escape may be partly responsible for attracting everything that happens to us. Our thresholds of pain are learned behaviors.

How can we be good agents of change — both the abuser and the abused? I will use a classic domestic cycle of abuse as an example of how it can happen:

A person becomes unhappy with his partner's behaviors. As a result, they use fear, shame, intimidation and threats — subtle or not. The cycle can begin anywhere; it is a machine in perpetual motion. People can go in and out of cycles at will.

Tension builds, and both parties participate. They get caught up, willingly or unwillingly, and start being divisive with their disease. Escalation from life's situations – jobs, work, sex, relationships, jealousy – create a volatile environment. Everyone walks on eggshells inside an explosive atmosphere.

When the abusive accumulation has nowhere else to go, KABOOM is followed by yelling, screaming, tongue-lashing and awfulizing from both parties. Globalizing ensues, and even dangerous physical abuse is possible.

Survivors internalize their suffering and shut down. The abuser tries harder to be heard. Everyone is scarred. Although the abuser feels momentary bliss, that euphoria is over quickly. All suffer deeply without anywhere to hide.

Then begins the "I'm sorry," "I'll never do it again," "I love you," phase which sometimes leads to the honeymoon period, where some hope is restored. Both parties begin to believe things could possibly be better next time. But the cycle begins again when tension builds, and mistrust on both sides perpetuates the abusive way of life.

Emotionally abusive relationships destroy both parties' self-worth and their ability to feel good. They spawn anxiety, depression, helplessness and isolation. The abuser may find momentary and convenient relief through poisonous tongue-lashings, but the feeling passes. It's hard to accept or tolerate. Both parties suffer.

My first step toward recovery in this behavior was to realize I was the perpetrator, the survivor and all the gray areas in between. My machinations were conditioned responses that created or permitted one or the other to happen.

When I sought help, I learned everything I could about both sides, so I became aware of how the cycle works — not as a way of blaming, but as a way of understanding abuse. In my lifetime, I have been beaten down and tongue-lashed to infinity, lost my self-esteem and then repeated those abusive behaviors, becoming an exact replica of my family's generational imprint.

The following is an overview of what the abused partner might notice: I fear my partner will come up with any reason to be angry at any time. I cannot talk about certain subjects, because my partner is unskillful in responding. I feel afraid of my partner a lot of the time. I feel as if I am doing something wrong from his point of view. I feel as if I deserve to feel bad about what he thinks of me. I feel depressed from being with and around my partner. I feel trapped and that my life is in danger.

Abusing others is an insidious disease. Yet the abuser is able to control his behavior, pick whom he will abuse, and make sure they are alone to do their business. He is also able to stop his behavior when it benefits him. Absolute power corrupts absolutely. Abusers can't give away their power to abuse, because it's all they've got.

Signs of the Abuser

They use anger and unpredictable temper. They make threats about cars, houses, money and children and bother their partners at work. They threaten to harm or kill themselves, or you, or your children, or people at work, or a suspected lover. They force or manipulate sex for power, control and humiliation. Abusers make their targets feel bad about how they look, always find something wrong with the way their partners do things. They constantly check up on their partners to see what they are doing, where they are going, or whom they are with.

Abusers blame their targets for having imaginary people of interest; they threaten and admonish. They are hyper-vigilant, micro-managing the partner's day-to-day life so they can feel safe and in control.

With passive-aggressive situations, both parties often create a feedback loop of resentments. They perpetuate their way of living together as a couple and call it a relationship.

The abuser's tool chest includes the following devices for control: humiliation, domination, isolation, intimidation, threats, denial and blame.

If You Are in an Abusive Relationship, What Can You Do?

It is important to note that most abuse in a relationship happens in a "closed system," where others do not see or know about it. It is a disease of isolation. The best solution is to get away, if you can do so without harm.

Escape usually requires a community of concerned parties to create a menu of options. If there is drug abuse or alcoholism, a few meetings with the abuser may be required. If there is anger and potential for great harm, a mediator trusted and approved by both parties could become involved, as long as the mediator doesn't take sides.

If there is a chance for a newfound spiritual epiphany based upon your need for safety, find a spiritual practice and start believing. There are online services and community-based shelters. The concerned parties could write up a "no harm" contract for your relationship with an agreement that either the abuser or the survivor will leave. But it doesn't matter. If you need to leave, leave.

There are Twelve-Step meetings for both parties to explore. Get a sponsor to guide you in safety. There is also free access to community-based therapists. Consider your medical benefits and your doctors' ideas and suggestions. Psychologists and psychiatrists can create a coping regimen of mental-health possibilities, including medications for yourself or the abuser.

Remember that both of you are equally in need of support. How can you make an environment where you both commit to doing no harm to each other?

Things the Abused Can Do to Seek Safety

Go to treatment or Twelve-Step meetings, and take anger management classes to learn what is going on with your partner and with yourself.

Trust that the process of change is pro-active. Running away from your problems usually makes them worse. Letting them build up over time without taking action makes both parties more complicit in the inevitable ending.

For emotionally escalating situations, take five-minute timeout periods, or whatever is reasonable and safe. Build a timeout period into the agreement. Take a walk, call a sponsor, clergy person or trusted friend. Work out at the gym, and let go of all that physical energy. Run, swim — it's healthy for everyone.

Get a support group. Go to Recovering Couples Anonymous or Sex and Love Addicts Anonymous to learn what others do in relationships. Go to a meeting for codependents, and see if it's a good fit.

Learn your legal rights to safety. What are the boundaries of pain and suffering your partner is willing to cross to violate your safety? *Do not* think you can stop abuse without a support group, the legal system, or police, if necessary. Use everything you can to do no harm.

Workbook Questions:

1. We all have bad habits we think are OK in a relationship. How willing are you to be courageous enough to ask others what they think you could work on?

2. In what ways do you control your partner's free time? How do you make them feel vulnerable about their self-care by spending time with friends?

3. In what ways do you snoop in your partner's business phone calls, emails, etc.? What are your reasons for doing that?

4. How do you make your partner feel "less than" about how they look in private or in public with friends?

5. In what ways is your leadership style in need of a tuneup? Do your fellow employees feel safe working with you?

6. How has your family of origin affected the way you abuse others and make it OK? Give examples of abusive techniques you employ for power.

7. In what ways are you coercive and manipulative in a relationship?

8. What expectations do you have of your partner? What are you not in acceptance about with your partner's behavior?

9. What secret ways do you use to control and exert power in your relationship? Are you the breadwinner? Do you withhold sex? Threaten to leave? Embarrass your partner in front of friends?

10. In what ways do you accept small forms of abuse and make excuses such as saying, "That's just the way she is"?

11. How do you stand up for yourself? Why do you believe your partner will leave you?

12. In what ways do you use the tactics of a bully to overwhelm your partner's point of view?

13. In what ways do you use your victim status to explain why bad situations and abusive people are attracted to you? Do you think, "Why me? Oh God, It's happening again!"

Acceptance

The word "acceptance" used to scare me.

When I first got into recovery, I had no clothes, no shoes and a frazzled mind. I lived around other people who suffered like me. I badly wanted admission to a recovery facility.

I was told that everything I always thought about myself and the world — all my empirical thinking — got me to a point of demoralization.

My choice was clear. I chose to change everything I thought. And I knew change was hard with my limited ability. I had to recognize the conditions and rules of the process ahead of me. I had to commit to change, no matter how hard. I had to accept that I am part of something besides my own dysfunctional concept of abundance.

That was a scary time with so many uncomfortable thoughts swirling in my head. At first, I felt as if I was in a negative situation, and my behavior was being observed by an entire community. I could not protest or keep holding onto my old belief system. My choices were to acquiesce or be put back out on the streets.

But that was my first experience of acceptance as positive stress. I had always been satisfied knowing I was a drunk, a drug addict, and a sex addict with a workaholic tendency. I had already accepted this as the only life for me. It made things easier. My attitude was, "Why bother? Who cares? Just give up. Forget it!"

When I surrendered and stopped struggling and resisting, when I accepted everything I thought with all my words and deeds — who was I? How could I let go? And in letting go, what will it take for me to elicit self-change thoughts? When I stopped struggling, resisting and hanging on so tightly to my thoughts and surrendered myself, I began to realize, *Oh, this is the way it is. It's not forever. It's just for today. I can do this one day at a time.*

In my new, cooperative state of mind, I was able to access serenity and peace. I had enough strength to make it. Then, "life" would show up again with trouble of some kind, and I had a choice. What would I choose? Finally, I recognized the option of not fighting but temporarily accepting pain and suffering as my teachers. I allowed them into my life. When I was finally ready, my teachers, Pain and Suffering, taught lessons, and I was able to walk over the burning coals of my life without being injured. I had to go through difficult or uncomfortable situations to get to the other side. No more running away or ignoring the present reality.

In the past, there were many disturbances, people, places and things that made my story line and belief system work. Someone had done me wrong, and it was unacceptable. When I righteously fought the good fight, I was only perpetuating my fraudulent behavior as a way of life. Only when I stopped fighting was I able to find peace and work with what I was given. This change was living life on life's terms. It required me to feel sensitive and vulnerable to create equity with my surroundings, instead of building walls to keep bad ideas and situations away from me.

As I grew in acceptance, I learned to love myself unconditionally exactly as I am. I hardwired my thinking and replaced my fighting instincts. I gave up making someone else's behavior the reason I didn't surrender. I fought and fought and finally realized I was just fighting against another's legitimate belief.

How could I make peace with the fact that everyone on the planet has a belief they believe is true — just like I believe my truth? When I was able to accept the idea that many truths can exist simultaneously, I made even more progress.

I chose "radical acceptance" with all things. I still go from Holistic to Ballistic in a nanosecond, but it no longer rules my whole being. I still have issues with intolerance of others' views, such as with climate change, our prison system, education, child abuse, and other causes. I will work on these issues until I die. I hope I can die with peace and acceptance.

To have a peaceful state of mind, we must learn to cultivate acceptance with the way things are. Acceptance works with all ideas, races, genders, ages — you name it. We can always find another way that does not harm ourselves or others.

Workbook Questions:

1. Name some ideas you have a hard time accepting. With your family? With your job? With your partner?

2. Are you competitive and like to win? What happens when your team loses and you find yourself getting angry about a sports event?

3. What kinds of beliefs do you have a hard time accepting? Deforestation, racial inequality, whaling, global warming? Do you believe the person who believes the opposite should have the benefit of the doubt that their truth is actually valid? Do you believe and accept that they really think their beliefs are true?

4. Do you accept your life the way it is? Are there unreachable things you want in order to be happy? What would happen if you were happy with things just as they are? What's the worst that could happen if you changed your thinking?

5. How do acceptance and forgiveness blend together in your world? With your hardened belief system, what stops you from being a team player and collaborating with others?

6. Does your religion stop you from accepting others' beliefs? What things are hard for you to accept?

7. Can you hold multiple truths and belief systems in your head at the same time?

8. Do you have imperfections with your body that you do not accept? How about your mental state? What are the things you don't like? Why can't you have peace with yourself just the way you are?

9. Do you judge others by the way they talk, look and act? If you are not in acceptance with yourself, how can you be a good judge of others?

10. Do you have strong, negative opinions and entitlements about other races that make you a bigot? What will it take for you to walk a mile in their shoes and come to terms with your hardened thoughts?

11. Do you simply accept your lot in life without challenging the ways you could change?

12. Have you been trying to get a job, a partner, a change in your lifestyle? What can you do to accept that those things are not happening right now? What can you do to make the lack less personal, and accept that this moment is like a cloud and will pass?

Advocating and Demonstrating for Life, and Getting Consistent Results

Change is in the air. We are at the crossroads of your life. There is a lot we can do to create a balanced transition that allows for change and growth without upsetting the flow of our lives.

To get started, pick one area to work on. Decide to work on it for an undetermined amount of time – let's say, three months. It takes a while to internalize any new techniques or teachings and practice them in daily life. For the sake of debate, let's choose this conundrum: "Do you want to be right – or be happy?" Choose to work on this for three months, and see what happens.

First, we choose our direction – our goal. Is it more important to be the one who's right? Or is it more important to be at peace with ourselves and others? Visualize the destination. Be clear and consistent with values. Perseverance is the key to success. A lot of things we yearn for require a lifetime of curiosity and discovery as part of the learning curve. Keeping an open mind for another person's truth is key to long-term conversations. Start with something small, almost imperceptible, and build upon it. Then move up to more complex tasks, and we will effect change.

Second, as we are taught in Non-Violent Communication, if you can speak in a way that others can hear, you are more likely to get your needs met. Demonstrating means standing up for what we believe in. We advocate for what we deserve in life and challenge unfairness. To be heard, we rise above the noise. We show we are capable of enjoying life, housing, safety, and the pursuit of happiness. We champion our cause to legal, medical, social and political mediators to prove we are worthy of healthy relations, job security, medical care, money management and good credit.

Trust is earned, not given. Through the practice of advocating and demonstrating, we slowly learn to be consistent and trustworthy. We develop Teflon skin and patience extraordinaire. We start out in murky water, and state our case to unbelievers. We get to hear NO, and process it as part of our life's journey. We get to take the long view, and work with years in mind – not minutes, hours or days. There is no instant gratification here. We get to work with all of our character defects as they come up, and as we do, we gradually grow into a person of value.

Active listening will become part of our communication habits. Giving and receiving information will become familiar. In active listening, we bring our eyes, ears, minds and bodies to attention to really comprehend what the speaker is imparting. We repeat back what we have heard, and ask if we heard it correctly. We then listen without agenda or emotional escalation. We want to keep a neutral stance and safety for the speaker, so he can impart what is important for him to say.

Then we repeat again what we heard to make sure we heard correctly. They may not need us to offer solutions; they may need only to communicate their needs to us. If we have a suggestion that might be helpful, we should ask permission to divulge our contribution. We let go of all attachment to our own perceived needs until it is time to speak. We receive the grace of truly hearing and accepting another person's truth, not simply reacting to it.

As we advocate, we will find many are unable to hear our truth, and we must persevere. Some people want exact facts with so much research that it seems counter-intuitive. For the greater good of our needs, we have the opportunity to rally, campaign, promote, propose and champion our cause for personal vindication. Then we can take a look at why we always need to be right and win – another form of addictive behavior.

With addiction, there is almost always stigma and mistrust in people's ability to truly change. "Oh, you're just an old (fill-in-the-blank)" – and whoosh! We are dismissed.

If we can learn to listen to another's truth and understand that they have emotion vested in their own beliefs, we can develop compassion and empathy and still hold our ground.

Some of my personal roadblocks to communication are my vested needs – to be right, to win, to control, to manipulate, to not be in acceptance, and to have expectations of others.

It's hard to hold still around an emotionally charged person while he is being a bully or a predator. With power over another in this fast-paced life, we abuse for immediacy and convenience. If the other person suffers as a result – oh, well. It took many years for our communication behaviors to develop into habits. Invest time and energy to slowly change to a new, healthier "normal."

Fear causes most people to react in one of two ways. The first type of fear sounds like this: "I have something I need, and I'm afraid you are trying to take away." This could be freedom, integrity, esteem, addiction, etc. The second form of fear goes like this: "You have something I want, and I'm afraid you won't give it to me." This could be love, relationship, trust, value, safety, sex, employment, etc. We all have succumbed to this type of fear-based thinking.

In recovery, loved ones and family members just want all the discomfort to go away so they can return to whatever their familiar "happy family" looks like (even if it's not especially happy). They want to feel safe in familiarity. They do not want to be inconvenienced or harmed by the behavior of a loved one. The stigma and problems created by a family member's addiction take all the bandwidth and seem to outshine the sun.

When we first confront a loved one's addiction, the addict typically will respond with Sustain Talk. They will tell you why they must sustain their addiction and why they cannot change. They'll explain why they must continue their behavior. When you hear Sustain Talk, it's actually a positive sign. Sustain Talk, also known as pre-contemplation, is the first stage of change. In response, all participants review the reasons why recovery could still work, despite the addict's resistance.

Sustain Talk allows family members to hear what the addict believes — sometimes for the first time. It also allows the addict to walk in the family members' painful shoes. In this moment, if anyone (or better yet, everyone) can suspend the impulse to judge and reject and simply listen for the sake of mindfulness, everyone can move into a groundless space where two truths can exist at the same time. Therein lays the precious choice of accepting another's truth. This enables the ability to sit and have a difficult conversation without pushing the other away. For the first time, you can agree to disagree.

In these early conversations, we will use and hear words that block, conceal, condemn, deny, disapprove, discourage, oppose, halt, prevent, undermine, assail, attack and/or criticize. These words are easy to use and don't require much critical thinking. It is also easy to emotionally escalate during these early moments of openness. When we emotionally escalate is when most of the hurtful words, acts of violence, blame, wars and killings take place in the room and on the planet. We don't have to live there. We can choose to be still, just for a moment, and listen.

It is in these messy and bewildering situations that most people get lost in the gray area. We now have a choice. Be an agent of change in our own lives. If we don't make plans for ourselves, someone will make plans for us.

Workbook Questions:

1. Make a wish list of all the nice things you would like to happen in your life. Include everything, even if it seems impossible: a job, a relationship, a car, healthy relations, money, and so forth. List at least 20 items.

2. What would be the easiest of those to work on? Pick something that is not emotionally charged and has no threatening or divisive qualities.

3. What things have you worked hard for in the past? Playing music, buying a car, overcoming mental-health challenges, getting a job, going to college? What did you do to acquire these? Write it down, and use it as a blueprint for what you now want.

4. If your best thinking got you into your current demoralized position, what new behaviors are you willing to try to move beyond your familiar disarray?

5. In what ways have you seen others do the work and get results in their lives? Are you willing to learn from the winners and ask them what worked for them?

6. Are you willing, just for today, to suspend your ways of thinking? Einstein said we cannot solve a problem by following the same steps that created it. What can you do to think outside the box?

7. Do you lack faith in the unseen and belief in the unknown? What would enable you to take a leap of faith and do the next right thing?

8. What behavioral responses can you agree to work on with your loved ones, your partner, your work colleagues? Are yelling, isolating, blaming, judging, divisiveness and people-pleasing part of your communication skills?

9. Make a list of healthy behaviors you know how to do. How can you use these as guideposts for your new way of living? What transferrable skill sets do you already use – in work, in play – that can help you in this area?

10. If you are willing to do anything for your addictions, why doesn't the rest of your life merit some effort?

11. What do you believe that you deserve in life?

Aggression

I was brought up by a father who survived generational abuse, cultural abuse and oppression. During World War II, one in every five Polish citizens was murdered. My family came by its aggression honestly. If we were driving down the road and another driver acted crazy or did something to endanger our family, my father met the aggression head on and made the other person swerve off the road. He always scared the hell out of whomever it was.

When I was growing up, my father had little patience for any variation of his instructions, and corporal punishments were meted out with swiftness. "This is going to hurt me more than it is you," was a popular pre-beating announcement.

At 17, my father joined the military and learned the ways of war. Self-regulation was used only to kowtow to men of higher rank.

My own education in aggression came via learning the ways of abuse and cycles of violence at home. With family difficulties and emotional trauma came direct fear of others, which heightened my behavior and inability to control myself. When kids are smacked at home while learning, they can develop the goal of misbehavior at school. The teacher was the obstacle that replaced my father's wrath. I didn't get hit or tongue-lashed at school, so the teacher was at a disadvantage to tame me. She called a school meeting where my dad had to do a fear-based corporal extension of the policy at home.

I became the aggressor, the victim and the perpetrator, all rolled up into one. When I could get away with it, I was the abuser. I treated everyone with disdain and disregard and had no healthy bonding with my peers. I always wanted to be the best at whatever I did and felt like a failure when I was not. I could never feel good with life as it was. I had to be treated as special just to feel normal.

Fear, shame, pain and discomfort increase aggression. The parallel is a dog being trained. If the dog is beaten, it will respond from a place of fear. If it is trained with positive re-enforcement and consistency, it will respond from a place of willingness.

In the past, if someone made me angry, I responded with sarcasm and stubbornness. I met any request by doing the least possible amount of work in the longest time to show them who they were messing with.

As a survivor of violence, I learned to be the most violent, a "killing" machine. I was a perfect generational imprint, passing on the legacy and halting everything else.

What happened to me as a child is over. Now it is my choice to keep engaging in negative behaviors. If I so choose, then my work colleagues, my partner, my kids and my spiritual community all will suffer from my choices.

It is not what happened to us that is important. What is of value is how we move into healthy ways of processing life on life's terms. The bold and positive words we can use to live a healthier way include:

- Initiating

- Enterprising
- Active
- Ready or willing
- Determined

We all have great energy we want to use to empower others. We can turn poison into medicine. We don't have to run away. We can go into our aggression to get kernels of truth, and accept pain and suffering as our teachers, just for today. We learn to breathe, meditate and respond to situations — not react like a bull in a china shop. We can be a universal observer to see how people use malaise and cause grief around them. We are learning that we do not have to fix them, help them, admonish them, or spin out with them. We are doing a great service by holding our collective conscious space. If we do our work, change happens.

Why do we fight? Why do we have to win? Why do we have to punish? Why do we have to outdo others on a job? Why do we have to win the beauty prize? Why we have to own the best car? These forms of envy cause great grief and suffering, which leads to outbursts and aggressive behavior.

Workbook Questions:

1. We all use forms of aggression either inwardly toward ourselves or outwardly against others. Name ways you harm yourself or others.

2. Are you quiet on the outside, but inside there is a nuclear world waiting to explode with seething contempt? Explain.

3. Do you think things such as "I wish you were dead," "I will crush you," or "I want to kill you"? If so, what triggers those thoughts?

4. In what ways do you use passive aggression to hold family, co-workers and others emotional hostage?

5. Name five ways you put yourself down harshly for not doing a perfect job or falling short of an unreachable goal.

6. In what ways do you beat yourself up and devalue your self-esteem?

7. Are you always ready to react strongly, waiting for the moment to do so when everyone else is having a good time? If so, explain why.

8. Are you stressed from taking things personally that really are not about you at all?

9. Do you micromanage others? In what ways? Are you hyper-vigilant, ready to pounce? What sets you off? Do you feel too close to the edge of losing it? Explain why.

10. Do you feel righteous about your feelings? When you are emotionally escalated, do you believe you have more importance than others? In what ways do you demonstrate that?

11. Do you feel as if you have righteous anger? Why?

12. In what ways do you get frustrated at games, sports or any other competition? How big is your ego?

13. Do you know how to lose a job or a partner with grace? Explain why.

14. Do you have a boss you want to do bad things too? Do you ruminate about something bad happening to them? Do you let them know how unhappy you are? If not, why not?

15. Do you believe your pain and suffering are greater than others? Explain.

16. Do you want to stick it to the man? Explain.

17. What do you notice from others who are not aggressive with you? Are you used to that behavior? Do you feel safe?

18. Are you aggressive with loved ones and hurt innocent bystanders when they get in the way? If so, why? How do you feel afterward?

19. In what ways do you use indirect hostility toward your coworkers or loved ones with whom you are angry?

20. Name a few ways you deliberately failed to finish work duties. Who were you angry with? What did they do to you?

Ambivalence and Discernment

It's OK to have a variety of feelings about a subject. Holding the paradox of our lives, holding truths and *responding* rather than *reacting* to life on life's terms, are the goals. Make the best decision for the greater good in your life based on everything you have learned so far. Being able to suspend our belief systems and realize we could have done things many different ways is liberating. This is how we make the best use of ambivalence and discernment.

When instant gratification and convenience are magical cures, we suffer from a delusional quick-fix attitude. Life happens. Shift happens. Change happens. How can we hold our own space and not be overly influenced by what others think of us?

We can develop the ability to safely judge what we will do with our future in mind. We can manage with our moral compass intact. We can see possibilities and make the best choices for the greater good. This virtue holds the longer view, using wisdom and judgment after looking at available possibilities and choices. We can take a stance and still consider other options as they naturally arise.

Developing discernment was a great personal achievement for me. I had decision-itis most of my adult life. I used drugs and alcohol and knew these substances were inanimate objects. I, the sentient being, made a conscious choice to alter my feelings and medicate with drugs and alcohol. If I had only one dollar, I bought alcohol, instead of buying food. Instead of paying my rent or car registration or insurance, I did drugs for the immediacy and convenience of forgetting. This sustained my world of "diminished returns." I lived in a netherworld of my own making.

Now that I have emerged from that place, I understand that I have choices and information. I no longer experience "poverty as a choice of the mind." I can explore and do the next right thing. And after that, I can do the next right thing again.

But how do we break free of those well-accessorized ruts and runways in our brains that worked for us so long? We negatively benefited and got used to numbness. How do we thrive?

I had to work to accept that conflicting feelings were OK. I learned to hold dual emotions – feelings about positive and negative consequences. I learned not to react, but to take time to process with a critical-thinking mind and make a best guess of the truth with a group of peers and teachers. Then I was coming from a powerful place of grace.

I learned to get past the learning curve of doing new things. Even though I was changing, the world around me often seemed the same. I got to practice daily all the principles I was learning in my life —or get my misery cheerfully refunded.

In a world where it seems to make sense to avoid conflict, some of us procrastinate and get stuck. Can you imagine what would happen if we freed up all the time we wasted? We could accomplish so much more. We would be immobilized so much less by shame-based thinking and worrying about what others think of us. We can learn to sit with the groundlessness of not knowing, and become comfortable with uncertainty.

Our Western culture teaches that we are the "good ones. "You know the sayings: "Put up the good fight." "We are right and must prevail." "Our God is good."

This entitled attitude of privilege comes with a hidden cost. It teaches that there can be only one winner, and all the rest either must be complacent losers or fight for their rights of equality.

With addiction, alcoholism and/or sex and relationship issues, we want to develop healthy discernment. Pay attention to what is happening around you. Healthy discernment requires us to suspend our beliefs and stop concretizing our thinking. Once we develop rigidity, we are less likely to consider other options or experiences.

We may also feel the need to defend a broken-down lifetime of experience when it is still painful to wear that burden. We are like moths to the flame, trying to receive comfort from our source of pain. How can we keep our minds nimble, open, flexible, willing and teachable with beginner's minds? This is our quest.

Things You Can Do

- Make a pro and con list of the reasons for and against things you feel strongly about.
- Write the worst that could happen, and why you are held hostage by your thoughts about it.
- Remember that what others think of you is none of your business.
- Assemble the facts and knowledge you have, and go over it with a trusted neutral party.
- Be willing to consider many truths.
- Do no harm to others, if at all possible.
- Be willing to agree to disagree.
- Be a good listener. You can learn everything about anything, if you are willing to listen.
- Have a strong support group that will call you on your stuff, if you make a harmful decision.
- Be willing to accept "No." Know that it often means, "Not now." It doesn't always mean, "Not ever."
- Be willing to advocate and demonstrate for your values.
- Be willing to change your mind as you develop resilient knowledge.
- If you feel stuck with intractable thinking, pray for the willingness to move beyond that place and into openness.

Workbook Questions:

1. Describe a time when you saw different sides of a conflict that others ignored or didn't think were important.

2. Why do you feel compelled to emotionally escalate with those thoughts? What would it take for you to consider another truth? What do you have to lose? Is your social status, your ego, your position of power at stake? Free-fall with pleasure and information-gathering. Have discovery and curiosity as defaults.

3. How do you learn to make healthy choices that create safety? Indigenous Americans honored Earth and families for seven generations ahead. What are you willing to do that takes a longer view of your life?

4. Do you feel morally obligated to create equity with your decision-making process? Do you hold a bias toward race, gender or other factors?

5. What are some examples of when you showed good judgment? Did you help others feel safer through your choices?

6. What are virtues that help you make sound decisions?

7. What thinking keeps you suffering? Do you pass judgment and hold resentments? Are you quick to anger? Do you let others have your power? Explain.

8. Does needing to feel safe and right hamper you from hearing others' truth?

9. Do you have trouble making decisions? Do you stay frozen in time with your thoughts? What have you done in the past to move beyond procrastinating?

10. Does your spirituality encourage you to look at all sides of a conflict and be a peacekeeper?

11. How do you handle people with strong belief systems that are rigid and unbending? How do you stay supple in your thinking and still make sound decisions?

Anger Management

Anger is a powerful emotion that is often misused. It's one of the spices of life that should be used sparingly and only when called for, then put away. Pick your battles and avoid fighting, if at all possible. War ends if you do not participate, in many cases. Use assertiveness and healthy boundaries. Advocate, demonstrate and model what you want to see in the other person. Play the long game.

These problems we have with communication do not crop up overnight. They are the result of needs unmet since the beginning of time. We sometimes fight our DNA and muscle memory to overcome the propensity to protect, defend, and control in order to get our immediate needs met, usually at the expense of others. Once we win, that immediacy is put in jeopardy. We then begin the opposite action of fighting for what we believe is right, instead of working on longer-term solutions to create equity and value.

In the United States, we live by a lottery of birth that has created generations of entitlement and privilege. The U.S. contains 4.25 percent of the world's population and uses roughly 24 percent of the world's energy. If all nations did as we do, we would need five planets and we would still destroy them all with our unmet needs of unsustainable consumerism. Once you get used to this privilege, you are willing to make others suffer to make sure your needs are met. You take and take and feel so deserving; then, you get angry and violate others' wishes for the same things you have. This self-perpetuating culture of entitlement feeds a cycle of conflict and anger that few of us are equipped to handle.

When someone feels they have been disrespected, deceived, robbed or disappointed, they use anger as a quick-fix coping mechanism. Usually when exploding in anger, we do a lot of damage that cannot be easily undone. We lose trust that takes years to restore. We ruin relationships that were healthy parts of our lives. We suffer from the loneliness and depression caused by our negative communicating. We are trapped and isolated by the seemingly inescapable nature of this way of life. Others avoid us, and we start avoiding others, and so it goes. We cry for justice and attention, and instead of getting our needs met, we are sometimes stigmatized as criminals for the methods we choose to express our feelings. It looks as if we are ruining our chances for change by having momentary outbursts of anger. We repeat this until we are shunned and marginalized by society.

Emotional regulating is a way we can start to change this unhealthy relationship with ourselves and others. By forgiving ourselves and others, everyone gets to feel safe, be free and live for today. When we learn to get into acceptance of "what is," we can stop blaming and judging others for our unhappiness. We can agree to disagree. We can evoke self-change thoughts in ourselves and others. We champion our ability to negotiate, and winning isn't the ultimate goal anymore.

With our newfound willingness to engage in positive, transformative thinking, we can reduce and replace all the ways we get immediate gratification from blaming. We take responsibility and know that anger is a feeling. If we detach from it and let it go, it is like a cloud in the sky that can pass us by.

When we over-indulge our anger, its chemical cascade of emotions fools and tricks us. Anger can feel righteous, even when it isn't, releasing feel-good hormones for a negative reason. No wonder we get so confused by it.

Anger management starts with the first things that trigger and undo your finest intentions. If you do not surrender the things that irritate you, they will always irritate you. By your stubbornness, you will keep attracting these situations and people as your modus operandi to re-enforce your belief system. You are setting up yourself and others for collective suffering. The anger that resides in us dwells within our unfinished psyche. It is this unfinished business in your head, about issues and subjects that irritate you, which causes your reactive confusion.

If you surrender and work with your issues of discontent, you become more resilient. You become more open to considering that if you feel what you are feeling so deeply, others may also have attachments to their thinking. All people want to feel safe like we do; this is what we all have in common. All people suffer like we suffer. It's when we attach to our suffering and refuse to let go that we become angry. The other person then feels the reflection of our discontent, and we breed this as our combined dissatisfaction. Anger feeds only itself. It never feeds healing.

Reasons to HALT Anger as Our First Reaction

If you do not work on your anger issues daily, you will not be in a flexible, willing, open and teachable platform of change. The first step is to check yourself and make sure you're not mistaking anger for an unmet physical need. You probably have already heard of the well-known "HALT" system. When you feel triggered into anger, ask yourself if you are Hungry, Angry, Lonely or Tired (HALT). If you answer yes to any of those, take care of them *before* you react. Also, ask yourself if you are irritable, discontented, vulnerable, horny, or depressed.

Now, take a deep breath, and greet your "perfect teacher." Your teacher, Anger, is always with you – on the freeway, at the grocery store, watching the evening news, with your co-workers, talking to your partner, trying to get your kids to do something, working on your computer.

Whatever you are doing that makes you feel vulnerable, sensitive, irritable or discontented, it's usually something you want to learn to do better. When you are dissatisfied and angry with yourself, your frustration is reflected onto others.

If you beat yourself up all day and feel guilty about what you have done, you reflect that depression and low self-esteem on others, and they reflect what you have perpetrated onto them. You are the cause and effect with your words, thoughts and actions. Try investing in new abilities, such as resilience, tolerance, faith, hope, and belief in the abilities of ourselves and others to change. Begin with forgiveness. You may notice that people reflect what you offer them. This is how you become the change you want to see in others. As the lyric goes, "Let there be peace on Earth, and let it begin with me."

Everything we try to do with our response is about making space before we react. First, make space by letting others know you feel angry, frustrated and vulnerable. You are trying not to make them feel what you are feeling; you simply want them to know this feeling is up for you. They are not making you angry; rather, the unmet needs you are vocalizing are upsetting you. People are not mind readers or magical thinkers. People perform better when they know what you expect of them. Then, you can hear how absurd some of the things you want them to do are – and how you violate others with your own unmet needs. It's an opportunity to work on yourself. Once you master yourself, you can be more patient with others. Play the long game of evoking self-change thoughts and seeking safety after the communication incidents are over.

Your environment triggers whatever easily offends you. I live in an impoverished part of an American city in the midst of gentrification. Seeing poverty and fearing crime can give you self-righteous, judgmental ideas. This bias creates a skewed platform to feel dissatisfied, name-call, and diminish a whole population of people who are just like you, trying to have a normal day. These people did not wake up this morning thinking of how they can "stick it to the man." Seek emotional safety and have designated moments for emotionally escalating subjects, then return to the ability for self-care.

Don't isolate – it only builds up resentment pressure. When you dwell on mental images of what you're dissatisfied with, you re-enforce these thoughts. You are like a hamster spinning in the wheel of your head. Your brain is wired to respond to what you are thinking. If you do not get resolution with your thoughts, you are rewiring your brain for a negative focus. Your brain thinks it deserves these angry outbursts and will reward itself over and over again. Your brain is not that smart. You have to make better choices to get better results. Many people with depression are stuck in this pattern. Your body cannot continue making stress hormones without feeling a diminished return with your well-being. Your toxic thoughts manifest in your body as stress, and stress kills all well-being.

Remember, anger is a luxury I can ill afford. It's too expensive for me to be angry. I am not coming up with any solutions for change. I am justifying my selfish experience of I, me, mine – not our experience together.

If you are in a relationship with kids, a partner, or a group who meets up after work, be aware of whether you are in an exhausted or triggered state. If you fight with your partner after work, you are the reason for most of your frustration. You might make everyone walk on eggshells because of what happened at work. You might project onto loved ones your anger and frustration from the day. You might not have the wick to deal with anything else today. People get into a rut and fight at night for years on end. You can stop this behavior. Wait till the weekend, or have the conversation at the time of day when you can be in your best mindful state. Make it a timed event when you talk for a certain amount of time, then put it on the shelf till the next opportunity. It took years to create this dilemma, and it might take a few weeks to find satisfaction for both parties.

Exercise and burn off your first, impulsive, adrenalized thinking. Get it out of your system with physical exertion. Then, learn to speak in a way that others can hear you, and you will be more likely to get your needs met.

Once you get excited, take a timeout. Say, "I don't want to cause harm with my thoughts and my words. I feel like my glass is full of muddy water with my emotions. If I wait a while, these thoughts will clear up, and I will be resolved to keep safety in the conversation."

Anger will always be your perfect teacher. No matter how skilled you get, someone can always undo your finest effort. We attract what we have not finished. This is an inside job, so keep a sense of urgency to be willing to participate with your assertive skills.

When you choose mindfulness, you increase positive emotions. You activate the ability to recognize and interrupt your triggers. Everyone experiences hard times and pressures. If you flex your anger muscle, it will get bigger and better at looking for things to feed itself. If you look for something wrong, you are apt to find it. If you look for something right, you can build that skill with all your opportunities.

When triggered or feeling self-righteous, think about what the Dalai Lama, Jesus, Muhammad or the Buddha would do. How would they handle it? Engage in that type of behavior. Fake it till you make it. Act as if you are having the experience of healing and well-being. Re-enforce this ability.

If you come from an anger response, you will attract the same from your partner. You also may add gasoline to their depression and frustration. Either way, you will not have the effect you were seeking.

Don't speak up simply because you hear something you disagree with. Don't start thinking about what to say before the other person is done speaking. Use a moment of silence to stop your righteous, "get even" thinking.

Look for the good qualities in the other person. Tell them about the great things they have accomplished and how you know they can overcome all obstacles.

Families are perfect breeding grounds for surrendering and making someone the "bad sheep." No one wants that label, and they don't deserve it. Stop this judgment with your kids, your partner and your parents.

Anger and stress eventually kill you. A compromised immune system and depressive mental health are a takeout order you place with your anger.

Anger drains you mentally and causes high blood pressure and cardiovascular disease from the repetitive stress of daily actions. Anger also drains you emotionally, keeping you in a hyper-vigilant, obsessive and compulsive state, where you do not access your good intentions. You come across like a bully, and your values and beliefs clash with your need to control others. Then you feel guilty, powerless and emotionally bankrupt.

If you are easily irritated, explore why. It is our responsibility to do extreme self-care and not harm others. If we can make it through a day without harming ourselves or others, we have done well. This is the platinum standard of well-being. Treat others as they want to be treated, and they are more likely to treat you that way.

Anger is a muscle memory we are accustomed to. We've been irritated and righteous for so long, our behaviors are smooth and seamless. They are our automatic response. Our brains reward us for this mal-adaptive behavior, and others are held hostage by our reactive demeanor.

Own that when you get angry, you over-emote and use colorful adjectives that are dismissive to your counterparts.

When you begin a dialogue with someone, follow these tips:

- I am working on my anger. It doesn't matter what we talk about; it is my work to practice these skills.

- I want to let go of my attachments to what makes me angry and choose to be happy, instead of being right about what I perceive as wrong. I surrender my judgment and righteous indignation.

- Let someone be wrong. We are working on our own side of the street. We can change only our own behavior and model how to respond. If we've been doing these behaviors our whole life, it may take the other party some time to evoke their self-change thoughts.

- We don't excuse other people's behavior, but we can let everyone have a free pass for a day when they might be emotionally challenged. We don't have to make their crisis our dilemma.

- It takes a second and a half before we can physically or mentally respond to someone or something. Practice making your response time longer and longer. That is what mindfulness is all about. Your mental health is worth the effort. The time you will feel good will grow longer, and you can always get your misery cheerfully refunded if you choose to follow your impulsive anger.

- Count to 10, over and over, each time you are triggered. The other person is simply trying to communicate. Why are you so easily offended?

- Breathe deeply, engage your peace of mind, and focus on releasing tension. We all hold tension in different parts of our body, and then we tighten up. Find where you store yours, and make it a policy of self-care to release it often.

- Distract yourself by focusing on the next five right things you can do. Think about how good you'll feel by continuous right thinking. It's an inside job and no one has the power to take your well-being away.

- Keep investing in a bank of well-being where there is no maximum limit. Keep investing in that, and you will keep attracting it. If you focus on what irritates you, you will keep attracting that, too. It's up to you.

- Exercise your body, and you will unleash a healthier brain chemistry. Your brain is the biggest chemical factory of well-being on the planet. It's like a muscle. It's a use-it-or-lose-it machine; the choice is yours.

- Your brain is like a Maserati in the Anger and Depression Garage. Let's stop this behavior, and take a road-test on the highway of possibilities that is your life.

- Use humor. It is the greatest way to heal with fun. It's distracting. It breaks the inertia of stuck thinking. It interrupts the cycle of making stress hormones and chemical cascades that create depression and adrenalized thinking. It stops a hardened, protective, serious demeanor and helps you to stay right-sized, appropriate and relaxed.

Only you can prevent emotional firing of neurons in your brain. You have all the power in this relationship.

Workbook Questions:

1. We all have challenging people who provoke us with their inability to comply with the most sacred and basic needs for interpersonal exchanges. How can we start to model the change we want to see in ourselves and quit looking at the "bad sheep" we have labeled and keep vilifying that they are wrong and the cause of our unhappiness?

2. Why do you let people have the satisfaction of keeping you emotional hostage? What actions can you take for emotional safety?

3. What people in the news irritate you? Does your news channel vilify a certain population that clashes with your own belief system? What stops you from turning the "bad news" off? What would you lose?

4. What judgmental belief systems does your religion have upon other belief systems? People of another country, race? People that have gender identities and preferences that differ from yours? Why does your religious belief system make it OK to villainize this population with righteous indignation, making it look like you are the good one?

5. What actions can you take to recognize your triggers, and own that it is your responsibility to deal with your own control issues and agendas that keep you irritable angry and discontent?

6. Are you willing to take Anger Management, or Mindfulness trainings to learn new coping skills?

7. What have you done in the past that has worked to keep your expectations of others from turning into resentments you feel justified about? What have you had success with that you can use again?

8. What domestic cycle of violence do you do at home with your family loved ones, or partner? Do you use threats, annoyance, verbal tongue lashings, secretive behaviors that keep your loved ones emotional hostages to your dissatisfaction?

9. Why is anger the answer to all of your problems? Why are there no other peaceful means to explore? Why are you so satisfied with this type of action and language that causes so much harm?

Assertiveness

Assertiveness is the ability to speak up and show the world what you have to contribute.

Being assertive might not be the only answer, but it can be a viable alternative and a beneficial choice we give others to help make informed, knowledgeable decisions. When we use healthy boundaries with active listening, we can mindfully traverse any situations with skillful collaboration.

We learn to state our needs in a healthy, respectful manner and listen to the first reply without defaulting to anger. We take the longer view, hold our space and advocate and demonstrate for our needs to be met.

If we are in an exhausting, long-term commitment, we may choose to move on from that uncomfortable situation. We may wish to make beneficial new choices for our lifestyle that may not include the other party.

To be able to respond with accuracy, we must be assertive listeners. We listen with our minds and bodies and do not make emotional or body cues when we hear something we disagree with. We let the other person know, "This is what I heard," and reflect back what the other person said. Then, ask if you understand the concept correctly.

For safety in conversations, we agree to disagree. More emphasis is put on understanding each other's requests and needs. To keep important points, both parties agree on summaries that encapsulate mutual benefits. The idea is to keep the "gray area" of possibilities and choices as a menu of options, coming from a place of respect and abundance — not intractability and scarcity.

We begin assertiveness by listening and really hearing another's experience. When it includes us, we back away from defensive mindsets and look for their pain. We do not make their situation or issue about us. That takes away from what they are saying. Underneath are kernels of truth and actual requests.

Resist the desire to fix others' problems or give advice. Let them express their truth. Then say, "Thanks for saying that. It took a lot of courage. I now see how you feel, and I will take a look at this behavior."

Remember that each of us has the solutions to our problems within us. By listening, we create a process that makes it about the other's experience. We have created equity and safety for them to be honest. It is a process. After listening, they might ask for our help, or we can ask if there is anything we can do. If they agree, with our needs in mind, we can begin coming up with mutually desired outcomes, solutions and coping mechanisms as we both elicit self-change thoughts in partnership.

When someone has a vested belief system, we can move beyond their need to protect what they value and still let a new thought or idea grow and take shape. We are assertive yet maintain a safe space to let them change what they know is not true anymore, without losing face or dignity. Our first impulse may be to feel devalued as a person coming from an unheard place. Then we may feel diminished about our position. But we can still claim our inherent right to the same values and benefits that others freely enjoy.

When we live our lives for the benefit of others and do service without obvious rewards, we have a voice that others can trust. This idea of service allows us to assert ourselves for the benefit of others. It does not mean we are the "good ones" or the self-appointed helpers. It means we come from a place that could change someone's experience in a helpful and non-threatening manner, where they have a choice and feel like it is partially their idea.

When being assertive, we may be completely off- base, miss the point and accept that the vulnerable place of speaking our truth is humbling. This vulnerability keeps us sensitive to others' viewpoints. We develop a thicker skin. Just because everyone is doing something morally and ethically wrong does not mean we should be quiet. We get to say, "No!" We get to process our helpless feelings amongst our peers or privately with people we trust. We get to feel the groundlessness of opposing the masses. It's OK. We can assert that we are sometimes wrong, and boldly ask for help without losing our power. We get to participate in humanity in an equitable manner.

We can assert empathy and compassion without the need for others to participate or agree. We can stand alone with our thoughts and be safe. We work with the assumption that all humans have something of value to say and contribute, whether it has a positive or negative impact on the immediate situation. We take each situation and do not pathologize or globalize another's thinking, keeping an open mind that consideration for another's needs can be complicated and unpredictable. After we assert our point of view, we can back off and make time for discernment to take place for someone else. Silence is a powerful tool, when used effectively.

When, Where and Why to Be Assertive

When: When should we be assertive? Timing is everything. We must pick our battles. Even though we may know we are right, there are times it may be wrong for us to assert our truth. It is helpful to be in the same room as our audience, so they can see our body language and personal inflections to denote our true intentions as peaceful or otherwise.

When someone derails a meeting with emotionally escalating personal points, we can defuse the situation and take them aside to listen fully, while the meeting stays on agenda. When we listen to others and keep the context on target, tracking other people's objectives with spontaneous openness, we are being assertive.

Where: We should make sure we are in a safe place where we have a power base and others are likely to listen. We must keep a neutral openness. We must know our terrain and be ready for engagement. We all feel safe and verbose when we are comfortable with our location. When we are in unfamiliar terrain, we should get to know our audience, their likes and dislikes. We can notice where we are and keep a place of empowerment, but try not to hold others hostage with a table, a car seat, a couch or a podium.

Why: What's our motivation? Is it to compromise someone else's integrity? Do we need to empower ourselves by making someone else look wrong, stupid or "less than"? Just because we know more about something doesn't mean we have to speak up. When we hear something we disagree with, we don't necessarily have to say something to prove we are right. Sometimes the truth is too painful for others to hear, or we harm others with our righteous assertions. That attitude will create an unsafe environment and erode the safety of others.

We must not make it a crusade to undermine others' thinking. We should assert in a manner that others can oblige without losing their power base. When we live our lives for the benefit of others, we empower others. Strive to create a "we" mentality where all buy into a collective, team-building experience. We collaborate and accept another's truth. We agree to disagree.

Our main objective is to state ideas without doing harm to the other. When we are assertive, we can state our boundaries and position of authority from a respectful place, not as a reason to diminish another's point of view.

"I" Statements

If we are emotionally escalated, we can use "I" language to share feelings without attacking someone else.

When you _____, I feel _____.

I feel unheard when you do all the talking. I would like more time to speak and be heard.

When you make demands, it makes it difficult to respond in a healthy way where we both benefit. I would like us to make collaborative choices and come to agreements together, peacefully.

When you ask me to do something, it feels like you are already angry with me. I would like to help you of my own volition and need to feel safe when I respond to your requests.

To Be Assertive, Value Yourself and Others

To be assertive, we must learn to value our own worth. Be trustworthy and help others feel comfortable saying their truth, no matter how strange it may sound to us. By stating our contribution out loud, we also may hear how silly some of our own beliefs sound.

Body language and gestures can give the look of mastery of our subject matter. Emphasize important points. Use balance to be a compelling storyteller. We can be like a musician who uses dynamics to regulate with a touch. However, we must be judicious with our gestures, so we don't look grandiose.

Personal appearance can add to our credibility. If you wish, dress to fit in with the crowd so you blend in and are not ostracized.

Use your voice to create impact with your words. Don't speak in a monotone. Speak loudly enough to be heard, and enunciate so everyone can hear and understand. We also must be culturally inclusive and welcoming.

Using negotiation and collaborative techniques creates equity and an atmosphere of willingness.

Equity-building and curiosity discovers how our audience might feel as a collective group. Then we can address the greater good to be achieved and be satisfied with small steps toward larger goals.

Help the persons you speak with to feel at ease. Create fun distractions that let everyone know we all make mistakes, and there is no such thing as a stupid question.

Work with your own issues, triggers and biases toward subjects that make us emotionally unstable. Know thy self.

After stating our truth, we must be willing to hear others' truths without feeling offended, violated or unhappy about their disapproval. Everyone has something to gain and possibly something to lose. We should keep our willingness to consider that if we believe what we believe, they also believe what they believe. Hold both truths for the safety of future meetings, based on openness and safety for all parties.

Be willing to accept that someone has honored our strengths and praised us because of our skills. Don't diminish their compliment by dismissing our abilities and their insight to notice our talents.

When we are comfortable with ourselves, we put others at ease. We are not concentrating on our fear-based thinking and what we might not get out of the conversation. We are already whole and complete. We are inviting others to contemplate ways to create more intimacy, trust, value, collaboration and tolerance of another's views.

Workbook Questions:

1. How are you honest and courageous enough to ask for help if needed?
2. When you think of something to say before the other person is done talking, how does that damage the conversation?
3. How do you express anger and annoyance?
4. How do you ask questions when you're confused?
5. When have you followed agendas that make others distrust your intentions?
6. In what way do your opinions keep others from being honest with you?
7. Do you speak up in trainings or meetings? Do you participate at all? How does this affect your status in the group?
8. Are you able to say no when you don't want to do something? What is the result?
9. Do you believe in yourself, your truth and your beliefs? Are you able to verbalize them?
10. Do you look at people when you're talking to them? How does this affect their response to you?
11. What makes it difficult for you to voice a difference of opinion with others?
12. When you feel offended or humiliated, what keeps you from voicing your emotions in a healthy manner?
13. When someone has an opinion different from your own, are you quick to defend or retaliate?
14. Describe "constructive criticism." Are you capable of accepting it?
15. In what ways do you get your points across without offending anyone?
16. How do you speak up to get what you want out of this life?
17. When you communicate, do you invalidate the contributions of others? How can you tell?
18. How do you paint yourself as a target and then reinforce your unhappiness by being assertive in a negative way?
19. When you "go with the flow" and avoid speaking as part of a group, how do you feel when your peers don't understand you?
20. Who are you when you avoid confrontation simply so you don't disappoint someone?

Attachment

We are creatures who put our energy into people, places, things and concepts. As we develop tenure and equity with those things, we start to attach them to our core belief system because of consistency and familiarity. These beliefs tap into our deepest feelings.

When we attach to a belief about a person, we create a storyline about them based on the event and our belief. These storylines create the highest love and worst destruction that humankind is capable of.

Sometimes we feel we must work hard to defend our storyline, confusing it with our safety and our way of life. We might feel deep frustration, seeing others enjoy abundance. How can we move toward detaching ourselves with love from the old and embracing new concepts?

For example: A man meets a woman and develops a relationship with her. He has his experience with his parents and family and is learning about her family's nuances, too.

They have a child. The child is biologically his creation, as the man was to his own parents. He wants his child to have the best upbringing, education and training for a livelihood, so the child can go on to live in abundance.

It is when things do not go his way, and he experiences life on life's terms, that he creates tension with his surrounding environment and rallies for his cause. He is in a form of conflict from not getting his needs met.

From our collective experiences, we have emotions that conflict with our abilities to be objective. Once we sided with beliefs that conflict with an event, our emotions spiral out of control. We want certain things to happen with people, places and things. We make it our personal crusade to right any perceived injustice. We are attached to protecting, covering up, and making others bend to our will so we feel safe.

This becomes dangerous when we use our religions and connections to a deity to look for differences in beliefs instead of similarities. Most wars are pivoted around fighting god against god in attached belief systems. Reasons could be political, racial or equity differences. People lost in their attachment have little interest in others' belief systems. We care even less when something we value is taken away, such as our feelings of safety, our natural resources, or our ability to make money.

Inflexibility creates conflict with active listening. If I believe what I believe, why can't I believe that *they* believe what *they* believe? There are usually three sides to a conflict: yours, mine and the truth.

Failure to have healthy attachments during our early years usually comes from conditioned learning with our parents. We learn in our social relationships and from our primary caregivers. We start having problematic social expectations and don't learn to deal with behavioral problems. We react from not getting love and attention, and we don't learn about inhibitions or boundaries. We try to make our environment fulfill our needs. We also react when we believe our needs are not being met and we are not heard.

Some of us protect ourselves by introverting and isolating, which turns into social anorexia. Social anorexia is the sustained avoidance of giving or receiving social, sexual or emotional nourishment. We also try to control others so we can feel safe in our environment. We may become perfectionists and judge ourselves harshly. If we think so little of ourselves, just imagine what we do to those with whom we become attached.

In our journey to find our own set of beliefs, we typically look for and attach to what we experienced as children. If we learned unhealthy attachments, it is no wonder we are drawn to those types of people. Yet we always wonder why we pick the most dysfunctional person in a room and keep having terrible relations with them. With our behaviors and our needs for safety and familiarity, we are drawn to people, places and things that make us feel at ease — even though it's not healthy for us. It's painful and dysfunctional, but it's all we know, and it feels safe.

Unhealthy attachment creates many of the conditions in the Diagnostic and Statistical Manual of Mental Disorders (DSM), which professionals use to diagnose us.

My own healthy and unhealthy attachments as a child were learned from living with my father and mother. I wanted more than anything to make my father love me. But he was brought up in an even more violent childhood than the one he gave me. I had it made in the shade compared to his story.

In school, I was comfortable with troublemakers. I thought being the class clown at least got me recognized by my peers. I started attaching to vulgar, violent and abusive people who mistreated me. From an early age, I tried to fill the emptiness in me, and that was what I gravitated toward.

I unconsciously looked for people I thought were easy targets who would give me love. I was confused and never able to fulfill my ambiguous ideas about life. I would look for people who either could take abuse quietly while inwardly hurting themselves or loudly while fighting back. The friends I chose used sex, drinking, drugs and thrill-seeking behavior as a cure-all to replace any healthy relations we could've developed.

Those relationships always ended in dissatisfaction when I learned they did something that wronged me, or I grew tired and wanted the next insatiable fix. I fought with, dumped or was left bewildered by my partners. But I always had a line of people waiting as human rain checks to take the place of the last person, after every disaster blew up in my face.

The physical violence and abuse I experienced as a child became my comfortable way to relate to this world. That was my relational cycle of violence. At work, I created problems and needed more attention than anyone else just to feel normal. I found fault in others and tried to get their jobs by any means necessary. I was a workaholic without healthy boundaries and made my work my life. After a while, I burned out. My cycle was to work non-stop; rise to the top of the food chain, be unhappy and then get fired or quit during an emotional meltdown.

To change our conditioned responses, we must suspend everything we think, say and do — all our thoughts words and deeds — and become willing to have a beginner's mind. Although it is counter-intuitive to every muscle memory and gut feeling we have ever experienced, it is the first step. It may feel as if we are free-falling from groundlessness. But we are developing a new belief system and faith in the as-yet unseen.

We will become fearless, courageous people with limitless thinking.

Let's re-parent ourselves, starting right here and now. Let's take that scared and confused inner child by the hand and slowly work toward oneness of person, while acknowledging our inner child's reality. Here are some ideas to get started. Add your own to the list:

1. Do No Harm to yourself or others today. Stop the cycle.

2. When you find yourself getting emotionally escalated with your beliefs, recognize your behaviors; resist temptations to attach, and recover your immediate experience. Stay neutral and groundless. Attach neither to highs and lows, ups and downs. Stay in the middle ground.

3. Look into the mirror and see who you are. Start repeating healthy and loving endorsements of your love for yourself. Be gentle. Even if your words feel inauthentic, fake it till you make it — dress for the life you want, not the life you have. Practice new behaviors now, and they will become your normal later. If you do this work, you will get the results.

4. Make a list of healthy things that help you make it through a normal day. Hold on to them and recognize them as good. Repeat them and add new ones, so you have strength-based, empowerment building blocks to create your future.

5. Make a list of ways you hurt relationships with others. Start working with a group that's committed to self-change similar to yours. Make yourself accountable. Write down what you do, and be responsible. Start making living amends to people who have suffered from your behaviors.

6. Let go. Do you want to be right or happy? What's the worst that could happen? Play the scene out in your mind until the end, and give yourself a happy ending.

7. Detach with love. It's scary at first. You have to sit with your feelings, and fill your emptiness with trust and faith that doing the next right thing is all that matters.

8. When you see someone get a job, a partner, a car, a home or a vacation, consider the abundance they have as your own abundance. Trust that if they can do it, so can you.

9. Look for what is behind your need for someone to do what you want. Look behind your need for someone to act like you want them to. In relationships, we get used to things happening in a certain way. When the behavior changes, we become concerned that our way of life will not be sustainable. Many of us want things to stay the same, so we feel safe.

10. Know what your bias, judgments, racism and righteousness are all about. These are the attachments that prevent you from joining others in partnership and collaboration.

Workbook Questions:

1. What kinds of thinking are you attached to? Do you have a bias toward immigrants; fighting wars, political parties and the like? Are you attached to groups that work to end racism or protect the planet? Name what you are attached to.

2. Did you have immediate attachment to your mom at birth? If you can, ask her. In what ways were your parents too busy or distracted to give you attention?

3. Did you learn from and attach to the television or computer? Did you play games instead of receiving parental guidance?

4. Did your parents use corporal punishment when you did something they did not like? How did that form of violence mold and affect you?

5. Did your parents overprotect you and not let you get into your fair share of life's bumps and scrapes? Did you look for friends and partners who would overprotect you as you got older?

6. Are you imprinted with your parents' beliefs, cultures and mental outlooks? Did you rebel? What was the result of either experience?

7. What do you know about healthy bonding? Name five ways to practice healthy bonding. Do you have any healthy friends as role models? Why or why not?

8. What do you know about re-parenting yourself, so you can heal from real or perceived childhood problems?

9. When you feel attached and intractable with your thinking, ask yourself, "Why do I believe this is true?" Then ask, "Who would I be without this thinking? What do I have to lose? How can I turn this thinking around?"

10. What image-breakers are you willing to do to step out of the box and into meeting new people and learning new behaviors? What do you find valuable about connecting with people who have what you want? What are your fears about being seen in a new light?

11. How do you stay neutral when you are emotionally escalated?

12. Do you find yourself joining in gossip about others just to fit in? In what ways do you detach from those behaviors?

13. In what ways do you raise your children or respond in a relationship with your partner that is different than what you learned from your parents? What things do you repeat that your parents did? Are you imprinting another perfect replica of dysfunction, based upon your bad experiences? What can you do to stop that behavior?

14. What behaviors would you like to detach from? Physically? Emotionally? In relationships? At work?

15. Which of your addictions can you relate directly to your family of origin? Did they do these types of things? Did you do them to rebel and cope with your feelings?

Attention Deficit Disorder / Attention Deficit Hyperactivity Disorder

Here is a view inside my own ADD. I am a thrill-seeking person who thrives in dangerous situations. When it is "just another day" of routine, I find myself bored. Nothing excites me, and that can lead to depression.

I am a megalomaniac, a multi-tasker from Hell. No matter how much I accomplish, it is not enough. I do not ever feel satisfied with what I have done. I am always looking for perfection. I judge myself harshly, and sometimes I judge others as harshly as I judge myself.

It is not uncommon for me to start eight projects and multi-task, so I always have something to do and won't get bored. It is a vicious cycle that creates its own unhappiness.

When I speak to others, I often use metaphors and parables. People cannot understand me. This is frustrating. I have low impulse control, and I over-disclose and speak in a Tourette's-like style that lends itself to anger and control issues. I have expectations and want everyone to understand that if they do as I say, everything will turn out right. If this does not happen, I get frustrated.

When I was in fifth grade, I drummed my fingers on my desk like it was a drum set. I listened to instructions and then tried to find quicker ways to complete the assignment without following them. I played dangerous games without thinking about the consequences. I also developed a tendency to speak ALL of my truth, even though it often was best left unsaid.

Today, I play drums, keyboards and guitar and am exploring the flute, clarinet and saxophone. I paint with watercolors, acrylics and airbrush in a variety of styles, both representational and abstract. Because of my upbringing, I know how to use a variety of tools and have done trade work, such as plumbing, electrical, HVAC, roofing, cement work, lock-setting, carpentry, window work and landscaping.

I also once was addicted to speed, weed, thrill-seeking, sex, and alcohol.

Even today, I struggle with the need to be treated as special so I can feel average. I have inaccurate self-observations of my worth that lead to low self-esteem. I wrestle with chronic anxiety, an anti-authority combative disorder, bipolar disorder, depression and trust issues. I am driven to distraction and can resist anything but temptation. My whole life has been one distracting mission creep after another.ADD and Its SymptomsADD, which stands for attention deficit disorder, is an older term used to diagnose individuals who are inattentive and often distracted. The American Psychological Association (APA) first coined the term ADD in 1980 to describe individuals who had trouble paying attention, were often forgetful, and had difficulty with organization at home, school, or work.Children with ADD have trouble focusing in school or appear to daydream, and can be easily distracted by small noises that most people tune out. They may also forget or lose things. These children often jump from task to task without completing them, which can lead to poor grades. Some have trouble "turning off" their brains at night and struggle to fall asleep.

ADHD and Its Symptoms

ADHD is a neural behavioral disorder in which an individual is unable to concentrate on everyday tasks. Individuals with ADHD, like those with ADD, have trouble with focusing and organization. They may have difficulty following a conversation, and, in some cases, they are impulsive or have a higher than normal energy level (hyperactivity). However, not everyone with ADHD has the same symptoms—in fact, how ADHD presents in any one individual depends on many biological and environmental factors.

Three Types of ADHD

Inattentive Type

An individual with inattentive ADHD has trouble focusing and completing tasks and is easily distracted. This individual may stare into space or seem to be "missing" from a conversation. With this type of ADHD, the person is often forgetful and disorganized and may make mistakes with the details of a task. For example, a child with inattentive ADHD may complete a math homework assignment, but forget to show his or her work, or make mistakes in the details of the calculations. An adult may not follow or recall points covered in a business meeting.

Individuals with this type of ADHD are usually not hyperactive, but are quiet and seem "spacey." However, individuals with inattentive ADHD are not really inattentive at all—rather, they are paying attention to everything at once (the hum of the air conditioner, the tapping of pencils, the ticking of the clock, the teacher speaking). This overload of stimuli makes focusing on one task difficult and leads to the assumption they aren't paying attention. This type of ADHD is often overlooked in the classroom or the workplace because individuals with inattentive ADHD do not draw attention to themselves.

Hyperactive/Impulsive Type

With this type of ADHD, the individual has a higher than normal energy level and great difficulty remaining seated, even for short periods. The person may fidget, tap their hands or feet, or get up and walk around. In severe cases, the individual has to be in constant motion, even when it is not appropriate. In some individuals, hyperactivity is expressed by nonstop talking.

Impulsivity is also present in people with this type of ADHD. The person may interrupt conversations or have trouble waiting in line or taking turns. Impulsivity also means that the individual may act before thinking—for example, a child may suddenly jump from a high place on the playground or hit someone who has made them angry. This makes these individuals more prone to injury and can have an effect on their social relationships.

Combined Hyperactive/Impulsive and Inattentive Type

Individuals with the combined form of ADHD have characteristics of both the inattentive and hyperactive/impulsive types. According to the CDC, this is the most common type of ADHD.

Adult ADHD

Adults with ADHD have typically had the disorder since childhood, but it may not have been diagnosed until later in life. An evaluation usually occurs at the prompting of a peer, family member, or coworker who has observed problems at work or in relationships. Adults can be diagnosed with any of the three subtypes of ADHD discussed above. However, due to the relative maturity of adults, as well as physical differences between adults and children, adult ADHD symptoms can be somewhat different from those experienced by children. For example, adults with hyperactive/impulsive ADHD are unlikely to run and jump around.

ADD and ADHD Severity

The symptoms of ADD and ADHD can range from mild to severe, depending on a person's neurobiology and environment. Some experience mild inattentiveness or hyperactivity when they perform a task they do not enjoy, but have the ability to focus on tasks they like. Others may experience more severe symptoms, which can have a negative impact in school, at work, and in social situations.

Symptoms seem to be more severe in unstructured group situations (e.g. on the playground) than in more structured situations where rewards are given (e.g. in the classroom). Other conditions, such as depression, anxiety, or a learning disability may worsen the symptoms of ADD or ADHD . Some patients report that symptom severity diminishes with age. For example, an adult with ADHD who was hyperactive as a child may find that he or she is now able to remain seated or curb some impulsivity.

The good news is that by determining your type of attention deficit disorder and its severity, you are one step closer to finding the right treatment to help you cope. Be sure to discuss all your symptoms with your doctor to ensure an accurate diagnosis.

Yes, I have accomplished much. But not in the mindful way most have done and which I would have preferred. That path is more likely to lead to predictable, safe lives with a prosperous retirement and pension.

What I Have Found

For me to really get something, to understand it clearly, I must attach in a healthy way to the source or teacher. To learn, I need to surrender all my racing thoughts by using breathing exercises. I have to clear my mental clutter. If I learn this one thing, it will lead to Good Orderly Direction — what I call GOD in my life.

When I am able to turn these things over and "let go and let GOD," I do not have the weight of the world on my shoulders. When I catch my brain over-tasking and spinning in a thousand directions, I remind myself, "Slow down. I am safe right here and right now."

I pray for the willingness to pray for the willingness. I pray for peace and quiet so learning can take place. I have to take small steps to build upon my learning; I realize a lifetime is spent learning new things. Eventually, I grew to the point that I am able to take in more complex learning.

I am committed to my journey. Daily I remind myself that if I live for the benefit of others, I can have all things. My spiritual house needs to be cleaned so it is in order for learning. I must stay open, willing, flexible, and teachable, with a beginner's mind. The decision is, "Do I want to be right or happy?"

During those times when I am learning and really trying to "get it," I make sure a lengthy amount of time is set aside and committed for real change to happen. I am willing to try through practice, practice, practice and realize that mistakes are a natural part of the learning curve. The fact is surrendered that I do not have a necessarily fair hand in playing this game, and if I try to compare my life with another's, I will feel despair. If I compete, I will feel defeat. The middle ground must be my road. If I get too "up" or excited — or I get manic and feel like Superman — the vicious cycle begins when I get depressed and feel bad. I am bipolar! Isn't everyone? I have to remind myself I am safe exactly as I am. I accept myself unconditionally right here, right now, in this moment.

Throughout this book, I encourage you to learn what works best for you. It can take years of commitment, but it is possible to change our neurogenesis. We can rewire our brains.

My ears are the gateway to learning; I often begin with what I hear. I write with my hands what I want to remember or explore. With my eyes, I look at the task I have committed to or at the words I've written. My voice speaks what I have learned. I practice, practice, practice. Traveling through the learning curve incorporates all five senses for the brain to fire together and release the neurochemical messengers. The more I access this way of my mind completely committing, the more focus is created for learning and remembering. I create my own brain's muscle memory. If you do not use your brain, it will atrophy.

Mindfulness Exercises

Make a list of important things you need to do during the day. Set an allotted amount of time per task, and get in the habit of starting and completing one task at a time. When you finish one, move on to the next right thing on your list. Let go of what you have accomplished, and don't try to be a perfectionist. Have an accountability partner to bookend with after a day of tasks. If you can't finish a task, make note of what it will take to complete it later.

Notice the times when you are not listening. You're too excited, talking too much, shutting down mentally, building resentments — these are distractions of the mind. Keep working your brain. Start with small, doable tasks such as waking up, taking a shower, brushing your teeth, reading the newspaper, ironing clothes and dressing for work. Allot time to get to work and begin on time. At some point, stop, notice and admire what you have accomplished so far that day. Persevere.

Things to Watch Out For

Defensiveness: Do you often feel you are at a diminished return? Things seem to pile up, and you can't get out from under the load. Let go of your defense, and accept that you have a problem. Until you deal with it, you cannot conduct normal business with others. It is an unfair exchange for both sides. Get help and start creating equity with those around you.

Learn how to actively listen with your whole body and mind. Watch the emotional cues of others, and believe them. You are not a mind reader or magical thinker. Let go of your agenda thinking, and sit with the discomfort you feel at your inability to pick up on clues. Develop the person's trust to be honest with you, and process their truth. Hang around people you can trust.

Impulsivity: You want immediate, convenient and instant gratification. When it comes to communication you blurt things out that you are sorry for later. You also don't take time to talk with your partner in buying and decision-making processes to evaluate the best thing to do for the greater good. You make impulsive moves without checking in.

You are driven to distraction and can easily start doing many tasks without getting anything done. "Can't you tell I've been working by the mess I made?" When someone shows you how to do something, your mind races to find a quicker, better way, one that is easier for you than the process that has been done for years and years. As a result, the task isn't done in a timely manner. You think you know it all.

People-pleasing: One trait of a people-pleaser is doing things for your boss that are not really your job. Know your own job description. Know your scope of practice. Know your limitations.

Don't let someone else's lack of preparation become your emergency or crisis. Don't become a disaster-recovery expert. Let others clean up their own messes.

Build estimable acts into your day to feel esteem. Make space for service to others as part of your healthy give-back. You will feel worthy and part of your community.

Notice when you are hungry, angry, irritated, lonely, tired and horny. These lead to distractions. Extreme self-care is paramount for staying on task.

Notice when everyone around you is distracted by your confusion. Recognize your behavior. Call a trusted partner. Resist the temptation to continue what you're doing, and recover your ability to stay on task.

Workbook Questions:

1. Everyone gets distracted. What are your emotional clues? Are you sensitive, vulnerable, stubborn, unskillful, easily offended? Name five. In what ways are you physically distracted? Your diet? Attractive people? Do you get a sweaty, adrenaline rush, or lazy, unmovable and confused?

2. What are your main work habits that people complain about? What about habits at home? Habits in conversations? As a team member? Intimacy and sex?

3. Do you think it is bad thing to have a mental-health diagnosis? Are you willing to work on common ways in which you can get better anyway? After reading this section, what would that look like to you? How can you demonstrate to your loved ones that you are in solution-thinking mode for the longer view?

4. Do you always defend your beliefs? More to the point, do you argue because you are unskillful at communicating effectively? What makes it difficult for you to accept another's truth? Why are they wrong? What can you do to surrender and work as part of a team?

5. Do you blurt things out and ruin all the work you and others put into a project, after working hard on it for months? How does this set you back with trust issues with others? They want to feel safe; what are you willing to do to stop your outbursts?

6. Is it fair to your family or partner when you buy things without asking? When you impulsively do things because you believe you are entitled, in relation to others, how does that destroy your life?

7. Are you unable to accurately read others' emotional cues? Why don't you believe what they are stating? In your opinion, why can't they be right and have their truth? What will it take for you to accept their point of view? Are the people you hang around with unsafe? If so, why do you continue to distract yourself with instability and danger?

8. Do you begin a lot of projects, get to a certain point and then have difficulty finishing? What can you do to finish one and then another, and enjoy the satisfaction of a completed task?

9. How do you feel about exercise, medication and learning about your condition?

10. Are you willing to take a few years to focus and get to know more about how your brain functions?

11. Is your job ideal for your brain chemistry, but things fall apart when you get home? Why?

12. Do you feel as if your partners, parents and loved ones are nagging you to participate in a recovery program, and you don't understand why?

13. How does your diagnosis work for you? There are perks, even for challenging diagnoses. What are yours? Some behaviors make you feel safe and as if you belong to something. How can you have the best of both worlds? Where is there discourse and confusion in trying to persuade others?

14. Do you let bills pile up, or get tax information to the IRS at the last second? Are you always just a few days away from having cable, phone or utilities turned off? What can you do better to give you and your family peace of mind?

Biological Vulnerability

Where did we come from? How did we become conditioned to need what we need?

Let's get curious about our DNA. We have tendencies that evolved into our appetites for survival. These can include sexual preferences, our drive to fight, hunt, gather, mate, lead and/or follow. Hormone levels and brain structure may continue the work toward what we are destined to do and develop our conditioned responses.

When did conditioned responses evolve?

In the evolution of the species, "Ontogeny recapitulates phylogeny." This means the birth of a new organism expresses all the adapting forms of its ancestors throughout evolution. As our new and demanding environments create the need for change, we adapt and evolve. Necessity is the mother of invention.

We develop survival mechanisms that become integrated into our being. Or we become hybrids who develop new behaviors and terminate old ones. This is basic evolution. Our collective consciousness and behaviors are destined to be our genetic disposition. Yet our environment can change that consciousness.

One hundred generations ago, someone fermented fruit —grapes or something similar — and created alcohol. Since then, humanity is pre-disposed to suffer from the side effects of drinking too much.

When do conditioned responses to actions such as drinking, warring and philosophy become part of our collective DNA? How can we edge the "hand we are given" for our life into something positive and nurturing and contribute in healthy ways?

My mother grew up among the dirt roads of Kansas. Her family lived off the land. My father is of Polish origin. Poland has experienced tumultuous changes in war-torn kingdoms since the 15th century and concluded with World War II. One of every five Polish people was killed by Germans or Russians.

I am culled from the genetic history of my parents. I am a survivor. I am able to adapt, morph and live anywhere off the land. I thrive with whatever society throws away.

I have chosen to evolve before I die and quit accepting scraps tossed under the table. I do the work to make sure that others evolve and carry on without repeating humanity's history of waste, violence, and disparity for Earth.

People react to specific stimuli. How do we change the association and prompt new responses to practice until they become our new muscle memory?

When the military teaches us to kill, we learn more harmful ways to demean and dehumanize the enemy so we can kill on command. We can turn this same mind-conditioning around and use it for positive change in our lives.

What if addiction is 50 percent pre-disposition and the rest is opportunity to change poor survival strategies? Our willingness has a lot to do with the end game. We live in a world where we can effect change in our lives. In some cases, choice becomes a poverty of the mind. In our addiction, we did anything to get our fix, whether it was a sexual encounter, food, gambling, thrill-seeking or gun behavior. Let's use that transferrable skill for healthy choices, and thrive.

By staying mindful and vigilant, we avoid entropy – or gradual decline – by our actions. We are metaphysical alchemists, changing matter from one thing to another. By our choices, we turn the poison in our lives into medicine. We work against the muscle memory of our upbringing to surrender everything we think, say and do – all our thoughts words and deeds. We are what we think. We digest our thoughts on a cellular level, and it becomes our organic experience. It's our choice, once we have been shown the way to do it.

We have used drugs, anger, righteousness, poverty, privilege and alcohol so much that we have rewired our brains for entitled ways of thinking. We can surrender that way of life and develop healthy choices to replace it.

Be the change you want in your life. Respond differently to life's opportunities. You can cleanse the area around you, so your destiny will be a legacy passed on to others. You will change their pre-disposition and eventually their DNA, when they learn how much benefit they will leave for generations to come.

Following are nine ways to work on being an agent of change in your life:

1. Be willing to suspend your thinking absolutely for the quest of alternatives that may work.

2. Be willing to actively listen to all sides of an argument. Do not judge, just listen. This is your only job.

3. Be willing to see things differently as with a new pair of glasses. Don't assume.

4. Close your eyes and start deep-breathing. Is anything really happening right now? Are you in danger? Is harm really all in your head? Is your mind really the only thing doing harm?

5. Be willing to walk one mile in another's shoes, and feel the emotion or action you thought was wrong. Is it wrong when *you* do what you do to survive?

6. Be willing to hold both truths – yours and the truth you want to activate. Hold the paradox.

7. Be willing to develop your diametrically opposed thinking, discernment and ambivalence, and to look for solutions that do no harm.

8. Be willing to agree to disagree. Be groundless. Feel that uncertainty and get used to its discomfort as normality.

9. If anxiety is the distance that separates you from your Higher Power, and acceptance is the answer to all your questions, can you become accepting of life on life's terms?

Workbook Questions:

1. What are the genetic traits of your family of origin?

2. What beliefs were handed down as conditioned family ideals that now seem almost genetic in origin?

3. What would you like to change in your genetic predisposition? For example, is there tendency toward diseases such as cancers, mental-health problems, high or low metabolism? Are there warrior, hunter/gatherer tendencies or thrill-seeking behaviors?

4. In what ways can you play the hand life gave you?

5. Where can you find help?

6. What will you do to change? Are you willing to give 100 percent of your life's energy to the effort?

7. Sometimes you must work against your upbringing and family values. What small changes are you willing to make to stop the spiral? What can you think of that will help?

8. Has your culture suffered from generational dysfunction and historical oppression? What small changes can you make to turn the tide? What is stopping you from being an agent of change in your life, your community or your country?

9. In most families, drinking is a family tradition that goes back many generations. Do you believe you're genetically inclined to drink or exhibit other behaviors, such as warrior qualities?

10. Do you have cancer in your family line that could be the result of eating and lifestyle choices? What can you do to stop such things from writing your epitaph?

11. What health conditions, such as diabetes, can you reverse by changing your diet and lifestyle?

12. How do your sexual proclivities genetically drive you to do things that are out of control? What are you willing to do for peace of mind and healthy relations?

Bipolar Disorder/Manic Depression

All diagnoses are relative and capable of producing great positive changes in people, if used as a guidepost for working on their lives. Our brains are a complicated array of chemical cascades that create how we feel, act and think. People are complicated and live in a hectic and unpredictable world. We should remember it is people who are real — not their diagnoses. Do not pathologize a person with his diagnosis.

At age 42, I was diagnosed with bipolar manic depression with psychotic features. It took me a long time to understand what that meant. I had many other problems that seemed harder to overcome than that diagnosis. But I needed the diagnosis to get help.

At the beginning of treatment, I felt like it was a chemical straightjacket, because I had to take medications and was told I would be on them for the rest of my life. As I grew to understand myself better because of the diagnosis, I slowly turned every weak link in my life into my strongest assets. I appreciate and value myself because of the starting place. Here are some ideas about what bipolar manic depression with psychotic features means.

I describe it like this: I went Up Up Up Up to the heights of extreme power and bliss, and then I crashed Down Down Down Down until I wanted to crawl in a hole and die. There was no gray area.

Here is a clinical definition: The disease affects changes in the mood from a soaring high of mania and elation, then plummets down to the darkest lows of depression.

Here are warning signs to look for: If you are able to regulate your mood swings, then you have more opportunities to be skillful with the chemical cascades in your brain. The brain sends signals and gives chemicals — or lacks the ability to produce the correct chemicals and can even block receptors to the chemical flow. When I found out what was physically going on, I had a chance and a choice to respond with different behaviors as I became master and commander of my life experience.

There are two major components of bipolar disorder:

- When feeling depressed, there are extreme lows and sadness. It seems that life is not worthwhile. There is a hopeless feeling and an inability to come back from that infinite sadness. There is helplessness before terror. A lot sleep is needed, and there is a general feeling of paralyzed nothingness.
- When the manic phase is in swing, people believe that they can move mountains, are excited, have unparalleled energy to burn. They forget to rest, eat well and sleep because they are on "a mission."

The two feelings of depression and extreme energy can happen at the same time. There are no regulations as to when, where and how they will be felt. They are uncontrollable and keep the person and their loved ones emotional hostages.

Some of my depressive symptoms included: crying a lot, sleeping a lot, low self-esteem, awfulizing, catastrophizing, globalizing, sadness, extreme apathy, negative emoting, inability to connect with friends and loved ones, suicidal ideation, chronic fatigue, sometimes appearing passive-aggressive in tone, guilt-ridden, unable to concentrate and coordinate my needs, lacking interests or pleasures, eating as a stress reducer, and scattered, metaphoric, tangential speech. When I started negative emoting, it seemed as if I attracted negative concepts into my life; they seemed to snowball out of control. I also took street drugs and drank alcohol to self-medicate.

Some of my mania symptoms included: hyper-grandiosity, hyper-sexuality, magical thinking, fantasy and delusional thinking, euphoria, thinking faster than I could talk, boundless energy, less need for sleep, trying to buy happiness through shopping, thrill-seeking behaviors for immediacy, convenience, hyper-vigilance, micro-managing affairs, low-impulse behaviors, impatient and fast driving.

I felt extremely creative. I felt like I could solve all the problems of the world in a minute. Eventually these things led to irritability with others to buy in or understand my thoughts, which introduced anger, irritability and blaming. I picked fights at the slightest criticism. I thought God was talking to me. I manifested voices or requests from people who weren't there.

Following are some things that helped me:

- Admitting that something was wrong, then surrendering to accept help from medical professionals.

- Willingness to be honest with my experience in front of trained professionals and to develop a loose diagnosis to begin my recovery.

- Ability and patience with trying medications that worked with my brain chemistry and physiology. It can take a long time to get the right mix of medications. Be prepared to change them as necessary, and be willing to try them for two to three months to make sure they are a good fit. I had to commit to being medically compliant for at least a few years to make sure I was in control of my life. Then slowly I advocated and demonstrated to wean off and experiment with my medical team to see if I could live without medications.

- Willingness to learn absolutely everything about my diagnosis from many sources. It was crucial to get a general overview of the experiences people had. Education is vital. I turned my weakest asset into my strongest ability.

- After my moods were stabilized with medications, I started to develop therapies to learn preventive skill sets, coping skills and thriving mechanisms. I learned to recognize my behavior, resist the temptation to act out and recover my mental ability to create safety for myself and others.

- In the same way I tested medications, I had to find a good fit with my psychiatrist, psychologist and therapist. This took time. I also started developing community by going to meetings with groups of like-minded people who were thriving with their diagnosis. I realized I was not alone, and my diagnosis wasn't personal or unique. I learned it is my choice to be responsible with the hand I was given with this life.

- I began living with new lifestyle choices, monitoring my episodes and learning from each one. I learned to live with less stress and maintain healthy boundaries with others. This disease will come and go, but my commitment to work with it mindfully will last a lifetime. I maintain my support system and keep learning new healthy additions to my lifestyle.

- I exercise regularly.

- Relapse of symptoms will happen. I stay flexible, open and willing to surrender my old thinking. I focus on goals and solution-focused therapies. I don't dwell on the episode, but move into healthy actions with a sense of urgency.

Workbook Questions:

1. Do people walk on eggshells around you, distrusting you because of past behaviors?

2. Do you revel in your diagnosis as if it is something romantic? Does it give you rock-star status like Jimi Hendrix?

3. Are you on medication? Willingly? Do you take it as prescribed or only when you have an episode? Do you expect it to work even though it takes weeks to get a proper dose into your body?

4. What are emotional cues that hint you are having a manic episode? What are they when you know you are having one?

5. What are signs of depression — chronic depression, not just one thing going wrong? Do things seem to bombard you when you feel down?

6. What good things did you accomplish when you had a manic experience?

7. What low-impulse things have you done that you regretted later? Did they involve a vehicle, a relationship, a job, your family?

8. What are you willing to commit to doing to keep your Jekyll-and-Hyde life of Chutes and Ladders under control?

9. Do you have suicidal or homicidal ideations? Do you have a place, a method and a time? If you answered yes to these, please seek immediate help. Go to an Emergency Room or dial 911.

10. What brought relief from your symptoms in the past?

11. Are you a part-time bipolar manic depressive? What keeps you coming back? Can you afford this recidivism in your life?

12. Do you believe you are more creative, poetic and artistic because of your diagnosis? Do you believe you have more feelings than others and would feel dull and "normal" without all your highs and lows?

13. How long would you be willing to commit to seeing a medical team and take medication?

14. What kinds of support groups are you willing to go to? What communities can you become a part of that give you feelings of safety, restfulness, serenity, health and exercise?

15. What method do you have in place to document your episode, break it into meaningful understandable bits, and then learn from your mistakes?

Body Image

With this topic, I address what we think of our self-image; what we are shown in advertising as the purported "ideal," and how we respond if we do not fit that manufactured image.

We are social creatures with genetic pre-dispositions to pass on to willing and capable hosts. We judge and compare, dismiss and diminish those who do not conform to the body standard of our culture. We also dismiss cultures and beliefs that are not our own in the same divisive ways. We will explore what's left for the other 99 percent of people who have blemishes and real bodies. Each of us requires and deserves the same love and attention that all sentient humans need to flourish.

My earliest experiences with body image were learned from baby-sitters. I got infatuated and developed crushes on them. I was a child of the 1960s, when there was rampant sexual freedom. My parents hosted sock hops and stayed up late with young people, moving and gyrating to the sounds of the times. It was a time of hot pants and mini-skirts. Women tried to be sexy, and men tried to be James Bond. Twiggy was the model for the era and set the bar for societal standards of American beauty.

And so it began for me: sexualizing, womanizing, misogyny, perfectionism, objectifying and chauvinistic tendencies. I viewed women as sexual objects for ego satisfaction, immediacy and social stature. I masturbated to images of women. I used them and then moved onto the next conquest. I needed women to fulfill all my needs, which were mother, girlfriend, sexual object and baby-sitter.

As has been the case in most, if not all, eras of American history, fat people were fair game for bullying and name-calling. Any people whose faces and bodies didn't conform to cultural standards of beauty were targets of cruelty and rejection as well. People of color were treated as if they were less than human, name-called, objectified and ignored as if they did not exist. Conversely, those considered good-looking had everyone wanting their attention and vying to be near the 1 percent.

I was brought up in and taught that way of life from society. However, my mom taught me to treat people of all shapes, sizes, and ethnicities with equity, dignity and respect. We were also introduced to gay people back in the '60s; some of my mom's co-workers were gay and a part of our lives in the government positions she held.

When I was in the sixth grade, my front teeth were knocked out. Girls stopped chasing me around the playground and started calling me "Silver Tooth." This was the time I learned how it felt to be treated differently. I spoke with a lisp after that and went to a speech therapist to address it.

My dad encouraged me to lift weights to be manly. Part of that manly image was being a rough guy who could fix cars; scale freshly caught fish; gather wood, mow lawns and repair anything. In public, I was loud and brassy. I was insecure and needed a lot of attention to make me feel safe.

From an early age, I had great diversity among my friends. I wore unisex clothes, trading silk and lace shirts with my mother and sister. I sported the latest fashions, with tight-fitting shoes and pants that showed off my crotch. I wore my hair in long locks and strutted around like a rock star. I was Adonis – a God-given ass.

However, despite all the ways I styled myself, I always thought competing was cosmetic hell. I was always caught up in compare-and-despair with others. I had pimples and greasy skin. Meanwhile, my mom seemed to try every new diet, and I realized she was never comfortable with her body either. Never enough.

When you look at yourself in the mirror, what do you see? Can you simply see you, as you are? Do you see what society thinks you should be? Do you look, act and respond to those beliefs? Do your perceived shortcomings overshadow what you love about your own body?

If you look at yourself and reflect on the fact that more than two-thirds of Americans are overweight, then what do you believe is "normal"? If being overweight is the norm, why aren't we all acceptable as we are?

Somewhere between what I think and the norms of my culture, therein lies my opportunity to develop my body image. Body image includes cultural norms, sizes, ages, disabilities and ethnicity. This is big stuff. It is our responsibility as a society to get honest with our belief systems and honor others for their inherent worth as sentient people who deserve the same privileges everyone enjoys.

Sometimes we suffer from body-to-mind confusion. Our eating habits and mental issues are connected. If I have a healthy sense of self and am comfortable with myself, what I look and how I live, then I am less likely to be concerned about what others think of me. As the saying goes, what other people think of me is none of my business.

Acceptance is the answer to all of our questions about "good" and "bad" body image. Let go of cultural ideals. Learn to love yourself exactly as you are right now, unconditionally, at this moment.

Workbook Questions:

Please do this work with trusted and responsible people who will help you process and move into healthy acceptance and immersion with a loving community. This is a disease of isolation.

1. Why are you hyper-vigilant about your weight, watching every pound like a hawk?

2. When you get upset or stressed, do you eat comfort food without being able to stop when you want? How does it make you feel, while you're eating and afterward?

3. What makes you feel healthy?

4. What is your cholesterol level?

5. Do people judge you because of your race? How does that affect the way you respond to others? Were you taught to hate others who are not of your race? Do you believe you know how to love, value and appreciate all others, regardless of race? How can you be the change you want to see in others?

6. Do you have cultural beliefs that make you feel uncomfortable unless you are with "your own kind"? If you want to change this, how can you safely communicate that wish to others?

7. People of privilege often don't even realize the inequities around them. They think others should just "pull themselves up by their boot straps." Why do you believe some persons have more trouble conforming?

8. Do you have a disability that makes you feel "less than"? Are you uncomfortable around persons with disabilities? When you see a person with a disability, do you make eye contact or avoid it? How can you work on welcoming people with disabilities into your life?

9. How many hours a week do you watch TV? Do you have any healthy hobbies? What are they?

10. Do you eat fast food because it's convenient or cheap? What are healthier alternatives?

11. How do you feel about eating healthy foods and exercising?

12. Do you have mental-health issues? Have you been diagnosed?

13. Do you have medical conditions that affect your daily life, such as diabetes, thyroid issues, or allergies? How do these affect your body image?

14. Are you into keeping up with the latest trends, fashions, phones, cars? What attracts you to that lifestyle? Do you believe this is your authentic self? Explain.

15. What physical quirks do you have? Are your fingers, feet, legs different sizes or larger or smaller than you wish? Explain.

16. We all have something that makes us feel vulnerable. In what ways can you become more comfortable with your vulnerabilities?

17. Do you have the metabolism of a hummingbird — no matter what you eat, you stay skinny? Do you judge others because you're skinny and they are not? What if the situation were to become reversed someday? How would you feel?

18. Do people treat you differently because of your skin color? How do you process this?

19. In what ways do you believe your language sets you up with a disadvantage? Are you aware of how intelligent you are because of your knowledge of multiple languages? Do you resent the focus on English in the United States? Explain.

20. Do you have a physical disability that leads others to ignore you or take advantage of you?

21. How were you treated as a child? Did that continue into your adult life? In what ways do you seek safety?

22. Explain how it might feel to have a partner who loves and accepts you unconditionally.

23. When you feel insecure about your looks, do you isolate and keep out of sight? Has staying under the radar become your lifestyle? Explain.

24. Are you willing to work to become comfortable with yourself around others? What do you believe would help you to achieve that?

25. Have you felt momentary increases in your self-esteem? Why didn't it last? Did one behavior feed others and, through repeated actions, become a way of life for you? How could you change a few things now for a different outcome?

Bookending

Because I have been a procrastinator for a great portion of my life, I know I need the accountability and support of likeminded peers.

When we write down our task lists and check in daily or weekly with an accountability partner while continually revising our goals, we have a 76-percent higher chance of fruition. Bookending means:

1. Check in with an accountability partner before starting a task or goal.
2. Do the work.
3. Check in when done.

There are methods to help us achieve goals, such as Paul J. Meyer's "SMART" system – commonly defined as Specific, Measurable, Achievable, Realistic, and Time-bound. But inside the closed system of our own self-will, our efforts will dissipate once the inspiration to use those practices is gone. With someone to call us on our stuff and keep gently redirecting us toward our goals, we are less likely to listen to that inner critic who says, "Why bother? Who cares? Give up! If only my true worth were known, the world would listen to how great my ideas are."

Oscar Wilde once said, "I can resist everything except temptation." Personally, by the time I do a few chores, put some food into my mouth, make a few phone calls and answer my emails, I am usually totally distracted. I will go on any mission creep to distract myself from following through on ideas. In addition to being distraction-prone, addicts are often perfectionists, which means they are never satisfied with any outcome short of a Nobel Prize.

Bookending helps us to recognize the small steps we make toward a larger goal. Repeatedly telling someone, "I did this little thing," enables us to realize that a week or month of "little things" adds up to real progress.

This concept is prevalent in the recovery community, because it prevents us from being ruled by self. We have a healthy community of colleagues with whom we create equity by being vulnerable and sensitive about our commitments. In return, they can bookend with us. This is an exchange of real power to call others on behaviors they want to change. Then, we are more willing to listen when they do the same for us. Our world could use more efforts like this to solve problems by using the power of collaboration. It's not a "me" problem; it's a "we can solve it together" opportunity.

Find someone who can relate to your effort toward change and recovery and wants to support you with simple check-ins. Follow through on your commitment to call – on time, every time – and check in. Your accountability partner does not necessarily have to respond. She or he is doing their part by simply listening to your check-in. They will get back to you when they can. I like to use the idea of "G.O.D." or "Good Orderly Direction" for bookending. I am working for G.O.D. I am safe. I am protected, and I am loved.

Bookending also helps keep us from isolating during vulnerable times. Loneliness and isolation will let our inner critic run amok, just waiting for the chance to stop anything positive from happening. By making our check-in call, our accountability partner is witnessing and supporting us and validating our worth. This kind of check-in is also a way for us to self-monitor. We need to be an agent of change in our lives and value ourselves through others. We must do estimable acts to develop real self-esteem.

Here are tips for success when bookending:

- Choose an accountability partner who has what you want – a happy life, recovery, a great job, some kind of spirituality, a good sex life, successful recovery or a diverse life. They don't have to be like you or act like a friend. They are accountability partners. They are mentors and spirit guides. They mirror your progress.

- Make an agreement about what you will do and what your accountability partner will do. Interview them as you would hire someone for a job. Make sure they are on board and have enough time. In your agreement, include things such as addressing certain behaviors, best calling times, and what you will be responsible for in challenging and changing your lifestyle.

- Do appropriate readings and research. Go to meetings. Find other people who are changing like you are, and immerse yourself in community. Be accountable by showing up consistently. Your community will know your stuff and call you on it. You will develop a thicker skin and learn to listen to others who suffer as you do.

- Make your bookends measurable and observable timed events, so you can gauge your progress. Remember, change is about progress, not perfection. It took a long time for your behaviors to manifest, and it will take some time to learn new ways to cope and thrive.

- Be honest, willing, teachable, open and curious — with a beginner's mind.

- Stick to it! You did your addictions 24/7. Why won't you put a little time and effort into improving your life? Persistence and perseverance are part of wisdom.

Workbook Questions:

1. What do you want to change about your life? What does your partner or family want to be different? What amount of work are you willing to do?

2. What communities can you contact to help you? Are you part of a house of worship? Can you reach out to Twelve-Step communities or MeetUp groups? Do you have health insurance that might offer communities that would be helpful? Do you have medical help by way of doctors or therapists?

3. What communities have worked for you in the past?

4. When you feel embarrassed or stigmatized, what would you like to change? Do you believe you are the only one with your problem?

5. How can you become more willing to trust someone with your most intimate and vulnerable characteristics? Do you believe others can change? What is stopping you from trusting someone? What will it take for you to move forward?

6. What have you successfully worked on in the past? What people do you have at work who can keep you on track and in whom you can confide for supervision? Could you imagine trusting another person in the same manner regarding your addictions?

7. What easy concepts of change can you embrace that do not shut you down? What are you willing to work on to develop trust? What are the taboo subjects you feel you will never be able to work on? Why?

8. Addiction is a disease of isolation. What stops you from picking up the phone and calling people? What stops you from asking for help? What keeps you thinking you are different from everyone else and can't be helped?

Boundaries and How to Set Them

Boundary: a line that marks the limits of an area. Boundaries, as the saying goes, are where "you stop and I begin."

How do we take control of setting our own healthy boundaries? We can start here and now by taking our "boundary inventory" and honestly acknowledging how we're doing. We may discover how we have violated or crashed others' boundaries. We will work with our passive aggression and pushy agendas.

Admitting that we all do certain selfish things to get our needs met is the first step to developing longer-lasting, meaningful and healthy relationships. We can turn our shame and weakness into our strongest asset and become extraordinary people of value.

As a result, we can garner trust from others and respect ourselves enough to have difficult conversations with others. We can listen to their needs and respect their beliefs and do no harm along the way.

Once we develop self-esteem and self-respect, we know better what we will or won't do. We learn to say yes or no to unappealing requests and develop a Teflon skin. We can hear another's request and say yes or no without our worlds falling apart. We become assertive, truthful and trustworthy in the community.

We can create equity with our healthy boundaries and partner and share power. We can delegate with integrity. We can do extreme self-care and still show up for the game of life.

After developing trust and tenure, we gradually will share more intimate and personal information when it is appropriate for both parties. We live within a partnership of agreed values and integrity.

With the opportunity of teamwork, equity-building and collaborating, we experience a fluid line of give-and-take that creates a healthy relationship of value for both parties. When we set good boundaries for ourselves, others have insight into our moral and ethical beliefs. When we say out loud what our needs are, we hear what our demands or needs are, and see for the first time how brittle and shortsighted they are.

It is important to know what we want and need out of life. People are not mind readers. We need to let them know. They perform better if we make requests of them. If we do not make plans or set boundaries for ourselves, others will gladly make them for us, as we are herded like cattle toward an ominous destination that destroys our self-worth.

Developing healthy boundaries will empower me to say, "I respect your boundaries and, in a healthy way, advocate for what I need in this relationship." Boundaries are what we agree or disagree upon to develop our interpersonal relationship. It is a give-and-take opportunity. We both have a choice and make inroads to meet each other's expectations or make a clear exit plan and stay socially amenable. The gray area in between is where we live with the results of our actions. Actions can be open, willing and flexible depending upon our character traits and our needs for change.

We develop those skillsets by actions. Here are some ideas to consider as you begin your own journey:

- Know thy self. Know what you believe about life, spirituality, self-care, work ethics, political beliefs, racism, sexism, mannerisms, sexual preferences, moral attitudes, fun and playfulness, openness, and closed-mindedness.

- Know your triggers. What makes you angry, resentful and emotional? How much can you handle before you overreact to compensate for your discomfort? Know what your mental capacity is before you feel dis-eased. Know what you can take spiritually before you question your beliefs and act out in anger or righteousness. Know your fears and deepest regrets. These help define what your limits are now and what you are personally willing to work on and expect of others while you decide your own ceiling of comfort about particular subjects.

- Take care of your needs first. Put the oxygen mask on your face before you try to help others on the airplane of life. Give yourself what you need. You deserve to have permission. You belong to the human race. You deserve a relationship where you are trusted, valued, appreciated and treated with respect and admiration. You are learning to present yourself so that people notice you and realize the mutual benefits of honoring your needs.

- Be firm, clear and willing to appropriately adjust your style to diverse personalities and cultures with different values than yours. Do no harm. Be willing to compromise to create a mutual, equitable experience.

- With difficult people in fear-based relationships, start with incremental small items that have no emotional attachment for you. You are beginning a relationship of give-and-take. You learn to agree to disagree. These are the kernels to elicit self-change thoughts. Build momentum and trust based upon earned value from your relationship and by honoring the basic goodness of which humans are capable. We like to give. Giving makes us feel good.

- Be as consistent as you can, and do not play favorites. Be mindful about sending mixed signals.

- Notice what makes you calm, serene, happy, excited, involved and belonging. Understand that you can have all of those values in your life. They are good, and you deserve them. But you have to let others know what you want. This requires that you express your needs. Value and realize that your past created your present, but you now have a choice as to what your life should be. Understand that others are moving past their experiences, too. Keep a soft boundary for changes to occur, as long as no one is being harmed. Keep a safe playground for all to benefit from your self-empowerment. It is for all to enjoy, not just you. It's an agreement — a binding of two parties. With healthy people, there is mutual benefit.

- Everyone deserves connection. People without boundaries can learn, in a safe environment, how to have them with you as a benevolent benefactor and trusted servant. Keep yourself safe and help them build their sense of responsibility. Trust them as far as they can be trusted, and move their opportunities forward through developed trust. This takes time. People who have violated boundaries the most need this help the most. Move beyond your superficial idea of safety, and get to work making this planet a safer place for everyone, not just yourself. Find people to practice boundaries with who are learning, connecting, testing and trying out healthy ways. When you speak your needs out loud, it puts everything into perspective. When you get feedback, you can re-adjust your requests so others can hear you in a safe and respectful way. If you do this work, you will get results. This is an investment. Everyone around you will benefit from your practice.

Workbook Questions:

1. What validations have you received from healthy boundaries?

2. What self-respect do you receive by letting others know what is important to you? Do you speak in a way others can hear you? What can you improve with your style and message delivery?

3. What healthy boundaries do you have? How are you with time management, responsibilities, speaking up for your needs, and asking for what you want from your partner?

4. How do your healthy boundaries keep others safe and able to come back again and again? What do you do that is honest and clear and makes others want what you have?

5. Do you have secrets and live a double life? Do some people harm you and, because you don't want to lose the relationship, you enable them? Do you have a partner who treats you unfairly in a way you would never accept from anyone else? Explain your deal-killers and the boundary relationships of your loved ones.

6. Do you want to belong to a group of people so much that you are willing to compromise your integrity and cross boundaries you would never dream of crossing? Explain what you feel vulnerable about and what seems unfair in your relationship with your environment.

7. Do you have beliefs that collide with your spiritual and religious thinking? Where do you need to make a boundary call with your religion or your true beliefs? What could happen with your community if you voiced your authentic truth?

8. Name five boundaries that others cross in your life. Race, age, weight, education, legal, the list goes on and on. See how many you can express.

9. What unhealthy boundaries have been violated by your children? Do they push against duties and limitations such as chores, room cleaning, studies, money, cell phones, and responsibilities? What will it take for you to stick to your guns and keep healthy ways to develop them instead of giving in or giving up from their persistence to balk?

10. Does someone at work expect you to do more than they do others? Do you help someone at work who is getting paid more than you yet you don't get any credit or money? Are you denied paid breaks because of the culture at work? Have you been sexually treated as an object of desire and are afraid of losing your job if you speak up?

11. Are you treated in a diminished manner because of your race or sex, handicap, partnership? Explain.

12. Have you become an enabler and are co-dependent on others? In what ways do you contribute to their continued dysfunction and dis-eased way of existing?

13. Are you enmeshed in others' lives and have no healthy boundaries for taking care of your own? What will it take for you to honor your life and value your own existence? Is it really compelling to help others in order to make you feel approval? Are you chasing future opportunity instead of looking at the cold, hard facts of your irrational behavior?

14. Do you use agenda, manipulation and coercion to cross others' boundaries so that you can get your needs met? Do you easily use guilt complexes to maneuver over another's life for your immediate gratification or your convenient needs? Why is this okay with you? What sense of entitlement and privilege make you behave that way? Do others deserve that kind of abuse? What can you do differently in the future to take care of your own needs?

15. Do you tolerate discomfort from your partner and stay quiet so that you don't rock the boat? Are you angry and violated and used to taking abuse or neglect? If your partner disrespects you, in what way does the creeping boundary violation affect other areas of your life? If you don't respect yourself enough to say something and set direct and clear boundaries, why are you upset with them? Why not yourself?

16. Do you "tell all" and over-disclose your life without really knowing another person? What do you get from that behavior?

Brain Chemistry, Neural Elasticity, and Chemical Cascades

For better or worse, humans have gotten to this point in history through the ability to use our brains. Our duty as responsible people is to learn to use our brains in an accountable and sustainable way.

Maintaining healthy brain chemistry is about creating better skillful means of dealing with ambivalence and discernment. As we are able to hold the truths of many realities, our ability for critical thinking increases. We can see the bigger picture and access our best wisdom to make healthier choices. This is neural elasticity in its simplest form. Once we understand this, we can begin to deal more effectively with our emotions and the confusing chemical cascades in our brains that are labeled as disorders.

Let's work with what makes the brain tick. We start by bringing different elements of the brain to attention.

Let's start with our eyes, "the windows of the soul." The way we read into, look at, are attracted to, or feel revulsion for what we see is all in our heads. It's all about how our brain perceives things. For example, we immediately judge whether we want to listen to or ignore a speaker via the way we hear that person speak. We use our mouths to let others know what we are thinking and feeling and how we would like the world to perceive us. We want control and safety. We have an agenda and expectations. We are not in acceptance of some aspects of life. We want to coerce time and space to bend to our will and commands.

Lastly, we write down what we want to happen and/or how we feel about life, which goes into different interpreting neural channels of our brains. This is the story of our lives, or the version of our lives we choose to believe. This is what creates DIS-EASE. When we realign those different pathways to be willing, open, flexible, and teachable with a "beginner's mind," we remove ourselves from our debilitating mental status.

Our abilities to look, listen, write and speak create an environment of awakening in the function of our brains. We can feel and evaluate at once the aspects happening in the many facets of cognizance that create our experience.

Our thoughts are digested on a cellular level in our brains. We are what we think. All these attentions together create an attentive brain. The more neurons that fire together at the same time create an ability to wire those new connections. We have more chances of eliciting and evoking self-change thoughts during our experiences. This leads to healing and increased abilities on all levels.

To achieve this fully functioning brain, we begin with some form of physical exercise for at least a half-hour per day. This gets all our muscles fired up and releasing "feel-good" chemicals in our brains. It rewards us for using our bodies as they should be used. We feel good.

We then do small, simple tasks that may seem almost imperceptible to us. Daily, we improve in increments. We work toward good, orderly direction in our lives. As we become more skillful with our newfound abilities, we start taking on more complex tasks. This is change. Consistency and perseverance are responsible for accomplishing more than simply being born brilliant or into privilege. We can effect change with the hand we were given in this life.

By bringing all these aspects into focus, we are able to handle any situational or peripheral distortions that come our way as we accept life on life's terms.

No matter how far we have fallen, no matter how little we think we have to give, we are already equipped with more than enough to begin. This moment, right here and now, is the only moment we have on the planet to be enlightened. This is the only moment we can choose to be happy and mindful. We can't change our choices in the past, and we can't make choices in the future. We have only now.

We now have fully utilized brain function and ability. We are able to be in this moment, here and now. This is what mindfulness and enlightenment have always been about. This is the only moment we will ever have any control over.

Poverty is a choice of the mind. What will you choose today?

Workbook Questions:

1. If you could be anyone or do anything, what would you like to be? What can you share with others? Are you shy, ashamed, or vulnerable about expressing your true self?

2. How are your well-being and ability to communicate with others isolated? In what ways are you ashamed of who you want to be associated with in current events? What is it about your true self or your angry thoughts that irritates and frustrates you? How are you driven off your life goals by impulsive distractions?

3. What do you watch to get you excited? How can you use that to expand your mental repertoire? How can you use mental sleuthing from crime stories to create hope and solutions for a safer way to live that does not rely on fear and gun ownership?

4. In what ways do you feel frustrated that you cannot communicate your story or belief system without fear of retaliation from your honest thoughts? How is your political stance creating frustration with others who might have other opinions?

5. In what ways do you love to be creative? Name 10 ways, such as swimming, music, geology, health, cooking, relationships, watching documentaries, art or creative projects, building things, woodworking, computers, online gaming, social media, working on small motors, etc.

6. In what ways do you feel like an expert without really doing any research except for the news you watch? Is there really any truth about your thoughts and others' ignorance? Why do you believe they are stupid? Don't they deserve the qualities you have in your life?

7. What would a successful conversation look like in which your partner feels heard? Why do you resort to anger as your first response? Belittling, justification and rationalization soon follow. How can you agree to disagree about subjects? Why is everything a hot topic for you, leading you to lose your composure and ruin any progress in creating safety?

8. Do you think you have million-dollar ideas for creating a better world? What happens when you write your thoughts down? In what ways are you afraid of being the one person who can change everything that is wrong with the world? We need you to help out. We all have a part of making the world a better place.

9. How can you practice what you want your kids to do? How can you lead by example your true intentions? Are you a "do as I say, not as I do" role model with drinking, smoking, anger, righteousness, or consistently being an "expert" on subjects that really just frustrate you, such as racism or sexism?

Burnout

It can happen to anyone, anytime, anywhere. A person does something too much and gets overloaded. That's when he needs to develop healthier boundaries, learn limits and — like most of us — practice extreme self-care.

We like to think we can handle life and its demands. We've heard it all before — the importance of taking care of ourselves. Yet we believe we are different and impervious to getting burned out. After all, we have more experience with (insert your challenge here) than anyone on the planet.

Does your job have unreasonable expectations? Although it was something you liked doing at first, now your tasks and arriving at work feel more like an obligation than an authentic interest of your heart. You believe you are needed so much that others have the right to demand and suck all of the mental, physical and emotional life out of you, leaving you feeling as if you didn't do enough.

The physical effects of stress are among the biggest killers of humans today, according to the American Medical Association. Being a workaholic just isn't fun anymore, nor is it healthy.

Do you have days when "enough" simply isn't enough? Do you feel dread, along with hopeless, resentful and angry emotions, then take them out on your colleagues and/or loved ones? Do you feel like you are alone and working overtime just to keep your head above water? Do you keep doing distracting things to keep busy? Do you internalize the stress?

Stress will take you out. Stress will make you weak. Stress will turn into dis-ease in your soul one way or another. If you are not willing to face the stress in your life now, you will sooner or later. Can you afford the long-term effects of doing too much?

Because we are hard-working members of a workforce, it is difficult to contemplate that we may be susceptible and vulnerable, human and fragile. Once we recognize these signs of stress, we will be more than halfway to stopping the repetitive stress injuries of our work habits. When we are stressed, we can talk ourselves out of almost anything and minimize what others say in their concern. We want to show everyone we can keep up our charade of having everything under control.

Our co-workers and loved ones suffer the most because of our stubborn clinging to what everyone can see but us. Yet we unwittingly expect the same unreasonable things from others and lose our healthy boundaries. We are burned out – burned to a crisp.

Ours is a cunning and baffling egoistic structure that will not admit defeat. Here are some signs that you may be on the verge and in need of resilient, helpful changes in your life:

- You can't see an end to your dilemma.
- Nothing you do will make a change. You think, *why bother, who cares, just give up*.
- You disengage and are driven to distraction while saying out loud, "I got this."
- Stress and pressure make you feel puny and small and that your efforts are insignificant.

However, there are ways you can circumvent the full-blown breakdown of burnout. Before you go to sleep, follow a ritual in which you mentally let go of everything that happened during the day, and put the demands on an imaginary shelf until the morning. Then, get a good night's sleep. You deserve time to mend and heal. This precious time dictates the kind of day you will have tomorrow. Tell your brain it is safe; it is OK to relax and to let go. Read, meditate, or write a gratitude list of everything you're thankful for. Watch some television or whatever you need to do to come down. Then wash up, brush your teeth and go to sleep.

After you wake, begin your day the way you want it to end. If you start with a routine that includes mindful ways to get your body and mind gently ready for a fulfilling day, that's the day you will likely have. If you wake up late to your alarm and find yourself cursing, hurrying and rushing everything to the last minute, then driving in a rush to work, that will likely be your pattern during the day.

Eat well when you awake. This is the most important meal; make sure it is a balanced breakfast. Meditate, do some light exercises, and listen to healthy and inspirational programs on the way to work. Your mind wants to be fed exciting things to break the monotony of day-to-day work schedules.

Take healthy breaks throughout the day and include a 15-minute timeout, which could be a nap or closing your eyes to re-coup your mental status. Take a walk or do other exercises. Your body needs food and exercise to make your brain chemistry healthy. If you feel good, you work well. This creates resilience, so you are better able to deal with whatever life brings to you that day.

Notice times when you are stressed. Write them down in a journal. This will help you figure out what is real and what you can let go. Find ways to balance your life. Find community and the support of like-minded people who are thriving. Find out what they are doing, and choose to live that way. There is help. Go and get it.

Know thyself. Know your boundaries, and practice interpersonal skill sets. Let people know what you will and won't do. They cannot read your mind. Be honest and flexible, and head toward the workplace you want by demonstrating healthier ways to be at work and advocating for those ways. This is a long-term plan; it will determine how you live the rest of your life. Be authentic.

In your downtime, make sure to do something just for you – something that excites you, such as art, music, writing. Be creative and use a different part of your brain. Your neurogenesis is up to you. Your brain is like a hot sports car. Do you want to keep it locked up in the "garage" of deprivation all day? Take it for a spin, and have the ride of your life.

If there are non-negotiable items in your life that you are not able to set aside, and they are killing you, then find a way to slow down. Seek safety and reach out for help to your community and Human Resources, and engage the medical opportunities available to you. Look for work alternatives. They may not be ideal, but will keep you healthier and able. You want to last as long as you can — intact.

Remember, it is not the destination, it is the journey you are on in this life. Find out what you really want, what makes you happy, and head toward this mystery. Forgive yourself and move on slowly. Recognize that you only have so much energy. If you lose all of it to mental duress, you have nothing left to give your life meaning.

Workbook Questions:

1. What are things you don't you like about your work situation? Write them down. You will never know how to deal with work issues until you hold them in your hand.

2. Do you feel obligated to work a lot more than necessary? Are you expected to do more than your colleagues? Do you feel you are treated unfairly? Do you feel under the gun? Do any or all of these things make you feel depressed? How does all of this affect your life at work and home, including your sleep?

3. What are your limits at work? What are things you will you never do? What do your employers and other employees expect of you?

4. Do you have healthy ways of communicating your needs? What are they? Do you feel safe to share them? If not, why not? What are you worried will happen?

5. Do you have unreasonable expectations of your co-workers? If so, how do you justify this behavior when you know they are also suffering? When do you believe this type of work ethic should be addressed and the madness stopped? Do you get paid to create suffering? Are you "only following orders"?

6. Name five healthy ways you combat stress.

7. What creative things do you do with your life – art, music, crafts, sports? How does creativity make you feel safe and healthy? Why do you believe you have too little time for doing healthy things? What would you need to make space for these life-saving activities?

8. What does resilience mean to you and to your work experience?

9. In what healthy ways do you use coping, thriving and solution-focused goals? What things can you engage in at work to stop burnout and aspire toward healthy habits?

10. Is it worth your health and life to stay in an unhealthy job and work environment? What would it take for you to achieve a different work experience? What are you afraid of losing?

11. What interpersonal skill sets do you have? List them. How can these help you to negotiate healthier working conditions? Are there others at work who will help you and collaborate on ways to make the work experience better for all?

12. What's stopping you?

Closure with Unfinished Business

What unfinished business do you have?

What needs to be done to fulfill a wonderful and complete life where you can die in peace, and your tombstone would read, "He lived his life to the fullest, helping others and thriving through it all … When hardships came, he worked through each one as if he were life's student and became willing, teachable, open and flexible, with a beginner's mind. He turned the poisons into healing medicines and taught others to do the same."

In the early years of my recovery I had to work on so much in my life, it seemed impossible that I would make it through. Here is a list of issues I started with:

- Homelessness
- Alcohol and drug addictions
- Abuse issues as a child
- Anger and domestic violence in adulthood (as perpetrator)
- Institution phobias
- Trying to get on Supplemental Security Income
- Hepatitis C
- No front teeth (cosmetic hell)
- Authoritarian Combative Syndrome (did not play well with others)
- Grief and loss (mother, drugs and alcohol, lifestyle)
- Being culturally inappropriate and not being able to process
- No healthy boundaries
- Inability to hold a job, under-earning, and workaholism
- Sex and love addictions (hyper-sexuality)
- Attachment disorders
- Abandonment issues
- Validation issues, low self-esteem (hyper-grandiosity)
- Internalized oppression (cultural)
- Sleep disorders (from shooting speed)
- Eating disorders (from shooting speed)
- Learning disorders (ADD, ADHD)
- Post-Traumatic Stress Disorder
- Survivor guilt

- Family reunification

Until you work through your issues, your mind will be preoccupied and distracted from letting you achieve any of your goals for this life. How do you get closure? In what ways do you process life, when life seems so ambiguous and intangible?

With a clear heart and mind, you will be able to receive the benefits and prosper from the fruits of your labor. You did this restorative work in your life, and now you and everyone around you will benefit from your efforts. You can choose your direction. You have the motivation to engage in result-oriented strategies of abundance.

Closure is as deep as you are willing to engage. Are you willing to be open, willing, flexible, teachable, and to surrender your old ways of holding onto the past? Why put a bandage on an expansive and complicated issue, when you can be full-measured and get the value of complete healing?

We bypass our inclinations toward thriving and connection based upon the negative things that happen in our lives. We live in fear that something will go wrong again—and that this is personal. We attract negative things into our lives from not healing and getting closure. We attract what we have not dealt with. We continue to suffer from old wounds from our childhoods and what has happened since then.

Without closure, we have a repetitive stress injury. We have open wounds that jade everything we think, say and do. Our life and those around us are held emotional hostages. They cannot get any closer because of the boundaries we set to protect ourselves.

People who are in a hurry and want quick closure will bypass authentic ways to accurately process their situational distortions. Grief and loss and emotional processes are time-honored healings.

If you need quick closure, it should be for things such as an immediate threat to your life, when you must make quick decisions or you and others face substantial personal loss. For example, in an accident, stock-market loss, or your job, you need to respond quickly so no more damage will occur. Cut your losses and move on. You can fully process later, when it is safer.

Others who need quick closure bypass long-lasting options and use predictable platforms to cut out the humanistic ability to hold all truths of discomfort. This refusal to process uncomfortable feelings outweighs the healthy, longer-lasting benefits of doing the work and getting results.

You may feel you're exempt from liability in the short-term. You may fear being found out and having to pay the price. These beliefs are harmful. The subject still rents valuable space in you and colors all decision-making about subjects related to this issue. You cannot be authentic in this condition.

Have you broken laws or the trust of your community? Do you hold different views about subjects that are real and valid but that create controversy? Then you may have a real need to protect yourself from subjugation, chastisement and/or imprisonment. This form of closure may not be traditional but can be valuable because you have changed and still want to participate on a level playing field with others. You have made peace with yourself and your issues and can be trusted to do no more harm.

When we choose to not get closure, we have to up the ante. We cannot be trusted servants because we have motivating factors that compromise our integrity. We have to lie about the lie we lied about. We are unclean and unclear with our lives.

Ways to Develop Closure

Allow yourself to grieve and process the experience. Fear, pain, anger and frustration will each have a role in your grief. There is not one correct way to grieve, but there are several safety measures you can take that include extreme self-care and healing with community. You cannot move on with your life until you process and have a sense of urgency for healing and self-care. We get only a short time on the planet—make it count.

Be full-measured as you move into dialogue. Create a pro-and-con list as you produce self-change questions, and answer them with your support group. Keep your work transparent, so it is no longer you alone playing the tape over and over in your head. No matter what happened, you get to choose whether you want to be "right" about the pain and suffering, or if you want to be happy and move on with your life. Pain will happen to all of us, but some forms of suffering are optional.

Optimal conditions for eliciting self-change thoughts create a menu of options. What would it look like to live without a mental handicap? Envision your world, your life, the way you would like it to be. Write down your power, the strengths you have and what it will take to make this happen. Keep a gratitude list of what you already have that keeps you in a positive, healthy state. Write down what has worked in the past with similar situations. You have assets to access and implement.

Work with your healthy ambivalence for and against change. Choose a number from one to 10 ranking how much you want change; then, ask yourself what it will take to move one small step closer to positive change. Use all the support available in your community; everyone has suffered in similar ways that we can all use to help each other.

Keep your work measureable, timely, observable and do-able. If you do not make a plan for yourself, you will be doomed to repeat what you know is not true anymore. Look for and work toward the similarities of possibilities and opportunities you want. Don't focus on what you have now as your experience. Quit focusing on what is wrong and complaining about what you cannot change. That is a waste of everyone's time. Take a leap of faith and belief in the unknown, and temporarily suspend your belief system. Take action.

Use rituals, spirituality and healthy reward systems. You must believe, and it will be so. Let your aspirations and intentions create a wholesome and more complete life. Remove things and thoughts associated with your grief, and give them new life with someone who will appreciate them and associate them with happiness. Choose the experience you want to have, and dress "as-if." "Fake it till you make it." In other words, "Dress for the life you want, not the depression you have."

Workbook Questions:

1. What are perceived benefits of getting closure? On which issues would you like help?

2. What are negative aspects of holding onto perceived unfairness and injustice in your life?

3. What things in your life need closure that are unethical, against the law, stigmatized, or keep you in fear for your safety?

4. What will you have to do to process your dilemma? Explain it clearly, and make a plan.

5. What will happen if you change? How can you become more honest and transparent? What's the worst that could happen?

6. What are the benefits of holding onto a negative contract with life? How does that sustain your faulty thinking?

7. What would you like closure about with a deceased person – or a living person you may not be able to contact? Write a letter telling them everything you want them to know. Make a ritual that has finality, trust and closure.

8. How are you stuck and living in the past in thinking about the loss of your partner? Are they with someone else? Did they pass away? What will it take for you to move on? Write it out, and be clear about what you need. Make a plan to let go and bring change in your life.

9. What rituals do you have that help you to have closure and finality by ending one process and welcoming a new way of life?

10. What little things can you do that will help get the ball rolling? Make a list of things, such as your strengths or your gratitude about the situation. Each little closure makes space for the next right thing to happen. Before you know it, you will be halfway there!

11. How does negative emoting about the loss of your loved one, a job or how you think keep you from taking bold moves toward change?

12. What are other issues in which you would like finality? Jobs, siblings, colleagues, sexual preferences, spiritual ambiguities, sports, arts, education? Write them out, and consider what it would take.

Conflict Resolution

Here are two forms of fear:

1. I want something from you, and I am afraid you are not going to give it to me — a job, your love, your cooperation, money, status, sex, trust.

2. I have something, and I am afraid you are going to take it away from me — my freedom, my belief system, my way of living, my happiness, my autonomy, my kids, my life.

Most conflict happens in the space between these two forms of fear. How can we come to this conflicted "party of life" with everything we need to make us happy?

We can come with self-esteem, with our trust intact, and with our belief system that is not reliant upon others. Compassion and empathy do not require the participation of another. It is the gift I bring willingly.

Fear of abundance causes conflict for all. Some people's need is so great, it outshines the sun; they take and take and feel so deserving. Others suffer because of the greed, sloth and envy that work together to perpetuate a fraudulent way of living.

There is enough for all of us, if we share. The practice of lack being reinforced creates all suffering on the planet. All wars are fought for these ideals. Freedom for one person may be forced internment, and for another it is cultural beliefs: I deserve this entitled and privileged way of living. We turn God against God with our belief that our cause is right.

A lot of times when conflict occurs in my life, it is by my own making. I have contributed in some way of feeling unheard, or I have fear of not getting my unreal needs met. By personalizing this as my pain and believing that my pain is or will be real, I am setting myself and others up for collective suffering. I attract all that comes into my life; in recovery, it is called "drawing your own focus." We do it through our choice of conduct. Through acceptance of my true present and forgiveness of what created my past, I am able to move past suffering, punishing, and judging others. I get to choose if I want to be right or happy.

When someone explains why they are emotionally embroiled, you have the option to sit back and watch them spin out of control. It is their experience; it does not have to be yours. As you observe, you realize pain and suffering happen to all of us, and our part in the suffering can be optional. We can honor the other's experience and say to them, "Thank you. I see how you feel. I'll take a look at that. I believe that you believe this to be true. Thanks for telling me. It took a lot of courage for you to say that, with all the emotion up for both of us."

Can both of our truths exist simultaneously? Can we hold the paradox of both truths? First, we can't take their experience personally; it belongs to them. Our role is to take care of our own contribution to the dynamic. We can clean up only our side of the street and maintain our own healthy boundaries.

How to Facilitate a Higher Level of Healing Consistency in Conflict Resolution

Conflict happens when truths that co-exist on different levels come into question, and one party feels the need to be more righteous or feels more unfairly treated than the other. This unfairness is where we look for mutual benefits that we can share and keep fair dispositions for all.

Looking at both sides and truths creates a level playing field. There is your truth; here is my truth, and between us we concede together our living experience. How we make these universal aspects of fairness for both parties is the mark of our craft.

If we consider both parties worthy and equal in some aspects, we seek mutual benefits to both parties. Concessions are part of the equitable give-and-take phenomenon that occurs when we work toward common goals.

If we have concerns only for our personal benefit, we use control, agenda, expectations, manipulation, coercion, denial and power as our contributions. This is not negotiating.

Unhealthy boundaries, people-pleasing, low self-esteem, and quick-fix solutions create more unbalanced and temporary answers and create a feedback cycle of dissatisfaction.

Apathy, neglect, omission, and complacent neutrality may be employed to avoid conflict but actually keep it alive and thriving.

Both parties should get to define the conflict. Define what the important facts are for each side. Develop goals that are mutually beneficial and do-able. Make plans and methods so both parties concede something and accept the outcome. The truth then becomes an ever-changing ambiguity as both learn and grow with compassion and empathy for each other.

Conflict arises from needs and beliefs. Being able to express both clearly and calmly with flexible authority helps avert the uneasiness that ensues when needs are unmet. Our troubles begin when we believe we are unheard and feel "less than" and violated in some ways. This unskillful communication is where we improve for the benefit of everyone. It's an inside job.

Ways to Engage in Healthy, Equity-Building Relationships

We all are human and have basic needs. There is enough abundance to share and communicate fairly. Collaboration is a process in which both parties mutually benefit by the connection.

Compromise is the ability let go of meaningful points of contention on each side for the greater mutual good of all participants.

Humans are social creatures and need healthy ways of creating interpersonal relationships that are genuine and authentic. These ways create value for each participant's inherent worth as an equal partner.

We all feel good when we give, and it sustains our well-being as a community to have an exchange of mental and physical goodwill. We learn to receive what good is given to us and accept that it does not have to look, taste and feel like what we thought it should. We are grateful receivers of the good we are given.

We become grateful for what we have now. If we have more than enough, we take a look at why we need more than others and why we need be treated as special to feel normal. It's our responsibility to be self-regulating. We become benevolent benefactors for others as part of our social grace.

We learn to have more difficult and complex conversations. We learn to ask why we are so thin-skinned, and why we personalize and globalize our experience and project our unhappiness upon unsuspecting people.

If we have little in our lives and even less faith that this lack will change, we can become willing to commit to a five-year plan of advocating and demonstrating our needs. We find ways to survive and thrive without harming others. We are enough, we belong, we deserve, and we have arrived. We will no longer sit under the table of life, accepting scraps, when there is a banquet on the table. We take our place!

We are capable of making mistakes. We advocate in a healthy way for new wants and needs and forgive what has happened in the past. We are resilient and able to move toward change.

We are able to be universal observers. We watch all aspects and stay objective without judgment. We suspend our thinking for the sake of argument, and then we agree to disagree for mutually beneficial outcomes.

Feelings will come and go. It takes conscious effort to not let them keep us and our negotiating team emotional hostages. We use "I" statements for our own feelings and take responsibility for cleaning up our side of bargaining opportunities. We all have feelings, so we should strive to use them to explain our needs without causing harm to each other.

We are good listeners. We actively use our ears, bodies (posture, eye contact) and minds to really hear the experience of our partners. This creates intimacy in sharing common interests.

We have healthy, flexible, emotional resilience. We know our limits and how to take care of ourselves in community. We process situational distortions appropriately.

We develop healthy ambivalence when processing hectic, unpredictable circumstances.

We take actions to meet our needs. We are humane and try to facilitate fair and equal practices with our community.

We let go of always analyzing and rationalizing our experiences. Instead, we come from our heartfelt experiences, working toward connections with others. We use compassion and empathy as a moral compass and move beyond a right vs. wrong, dualistic world where someone needs to lose. We take responsibility and choose to process our feelings of loss and unmet needs. We use joyful exertion toward being in the groundless moment, staying balanced and creating a safe place for others to join us on the journey.

What are you willing to do to create equity right now? Really do this work. It will save the planet, and it starts with you.

Workbook Questions:

1. In what way do you have trouble accepting that others possess more or less than you? How does this color your ability to have dialogue with others, if you come with those judgments right from the start?

2. What are your best techniques for resolving conflicts? Are you a kind person with a formal education? How might this distance you from someone who learned in a different manner and has a dissimilar "less-than" experience? Does this make you more entitled with your needs? Are they less deserving?

3. What are your issues and triggers when you try to effect change with co-workers? Do you think they know everything about you and can easily keep you subjugated? Explain.

4. How do you believe your strengths are considered weaknesses at the bargaining table? What are your weaknesses and strengths?

5. Name a few instances in your life when you had success with conflict resolution. Write them out in short stories, and share with your conflict-resolution group.

6. What are reasons you always have fights and conflicts with others? Of what parts can you take ownership? Who would you be without having to give in to these behaviors? What's the worst that would happen if you relaxed and trusted the process of change? What are you afraid of losing — pride, dignity, self-esteem?

7. What are you willing to concede? Do you believe you will suffer true pain if you do not get your way?

8. Are you generally happy without needing others to do something to make your happiness possible? Does your experience rely on outside influences? Explain. Do you often blame others for your life and circumstances? Does this come easily to you? Please elaborate.

9. What is your part in conflicts with loved ones? What is your style for closure? In what ways do you harm your loved ones? Do you seek complete control of both sides of the conversation? What happens when you sit and listen without thinking of a rebuttal?

10. How does conflict keep your power base going at work? Do you use gossip, slander and use character assassination toward peers who do not give you what you want or bend easily to your needs?

11. In what ways do you thrive with the inequity that others have to tolerate? Are you part of a privileged class who has never felt unsafe in the workplace because of race, ethnicity, gender, degrees, or other factors?

12. When you negotiate for change, what are you afraid others will deny you? Respect, a job, their loyalty, your feelings of connection? Explain.

13. In what ways do you use active listening? What are your downfalls? Do you try to fix, speak up with solutions, and create plans? Is it hard for you to simply listen and say things such as, "That sounds difficult," or "Thanks for sharing"? Explain.

14. How do you use the mob mentality of sporting events or political issues to get your point across? Do you fall into the mob mentality of your party or team?

Consequences

We all live with consequences, either in our own lives or those we created for others.

So often in life, much of what we have is the direct result of our own choices and actions. Kind of like karma, what goes around comes around. The saying, "truth or consequences," leads us to believe if we follow the truth, we will get one outcome, and if we do not, judgment awaits.

Since birth, we have incremental ideals we strive for with our actions to make our lives richer and fuller. I encourage joyful exertion toward healthy, preventive, holistic ideals. In this way, we are able to slowly change the hand we were dealt – includes the cards we chose for ourselves. In recovery, we do our daily work and keep our spiritual maintenance as a priority, or we get our consequential misery cheerfully refunded. We slip back into flux and entropy, feeling hopeless and lost.

When we fall from grace, we accept scraps that have fallen under the table and forget about the banquet taking place on top, where we belong. We deserve to be at the banquet. Simply by our inherent worth as human beings, we are invited to partake. No matter how far down we believe we are, the moment we realize our worth is the moment we can change our lives.

Right now, by our ability to think, we are digesting our thoughts on a cellular level. We are what we think we are. We can change our outcomes by using painful moments and accept the suffering as our teacher — just for today. One day at a time — sometimes quickly, sometimes slowly. It is perseverance that creates timeless wisdom. We can change our relevance and turn poison into medicine.

Sometimes we procrastinate most of our lives away. We have many reservations as to why we can't comply with a new way of living. We have excuses such as, "I'll do it when things are better." "I'll do it when I have more time." "I'd like to, but I can't." And the list goes on.

We are Velcro for bad things that happen to us. Bad things stick to us and create unfathomable, infinite sadness. We get used to it. To change a life of consequences, we can begin with small gratitudes of what we *do* have, what we *can* do. Begin with small, almost imperceptible changes, and build upon them slowly. Add more complex daily challenges, and process your experiences with peers and supporters.

The weakest link in our lives, whatever the consequences, can be our strongest asset, if we become willing, open, flexible and teachable. We can become an expert on our consequences and change them into parts of fulfilling lives. We can create value out of disasters. We can accept life on life's terms and move forward to create our destiny and understanding, our mythological journey through the passage of time. We become the heroes of our own lives. Poverty of the mind is a choice we make daily. Let's start making better choices.

Workbook Questions:

1. What are the consequences you experience for your behavior? Were you born into unfairness?

2. What consequences do others experience because of your behavior? Are you in a place of power? What can you do differently to create equity and fairness for all?

3. Do you have internalized oppression as a consequence of your life, either as the giver or receiver? How do you rise above the static and noise of our unhealthy society and its values to find your own place in the sun and thrive?

4. Do you have habits such as drinking, smoking, anger, righteousness, privilege, poverty, drugs, promiscuous sex, adoption of the victim role, low self-esteem, overeating, drugs, obsessive-compulsive behavior, mental-health diagnoses, workaholism, people-pleasing? Name more, and explain how they create familiar distress that you want to change.

5. Control issues, expectations of others, refusal to be in acceptance of your situation, the urge to manipulate your circumstances: How do these create consequences in your life? What can you do to change these?

6. Do you have a family dynamic that is sometimes overwhelmed by generational dysfunction? It took a long time to create this complicated mess. How can you change those detriments into a lasting legacy of pride and goodness?

7. Do you get consequences from simply hoping and wishing for luck with your partner regarding certain issues? Do you hope she will become a mind reader and know what you want from your experience with her? Do you believe wishing and magical thinking will give you desired outcomes? What can you do to develop real intimacy with your partner and change the existing dynamic?

8. Do you have problems with your kids listening and obeying you and with your partner working toward team-building? Do your colleagues make you feel or look obsolete and disposable? What can you do today to change these things in a hopeful way?

9. How do you buy into negative emoting and accept scraps under the table? Do you procrastinate and have reservations as to why you cannot change your negative contract with your life? What are you willing to do so you will never return to those kinds of consequences?

10. Do you perpetuate or experience stigma because of your race, sex, sexual preference, age, weight, and/or mental-health issues? What can you do to empower your experience and change those things into healthy goals in your life?

11. Do you break the law in small ways and get caught over and over again? Do you believe you are privileged, and you must live with the negative byproducts of getting caught?

12. Are you in the habit of accepting undesirable things in your life? "That's just the way it is." "It is what it is." Have you given up hope? Explain what a path out of this misery looks like for you.

Control Issues

Control freak: a scared person who wants to feel safe by having power over others without their consent; an overbearing person without healthy boundaries.

If you don't make plans for yourself, someone will make plans for you. Sometimes we let our culture control us by omission – by not choosing for ourselves. Then, we blame others when situations do not turn out well. This is a form of passive control.

Nearly everyone feels safer when they know what is going to happen next. It creates the illusion of having a little control. However, in the same way as power corrupts, control corrupts — and absolute control corrupts absolutely.

In my personal life, my biggest daily surrenders are being in control, not being in acceptance, having expectations, having an agenda, and manipulation and coercion of situations and others. That said, the problem comes down to me wanting to control my environment at the cost of others' feelings and peaceful choices. What separates me from acting authentically is my attachment to wanting to feel safe. I have reservations that the situation at hand will not turn out to my benefit. As a result, I respond from a place of lack and desperate neediness, which is a response from childhood experiences. Whether I'm being a control freak or a passive-aggressive, reverse-pride victim/monster, the sucking sound is still me, outshining the sun with my single, dark cloud in the sky.

Even when I have complete control, it becomes more glaring that I do not know what to do with it. I get confused and don't participate with others. I isolate because I cannot create equity at the expense of others and still act like I am a good, helpful person. This is the single greatest tragedy of governing ourselves and others.

We all want to feel safe. We respond to feelings of uncertainty either inwardly or outwardly. Yet either is a form of not participating with others on a fair and level playing ground. Everyone has power, whether willingly or passively.

Nearly everyone has had the experience of asking a friend what he wants to do, but he doesn't know. That is power and control in reverse. We are still held hostage, but this time by the friend's unwillingness to choose. If we can help the control freak to tone down and invite the quieter, yet still powerful person to be vulnerable by participating in a healthy way, we create real equity. Both parties possess the power of control. Both want to feel safe. How can we create equity without blame and begin healing?

I don't like the dualism of one person being "bad" and another "good." Let's work toward empowering everyone with a menu of options and then get into complete acceptance, forgiveness, compassion and empathy. We are all affected by each other's responses.

It is our responsibility as a society to be able to handle discomfort and dis-ease. It is our duty to interrupt our storyline and suspend our belief systems, so we can participate in real-world peace through the ability to have difficult conversations and be in acceptance of where we are right now. Sometimes, that means interacting with a person of value who has control issues.

How can we move ourselves out of the way of the "dirty fan" and not paint ourselves into a belief corner where we can say, "Look, they did it again"? Fool me once, shame on you; fool me twice, shame on me — and fool me a third time? Shame on me again. This is a shame-based, fear-mongering system that can never move us toward healthy equity. Blaming others for our predicament brings instant and momentary bliss that fades, and then our misery is refunded.

How can we regulate the space around us and cleanse it, so we have done our part to create an unblemished, safe, powerful space of trust and inclusion? We draw our own focus. On some level, we attract almost everything that happens and everyone we meet.

Many people have been in love and keep finding that their tendency is to attract the same type of broken person back into their lives. This is our part of the codependent quagmire.

How can we do the real work of keeping our area safe and clean, leave no scraps, shut the door completely, and state to others that if they do no harm, they can come and play — but if they do harm, we will leave? When we are in the midst of an emotionally charged conversation, safety is often thrown out the window.

A solution could be that we talk for an agreed-upon period of time, like five minutes, and then move on. When we speak with people who have no healthy boundaries, we use the five-minute method and then excuse ourselves and leave. We have control. We have power. If we know we are with someone dangerous, we should always keep our chair by the door for our safety. We can take responsibility for our own safety, so if something goes wrong, at least we know we did our best to protect ourselves.

People with control issues have a sort of "cancer" of unhappiness. Would you yell at a person dying of cancer? When someone attempts to control your choices, try communicating gently and patiently. Say, "Thanks. I hear how you feel. I'll take a look at that."

Such a response does not mean you agree with them. It means you genuinely listened and processed the demons in your own head. Repeat your response until you feel prepared. People want to feel heard. Active listening with compassion does not require the participation or approval of the other person.

Many of our control issues spring from having a flashback to a time when our parents or other persons of power abused our safety and trust. We were innocent back then, and we were violated. But now we are grown and responsible. We have power to dismantle our childhood remembrances. Remember that you have all of your power. Breathe and loosen your tightened muscles. Your brain is tricking you into having a fatal peril response. You have the power to thank your brain for protecting you and then tell it to calm down.

If we find ourselves constantly thinking people are trying to control us, then this is the perfect moment to learn and heal. We can finally heal.

In my life, by fighting back I developed an "anti-authoritative combative syndrome." I kept perpetuating the sickness by buying into the myth of being controlled.

Remember, if we do not make plans for ourselves, someone will gladly make plans for us. Take responsibility for your life. That takes diligence and perseverance. Gradually we will begin to see the "dirty fan" blowing and step out of the way. We will become the "universal observer" in our safe and empowered lives and will no longer need to blame others for our unhappiness. If we are healthy, they will either respond in kind with healthy tendencies, or they will know we are not to be messed with, because they have no power over us. Voodoo works only when people believe in it. When we take good care of ourselves, everyone else will fall in line.

Workbook Questions:

1. What healthy reasons do you have for wanting control over others and how they live their own lives? What do you get out of it — safety, power, money, status, pride, ego gratification, leadership?

2. What are your fatal-peril responses when you feel you have not been heard or feel abused, neglected, or not privy to information?

3. When life shows up with a physical- or mental-health issue you have no control over, how do you respond? Do you say, "It's not fair," "Why me?" "You got the information wrong," "This can't be happening to me"? Explain.

4. What is your leadership style? Do you lead by example, or is your attitude, "Do as I say, not as I do"? What do you do when you do not feel respected or heard?

5. How do you surrender to what is and still feel vulnerable and sensitive by showing up when you feel unsafe?

6. Name five ways you need to be in control to feel safe.

7. Name five ways you can seek safety when others are controlling your life and abusing you.

8. What do you always have control of? Your response? Your anger? Your entitlement? Do you have privilege that keeps you from participating?

9. If you had your critical eyes removed and installed new ears for active listening, what would change in your life?

10. Do you follow orders well? Do you listen attentively to instruction? Are you the rebel archetype? Explain why you do what you do.

Co-Occurring Disorders and Triple Diagnoses

I was a homeless, marginalized, invisible person. I seldom, if ever, went to the hospital. I had to have bones sticking out of my skin or be half-dead with disease to even consider going to an emergency room.

During the course of 20 years, I had two low-grade infections caused by my teeth, and my gums oozed pus. This was normal for me. Finally, at age 42, I tried earnestly to get help, but I was rejected because I was not "on the books" – I had no documentation or identification cards to prove my existence. To complicate matters, I worked for pay under the table and therefore wasn't on anyone's payroll or health insurance.

I didn't understand recovery and all it entailed, and I had never been officially diagnosed with a mental illness. I was not willing to seek and pay for treatment on my own.

In a San Francisco homeless census in 1998 to determine who received services, an estimated 16,000 homeless people were counted. That year, 157 homeless people died in the city, many right on the street. The average age of death was 42 – my age at the time.

Despite knowing that, I was neither reachable nor willing to go. I didn't know what getting services meant, and I did not trust the government or medical community. I finally got help in August 1998, after correctly diagnosing myself with hepatitis C.

Facilities had just started working with "co-occurring disorders" or "dual diagnosis," by which they meant mental-health issues combined with substance use. Some people, like me, were triple-diagnosed, with a physical disease added to the mix. I had multiple mental-health issues; multiple drug and alcohol addictions, and hep C. There were many other things wrong, but the professionals helping me focused on these major issues first.

When I was finally diagnosed, I realized I had multiple needs. My intervention required a whole village to care for me. I had the use of psychiatrists, psychologists, therapists, doctors, dentists, addiction specialists, counselors, nutritionists, advocates, money managers, spiritual helpers, Alcoholics Anonymous, Narcotics Anonymous, and Sex and Love Addicts Anonymous.

I soon learned it was best to get my care and services in as few locations as possible. My treatment resembled a shotgun blast of approaches instead of a single magic-bullet theory. As I matured in my recovery, I was allowed to share in the decision-making and choices, methods and treatments. I slowly became responsible for my life.

When I learned where to go for help and how to get help, I maintained that precious gift. I sifted through all the teachings, medical advice, and counseling disciplines at hand, then created my own truth through the knowledge gained. I knew I had a lifelong opportunity to work comprehensively on all my issues.

When you decide to start this work of recovery and wholeness, know that you are beginning the work of a lifetime. As you get better, you will realize that maintenance keeps you from choosing unhealthy alternatives. Do your spiritual upkeep, or get your misery cheerfully refunded.

Another aspect to remember is that you are a person, not your diagnosis. You are a complicated creature living in an unstable, hectic and unpredictable world. Be gentle with yourself. Find community. Be willing to listen to what works for others; accept the work of healing your life.

I made a lifetime commitment to work on the issues listed below. After 16 years, I am doing much better. My life is maintained now in a preventive way to keep destructive aspects on hold.

- Case management: There was a program and team in place to help me with specific goals and measurable outcomes. They held me accountable and gave firm guidance and supervision.

- Illness management: My initial diagnoses were a starting point. I was given a trusted team to work with, and I had to be willing to follow directions and understand that I was in a groundless place of surrender. We worked with different medications and treatments. It was done gently, as my body responded one way and my brain responded another to changes and adjustments.

- Pharmacological treatment: I had to be willing to try medications and stay on them for at least three weeks to see how my body felt. With some, it was possible to adjust and dial in with the different medications and how they affected my stability. This was one of the hardest things to figure out – which appropriate medications worked with my metabolism.

- Family-of-origin reunification after 30 years.

- Owing the IRS $28,000.

- Multiple mental disorders: Bipolar/manic depression with psychotic features was my ultimate diagnosis.

- Homelessness integrated into housing management: This was a learning curve. I had to eat, sleep, participate, and relate to others as I moved through the gauntlet of early housing developments. I had to learn how to relate to my environment and triggers.

- Alcohol and drug addictions.

- Anger and domestic violence (as both a survivor and perpetrator).

- Institution phobias.

- Hepatitis C: Getting diagnosed, learning about my disease and how my body relates to the treatments and medications.

- No front teeth – cosmetic hell.

- Authoritarian Combative Syndrome (did not play well with others).

- Grief and loss (mother, drugs and alcohol, lifestyle).

- No healthy boundaries.

- Inability to hold a job alternated with inability to stop working (workaholic).

- Sex and love addictions (hyper-sexuality).

- Attachment disorders.

- Abandonment issues.

- Validation issues – hyper-grandiosity, low self-esteem.

- Internalized oppression (cultural)
- Generational dysfunction.
- Sleeping disorders from shooting speed.
- Eating disorders from shooting speed.
- Learning disorders (undiagnosed ADHD).
- Post-Traumatic Stress Disorder.
- Survivor guilt.
- Social Security Income. Getting on it and getting off it.

Workbook Questions:

1. Which issues from the preceding list can you relate to? Are there other examples more familiar to you that you can write down?

2. What are the issues in your life? How do those translate into disorder?

3. What are your dreams and unfinished business? What lifestyle choices have prevented you from achieving them?

4. Do you have medical issues? What are they? Name everything—be full-measured.

5. Do you have diagnosed mental issues? What are they? Do you think you might have other issues? Flesh out what they could be, such as anger, rage, jealousy, and co-dependence. Write down anything you think could keep you from achieving your best outcomes.

6. What social issues do you have with gambling, shopping, porn, eating? Can you name others that might change from fun to painful consequences for you and your loved ones?

7. Do you have Post-Traumatic Stress Disorder? Did you experience childhood abuse? Were you sexually traumatized? Did bad things happen such as crashes, natural or man-made disasters, losing loved ones? Be explicit if you safely can.

8. Do you have cultural stigmas that create suffering in the areas of race, ethnicity, gender, sexuality, culture, disability?

9. Do you have negative consequences from generational repetition of conditioned responses that create failure to thrive? What does this feel like? Can you break those unhealthy ties and still have the love of your family?

10. Are you constantly depressed? Do you get stressed easily? Are you at your wit's end? Why? What do you think you should do about it?

11. Do you have unresolved grief and loss issues? Did you lose your home? Lose a loved one? Lose a job? Sometimes multiple traumas occurring at the same time create serious, uncontrollable feelings. Name what you feel.

12. Are you dealing with dangerous and unstable people? What issues do they bring up for you?

13. Are you living in a dangerous neighborhood where you feel challenged just going to the store? What are other challenges about living there? Does living there create disorder in your life?

14. What relationships do you have? Think about your family, a partner, work colleagues, team players and musicians. Do you have disease around any of them that could create notable disorder in your life? Name what you think it might be.

Coping Mechanisms

We all cope the best we can with our own behaviors. You might be a workaholic, act out with fighting, drinking, avoidance, drugs, or and sexualizing your stress. You might be a shopaholic trying to fill a hole of dissatisfaction in your soul.

It can be hard to figure out the association between anxiety and acting outward or inward with all our trigger mechanisms. Our hard-wired defense mechanisms make us feel safe. It might be self-destructive or damaging to others, but we confuse these outcomes with safety. It's all we know.

We come to believe this is the only way to proceed, and then we defend our chosen behavior as we try to control our environment. We have had terrible things happen to us, so we relate to everything from a position of self-protection and fear. We respond from a place of Post-Traumatic Stress Disorder.

We respond with resentment, which creates a feedback-loop in the confines between our ears. We use passive-aggressive behavior when speaking with someone with whom we are having a "moment." We have flashbacks.

These mechanisms of responding in our maladaptive ways bring only momentary gratification. We are soon reduced to suffering because of those behaviors.

Up until this moment, you have actively chosen this poverty of the mind. You live with fear and shame-based choices that you accept as less than enough, and you fight over the scraps.

We all have well-developed ways of being OK. With addiction, we have a well-accessorized system that has worked as a survival strategy and gotten us to this point alive. We self-medicated for comfort.

Yet, somehow, we have made it to this point of choosing recovery. So with newfound knowledge, we are interested in using transferrable skill sets to choose safer, healthier, more productive and estimable behaviors so we can thrive and be successful in longer-lasting ways. We already have the answers within us. Our journey is to uncover and access what we know is true and take a leap of faith. Feeling vulnerable, we make peace with our environment.

What are healthier choices you can make? How can you access them and come to believe that they are worth learning? How can you take the first awkward step toward your lifetime of change?

Is your quest to live life on its terms, to solve your own problems without medicating, acting out or acting in, or going crazy? How can you tolerate stress and disease and achieve conflict resolution without doing harm?

When we come from a place of defensive posturing, we will always see diminished returns. People will participate from a dualistic place of who's right and who's wrong. If someone loses face, it is not a win-win situation.

However, if in our minds or with our fellows, we believe the war is over, there is no reason to continue fighting. We hold both truths as equal partners and find a way to not escalate or do more harm.

We have been habitually conditioned to respond in social situations as needing to be right, needing to be heard, to have our truth venerated, and to ultimately win. This is the cause of so much grief on the planet. When we listen to another's truth, we create openness for change to happen for both parties.

Following are some coping strategies. Take what you like and leave the rest—add them to your own list of solution-focused therapy.

By surrendering everything I think, say and do— all my thoughts, words and deeds — I am able to loosen my grip and release a lifetime of broken-down thinking.

By my unconditional acceptance of who I am, exactly as I am, right here and now at this very moment, warts and all — with low self-esteem, anger and contempt, fear, drugs and drinking — if I accept myself, I am no longer in a closed system with shame and stigma defining who I am. Acceptance is the answer to my questions. I totally forgive everyone and everything. It is my negative attachment to what went wrong that separates me from being genuine and authentic with my daily environment and those I deal with.

By focusing on the solution and not the problem, I am able to move beyond judgment and into working opportunities. I move beyond my fear-based thinking.

I accept that I will make loads of mistakes during the learning curve. While the seeds of change are growing beneath my feet, I will not stomp on them and scream, "This doesn't work!" I will say only, "There I go again. Wait a second, and I'll make another mistake. Oops, there's me—Jackass in the Box." It's who we are right now, not forever.

I compare myself with others. Sometimes I despair about what they have that I don't. This brings anger and stress. Even when I win, I don't feel safe, because winning is impermanent and can be taken away.

Change happens. This is all there ever is; nothing stays the same. It's hard work to make this recidivism continue, generation after generation. Let's stop the historical oppression and generational dysfunction.

When I compete with others, it leads to an inability to cope with defeat. We all want to win and have it all. There can be only a few who have this, and billions who don't. This is an unfair system I will no longer support. I am enough right now!

I can change my reaction to life's stressors. I can heal with humor, be gentle, and sometimes laugh at absurd ways I choose to tightly grip "mine" and accept scraps under the table, instead of dining at the banquet table of life.

I can bring everything I need to the party; no one can let me down. It's OK. I brought it with me. It's not about someone else not meeting my needs. I meet my own. Now, if I can accept you exactly as you are unconditionally, you get to deal with your own feelings. They are not mine to hold and stress about.

I can educate myself with knowledge and support groups and have accountability that is observable and measureable in a timely manner, yet with a sense of urgency. I can let go of procrastination, which keeps me immobile.

I can work or exercise to create healthy, appropriate ways of releasing stress and anger. I do not have to react to something I don't agree with. Rather, I can respond and take my time to think about what to do next.

I can be willing to have a beginner's mind to try new behaviors and go through the learning curve. I can choose to feel vulnerable and sensitive and know that I am safe and have all of my power. I do the new work along with the ordinary work in my life, and I become an extraordinary person of value.

I can accept pain and suffering as my teacher, just for today. I know I am totally responsible and can clean up my side of the street. That is my real job. I realize that NO doesn't mean no forever — just not right now.

I can turn everything over to a Higher Power. I like to use the acronym GOD, or Good Orderly Direction. I can let go and let GOD. I can let GOD love it because I can't. I can let GOD carry it because it is too heavy a burden for me. I know that tension is a luxury I can ill afford and that the stress monster is too expensive to keep inside me. I choose to surrender to GOD.

I can use proactive, preventive strategies. The teacher of life will always show up—I need not go anywhere. If I am ready, I can cope, maneuver through the quagmire and turn life into an opportunity.

I can take extreme care of myself during stressful situations, by getting enough sleep, eating well, exercising and relaxing.

I can quit painting a target on myself and playing the victim. I can accept that disasters and crises happen. What shows my character to the world is not what happens to me, but how I respond. I can perform honorable acts to create self-esteem.

I can do service for others so I can get release from my egocentric thoughts.

I can stop doing actions that cause harm to others: Do No Harm, in everything I do.

I can stop running away and accept my station in life, right here and right now. I can stop all avoidance and denial and just accept. What's the worst that could happen? If I close my eyes right now and just breathe, I find that nothing is really happening except for my next breath. I am not in danger. My eyes are closed, and I am just breathing—that's all.

I can do the next right thing, then pause and breathe and do the *next* right thing. I can know in my heart that I have done enough and accept that the next right thing is all there is to do, no matter what happens.

Workbook Questions:

1. In what ways do you self-soothe when you feel tension? Do you eat, run, become angry, depressed, and resentful? Do you pray? Explain.

2. In what ways do you respond to fear, death and dying, grief and loss, losing a job or a relationship with a friend or lover? Have you exhibited the same behaviors for all of these interruptions in your life?

3. Do you turn your tension inward toward yourself and hold it in as a coping tool? Do you let tension turn into a disease that your whole body feels? Why? What can you do to get it out and let go of unnecessary tension?

4. Do you find that it works to blame others for what is going on in your own life? Do you find yourself easily offended when having conversations that others seem to handle in a less conflicted way?

5. What healthy boundaries keep you safe while in a business meeting, a political rally, on airplane trips, fighting with someone, a family gathering?

6. Name five healthy coping skills you know right now that will work for you.

7. When you focus on the problem, you see only what the problem is about. You cannot use the same energy to get relief from the cause of your pain. How will you solve this quandary?

8. If you know you will be with someone who always gives you grief, how can you take care of yourself and skillfully be in the same room, working toward healthy alternatives that keep both of you safe?

9. How do you stop the power struggle with a person of power? How do you create equity without giving up your own power?

10. Do you want to be right or happy? How do you stay safe in battle?

Critical Eye – Criticism

When we meet someone, we start having a conversation in our heads based on certain characteristics we believe we "know" about whom this person is, what this person wants – and what how we feel about all of that.

We have formed contempt prior to investigation.

With our critical eye, we can almost predict the news of the day before we turn on the TV. We assume and judge. By doing so, we create safety and space for ourselves to exist without having to change or recognize the inherent worth of the subject of our judgment.

As a society, what do we get from quickly judging our fellows, our situations, and our ways of life?

There are two schools of thought. First, there are those who feel that criticism is the way to maintain our power base and keep control over others. It is a form of manipulation, coercion, agenda-thinking, having expectations and not being in acceptance. We keep the other person in a constant state of disorientation. By continuously putting down others, this type of critic starts to believe the others' inequity is real and puts them in place as a "have-not" person of lesser value.

The second school of thought: By skillfully empowering others, there is less need to maintain control over others. By delegating work, equity is available and power is granted. If you speak to others in a way that they can hear you, you are more likely to get your needs met. Power through delegating creates healthy societies; we all can help with everything that needs to be done.

Constructive criticism should be crafted to help others use their skills and develop ways to maximize their efficiency and value. We are taught to be unique, independent, one-of-a-kind people to the point of exhaustion in a workaholic society that uses people up and replaces them with the next contestant.

Your parents likely had few parenting skills taught to them. When you were a child, they did the best they could with what they had. You were taught how to do everything for your early survival. When you did something wrong or put your life in danger, you were shown a different way or harshly reprimanded. This dictated how you evolved and treated others. You learned to do what was done unto you. You need to evolve again and stop being punitive and dismissive of others as the way to get your needs met.

We receive information the way it is given. Methods that use healthy interchange keep both parties safe. Healthy interchange is a give-and-take of information and goods to create equity and sustainment. If you communicate with safety in mind, others will have the opportunity to respond in kind. When you educate and do not withhold power and knowledge, there is a chance that the world will evolve instead of fighting. The devil is in the details.

We have a chance to look at learning as having more value than one-upping your colleagues for advancement, power and money. The real truth is that the more you know, the more you know how little you know. So if we fight over the scraps under the table, there is little chance right from the start that we can evolve with such an archaic policy in hand.

How can we learn to take criticism as the gift it really is and figure out what kernels of truth to keep and which to let fly if they do not apply? How can we honor the truth of a skillful, honest person who cares enough to say something that might actually help us? They spoke up while others just let us sit in our dirty diaper. Which person is more truthful? Why are we so thin-skinned when it comes to hearing another's truth about ourselves? It is their truth to tell us. If they are not gossiping or performing a character assassination or slandering us, why does it bother us so much?

Consider what happens when someone gives you a compliment. Why is it so hard to say thanks and honor them for their good taste and good will? We are so harsh about receiving compliments that, in turn, it is hard for us to give them. We need more work to stop reacting negatively and learn to trust that others have good intentions for us.

How can we learn to digest others' painful thoughts without speaking reactively?

Let's go back to our main topic: Critical Eye – Criticism. When we walk into a room and meet someone new, why have we already made up our minds about who, what, when, where, and why the topic is important or trivial? Why do we accept or dismiss someone completely?

We judge ourselves harshly and expect perfectionism, never satisfied with our own work. If we cannot honor those times when we have done our best, what good are we to ourselves and others? Think about it. If we judge ourselves so harshly, just imagine how we judge others, yet they don't even know why they are being criticized. Why is there always one little thing that was not correct? Such a thought disaffects all the good we did.

I believe I learned this behavior pattern from my parents. Perfectionism exemplified what I was taught as my measure for others. If I want to change my thoughts about myself and others, I have to unlearn this. If you are the same, you will, too. How do we do this?

Ideas to Slow Down Your Critical Eye
- Be gentle with yourself. Know that you are doing the best you can.
- Don't judge, lest ye be judged. If only for that reason, you can stop a large portion of self-infliction and doing harm to others with retributive acts.
- Do esteemable acts that do not require anything but unconditional, positive regard toward the other.
- In Recovery, A helps B and, in the process, A gets better, even if B doesn't.
- Make affirmation lists of positive aspects of your life instead of focusing on one bad thing that happened.
- Be like Velcro for the good that happens in your life and Teflon for the bad.
- Quit globalizing, catastrophizing, personalizing and awfulizing when something doesn't go your way.
- Learn to sit with pain and suffering and accept them as your skillful teacher. Know that pain and suffering will pass. They must come and visit from time to time for balance in your life.
- Develop appropriate awareness to peripheral distractions in your life.
- Learn to analyze with curiosity and a sense of discovery.

- Your energy, compassion, and empathy do not require the participation of the other party. You do it because it's the right thing to do.

- Make a "love sandwich" with your constructive criticism for another. Start out with something good about the person or job, then gently guide into the improved or desired behavior. End your paragraph by complimenting the ways in which they have easily done these kinds of things in the past. Yummy.

- Be of service to others, and Do No Harm.

- Blur your vision to see supreme happiness. Realize that the rest is judgment.

- Revisit evaluation without getting overwhelmed. The ability to reconsider keeps you flexible and pliable for change. Don't take yourself so seriously. Remember, you can learn new things without feeling bad. Be open to learning, to revising and changing, and surrender everything you think, say, and do—all your thoughts, words, and deeds.

- Keep in mind that you do not need to speak up just because you see something you disagree with. What are your motivating factors? Do you wish to compromise the other's integrity?

Workbook Questions:

1. If someone is easily offended, how can you skillfully develop healthy and constructive ways of integrating and eliciting self-change thoughts without judging the person's value? What do you get out of this? Is it easier than taking the time to teach and empower your colleague, partner, or child?

2. Who appointed you judge, jury and executioner of others? Are you trustworthy for this job? Were you just following orders, like the Germans during World War II? Does that make it OK?

3. What is it about you that wants and needs to look for something done wrong so you can correct it?

4. Is there a way you can start self-regulating your needs, instead of feeling better by judging others?

5. Why do you need to be "the good one," "the one who can help others," the one who has the final word?

6. What do you get out of criticizing and making another feel small and "less than?"

7. Do you judge your own work with harsh measures that leave you feeling bad and debilitated?

8. Do you work harshly with children?

9. Are you afraid of losing your power base of entitlement and privilege that you believe comes from your education?

10. Do you use, gossip, slander, and/or character assassination as forms of power to keep your position of authority?

11. How can you learn to digest others' painful thoughts without reactive speaking?

12. How can you learn to appreciate the one kernel of truth that was yours to receive, thank the person who had the insight to help you—and then surrender everything else that was said? How can you stop escalating emotional attachments? How can you work to be the bigger figure and let it go?

13. When you get to work or come home from work, why do you feel inclined to start and end the day with your dissatisfaction about something or someone's worth? What do you get from this behavior?

14. What do you know about non-violent communication? Motivational conversations? Empowering others? Receiving power through delegating strengths to others?

15. Does your judgment create a kind of social slavery and subordination of others? Explain.

16. What can you do differently today when you notice that you are making others the brunt of your experience?

17. Name five ways you can look for the good in what others have done.

Cultural Sensitivity, Diversity, Inclusivity and Competency

Realizing — and admitting — how little you know about other cultures, customs, values, communities and spiritual beliefs is the perfect place to begin understanding ourselves and others with an eye toward recovery.

My wife and I lived in the San Francisco Bay Area, where more than 110 languages are spoken. Amid this beautiful diversity, a disparaging amount of people live below the poverty level.

Let's get to work on the idea of the United States being the "land of milk and honey," where "freedom and prosperity" can be found for all.

Contemplate this scene: You leave the nation that was home. The color of your skin – or your sexual orientation, or your hijab – changes everything about the way you are treated in this land, where you had so much hope. Then, add this nation's mob-mentality racism, fear and bigotry.

This is where we begin.

When working with others, looking for similarities is a good place to start. For example, we all eat, drink and sleep. We appreciate having jobs with the availability to be upwardly mobile because of an education. Everyone wants safe places. And we all share a bloodline that goes back to prove there is no genetic difference that separates us. We are one village on a very small planet.

My parents tried to raise me as an egalitarian and peace-loving person. Many cultures were part of my life. My siblings and I were raised near military bases that provided a culturally inclusive playground for learning. My mom worked in Civil Service, which was also a place of ethnic and cultural diversity.

But pursuing cultural diversity in a nation founded on genocide, abduction, land theft and slavery is complicated. My family also communicated some messages of racism, bigotry, misogyny and ridicule of homosexuality and obesity.

As I got older and made my own way, I became a drug addict, alcoholic and sex addict. I developed looser morals. I spent decades working with a prison-release population in the construction industry. I noticed the differences in the way people were treated.

As a nurse's aide in Bay Area hospitals in the 1970s, I saw how differences in race, class and education affected access to health care. For example, a black person who broke his leg was more likely than a white person to need a cane afterward because of the shoddy medical care he received. Black people I knew were afraid to go to the hospital in general.

In other areas, too, unequal access is the American rule, not the exception. In the 21st century, U.S. public schools are getting more segregated again. In California, 23 prisons were built between 1982-2000 to accommodate an exploding prison population. Nationwide, 37 percent of male prison inmates are black. In a system that places human warehousing above rehabilitation, these young adults are released into a society that offers little but barriers to housing and employment, often forcing a return to crime merely to survive. We are not investing in this youthful population in ways that will change our broken system.

Our national bias toward white Christianity can also be seen in our entertainment industry. Hollywood has long shown a bias in favor of white people and our experience. Movies showcase whites as heroes and saviors of other cultures, in whatever limited ways those are deemed valuable. As one of countless examples, in Westerns, heroic and righteous whites routinely kill Indigenous Americans, who are portrayed as "savage" to support the national pro-white narrative.

Our country's systemic, institutional racism touches every aspect of American life, from entertainment to education, housing to healthcare, personal finance to the toys our children play with. Studies conducted in the recent decades have proven that black children, offered the choice between a white doll and a black doll, often choose the white doll because society's constant, pervasive negative messaging about people of color brainwashes even toddlers into believing that white is "good" and black is "bad."

If you – like me – are a white person, that means you have lived with some level of privilege. I know some white people don't understand that, or we get defensive and can't hear or discuss it. Or even worse, we know it's true, and we believe, for some reason, we deserve privilege.

You also might say you didn't do anything to create our centuries-old, still-in-progress system of privilege because you weren't even alive when U.S. slavery was legal, so you didn't own slaves. Well, that much is true. But if you're a white American, then you and I still benefit daily from institutional racism. Because when slavery ended, a series of racist – but still legal – systems took its place. (To find out what those systems were – and the system that's in place today – read, "The New Jim Crow: Mass Incarceration in the Age of Colorblindness," by Michelle Alexander.)

White people – yes, including poor white people who have to work hard for everything we have – reap the benefits of systemic racism. We reap more benefits than people of color via access to jobs, education, housing, healthcare, police protection, life expectancy, and overall well-being.

Don't take my word for it about all of these issues. You can learn the hard facts by asking a public librarian near you for recommendations of books and articles that are available for free, to stream on your device or read between two covers. None of us have any excuse to not educate ourselves about what is being done in our names by our governments and our fellow residents.

Faced with such an Everest-style mountain, how can we be the people — how can you be the *person* — who comes to grips, wakes up and makes sure that ours is the first generation that will not tolerate those behaviors?

In short, we are a biased country. Now what?

Include, Invite, Tolerate, and Be of Service to Diversity and All that Comes with It

We can show others the same respect and give them the same dignity for their lives that we feel for our own. This will be a way of living with tolerance and deep admiration for others whom we recognize have the same wants, needs and abilities as ourselves, so we may all achieve what we desire.

In our journey toward recovery, we learn together about our threshold of comfort with others and their behaviors. We learn to broaden our expectations of others. We can all have our powerful expressions of peace without depriving others of their peace.

Underneath most people's intolerance is a survival instinct seeking to protect our way of living. The fear is that something or someone we don't like or trust will take our power or freedom. Yet, if we stop and look at those with whom we struggle, we will see similarities. We all must collaborate and create partnership. If we look only for differences and disagreements, we will surely find those divisive things.

In what ways can we look at our "status quo" ideas and move away from conflict and prejudicial mindsets? In what ways can we move into the groundless state of accepting that we all live on the same planet? It is our destiny to remove human suffering and create equality in our minds as well as in our neighborhoods.

We can start where we are and develop healthier strategies based on our experiences, instead of our fear and reactions. Those we guard ourselves against are looking right back at us with fear and distrust. However, their fear is based on generations of oppression and cruelty.

Cultural Sensitivity

The knowledge we have of cultures other than our own gives us insight and understanding about their norms and helps us to stop generalizing the entire population. In becoming culturally sensitive, we develop skills to understand the cause and effect of our interpersonal experience. We become mindful about what hurts others and what inspires them. This exchange leads to trust and movement toward a common, shared truth.

The more we develop our sensitivity muscle, the more we stretch our ability to respond with solution-focused strategies, instead of reacting with anger or defensiveness. Even after multiple negative experiences, many people still respond positively to empathy, trust, validation and acknowledgement. This respectful exchange grows in value, and we start making inroads toward connection, which leads to our ability to talk to all cultures and become curious about all backgrounds. We are all bound to whatever conditioning we were taught, but we can make changes and take responsibility for not acting out on our unskillful upbringing. As long as we are still breathing, there is hope.

What is normal for my culture is not normal for many other cultures. We can learn more about our similarities and our need for connection by looking beyond the superficial and becoming genuine. We can stay curious without generalizing and pathologizing a whole culture.

We understand more as we learn about each other's eating habits, medical beliefs, social interactions, needs and spiritual values. Start with fun ways of connection that don't deepen confusion. Connect with humorous, lighthearted ideas. Find out about music and art, sports and other interests. Let go of preconceived notions and acknowledge that others have as much belief in their own cultures as we have in ours.

Many first-generation immigrants who live in the U.S. know two or three languages fluently. Many endured unbelievable hardship to make their way to the U.S., and once they arrived, they approached American culture with open minds and acceptance. How many languages do you know? What work did you do to *earn* your U.S. citizenship? Let's get in the game of curiosity, respect, acknowledgement and admiration.

Thoughts About Dropping Our White Defensiveness

1. We white people must admit we often are guilty of supporting unfairness through either active or passive acceptance of injustice. We turn a convenient blind eye.

2. White people must process our intense, conditioned responses of distrust; fear of losing what is "mine," and perpetuating fraudulent messages. We must become mindful and conscious of our words, thoughts and actions.

3. How can we place value and honor on a culture of which we have learned nothing? We are in a closed system when we have not made any inroads or gestures toward another culture. Change cannot occur in a walled-off environment.

4. If we judge others from a place of dualism and assign good-bad-right-wrong-winner-loser labels, we will always be in competition. One will always live in fear that the other will win. If we come looking for something wrong with another, we will find something wrong. If we look for something good and similar, we will find the good. What are you looking for?

How can we change our internal values and attitudes toward others? This is hard work. To work together, we must be flexible and open to another's cultural practices and beliefs, even though it may be slow going at first. Look yourself in the eye and ask if this actually has nothing to do with the persons you're judging and everything to do with you.

The Abundance of Others Is My Abundance

Instead of fearing that other with less than you may take something away from you, sometimes the opposite is true. Sometimes white Americans look at other nations or cultures, resent their abundance and fear their intent.

For example, at this point in time I am working with my own bias toward another large nation becoming a world power and the richest country in the world. Pollution is my biggest concern, but I err toward globalizing and entrenching my fear-based thinking. I try to prove that "this is bad," and, "we should do something," and it goes on and on until there is no way to communicate effectively what is *really* on my mind.

What I really mean to say is, "Please stop polluting the whole world with your abundance." Yet at the same time, I know that the United States has belched horrifying amounts of pollution into the Earth's soil and waters from the Industrial Revolution until today. The U.S. holds one-fifth of the planet's population and uses 24 percent of Earth's resources. We are now in the early stages of a climate catastrophe and Earth's sixth mass extinction. Before I look at pollution from other nations, I have a lot of work to do around my own nation's pollution – as well as my own personal carbon footprint. At this moment, there are countless residents of other nations looking at the United States with anger and blame about the climate crisis. But as with all other crises, the solution does not lie with anger and blame. The answers are found with collaboration, cooperation and mutual support. And that need brings us right back to cultural awareness, sensitivity and diversity.

Cultural Awareness

How can we change our thoughts and attitudes and what we think collectively about another culture? When do we consider being open and flexible and letting go of our fixed ideas about entire cultures based upon stories we are told? Start where you are. Maybe a family or a neighborhood with a culture different than your own is nearby. If you know nothing about them other than rumors and negative stereotypes, just a few hours of homework can really open our eyes. Facts are free at your public library. Look for books and film about their culture; be open and curious.

Then, bring it closer to home. Do you know even one of them personally? Can you go to a house of worship, a store, a community event or a library and strike up a conversation? Humans are humans. Making a new friend works pretty much the same, regardless of our differences. Smile, say hello and introduce yourself. Ask respectful questions about what's happening in their community. Are their issues the same as yours? Are they shockingly different? Tell them about your own life. Keep showing up. Make a genuine effort to be open and supportive. At some point, that scary unknown "other" you said hello to may become a friend. This is how we begin. This is how everything changes.

Ways to Improve Your Work with Other Cultures, Beliefs or Values

- Cultural competency, inclusivity and diversity
- Observe without judging.
- Negotiate without assigning blame.
- Suspend all thinking, and just watch and listen.
- Express mutual needs and ways to collaborate and develop trusting benefits.
- Think outside the box.
- Be solution-focused.
- Visualize that others have all the answers to their problems within themselves.
- Look at their problems as opportunities.
- Find similarities in needs and feelings.
- Be vulnerable in expressing your position.
- Create equity and safety for both parties.
- Recognize the inherent worth of all beings as a starting point.
- Do not be motivated by guilt or oppression.
- We are not responsible for others who are irresponsible with their own feelings of guilt.
- Behind the use of guilt is the ability to take responsibility for your feelings.
- Give from the heart, not out of guilt.
- Behind every judgment is an unmet need or fear that needs to be addressed.
- Don't blame others for what's wrong; ask that your needs be acknowledged.
- Develop what you need from another in conflict. What is your request of the other party?
- Rationalizing and blame are the roots of dissension and unhappiness.
- Talk about what you need, not what's wrong with someone else.

Workbook Questions:

1. What do cultural sensitivity and cultural awareness mean to you?

2. How can you better develop your cultural awareness?

3. Does thinking about a particular ethnicity, nationality or religion fill you with anxiety, fear or hate? Do you have an opinion about an entire group of people based upon the actions of a few?

4. Do you use racism as a way to feel safe?

5. Do you have a "token friend," someone you maintain a superficial friendship with because they are different than you? What do you really know about your token friend's life? What would be a reason for you to take time to develop a rich and wonderful relationship with this person?

6. Sensitivity begins with the understanding that there are differences among cultures. Cultural sensitivity includes placing value on diversity. What is the culture you judge most harshly or fear the most? Every day, spontaneously state five positive aspects of that culture. This way, you can change the muscle memory of bias and judgment.

7. What community groups can you join to find fellow travelers on this cultural journey of wellness and connection? What groups can you join to learn more about another culture?

8. How can we become the people who embrace humanity? How can we return the openness of teaching the world to sing in perfect harmony? How can we listen better to the music of others' lives, and sing along?

Curiosity

We have evolved to this brilliant state of being through curiosity about who we are in relation to our environment.

The first question a 2-year-old may ask is, "Why?" Our desire for knowledge helps us develop discernment and ambivalence about life. We either ask others or stumble blindly. We make observations and learn, or we repeat history because we did not learn the important lessons.

We are attracted to what interests us. That can be anything — and it can change in a heartbeat. Sometimes with curiosity we want to be careful what we ask for, because we might get more than we bargained for. Remember the Latin phrase, "Caveat emptor"— let the buyer beware.

Sometimes when we are attracted to bright, shiny objects in our lives, we find that our obsessions can lead to pain and suffering. Everyone wants a faster way out of negative experiences. We must be careful with important life decisions. If we want big-ticket items, we should think of them along the same lines as wanting an elephant. There will be a lot of poop to clean up as part of the responsibilities and upkeep.

Our senses are on full alert when we are curious, and we are excited to observe and maneuver our way into our new interest. This is where we can be tricked by confidence scams. Sometimes we get the thrill of our lives. We want to lean toward fun, exploration and safety for everyone involved.

Sometimes with love interests, we are drawn like a moth to a flame, trying to receive comfort from the source of our pain.

Curiosity is a cure for boredom. It relieves tension, giving our brains a reason for existing, which brings happiness most of the time. Our lives become rewarding when we are able to make healthy choices and understand the consequences of our endeavors. We move forward with courageous, limitless thinking. We can solve more problems with curiosity than we can with negative emoting and blaming others or situations.

Would you want a partner who is curious about what you think and do, rather than one who is bored or judgmental? Curious people want to know what makes others tick. This attitude creates more intimacy when developing healthy boundaries with another. There are more options because there are more interests – more reasons to fully engage in life. Curious people often love science, philosophy, art and music and want to know how and why things happen. Their lives are enriched by the journey.

When we feed our brains, we are rewarded with healthy, feel-good chemical cascades. That sensation makes us more likely to keep using our brains, which in turn can make us smarter. If we don't use it, we lose it. People who have lost curiosity are apathetic and give up. Curious people remain alert, grateful and joyful about the precious time they have on the planet.

When we make our lives a joyful exertion, the benefits will outweigh the bad moments. We will develop wisdom through open and willing searches for our own mythology – the story of who we are and why we are here.

Workbook Questions:

1. What are your interests? What initiated your life-changing events?

2. What would you love to learn about? What excites you about that?

3. Which relationship ideals would you like to explore? Are you satisfied with your place within your family, loved ones, co-workers, colleagues, community? What would you like to change?

4. What types of intimacy would you like to develop – new ways to love your partner, honor, trust, keep the honeymoon going?

5. How does your body respond when you are excited and on a mission of discovery? Where do you feel it? Is it like butterflies in your stomach? Are you itching to jump into learning? Is the excitement connected to your brain? Is it sexual?

6. What has been a typical reason you procrastinate exploring with pleasure and information-gathering to go for your dreams?

7. How have you been hurt with curious endeavors in the past? Were you gullible? Did you believe everything about the good parts and dismiss the dangers of your thrill-seeking? What will it take for you to heal and find fun again?

8. What kind of partner do you have? Do they care about and support your interests? Does fear that your children may get hurt stop your playful curiosity? How can you retain your childlike innocence with your family and enjoy all the benefits and knowledge that curiosity brings?

9. How does your brain reward you when you feed its desire for learning and knowledge? Explain the feelings you have when you make a discovery. What might happen if you suspend negative thinking about a certain subject and look for healthy reasons to engage in an activity that others have found to be beneficial? Are you hesitant about swimming, playing games, science, art? Name five things you have reservations about because you have been hurt or told you were not good at them.

10. Do you bring out curiosity in your family, partner, colleagues? How can you excite others with your contagious fun and exploration? What do you have to lose?

11. What will it take for you to stop taking life so seriously and have some fun?

Death and Dying

So far, we are survivors in this life. If we live long enough, we will have the opportunity to watch and participate in the loss of friends, colleagues, and loved ones. We may feel communal loss in hearing about disasters around the planet. We might even be facing our own mortality through a slow process of disease or age.

We all go through a waiting process. It is during this time that some of us process the forthcoming fate that we will personally feel with our own death or that of a loved one.

There is no one right way to deal with grief. Grieving is as personal and individual as the people involved. It's helpful if you Do No Harm to others while having your own experience. Our minds are complicated machines. We try to reason and make our experience palatable. The stages of grief, loss, death and dying are a cascade of emotions that include denial, anger, bargaining, depression, and finally — we hope — acceptance of what will happen.

When we witness someone struggling with the loss of a loved one, sometimes listening and being available is the best medicine. Let them cry and process their mixed feelings for what they are. If they do ask for our thoughts, we might consider honoring and acknowledging the great, fun and worthy times their loved ones contributed to the planet. If appropriate, celebrate along with others' loss and mourning to keep emotions in perspective. Sadness is one of many feelings we experience.

Life is not convenient or fair. How we accept our losses is something we can start doing right here and now. How do you process failure, loss, grief and death? Would you change your thinking if it benefitted yourself or others? They say a spiritual moment is when things are not going the way we would like. This is the time we can access our faith and belief and choose to participate in life differently.

Like most people, I would like to feel peace at the moment of death. There are ways we can facilitate these aspirations. We can have our process and still die with dignity. This can be a healthy and natural part of our experience on the planet.

We lose perspective when we make death and grief about us and attach to our beliefs. People all over the planet are dying at this moment. They are experiencing suffering. We can connect with this universal experience and be part of a bigger picture.

We are resilient beings. It is healthy and natural to accept change and to process and move on. We do not need to stay stuck with the omnipresence of death. When our loved ones are dying over an extended period of time, we do not have to mourn for years waiting for them to die. We can grieve and also be joyful with the entire process.

It is important to have closure with someone, so we are OK with our feelings and don't regret holding onto negative emotions. The attachment to unfinished business makes us sad and depressed about not doing due diligence earlier.

Suicides are a daunting process. We try to notice signs and be aware of our surroundings and how we influence others. By our mindfulness, we could be the right medicine to prevent suicide. We all suffer when someone chooses to take their life. The media is full of news about people who feel unheard, who take the lives of others and then themselves. We can do a lot as a society to prevent these kinds of behaviors. Start now and be part of a preventive culture.

We can bring peace to the living and the dying by asking questions about what they would like to happen while they are still alive, and to bring peace and dignity to their dying. Finding out about what their unfinished fulfillments are will help us maneuver and develop solution-focused closure with life.

As the moment of death comes closer, we need to maintain healthy boundaries and don't make the situation about ourselves. Their process is paramount. Remember that others around you are processing, too. Make sure you do not deny their experience any more than you would your own.

When we make another's death about how *we* feel, it is unfair to anyone else who is experiencing authentic feelings of their own. We are all in this together.

Following are paraphrased Stages of Death or Grief and Loss:

1) Denial

When we lose a loved one by accident or find that we are dying of cancer or we lose a lover or a job, we go through a process of denial. "Why me?" "This can't really be happening." "This is so unfair." "Maybe they got the diagnosis wrong." Through this defense mechanism, we refuse to accept and believe that the painful time is happening in our lives. "There must be something wrong; check it again." After finding out there is no escape, we move onto another step.

2) Anger

We blame God, ourselves and others. We internalize our loss and lose our ability to be objective. Who did this unspeakable thing? We rage and try to find out when and why this happened. What was the source? Who's responsible? What causation led to this happening? Why me?

3) Bargaining

In bargaining, we have "fox-hole prayers." "God, get me out of this one and I will (fill in the blank)." We do things that compromise our integrity to look good or keep a job or save a marriage, or to keep our son/daughter in the house. "Take me, God, not my loved one!" "I will do this and be so good. I will be spiritual and do service for others." Fate is not chance. "Just give me one more chance." It would be nice if death was about chance, but it's about reality and our coming to terms with life on life's terms.

4) Depression

Depression is the aftermath. "Oh, no. Everything is crystal clear and right now. There is no escape, no bargaining, no blaming." We feel it now. This is reality, and we respond to our loss, sorrow, and regrets about not showing more timely love and putting off saying important things. We feel infinite sadness with what is, a powerful feeling that gets mixed up with coulda, shoulda, woulda — regrets and shame-based faith.

5) Acceptance

"Oh, I get it now. Wow, this is real. It is not personal, it just is." We accept that we have lost our son, lover, wife, job, arm, car, or our own life to a disease. We take ownership of what happened and know it is our process that will determine how we will inevitably respond — sometimes quickly and sometimes slowly. Grieving happens in earnest; we have a choice to accept all that is. We realize with wonder how precious life is and how sometimes we must forgive ourselves and/or others or we will keep carrying a poison sack of resentment that clouds our efforts to recover. We move on.

These stages can happen independently in any order or all at once as we develop discerning wisdom about how we move forward in life.

Workbook Questions:

1. What close experiences with death and dying have you had? Have they been with family members? With friends or colleagues? What were the differences like? How did you handle the experiences?

2. How have you used the Stages of Grief and Loss in your life? Did you skip around the steps? Did you get to acceptance without going through every step? How did you do this?

3. How did others around you respond to the death of a loved one? Did they seem to have it all together? What did they do that made them so prepared? Or did they lose it completely? Did they fight about who loved who more?

4. How does your choice of faith encourage you to deal with death and dying? How does your community participate with those trying times?

5. Do you have survivor's guilt about losing a loved one in a situation where you could have died as well?

6. Do you know anyone who committed suicide? Was there anything you could do better now to prevent this kind of death and dying? Are you afraid of intimacy with people who are that distraught?

7. Have you had the privilege to see someone die with grace and dignity? How did that affect you? What will it take for you to have that experience?

8. What are your feelings about your own mortality? Would you have closure if you died today? What would you like to happen in your life to feel complete and die in peace? What stops you from engaging in those behaviors? Are you too busy?

9. Name the people in your life whom you are going to share and experience this special end to their lives. Are you ready? What would you like to say to them to make your own experience have closure? Why wait till they are dying to get the peace you could have now from complete forgiveness?

10. Do you have inordinate fears that your children or spouse will die and be taken away from you? What will it take for you to feel peace about that concept?

11. How do you care for yourself when you are feeling depressed about losing something? What techniques can you learn to be more prepared? Do you have a spiritual community to help you process loss?

12. How do you skillfully help others who suffer from loss? How do you stay patient with the grieving process? How do you take care of yourself so that you do not burn out?

13. Are you a caregiver for a loved one? How do you do extreme self-care and keep your life in balance and order? Do you get help and have someone to talk to when things get rough? Do you feel you have to be the caregiver and that you are alone? What community can you call to get help? What stops you from reaching out for help?

Discovery

The world is brand-new, if we believe it is. The war inside our heads is over, if we believe it is. Everything is in motion, and change is always in the air. Our minds give us the first chance to be part of the evolution of our times. Our minds are open and flexible.

From childhood, we engaged our learning process by observation. We learned what to do and what not to do through our parents — or lack of parenting. We learned about hot stoves and boiling water by discovering dangers inherent with the stove.

Our lives are all about discovery.

Sometimes we discover that our thinking is brittle, thin-skinned, biased or racist. We will find that change is possible if we let go of our hardened belief system. If we stay curious, we are more likely to understand more things. This state of openness keeps us willing to consider and contemplate other truths.

A state of openness includes keeping an open mind to be willing, flexible, teachable, open, honest, and not attached to a dualistic outcome of right and wrong. It means letting go of agenda-based thinking and maintaining a moral and ethical compass unto ourselves.

When we were children without any pre-conceptions of the world, we were truly free and without judgment. We were taught someone's idea of right and wrong through laws, spiritual beliefs, and daily choices. We were introduced to a world of consequences for certain behaviors. Our freedom was curtailed to the morales, laws and ethics of our colloquial area or country. We assumed the customs, rights and rituals of our tribe.

When learning something new, it is best to come with an open mind and develop what we relate to. Children of every ethnicity play together and have no attachments to race, class or social status. They co-exist. Only when they are taught that someone is different or less deserving do they attach to that belief.

For us to succeed in recovery, we need to suspend our empirical belief system and all of our thinking and come from a place of openness with a beginner's mind. This is where all things can happen and change. When we are able to hold simultaneous truths, true wisdom occurs. Change happens when the paradox of diametrically opposed sides becomes congruent. This is the only truth — change happens. Nothing ever stays the same. Things evolve. Nothing works every time, because some factors will always change. We are in a constant state of flux; we have the ability and resilience to become comfortable with uncertainty.

When we can grasp the understanding that someone believes in what they do in the same way that we believe something, we will discover there are many truths. We must hold all these truths as precious and valuable until we learn otherwise, and help educate others without agenda. We each discover our own truth. We surrender and willingly hold the paradox of both worlds.

With our best thinking getting us where we are right now, it is good to be in groups where we take on the role of a "think tank. Everyone throws their thoughts into a pond and gets to agree to disagree, letting the collective mind process controversies and questions. In a group experience, we can come up with the "greater good" based upon what we have learned. We have compassion for another's truth, and our truth may change with this open system of discovery.

With our self-discovery and collective truth, we are more capable of retaining knowledge and concepts. Without dualistic beliefs, we are more capable of imparting information with no attachment to the outcome.

A person who thinks he knows everything cannot learn anything.

Change happens. Nothing stays the same. Nothing works all the time.

Workbook Questions:

1. How do your beliefs about past pain and suffering make your mind rigid and brittle when considering new truths or another's experience? In what ways would you like to change? Why or why not?

2. Why is it hard for you to hear another person's truths about politics, religion, spirituality, health, psychology? Say more.

3. In what ways do negative personal experiences shape your future? What would it take for you to believe your future is spotless and unwritten — blemish-free? Explain.

4. In what ways do you keep yourself from enjoying and being curious about life? How do you globalize and "awfulize" situations so that you continue to sustain your way of life? What is the worst that will happen if you suspend your concretized thinking?

5. How does having control, agenda and expectations keep you from enjoying the serendipity that can occur when you let go and surrender your old ways of communicating?

6. How does attachment to your ideals keep you from being in wonderment? What happens when you suspend your belief systems? Can you be mindful and groundless without feeling like an exposed nerve?

7. In what ways does being jaded, coercive, and having all the answers give you an upper edge, but prevent you from hearing another's truth?

8. In what ways are you uneasy being an observer and only watching events unfold? Why do you feel the need to control outcomes?

9. When you are having a problem-solving moment, what stops you from listening to all input from friends or colleagues — no matter how silly some of them might seem?

10. When troubleshooting a dilemma, do you look up on the Internet all the ways in which others have processed your dilemma? Explain.

11. When you are in nature, do you feel discomfort when you see bugs, snakes or birds? Or are you curious about their lives? What are the limits of your curiosity?

12. How do you view danger and curiosity? In what ways do you find out the difference without getting hurt?

13. When you discover something you enjoy, how do you proceed after the excitement wears down? Do you desire to keep the discovery going? In what ways can you do that and stay open?

14. Are you curious about musical instruments? What stops you from wanting to find out more or learn how to play one?

15. What foods do you like from other countries? Have you tried any? Have you eaten a meal with your fingers? If so, what did you find out about your experience?

Ego

My ego is a hard-working gorilla doing pushups to kick my behind at the next available opportunity. It wears a T-shirt that says, "Doesn't play well with others." My ego needs to be right about things. It is pushy, authoritative, and retributive.

I have such low self-esteem that I wear a target on my back and front so I can conveniently be a victim when and where I need to be. Therefore, everyone can hit a bull's-eye on me. I am so thin-skinned that I am easily offended, and then I get labeled that way, so my reputation does the work for me.

I have "contempt prior to investigation," which puts me in position to be offensive and defend a broken-down lifestyle that has never worked, just so I can be right. I need to be treated as special or at least better-than-average simply to feel normal. I use reverse pride to expend as much energy as an egomaniac.

I always need to be right, win, control, reject acceptance, and keep expectations of others. I always have an agenda. I play unfairly, and manipulating a situation comes easily to me.

Those of us with demanding egos come from a place of "poverty of the mind." We all must deal with mental scraps from under the table, not accessing the banquet before us, and attempting but never attaining healthy boundaries or fruition of ideas.

We thrive in being the underdog. We are perfectionists, yet never able to attain our goals, so always unhappy and unsatisfied with outcomes. If we think so little about ourselves, just think how little patience we have with others. Our egos love to win, but even when we win all the time, we remain unsatisfied and find a way to destroy our own happiness.

Our egos want to get laid all the time as a testament of our worthiness.

Can you hear that massive, sucking sound coming from between your ears? It is our egos sucking the life out of every living thing around us, leaving desiccated bodies of no use to ourselves or anyone else.

To develop a healthy ego, I had to break down all of the above thinking and build a foundation of acceptance. I accepted that "pain and suffering" would be my teacher. I accepted that this time, right here and now, is the only time I have on the planet to be happy. I accepted that others have their own truth, and choosing to not accept their truth will make me unhappy.

I also learned to honor and accept that the position I am in is my station in life, at least for the moment. I accept and agree to disagree in all of my affairs. I acknowledged that my hand would get stuck in the candy jar, and I could not have all the candy at once or my hand would come out empty. I had to admit that by doing estimable acts, I would cultivate my own esteem. I recognized that by doing service for others, I was put in a position to get out of the egoistic structure inside my head just enough to not be stuck in myself for the day.

With the ability to break down all of our thinking and suspend our judgment and beliefs, we let go of our reasons for clinging to ego.

Our ego wants to over-protect us and make sure we win. It's connected to the reptile part of our brain, creating safety for us to live, sleep, eat, and propagate. But the reptile instinct leads to unwanted power, control and a feeling of safety at the expense of others. Ours is a world of dualistic thinking of mine vs. yours, right vs. wrong, winning vs. losing, good vs. bad. Our ego wants to win — not accept life on life's terms.

Workbook Questions:

1. In what ways will you work to develop a healthy ego? What purpose will it have in your life?

2. Who or what regulates your egoistic structure? Your values? Your community? Your spiritual beliefs? Your capitalistic tendencies?

3. You are what you think, and it develops what you do. What do you think about that brings you grief? Explain the ways you want something good, but it leaves a bad taste in your mouth. Explain the mistrust you have when someone compromises your integrity.

4. In what ways is your ego healthy? Name five values your ego has. How do you monitor and maintain balance with your ego when it feels threatened and violated? What ways do your community, spiritual values, and social interpersonal skill sets keep you observable and measurable in contrast to your environment?

5. What's the worst thing that could happen if you let go of your egoistic, entrenched thinking? How does your brittle armor keep you from attracting good things into your life? Your ego was meant to protect you, but now it protects only itself. What skills can you use to work with this paradox within your mind?

6. Are you the good person who always helps others because you are on the righteous side? Do you have a God that makes you do things to stop others from having a sense of safety, well-being and belonging? What purpose does this attitude serve? Is it self-serving? Do others deserve the feelings in their lives that you plant in their souls? What are you willing to do to create equity with others?

7. Does your ego have a strong sense that you are entitled to freedom and the pursuit of happiness? Are you one of the privileged few who've always had access? Do you deserve more than others? Do you judge others who are different and create a separation that looks politically, racially, or morally self-serving? Do those others deserve the happiness you want in your own life? Are you willing to wish your happiness upon them? Explain.

8. Do you believe your ego's needs are more important than the sustainability of the planet?

9. Is your ego measured by whether you own an iPhone, a car, the way you dress, the places you eat? Explain how your ego works —be full-measured with how you conduct your business.

10. Is your ego more important than any relationship — personal, business, or social? Explain how you must have all the trappings to feel normal around others.

11. Do you need power and control? Do you have an agenda with others to let them know whom they are dealing with? How does this serve your ego?

12. What does being an egomaniac mean to you? As an extrovert or introvert, how do you use your desperation and neediness to cultivate more than your fair share from others who want an equal relationship with you? Why do you need more simply to feel normal?

Emotional Enmeshment

When I abandon my own life and live for another, it is called enmeshment. We take their ups and downs, wins and losses, and claim them as our own worth. We try to fix them, help them, and create solutions for their lives. We become one with the other.

All of that can feel fulfilling at first, but as you stop having your own feelings, you find you are reliant upon another for your happiness and/or sadness. No longer are you an autonomous person capable of having your own life.

I define this as two broken, half-people trying to make one whole person.

What I need is to be one complete, whole person sharing my experience with another whole person. They can stand alone, and we value that trait. We are able to have a healthier, more intimate relationship because of it. It's healthy to have our personal thoughts, livelihoods, communities, creative processes, and beliefs. It's healthy to contribute our love to another who has a life as full as our own. This is what creates diversity; otherwise, we would all look and act the same.

When we base our worth and value upon what our partner or family thinks about us, we become reliant upon them to make or break our esteem. We use a reward system and neediness for their resolve about what to do to complete us. Without their approval, we believe our worth is threatened or lost.

When enmeshed, we feel obligated to be hyper-vigilant and micro-manage the affairs of our loved ones, their purpose, growth, and personal choices. Our happiness depends upon them to do as we say so we feel safe. We receive power and control through our requests of them. We feel either completed or threatened by their compliance to our will. We will use any tactics to keep them, including no privacy, no personal space, guilt and fear to make them kowtow in submission. We become the victim and the martyr. We don't take care of our own needs and desires. We become rescuers and create false reasons for others needing us.

How to Begin Healthy Relations with Others

Love, appreciate and value others exactly as they are right now.

Take care of your own needs. Bring everything you need to this party of life, so you are not reliant upon others for your happiness.

Be genuine, authentic and comfortable with your own needs. Be flexible enough to trust your decision-making process and to respect your partner's methods and techniques by relying on trust.

Develop equity by having different friends, interests, hobbies and musical tastes. Create diversity by encouraging your partner to enjoy new, creative relations.

Learn to let go and appreciate without holding your partner as emotional hostage.

Do small acts of letting go of trivial annoyances and fears. Build upon these and develop complex surrenders of true compassion and empathy for your partner's experience, based upon faith.

Create an inherent belief that your partner is a capable and worthy person of value who makes healthy choices. Trust that they will come to you for help if it is necessary.

Pray for the willingness to love and honor your partner exactly as they are right now. Pray, especially when you try to control and persuade them to your will. Pray for the willingness to pray for the willingness. The spiritual moment happens when you do the right thing, even while your life is hitting the fan. Your job is to move away from the fan.

Be willing to listen and heed what real friends have to say or inflect about your behaviors. Have a community that will call you on your stuff. Be willing to consider that you truly are doing the type of behavior they bring to your attention, and that you have the choice and power to stop this recidivism.

Start noticing when you are being co-dependent or an enabler to another's life. Consider the worst that could happen, and ask yourself if it really is your responsibility to engage them. Pick the times that you need to state your view. If you need to state your belief when it is not warranted, reflect on why you need to do this.

Notice when you are getting jealous, nervous, and/or envious. You are allowed to have those thoughts, but it is not fair to your partner to put your own fear-based control on them. You are allowed to have your privacy—as they are theirs. Mutual respect dictates you ask permission to pry, but they are allowed to say no. The decency, privacy, thoughts and views they hold dear are none of your business. The idea here is to Do No Harm. How do your motivating factors compromise the integrity of your partner's autonomy?

Be willing to consider the value and need for keeping thoughts in a secretive manner. Is it really healthy? What's your part in the intrigue? Why do you need to uncover every single item? Some things are better left alone and can destroy relationships. Always ask permission of your partner and state why you make the request. Be willing to hear and process a "yes" or a "none of your business."

You are complete, whole and healthy by yourself. You meet halfway with your partner, who is complete, whole and healthy. Trust is developed by this process.

Realize those times when you transfer and project your experience onto your partner. Take responsibility for creating the irritation. Sit with your experience without blaming someone else to make you feel whole, complete, or better.

Work on harmonic balance and collaboration as bargaining chips.

Let yourself spin out of control with emotional cascades sometimes, and then process your experience without blaming anyone else. Let your partner spin out, too, without enmeshing or trying to help, fix, solve. Just sit with the discomfort, and let them come to a reasonable state. Patiently wait. Be there, waiting to greet them when they are done. It's not about you; it's their personal experience.

Learn boundary-setting and know your limits. Make Do-No-Harm contracts that you will adhere to for safety and health in your relations.

Learn to love and accept yourself. Know that you are loveable and belong. You deserve. You have arrived at your destination to share your journey as a gift to others.

Honor and value that great sex is an indirect by-product of a healthy relationship built upon trust.

Workbook Questions:

1. Do you monitor your loved one's voicemail and/or email? In what ways do you check their bank accounts and other personal business without permission, looking for something wrong?

2. In what healthy ways do you recognize your behaviors? In what ways do you regulate yourself? Whom do you serve?

3. What healthy boundary-setting do you implement to keep relations safe and open? In what ways do you veer away from closed, enmeshed settings where things go astray?

4. Name five autonomous values or qualities you exhibit that would make someone believe you are trustworthy.

5. How do you judge your friends and their decision-making processes? What power do you get out of that encroachment? What can you do to keep yourself open and create a safe way for them to disclose, and then for you to hold your space without enabling or fixing their problem? Did they ask for help?

6. What do you complain about that sounds like a broken record to your partner? Do you harp on and berate them for your unhappiness? What can you do to take care of your own needs and not control your partner for your own comfort?

7. Do you believe it is your responsibility to tell your partner what you are unhappy about, what needs to change, show them how, why and when change should happen? Do you control their life and make them feel powerless by your violating behaviors? Explain.

8. Why do you feel it is OK to judge harshly your loving partner? Do you get feelings of power and control or convenient and immediate satisfaction? Do you feel better after beating them down and letting them have it? Explain.

9. How do you try to fix, help, and/or create solutions for others? Are you a good, trustworthy resource? Have you worked on your own healthy autonomy and boundary-setting? Are you breaking your own values because "this situation is different"? Say more.

10. Do you believe that, because you are a parent, you can enmesh into your innocent child's life and create a perfect imprint of your dysfunction so you are not alone? Are you a controlling parent who needs a child to love you unconditionally?

11. Do you believe you have magic powers to help others? Are you the "good one" who is there to help? Name five ways in which you are the "good one" who can help others in their suffering. Are you capable of working on or being open to listening about your own character defects? Are you willing to self-regulate? Why do you not have magic healing powers for yourself?

12. Do you enmesh with others to create a power source? Do you use people for different reasons and benefit from divisive techniques? Do you make yourself out to be the expert in the field and charge money to others while your own personal life is unhealed and unresolved?

Enabling and Codependency

Enabling can be part of a healthy, empowering, give-and-take relationship built upon trust and belief in the partner. This ideal lends itself to accepting that your partner is trying hard, deserves support, and can safely make mistakes and be forgiven. For healthy enabling to occur, you must have mutual trust and take a leap of faith when things look unstable.

Unhealthy enabling and codependency begin when safe boundaries are lost through broken trust. It begins when people want a situation to get better, no matter the cost, and you are willing to sacrifice your healthy autonomy to enmesh with your loved one's addictions or destructive behavior.

This method of coping makes the "helper party" vulnerable on many levels. You will go to almost any lengths to cover up, make excuses, support with money, and threaten your mental, physical, spiritual, and financial safety. You will endanger your relations with family, friends, and the law and strive to make sure your loved one is safe and free from accountability, pain, responsibility and legal actions. When this occurs, we have earned the diagnosable disorder called Enabling and Codependency.

How It Works

A person is addicted to something. It can be drugs, alcohol, anger, sex or gambling. He has a great investment to keep his world stable and be able to maintain his way of life. To do this, the addict, as master manipulator, is willing to take emotional hostages to attain his immediate and convenient gratifications, no matter the cost to the family or loved ones.

This manipulation is a learned behavior for the enabler. The enabler is at risk of losing the affection and company of the addict, including through the addict's threats of suicide. The enabler is well-practiced with veiled threats, saying others cause him to do such-and-such by not accepting him as he is. Facing this behavior over and over, the loved one or family member has few healthy options.

The abuser will create the delusion that there is hope, playing on the emotional vulnerability of the family member. The addict will use anger and fear to make the loved one feel threatened and embarrassed and blame the loved one for feeling endangered and creating the threat of abandonment. The addict uses guilt as a weapon of enslavement against the family's good will and ups the ante with higher and higher emotional ransoms. The addict will play on the sympathies of otherwise healthy and loving people.

What the Loved One Can Do to Create and Hold Healthy Boundaries

Stop being the victim of this abuse. Stop covering up the abusive behaviors. Stop making excuses for the abuser when you feel vulnerable. Put your loving kindness, care and devotion into people who respond in healthy ways to your time, investment and money. Recognize the discomfort, shame and stigma you feel, and get help with others who suffer from codependent behavior.

Be pro-active and connect with other loved ones to develop strategies to get free of this toxic relationship. It destroys everyone who partakes in the codependent poison. It affects children and teaches them unhealthy ways to live. It creeps into other relationships, creating mistrust and disease.

Quit giving away all of your power to a loved one who will not take care of himself. Put the emotional "oxygen mask" on your own face; only then can you hope to help another. Self-care comes first.

Invest in the longer view. This can take years of the enabler learning more and more about why he does this behavior. Spend the time; your lives are worth it. Adjust your moral compass and get back into healthy values with people who have dignity and pride and who will honor your trust and have your back in times of need.

Hold still to feel the incredible loneliness of losing your loved one. Have a mock funeral; let go and forgive every bad thing that happened. Surrender your thoughts, worth and deeds. Don't pathologize the addict – address his behaviors. Then address the behaviors for which you are responsible.

Workbook Questions:

1. Explain how you will go to any length to pursue a person with disruptive behavioral traits.

2. How much of your mental health and safety are you willing to sacrifice for your precious loved one's "little problem" with behaviors or addiction?

3. Do you take emotional abuse from your partner and feel manipulated about your time, spending, support, and right to make decisions that are not based solely on their needs?

4. In what ways do you comply with people's unreasonable needs simply so you do not rock the boat?

5. In what ways are you afraid to ask for raises, because you fear the wrath of your boss and his views about work compensation?

6. How do your friends or partner play on your sympathies to manipulate you on various subjects to get their needs met?

7. In what ways do you engender and promote healthy enabling possibilities with your loved ones?

8. How are you secretly ashamed about your part in this unfair treatment?

9. When will your mental health and safety be more important than giving away your power and esteem?

10. In what ways is it painful and uncomfortable to stay in this relationship, but the fears of leaving are even more paralyzing?

11. What is your part in this? Do you get sex? Money? Prestige? Power?

Family Psycho-Education

Generation after generation, we all got here from somewhere.

We are the survivors out of all that has been, since the beginning of time. Yet with all those survival smarts, we still have a lot of problems to work on with interpersonal skill sets because of generational dysfunctions.

As addicts, we have problems that may be obvious to everyone around us. The idea of every one of us having 3.2 co-occurring disorders creates a sense of unity. I like to ask the question, "What's in your wallet?" We are humans, not diagnoses. We are complicated people living in a hectic and unpredictable world, which makes it imperative that we work on solution-focused, people-centered strategies.

Have you ever heard, "Well, at least he comes by it honestly"? How can we stop our generational dysfunction and historical oppression and move toward promising lives? How do we plan ahead the same way as Native Americans, who considered the effects of everything they did seven generations in the future?

The best way to begin is to stop finger-pointing and judging each other. We all have earned our place at the table of life. No one here gets out alive. We can realize that, with love and understanding, we work better together in the short time we are given on this planet.

By and large, there were no "how-to" books for our parents. They did the best they could, figuring it out as they went. Lines blur when we consider which family member has what addiction or personality disorder or physical, medical or mental-health status. Through family psycho-education, we learn to communicate our messages safely without doing harm to those we love. We can learn to agree to disagree. We hold our space and feel safe while learning to actively listen. We learn to respond by saying brave words like, "Thanks. It took a lot of courage for you to be that honest with me."

In our culture, most families like to look good in the public and social eye. There is stigma attached to those who suffer from anything. As a family, we want to keep issues private. *Don't let others know. Keep the problem a secret, or our social status will be damaged.* Despite struggling with problems, the family wants to bond and stay together. There is shame when everyone knows your family member struggles with addiction. There is stigma attached to not being perfect, which leads to the need to hide anger, drinking, drugs, sex problems, gambling and/or eating.

Through family psycho-education, we learn there is a way to break down the walls and talk about problems without inflaming situations.

With transition from the old to the new ways of dealing with challenge, opportunities arise for everyone to process and heal from old wounds. We can often heal with the support of a neutral support group that has no family ties to stir up emotional turmoil.

For families to successfully unite, these things are necessary: resolute perseverance with all "agreeing to disagree" – to suspend judgment and the tendency to "fix" or "help" or "solve." These are all ways we make *ourselves* feel better, as opposed to resolving issues for the family group. Sitting and listening are sometimes the most valuable things we can do. Silence has power. Putting responsibility back into the hands of the suffering member and giving them an opportunity to make better, less harmful choices can lead to healing.

When a person understands they are disruptive to their family, they have the chance to hold still and face the challenge. They can choose to hold their feelings in a safe place surrounded by those who care in a nonjudgmental manner. No one truly wants their loved one to suffer. Family consultation creates an environment where solutions, strategies, education and empowerment surface with safety options while eliciting self-change talk.

Families who desire to unify require a skillful craft to deal with the stages of change and transition at every step. Every family member will sit with their own share of discomfort, because everyone is required to focus on staying neutral, vulnerable, and sensitive, keeping healthy boundaries in place.

When those we love don't make positive choices, there is a skill to developing a healthy ambivalence and discernment about tough choices. The rest of the family needs to make tough choices, too, when they are left to pick up the pieces. They must seek collective safety without destroying the fabric that holds everyone together.

Often when a family deals with a loved one's destructive choices and behaviors, it becomes all too clear that they are ill-equipped for the long haul. They need a quick fix. They like to put a small bandage on a large, festering problem. Rarely do we have the impetus, insight, and patience to take a longer view and make a five-year plan. Behaviors took a long time to develop. Chances are, they will not go away in a minute. Make sure everyone is on board to make this a lifetime of work and opportunity.

Instilling hope in the family is the greatest goal we can cultivate— a sense of everyone learning to be willing, open and flexible, with a beginner's mind. That attitude helps the loved one to respond in kind. Persistence is the lubrication that creates an environment where everyone can get on board and thrive.

Complete forgiveness for everyone helps facilitate openness and healing. If we do not forgive our loved ones, how can we expect them to forgive themselves? This idea creates willingness for everyone involved to do the work at hand and not expect the suffering loved one to magically heal.

Here are some options a family can pursue with the help of a trained professional:

- Twelve-Step programs
- Therapy
- Medications
- Rational emotive behavioral therapy
- Cognitive behavioral therapy
- Dialectical behavioral therapy
- Mindfulness
- Motivational conversations
- Spiritual opportunities

Remember that we are working with human beings who have made poor choices. Our job is to create a menu of options, elicit self-change thoughts, start where the client is, and be there for the longer haul. It is a lifetime's opportunity.

Workbook Questions:

1. What solutions does your loved one have that can elicit self-change thinking and facilitate forward-looking strategies?

2. In what ways do you sabotage your family's connectiveness?

3. In what ways do you gossip, slander, and/or character-assassinate your suffering loved one's behaviors?

4. In what ways have you kicked your family member out of the nest? Have you used threatening and separating behaviors?

5. How have you contributed to the malaise? In what ways do you try to put the fire out with gasoline?

6. What spiritual work do you perform to take extreme self-care during emotionally escalated episodes?

7. What sort of things do you expect that may seem unreasonable to your suffering loved ones?

8. Explain more about your need for control, expectations, having an agenda, and not being in acceptance of your loved one.

9. What can't you forgive about your loved ones' behaviors? Why not?

10. What feelings of safety do you get about being in complete control? In what ways does that make it impossible for change to happen safely for others?

11. How does your childhood upbringing affect your ability to stay neutral now? Was there dissension in your family? Did the family play favorites? Did everyone have to pick a station in life and feel obligated to be typecast? Did you process the resentment these things created? Do you still respond from that wounded place?

12. Einstein said, "We cannot solve our problems with the same thinking we used when we created them." In what ways can you think outside the box and move beyond that type of thinking?

13. Sometimes the problem that repeats itself over and over is not the problem. Let's go deeper — what is at the bottom of your reactions?

14. In what ways have you maneuvered through similar situations? What worked? What didn't?

Family Reunification

In some ways, we are all estranged beings – estranged from family and unity. We feel separate and unique, no matter how close we feel our family units are. It's our Ego that wants us to be special and different.

Family settings are great proving grounds for all sorts of problems. For a lot of us, those problems are a mixed bag of unfinished business.

How can we do the work with ourselves and improve our lot in life, while objectively holding our space and knowing that others did not change, will not change, and have no inclination to even think about it? How can we model our behaviors without expectations of others? How can we become accepting and OK with all people exactly the way they are? What is it about us that wants them to change, so we feel safe about our stature, security, mental health, bonding and acceptance?

Many of us have different experiences of loss and being unconnected. We have built our lives trying to change, remove, and cover up ties to our family of origin.

How can we reconnect – or connect for the first time in our lives – with our families in a healthy way? How can we model the effect of the work we have done on ourselves without challenging or doing harm? How can we instill hopes and aspirations in others, so they may find and follow their own paths? How can we learn patience, while they explore and do research that doesn't require our approval or participation? How do we become great observers of our lives while engaging in the family dynamic?

For those raised in a closed-system family dynamic, when no one on the outside knew what went on inside the privacy of your home, you might have experienced some of the following incidences:

Many families argue. Some experience physical abuse, including hitting, pushing, and slapping as part of corporal punishment. There are lots of threats, with promises of punishment if certain needs are not met. More people have punishments and threats administered by family than by strangers. Those who were violated as children with violence, tongue-lashings, sexual abuse, and the like are likely to replicate those acts as adults with their children and partners.

Let's begin developing strategies to bring family together. Let's do what works.

Start with openness, willingness, teachability, and being a great listener with a beginner's mind. Begin with curiosity and a sense of discovery about our lives. We come with courage, fearlessness, and limitless thinking. We don't need to play that old tape of what happened in the past.

The war is over, if you believe it is. The end of it is an inside job that requires one person who chooses not to participate, because it's too expensive with their own mental health and a luxury the family cannot afford.

We are as happy as we choose to be.

Come with gentleness, unconditional positive regard for each other, and radical kindness with patience for the process. This plan will take a lifetime of consistent healing.

Here are things to consider, if you are trying to have a family reunification:

1. Make sure everyone uses "I" statements, such as I feel, I think, I want, and, "When you do this, I feel that."

2. So that all feel a part of the reunification, make sure leadership is shared equally among the family.

3. Ensure the willingness of all parties to agree to disagree without harming one another or using judgment and shaming techniques.

4. Agree to work for a specified amount of time, and then resolve to let it all go until the next time. Keep peace in your heart.

5. Agree to work on small, incremental tasks that are doable in the time at hand.

6. Strive for all parties to have an equal, common reason to meet halfway, to let go of old wounds and trauma from earlier times, to be equally vulnerable and sensitive to each other's needs.

7. Endeavor to work as a team. Collaborate with everyone's ideas, and be solution-focused with an emphasis on using each other's strength-based abilities.

8. Ask everyone to promise to create a safe place to have feelings and process them. Take timeouts, and come back to the table after an undetermined amount of time to resume the process. This will not look perfect. Apologize and start again. Give others the same opportunity.

9. Agree to look for the similarities and needs for communing together. Work with strengths for unity.

10. Agree to actively listen without drafting your rebuttal. Just listen. No fixing, no solutions. When requested, strive to hear someone's disagreement, and do not respond with reactive speaking. Simply say, "Thank you. I'll take a look at that," and, "I see how you feel about this subject."

11. Keep safety in mind for everyone's emotions, mental stability, and physical presence.

12. Develop healthy boundaries together. Promise to keep trying. Show up for each other.

13. When emotional turmoil does come up, have a safety plan set up for self-care and processing for the rest of the family.

14. No matter what has happened, keep forgiveness as a top priority.

15. Even if a family member is lost to uncontrollable life issues, do the work to process your own mortality with this issue. You develop and grow, so if the chance arises, you can be ready to navigate the process as your loved one becomes more capable.

16. Be willing to be in acceptance of whatever happens. Keep an open door for more to happen. This is the process of a lifetime. Don't rush it.

17. Let go of agendas, the need for control, expectations, rejection, manipulation, and coercion.

18. When controversy arises, use problem-solving skills and critical thinking. Make sure no one brings a can of gasoline to the fire.

19. Observe patience. Complement each other for being collaborative.

20. Agree that you will not personalize what the other is saying, even when it sounds personal and blaming. It's their thoughts and not your experience, unless you make it about you. Let go and trust the process. It may take six months, but people usually can see the error of their blaming judgments, after repeating them over and over again.

Workbook Questions:

1. Think of ways to improve your family's resilience and tolerance for each other. Name five ways you think would work.

2. Why does anyone in the family need to be labeled the black sheep? Elaborate on this.

3. Who is overpowering and typically comes in with both guns blasting and with no regard for others' feelings?

4. What are you afraid of happening with a reunification? What has worked in the past?

5. How can you forgive everyone for everything? How can you honor that everyone did the best they could in the past with what they had?

6. What emotional turmoil do you suffer from? What do you fear might happen?

7. What has worked in the past to create safety and unity with your family unit?

8. What stops you from active listening? What will it take for you to handle the truth? What will it take for you to listen?

9. What skills can you count on from other family members? How can you let them know you value those skills?

10. What safety nets can you put into place to make sure everyone has an equal platform to speak?

11. What does "active listening" mean to you?

12. How can you "skip the record" by doing an "image breaker" exercise with your family? In this type of exercise, each member takes on a new role usually reserved for another figure in the family.

13. Can you listen without reactive speaking, once you hear something you disagree with?

14. What are issues for which you fear you will never be forgiven? Have you forgiven yourself? What will it take?

15. In what ways do different members of the family use "passive aggression," started by one member with others joining in right on cue with a can of gasoline to throw on the blaze?

16. Was there abusive language and violence in your early years? How does that affect your views now on family discussions? What can you do to take emotional care of yourself?

17. How can you be the peacekeeper and Do No Harm to others when the journey begins?

18. What are triggers you can work on before the meetings?

Fatal Peril and Fight-or-Flight Syndrome

I was taught violence at an early age. When I did not do as my father expected, I was punished. I lived in fear. I knew he would emotionally vent and use corporal punishment as the explosive end to our vignette.

It was always about telling him the truth. My father wanted power over everyone, so he felt safe. He wanted it over his superiors, his wife, his friends, people to whom he lent tools. He always was grumbling about trust being broken or not trusting someone from the beginning. He was already locked, cocked and ready to pull the trigger. He would explode inwardly, and no one even knew it was coming. Or he would build up in the traditional domestic cycle of violence and then return to a brief honeymoon period when we held our breath until the tension started to mount again. This cycle – taught by previous generations – dominated our family experience.

As I develop friendships I had this generational violence inside my head. I did not trust others, including my brother, sister, and mother. I learned how to talk back, use foul language, act out, yell, create a confrontation, and then reverse-chase. I would run away or abandon a relationship because trust was lost. I finally ran away as a child.

As I grew older, I would use every form of coercion. I would yell louder, name-call, break things, and smash my own personal objects to make a point. I would threaten, physically restrain and hit people, or block doorways. I would beat myself up worse than anyone could beat me.

I held others responsible for my happiness. "If only all the actors would do as I say, this play of my life would be a success." I would scream louder than everyone else and make public scenes. I would push others mentally till they flinched and walked away from the psychotic breakdown I was having. I diagnosed myself with "double-psychotic, paranoid schizophrenia." I was a reverse racist and made anyone who was simply a white supremacist run for their lives with all the hate in my soul. I hated myself so much, it was easy to hate and violate my own race. I had a reason and person and a time for the venting. I used ideation to create mistrust and seething contempt prior to investigation.

I had a high threshold of pain, so I thought others should learn more about my pain, so they would understand they were fake, fraudulent phonies and cowards. Eventually I found it easy to violate others. In relationships, I would repeat over and over, louder and louder, the same excuses of why I had the right to ignore, hit, violate, overpower, and act out. I had "authoritarian combative syndrome." Mentally I was a danger to myself and others, I could not fit into jails or psych wards because of this.

This was where I would start relationships with others. I would want trust as part of our agreement, then make trust an idea of broken promises no one could ever live up to.

I lived in fear and created this same fear in others so I would feel safe. I projected my experience so all suffered equally for my reactions to life. I lived with so much tension you could cut the air with a knife. My adrenaline was always up. I would either try to overpower a situation or be ready to run for my life when violence, guns or knives were drawn or the police were called.

You cannot stop reacting from this form of fear till you do some real work and dedicate time and mental resources toward recognizing this behavior. Only after you have written down your fears can you really hold them in your hands and see what you have been reacting to your whole life.

Up to this point in our lives, we were willing to be thrill-seeking people unable to stop at the warning signs. We went headstrong into righteous indignation. With low-impulsive behavior, we made our stand and got ready to run if we needed to get away in a hurry.

Manipulation and coercion are the tools we use to try to sustain our way of life. By forcing others to do our bidding, we bypass necessary trust-building and long-lasting tenets of relational importance. We make it all about us and our needs. We are easily thrown into the moment of shock when we do not get our way. We are willing to fight and defend till the end or run away in cowardly shame to fight another day. We feel entitled to this anger and frustrating way of life. It's personal. We feel superior and righteous about our station if life. Our threshold of pain and fear is higher than most people's, and we run amok like a bull in the china shop of others' lives. It is a cycle of violence, and we are caught up in the recidivism of fatal peril.

When a violated person is so easily offended, he is always on the edge. This idea of playing the victim role and painting the target on yourself creates the tape loop of your experiences, ending up the way you set the storyline. It correlates with your belief. By choosing this recidivism behavior, we actually attract these negative emotions into our lives. In recovery, it's called "drawing your own focus."

Once we feel backed into a corner, that's when we do harm to others. It's a corner we know so well. In a way, we have a lot of control over what happens next. We have our adrenaline running, and we are ready to attack or run. So when the moment of triggered bewilderment happens, we defend this line in the sand, or cut our losses and run away so we do not have to deal face to face with our consequences. Once dominance was lost, we became invisible, disenfranchised and unavailable to the tenets of this world. We mutter under our breath, all fairness and trust lost. We use blaming behaviors toward others, and judge ourselves and our loved ones harshly. We sink deeply into depression, stress, anxiety and fear and no longer can be trusted with good judgment.

For others, there was the escalation from something small and manageable to the ballistic perpetrator. This keeps all at bay, and we can abuse, manipulate, and work the feelings of our emotional hostages till they get smart and avoid all contact with us. With new and innocent people we don't know or trust, we feign minor violations and then escalate to responses of violation and domination with name-calling, pushing, shoving, and sometimes uncontrolled physical violence.

Workbook Questions:

1. What puts you into the fight-or-flight or fatal-peril modes? Bullies, work partners, your love partner, your children, your parents, yourself?

2. Rewrite parts of the above reading that speak volumes about your body's response to danger.

3. What do you do to prepare before you go into harm's way?

4. How do you relax and come back to a normalized state of being?

5. How do you use this fear as a way of staying on the edge, always suspicious of others' intentions, never trusting?

6. By your inability to trust others, how do you attract the same kind of distrust from others?

7. What happened when you were a child that created your first fear?

8. What happened in later adult relationships that befouled your ability to be resilient?

9. When did you change from being an innocent victim into a predator?

10. How do you benefit now from your unhealed core issues? Do you distance loved ones and work colleagues? Are you a workaholic with unreasonable expectations of others?

Generational Dysfunction

My experience with generational dysfunction began three or four generations ago.

The family unit was always on the run once the young men turned 15 or 16. Family training was done in an abusive environment. Violence, anger, vulgarity, workaholism, infidelity — these imprints were passed on perfectly intact.

In my family, there were addiction, emotional instability and unhealed wounds. How I healed from my predicament was to make sure that after 44 years of life, I would surrender that way of living. I would make sure no one else had to go through that turmoil. I surrendered to the idea that my life's work would be service as a vocation and help others who suffered the ways I had.

Now, after many years, I have compassion. I am able to work with suffering people and instill in them a sense of hope to develop healthy goals, which in turn evokes self-change thoughts to help them live a lifetime of healthy choices.

Part of the process is that I model how to make mistakes and move on without doing harm to others. I offer survival strategies, coping mechanisms and thriving opportunities to encourage the idea of working with what we are given. We demonstrate and advocate new ways to move beyond the trauma we experienced.

It took many generations to get to this point of dysfunction we face. Therefore, we must be around for a longer view and take our time, while realizing our opportunity with a sense of vigilance and urgency.

Native Americans look forward seven generations. We should have that same sensibility when dealing with our opportunities. We can control only what we do — our own choices. When our choices were a "poverty of the mind," we responded in kind. Now that we have a clear sense, a better life, and a safety net for our loved ones, we value and treasure our freedom.

In raising me, my father repeated what he was taught by his father. I ran away from home, carried that scar and became just like my dad. We both had resentment, anger, PTSD and violence as our learned experience. We passed down our family influences. As we choose now to be "agents of change" in our lives, we also choose education, diligence, resilience, self-help, relationships, and love and sex awareness as the way we conduct our business.

Through introspection, we can change what we are attracted to. Then we notice that once we are attracted to something, it makes us accountable. This newfound choice in our lives causes us to respond differently. We are no longer who we were.

In the lottery of birth, we are given great qualities. We have beneficial survival strategies and work values. With effort, we sometimes turn some of our negative qualities into transferrable skill sets. When we choose to do the work at hand, we invest in future generations — their coping skills and survival strategies.

In our self-efficacious world of immediate gratification and convenience, selfishness takes away the value of a future where mindfulness is exercised. One person can change herself, and the world will be a different place. Break the curse of repeating generations with their conditioned responses that become our epitaph. Encourage great aspects of our unique heritage — our gifts of art, music, dance — when we learn to have joyful exertion. What we choose to value in our future becomes spotless, and we are able to live beyond our shame-based, pain-body experience.

A child is a reflection of the people who raised him. He responds in kind and reflects the type of consciousness in which they were raised. But change can happen with daily small gestures that build upon each other and create equity with their environment.

What can you do right now to change yourself? The world is waiting. When will you take your place and be seen?

This very moment, right here, is the only moment we ever really have to change things. It begins with a precious breath. We do the next right thing. After that, we do the next right things. We complete small tasks. In doing so, we change what was firm and rigid and exchange it for new neurogenesis, new brain elasticity. We cannot change what happened in the past, but we can invest in a future where work gets results. The results may not be what you hoped for or expected; however, it is a real future of value where things are different. Life is curious. Try not to have exact expectations of what you think your goodness will be. Remain open while the layers of your life's mystery reveal themselves.

Positive Things You Can Do to Impact Your Life, Your Family, and Your Community – It All Starts with You!

- Gain access to knowledge about your dilemma. Check out your house of worship and your peers who do a great job in their own lives. Ask them how you can make changes, and write it down.

- Start hanging out with and befriending people who live differently, so you are called on your stuff when you are heading down the wrong path. Stop hanging out with people who abuse and repeat their misery. Misery loves company. Move away from enablers and codependent people who won't change their lives. Stay away from people who gossip, slander and character-assassinate others. Be the change you want to see.

- Be part of education and awareness with your community. By practicing and helping others, you are less likely to repeat your habits. In recovery, helping someone helps you get better. You won't be perfect, but you are living your life as a yearning toward change.

- Disrupt your thinking when you are triggered. Continually suspend your old ways of thinking with insight and humor. You can laugh at yourself and your predicament, then move forward with dignity and grace.

- Be willing to call others out in a powerful, safe and loving way that does not embarrass or shame them. Help others by giving hope and encouraging responsibility. Offer a way that has skillfulness and craft that will last a lifetime. It is your gift to know what it feels like to be stuck and then to help another who is stuck; to think about ways to do less harm for the greater good. It requires building trust and being courageous. It requires fearless, limitless thinking.

- Seek professional help with your medical community in all aspects of your dis-ease, if you can.

- Take a parenting class, a mindfulness class, a meditation class, a dog-training program with your dog. Spend quality time with your kids and family and others. Have fun outdoors and learn from people you admire. Follow their values that speak to your situation.

Remember, this journey begins with one step and then another toward doing the next right thing. It took generations for today to be our reality. It may take a lifetime of skillful self-change thoughts to make a small difference that can be passed down to our children as our legacy, in exchange for the one we got from birth.

- Join an accountability group of like minds. Start your own group with others who suffer as you, and connect. The disease of isolation is fear and shame-based. Break away with others, and change the world.

- Do new things that you have never done before. Go places you've never considered going. Choose activities and places that are not conducive to escalated emotions and violent reactions. Go to a park, the beach, the zoo, and long walks to get away from the triggering environment you might live in. Perform service and help a church or feed homeless people at a facility. In order to feel self-esteem, you must do estimable acts.

- Make a list of experiences that went well and not so well. Write down skillful ways that others seem to use to effortlessly deal with the same issues you have. Make a list and keep it with you, so you will know how to react with harm reduction, motivational conversation and Non-Violent Communication (NVC). To paraphrase NVC, if you speak in a way that others can hear you, you are more likely to get your needs met.

- Bring your brain to attention when you know danger is near. Step away. Take a walk. Count to 10 and compose yourself. Remember, this feeling is flashback trauma that you are trying to work with and heal from, not perpetuate with another generation.

Workbook Questions:

1. For the past three generations, what is the history of your people? Find out what happened that was good — and not so good. Be full-measured in your inquiry, because families generally only like to talk about good things that happened, not shame or stigma.

2. What is the experience of your family members? Are they functional? What family repetition do you notice that is harmful to your loved ones?

3. Do you have problems with weight? Energy levels? Food issues? Gambling? Drinking? Obsession-compulsion? Anger? Sexism? Racism? Failure to thrive? How do any of these things contribute to your life and radiate onto loved ones around you? How did the generational card play into the way you handle this aspect of your life?

4. In what ways do you repeat things your parents did that you swore you would never do? With your partner? With your kids? With your pets? With your friends?

5. Do you recognize how tragic and destructive this behavior repetition can be for your loved ones?

6. If nothing changes, what are you willing to do right now for accountability, observability and measurability?

7. How do you know that you are doing harmful behaviors? Are you willing to listen to others and accept them as your team helper? How about family? Are you willing to come to a beginner's mind and be vulnerable and sensitive?

8. What awareness can you engage to know when you are doing harm?

9. What therapy can you access? How much can you afford? Are you willing to go to free Twelve-Step processes that deal with things in your life that taste like, look like, and act like dysfunction?

10. Do you realize that awareness without help or therapy is just another way of perpetuating the "Groundhog Day" repetition in your life?

11. What does ownership of these ideals look like to you?

12. How will you interrupt your vicious cycle of violence?

Grace and Surrender

Grace. The idea of walking over the burning coals of your life and not getting burned. How did we make it this far? What acts of chance and fate have delivered us to this moment?

The idea of faith is likened to following car headlights in the dark. We can see only where they end, not ahead to where we are going. But if we stay on track, we can follow them all the way to where we want to end up. Faith in the unknown, a leap of faith, belief in the unseen — these are what transports the disbeliever into a graceful state of serendipity.

Accept life on life's terms and work toward a future that is not ruled by karma running into dogma. We do the next right thing not because it is easy, but because it is the way to a future that does not repeat itself. We can learn a lot from history. Why we don't is no mystery: the longer view is where immediate gratification gets bypassed with a choice toward an investment in new values.

By our act of surrender, we do not lose. We accept, we join together, and we have power over more than self-doubt, deprecation, mistrust, and loneliness.

The pain we feel is no longer necessarily our own by the act of joining together. It is a universal truth that must come and visit once in a while to teach us its value. Pain in life will happen from time to time, but our ability to respond appropriately gives us a chance to not suffer quite as much.

If we can accept pain and suffering as our teacher, just for today, we know the precious, timed event has value. It is not personal; it is a universal teacher. If we can wish others well with their abundance or job promotion, even though we didn't get one, we are paying forward the idea that "your abundance is my abundance."

We are not separate. If we use our compassion and empathy for all suffering sentient beings, we include and acknowledge all that feel pain, anger, and loss. Those uncomfortable moments become universal truths, and we become part of universal observers who watch as life spins out of control.

Disasters and crises happen to everyone. The acts are not personal. We suffer when we personalize our troubles and globalize our experience. In order to end all suffering, we completely forgive our experience and all the bad things that have happened — one and all.

By this act of grace, we lose our attachment to the story line, belief system, and dis-ease we feel from our past. We are no longer willing prisoners of what happened to us. We open our eyes with a beginner's mind and see the world for the first time with wisdom as our teacher. Once we let go of all attachments, the events are not personal anymore. Once we set the perpetrator free, the situation free, our pain free, we can live without resentments. We no longer have to replay that old tape of what happened and respond from a place of injury and pain. We stop judging people and attracting scary scenarios back into our lives from our fear-based resentments.

When I say my daily prayers, I feel grace. My surrender goes something like this: *I surrender everything I think, say and do; all my thoughts words and deeds. I pray for the willingness to let go absolutely of all my old thoughts and ways of thinking, just for today.*

Then I do my daily, immediate surrendering. Here's an example:

I surrender my feeling of abundance. I surrender my fear of not being enough. I surrender my lack of faith. I surrender my negative emoting. I surrender my judgments of others. I surrender my ego. I surrender my lack of trust. I surrender what I get done today. I surrender what others think of me. I surrender money issues. I surrender being miserly. I surrender my racing thoughts. I surrender waiting in line at the store. I surrender slow drivers. I surrender how easily I am willing to be judge and jury and to execute others with my thinking.

With this opportunity to surrender, we need to remove what is in the way of surrender. Usually it is our ego and the two forms of fear. The first form is fear of losing something we have or having something taken away. The other fear is that someone has something we want and will not give it to us. I use the acronym G.O.D. — Good Orderly Direction — to remove my suffering. I accept that it is taken away, and with grace, I am thankful that it has been removed from my existence. The idea is asking a higher power other than yourself for help and stating what you would like to have done, along with the act of trash removal or surrendering. Finally, the grace component, or the act of accepting that it has been done, leads to faith. Faith is the most important step of surrender and grace.

With your attitude of gratitude, you say, "Thanks for it being done. I now claim this inherent right to abundance and well-being."

You must believe! Otherwise, you still perpetuate the recidivism of your dilemma. Stop the cycle now. This is the first step that begins your new journey. The destination is not where you end, but the graceful way you maneuver your journey.

Workbook Questions:

1. In what ways do you easily surrender to the flow of life?

2. What do you believe you will lose if you surrender your angst toward a person, culture, and/or society? Does the bias toward another really serve you?

3. In the song "Amazing Grace" are the words, "saved a wretch like me." Is there something that rings true from your own experience?

4. What are you afraid of losing by gracefully surrendering things that don't work for you and cause your loved ones pain and suffering? Why do you continue down that road? What will it take for you to stop?

5. Without the spiritual context, what does grace look like in your life?

6. Are you willing to join with others on this path of life and commit to creating equity and space, while surrendering control of your egoistic belief system?

7. Have you been given a moment of grace when you thought you felt overwhelmed and made it all too personal, but the situation was really just life on life's terms? Explain.

8. If being forgiving creates an environment for others to be graceful, are you willing to take it up a notch and be more mindful about moments of tension and uneasiness? To be the bigger figure?

9. When you are in a frantic situation and want to freak out or engage in unhealthy responses to insulting speech by people you do not trust, how do you get calm and back into the moment? Do you consider these responses to be grace and surrender?

10. What do people do that really makes you angry? What is graceful turnaround thinking you can engage in?

11. Without religious connotation, what are the coincidences in your life that you believe are graceful transitioning? How? Do you notice small blessings? In what ways do you always need to see big, obvious signs to feel "miracles" in your life?

12. Have you lost control of your body in some way — function of organs and/or limbs? How can you use the concept of grace to embrace this dilemma?

13. We all are getting older. How can you age gracefully and show others your powerful expression of acceptance?

Gratitude: It's an Attitude

I know how to say what's wrong and what's been wrongfully done to me. I know how to look for negative components in life and attach to them. I have Velcro for the bad things and Teflon for the good.

How can we change this so we attract good in our lives and change the dynamic entropy? We have vested our entire being into finger-pointing and trying to rally others against wrongs done to us. We have learned to manipulate with gossip, slander, and character assassination. How do we emulate the goodness and abundance available within all of us and share that universal oneness? How do we change?

If we can bring our minds to attention where we are going astray, then we are more likely to not repeat those damaging behaviors. How do we stay aware, vigilant and accountable for our side of the street? We can only change ourselves — we can't change others. It is our responsibility to be mindful and do the work at hand. Doing so helps us keep an attitude of gratitude.

When I made my first gratitude list, I did not truly understand what I had gratitude for. I started out with: *I am breathing, I have 10 fingers, I have two legs, I am at a meeting with my peers, I have a place to sleep.* I found that by mouthing new words, I eventually believed.

When my wife and I pray with each other, we pray for the willingness to love and accept each other unconditionally exactly as we are right here, right now, in this moment. That moment can be filled with irritation, conflict, and emotionally escalating, juicy stuff.

It took me years of mouthing words of gratitude to be a team player. But one day I actually felt belief that the truths were possible and available to me, that the abundance was mine to share on the planet. I now live my life for the benefit of others. I do service as a vocation.

Spiritual tithing is a proactive, daily reprieve from the idea that suffering is a personal choice and all about me. It is not about me when I live my life for others. It's not a me thing; it's a we thing. Once we get out of ourselves and into others, we become more willing. We do the extra part of life and the ordinary and we become extraordinary persons of value. If we bring all we need by doing due diligence in life, we are no longer waiting for someone to do good back to us. We know that others have lack and we accept them exactly as they are. We bring enough goodness for all to share. The abundance was given as a birthright — this indwelling goodness of well-being has no upper limit. We gladly do the right thing simply because it's right. That's all.

When we completely suspend our normal critical thinking and close our eyes to see what is really happening right now, right here, at this moment, we can breathe in and breathe out. We notice that nothing bad happened and we are safe, right here and right now. This is the only moment we have. This is our choice. We choose to be happy or sad. This precious moment is the only moment we have to be enlightened on the planet. What will we choose? "The war is over if you want it," to quote John and Yoko.

We have done research about the effects of negativity. We can change things and acknowledge, right here and now, the benefits of gratitude. Yes, bad things happen. However, we are less likely to attract them if we are not wearing a weary target of disbelief in the arena of accepting life on life's terms.

What is the negative effect of accepting life? Acceptance circumvents unnecessary pain and suffering. Bad things will still happen, but sometimes suffering is optional. We owe no one anything. We are not in debt to anyone. We do what we do because we feel better when being of service — and that's it. The rest is paying it forward with unconditional, positive regard for others and radical kindness.

What do you think? What future do you see when others are gladly helpful, more trustworthy, less fear-based and more culturally inclusive?

Change happens.

Workbook Questions:

1. What are you grateful for? Make a list of as many things as you can.

2. Is your gratitude self-centered and about things that give you control over the immediacy and convenience of your experience? That's OK; just write it down and notice. We are learning to ask for new beliefs and feelings.

3. When you see someone suffering —say, with an injury — are you grateful that isn't you? In what ways could you go up to that person, ask how they are doing, how their day is going, and skillfully wish them well? Elders, people with mental-health problems and people with disabilities are often neglected. Name ways you can include them in your daily routine.

4. Why are you happy and grateful when things go your way? What can you find to be grateful about when you are inconvenienced? For example, in slow traffic when you feel personally slighted, do you feel road rage? Do you think of others and realize that someone might be hurt in an accident up ahead? Where does your energy go? Where does your gratitude lie?

5. Why do you believe you are too busy to take time for gratitude? Why do you feel as if it's something that could be taken away? Why is your gratitude reliant on your circumstances?

6. Do you feel most gratitude when you are kind with yourself or the efforts of others when they are kind to you? Why is your gratitude personal?

7. In what ways can you build more gratitude into your life?

8. Why do you always look for things that are wrong or didn't go as you wished? Are you a harsh judge of your own efforts but kind toward others' efforts?

9. What parts of your negative emoting are you willing to let go of? What will you be happy about by letting those go?

10. Do you believe your pain and suffering is personal? Are others responsible for making you happy? Do you think, *If only they would…*, or *If this would happen, then I could have gratitude…*? Why not now?

11. Name five things you are grateful about that others do freely.

Example of a Gratitude List:

I am so happy and grateful for: my health

I am so happy and grateful for: my spiritual practice

I am so happy and grateful for: my partner and family

I am so happy and grateful for: my mental health

I am so happy and grateful for: my place to live

I am so happy and grateful for: my neighborhood

I am so happy and grateful for: my weather

I am so happy and grateful for: my animals

I am so happy and grateful for: my credit

I am so happy and grateful for: my music

I am so happy and grateful for: ability to help others with service

I am so happy and grateful for: my sex life

I am so happy and grateful for: having fun things I like to do

I am so happy and grateful for: good movies

I am so happy and grateful for: good food

I am so happy and grateful for: great music

I am so happy and grateful for: sports

I am so happy and grateful for: my art

I am so happy and grateful for: free time

I am so happy and grateful for: the ability and freedom to do what I like

I am so happy and grateful for: feeling safe

I am so happy and grateful for: my hobbies

I am so happy and grateful for: stability in my life

I am so happy and grateful for: good habits

I am so happy and grateful for: my vehicle

I am so happy and grateful for: my heartbeat

I am so happy and grateful for: teachers, helpers and guides

I am so happy and grateful for: my vacations

I am so happy and grateful for: education

I am so happy and grateful for: my abundance

I am so happy and grateful for: being alive

Grief and Loss

Allow yourself to be in the place where your feelings are and process them. It is a long and full-measured opportunity. Time heals everything. We can process all things through complete forgiveness of ourselves and others.

When we do the work of being angry or sad – of screaming and crying after the floodgates are open – we have the opportunity to realize that we are responsible for our extreme self-care. If we do not put grief on a shelf to process slowly day by day, it can overwhelm us. The waves of grief and loss sweep in, as relentless as the tides. Emotions can escalate from small waves of discomfort to all-encompassing, destructive tsunamis.

We have the option to shrug our shoulders, take a deep breath and let go of attachments. We tend to cling to what we want to happen. We want our truth to create a form of safety. Life on life's terms is an immediate part of that moment. If we can allow ourselves to truly feel our sadness, we realize grief is actually a timed event. We can eventually get to the point when we realize grief is also precious. It enables us to feel the happiness that comes after those depths of sorrow. Most of our suffering is a result of the attachment we had to people and our thoughts about them. When we let go, our thoughts will pass like storm clouds after they've been spent. Detach with love.

Allowing yourself to cry is courageous and brave. We stand bewildered before our wounded self and invite our soul cleansing to take place. In our heads, we know what happened. In our hearts, we've attached to a brittle shield that was supposed to protect us, but has let us down. We want to have an open heart and surrender our experience.

When we lose a loved one we can't live without, our hearts feel broken and undone. After processing grief, we get to open up to the life that is waiting for us. We learn to be happy even with the deep pain we feel. This is grace and acceptance.

With our dreams and wants of loved ones and life, we learn to let go and accept not what's right, but what's life. We learn to accept things we didn't want to happen. This is the learning curve of accepting: just for today, pain and suffering are the teachers. We don't have to travel far. The teachers will find us; seek us out, and give us our fair share of life lessons. We need both happiness and pain to cross the finish line. No one here gets out alive.

No one can know the exactness of our pain or how we will survive. It's not fair, and it's not a test. It just is, and that's all. I don't need anyone in judgment of how I process my pain. It's a selfishness I own right now, and it's mine to hold until it goes away.

Ignoring our feelings does not make them go away. Doing so creates an unfinished forum for us to transfer, counter-transfer and project our unfinished thoughts onto others as we go through our days — sometimes in passive aggression.

Everyone around us suffers, unless we do the valuable work of processing pain. From our privilege in the Western world of having everything, we are ill-equipped when something happens that we don't expect. When we lose control, it feels like the end of the world. We even associate real pain with the loss of games by our favorite sports teams. It is real pain that will affect our days. Then, when something really catastrophic happens, we are ill-equipped to process distress.

When we lose a child or a lover, they are still in our hearts. Our mind knows they have left or are gone, but the heart's hope dies last. This is an attachment that is healthy for humans, and we need more skill to process those situational distortions accurately.

We must empty our cup of grief and loss so we can be filled with grace, acceptance and new wonders to behold.

If we stuff our feelings, they will become toxic in our minds and bodies. We digest our thoughts on a cellular level. Disease and discomfort are meant to be naturally processed. We can't get to the other side unless we go through the process.

In the following section, I have paraphrased the Five Stages of Grief and Loss by Elisabeth Kubler Ross and David Kessler. It is a process we go through until we finally get peace and come to terms with our losses. Be gentle, and notice what you are feeling. Observe your discernment for and against what has happened to you. Remember that it's not personal — it is just life happening this moment, and this moment will change. Try not to attach to anything in a concretized way of thinking.

1) Denial

When we lose a loved one or learn that we have a fatal illness, or we lose a relationship or a job, we may think, "This can't really be happening. Maybe they got it wrong."

Through this defense mechanism, we refuse to accept and believe that this painful time is happening in our lives. There must be something wrong; check it again. After finding out there is no escape plan, we move onto stage two.

2) Anger

We blame God, ourselves and others. We lose our ability to be objective. Who did this unspeakable thing? We rage and try to find out when and why this happened. Who's responsible? What led to this happening? Why me? Why, why?

3) Bargaining

In bargaining we speak "fox-hole" prayers. *God, get me out of this one and I will (fill in the blank)*. We do things that compromise our integrity to look good or keep a job or save a marriage, or keep our child in the house. *Just give me one more chance.* It would be nice if this was about chance, but it's about reality and coming to terms with life. Fate is not chance. *I will do this and be so great and do service for others.* Good! You should be doing acts like that already. But understand that the service will not undo your loss or excuse you from your grieving process. Get it?

4) Depression

Everything is crystal clear, real and right now. There is no escape, no bargaining, no blaming. We are feeling it now. This is reality. We respond to our loss, sorrow, and regrets about not showing more timely love and saying important things that we put off. We feel an infinite sadness with what is. Powerful feelings get mixed up with could 'a should 'a, would 'a — regrets and shame-based faith. These help little.

5) Acceptance

Oh, I get it now. Wow, this is real. It is not personal; it just is. I have lost my [child, lover, partner, job, arm, car]. I take ownership of what happened, and I know it is my process that will determine how I will inevitably respond — sometimes quickly and sometimes slowly. Grieving really happens – acceptance of all that is, the wonderment of how precious life is and how sometimes we must forgive ourselves or others. We will carry around a poisoned sack of resentment that clouds our efforts to recover, if we don't move forward.

These stages can happen in any order either independently or at the same time as we develop our discerning wisdom on how we move forward in life.

Workbook Questions:

1. What losses have you had that were unforgiveable? What do you remember that bothers you the most?

2. What has worked for you to process this kind of deep loss? Was it a healthy practice, a spiritual practice, a community that helped, a close friend, a religious experience?

3. What does denial look like for you when you hear something you don't want to hear about your health?

4. What parts of life are you in acceptance with? Death and dying? Grief and loss? Loss of a job or partner? Name some others.

5. When you become angry about things, how do the five stages of grief and loss fit into what you are angry about? Can you see a correlation between the stages and your anger? What would it take for you to move on and get into acceptance?

6. In what ways do you have "fox-hole" prayers when something goes wrong or someone you love is hurt? How do you try to bargain with fate or with God? What do you say? Why do you pray only when something is wrong?

7. Do you believe suffering is personal, and life is trying to make you suffer more than others? Does your experience seem more intense than what you see of others handling pain and hardship? What would it take for you to see that life happens to all of us? How can you learn to respond better, instead of grabbing onto reactive thinking?

8. What are you afraid of losing in the future? Does living in fear distract you from whole-heartedly living in the moment? How can you stop grieving for something that hasn't happened yet — and might not ever happen?

9. What dreams for your life are unfinished? Do you already grieve that you will never be able to fulfill your dreams? Do you believe it's too late to do anything about them?

10. How do you help others who suffer? Why don't helpful suggestions you offer to others work in your life?

Habitual Reactive Response

For most of my life, I reacted to life. I tried to cheat the devil, stay one step ahead of the wolves, and take the quick path to the top. My line in the sand kept getting less honorable and more conveniently mobile for my immediate and selfish needs, ego and pride. I was quick to respond to danger, employment and sex, but slow to accept the normal ways that others went to 9-to-5 jobs and related to each other. I was free. But I did not belong.

How do you show up at the Party of Life? How do you respond to life on life's terms? What happens when things don't go as planned? What happens when you get caught doing something wrong, but fun?

When hurt, I responded by lashing out, being aggressive, and painting a target on myself. I started to believe this dysfunction and mayhem was where I belonged. I lived under the table, accepting the scraps of life, never showing up and taking a seat at the table where the banquet was spread. That thinking became a conditioned muscle memory in my brain and led to responses that have lasted a lifetime with my belief system — or rather, my disbelief system.

Over the course of our lives, we develop habitual reactive responses. Our habits are so smooth and comfortable, we hardly notice that we are bulls rampaging in the china shop of life.

And yet, by our reactive responses, we can attract our experience. We draw life to us and are responsible for much that happens to us. Now we need to look at how our agenda-thinking keeps that vicious cycle going. How and why are we like a moth flying around a flame, trying to receive comfort from the source of our pain?

I finally surrendered to change after being sick and tired of being sick and tired. I was done with the insanity of doing the same things over and over and expecting different results. I accepted the comfort of uncertainty and groundlessness.

For me, the destructive cycle can start when I see something I want or am triggered by someone's behavior. I stop and ask myself, "Why do I react? Why am I so thin-skinned? What egoistic benefit will I receive? What social status will this illuminate?" My mind is driven to distraction; I can resist anything but temptation.

What motivates us to think, "I need this, and then maybe I will be fixed, complete, or accepted"? Why don't we belong right now? Why are we incomplete? Why do we have an empty God-hole in our spirits that needs to be filled? How can we be impeccable with our inner dialogue?

First, let's slow down and ask for what we want in life. How do we ask? We come to the dress rehearsal of life with expectations and agenda, wanting control, not being in acceptance, wanting to manipulate time and space and fit that square peg into a social circle. Yet when we do this, life responds with those same tenets. We have the opportunity to completely surrender everything we think, do and say, just for today. We ask the universe for what we want. If we keep in mind that doing service for others is our vocation, we will surely be fulfilled. We learn daily by accepting what is. When we accept life on life's terms, we are in rhythm with our place in the universe. We head toward our goals as we live our lives as an aspiration.

So, we show up to the party of life and audition for our place in society. When we make an entrance, people will look and quickly judge and assume who and what we are before we speak our first words. Dress is so cultural. Keeping up with the "unsustainable Joneses" with our phone, clothes, shoes, makeup, hair, satchel, car — these are all factors put into play before we even open our mouths on stage.

This is how society works, even in houses of worship or meditation. We seek to be naked before our idea of God, with supplication and genuflection occurring alongside judgment from our peers.

We have a highly regulated habitual response from years of being judged. We have learned to use it as a form of power and safety. We take our places. In what ways do we put on a fool's mask instead of revealing our genuine and authentic self?

When we are scared or respond from fear-based thinking, it is seductive to react with "fatal peril" or "fight-or-flight" responses, rather than with mindfulness or emotional intelligence.

Here are a few things we can do right now to create equity in any room we enter. Say these things to yourself: I am enough. I deserve. I belong. Many have gone before me, and I am not alone. This is not personal. This is not about me. I can meditate or count to 10, take a walk, anything to lengthen the time before I react.

Our entire lives are built upon making our time-before-reaction space longer and developing our ambivalence. We hold everything in our hands through our reactivity, but we own nothing. This is a space of peace; it is mindful. It takes nurturing, cultivation and feedback from our trusted circle of like-minded peacekeepers.

When we cleanse and condition our space and the air around us by sweeping up our side of the street, others may have a moment of reacting only to their own discomfort. We no longer have a target painted on us. We put the burden of change back into their capable hands.

When dealing with our personal demons, adrenalin is great for getting us in motion. But we need to keep our heads on our shoulders, so we do not freeze up, get tight and let that lump in our throats deplete all the timeless wisdom we have to share.

How can we develop longer-lasting strategies of change that will become our new, flexible muscle memory? How can we feel at home with ourselves, so others can feel at home and relaxed with us?

1. If we do personal work on our issues, we are more likely to speak in a way others can hear us, and we have more of a chance to get our needs met.

2. If we do service for others, we help others to realize their highest selves.

3. Breathe out fear, and breathe in trust, faith, hope, relaxation. Breathe out troubles with given situations, and breathe in belief in our goodness and benefit to others. Our little light loves to shine, so let it shine. Breathe out worry, what-ifs and how-comes and breathe in, "I can, I will, I must" with joyful exertion for life's vitality and worth.

We get a few moments peace. Then life happens again, and we find that we are groundless with unexpected frustration and unpleasantness. (See, it really is us and not what happens to us.) When we are emotionally responsible for our actions, life can happen. We can stop, breathe, take a moment, take a walk, and get back into the trigger situation with calm repose, instead of rushing in with defensive moves that halt all growth and integrity for positive forward motion.

As we become more aware, conscious and mindful, we can begin to notice where we feel physical tension. Those spots could be in our backs, our necks, a headache, our shoulders. When we can recognize, resist and recover, we will have more control over our part of the situation.

For example, we recognize that we are triggered for the 10th time that day. We do our relaxing and breathing and begin ownership and grateful affirmations toward our sentient goodness. Then we maintain our recovered sense with urgency, knowing it is impermanent. We do the next right thing, and then the next right thing.

When we are in our addiction or habitual mode, our well-accessorized rut in our heads has everything in place. This neural pathway is a well-traveled road in our minds. How do we take another path? Just 'cause that rut feels good doesn't mean it's OK; just 'cause it's comfortable doesn't mean you have to travel it.

Every day there is a chance for us to get triggered by life. Someone steps on our feet as they cut in front of us in line. Someone takes "our" parking spot. Someone cuts us off in traffic, or steals our ideas and gets the job promotion, while we sit unrewarded.

How can we notice our body's reactions and the tension it holds and spontaneously begin breathing and reminding ourselves that the trigger is not about us, it's about what the other is doing? How can we become the "universal observers" in our lives and only watch as disasters happen and crises manifest, instead of participating in the malaise?

We can stay in the moment, stay with our breathing and remind ourselves of our aspirations and intentions for our lives. We can realize the person we are dealing with did not wake up looking to make our day miserable — and we do not have to choose misery.

Are you buying this? Let's get back in control of our existence and master these skills. Let's enjoy real freedom in all we do. We must stop bringing gasoline to put out fires.

We can change only ourselves; we can't change others. We can model ourselves and let others take what they like and leave the rest. We can craft our skillful message and elicit self-change thoughts for others, and then let go of the outcome.

Workbook Questions:

1. What actions do you do over and over again while expecting different results? Anger? Judgment? Expectations of others? Need for control?

2. Do you eat when you are frustrated?

3. Do you sexualize your stress with your partner, instead of working on healthy relations?

4. Can you wake up and know what the news already is and globalize our human experience?

5. Do you experience a form of road rage when someone cuts you off on the freeway? Do you hold in that anger and frustration or externalize it upon others?

6. Are you obsessive and compulsive about things others seem to perform normally? Explain. Name five ways in which you do this.

7. What are your personal triggers that create reactive actions that do not serve anyone in a healthy manner?

8. What are some coping skills you can engage when you know you are in a habitual-reactive-response situation?

9. In what ways do you recognize your responses? Do others wonder why you react so badly? Are you afraid to ask? Are they afraid to tell you? Why?

10. Do you take constructive criticism well? What will it take to make you feel safe enough to listen to the wisdom of others?

11. When your boss wants to talk to you, what physical triggers do you notice? In what ways does your brain trick you into thinking the discussion will be about something you did wrong and will be reprimanded for?

12. When your partner is unhappy with you about something, do you go into a sullen state and feel as if you are not being valued as a quality partner? If so, why?

13. When your kids do normal things that kids do, do you take their behavior personally? If so, why? What is triggered regarding your worth, value and esteem, that makes you have that experience?

14. Are you hard on yourself when you lose a game or sing a song off-key? If so, explain why.

15. What healthy things can you do to honor your worth and strength-based skills? List them here.

Happiness and the Pursuit

If someone told you all you had to do right now was to choose to be happy, no matter what has happened to you in the past, would you do it?

Your choice is telling. We have such concretized and reserved thinking that we do not allow ourselves to relax and simply be happy.

Worry is a built-in mechanism meant to keep up safe and alive. But it has been misrepresented by our culture to keep us from accessing real happiness. There are people all over the world who live under oppressive, punitive government leaders who quash their freedoms, and they have still chosen to be happy, regardless of negative impacts on their lives. Why? What does that attitude serve? How does that choice help us to cope more effectively than worrying? What health benefits does a cheerful heart encompass?

Do we choose to follow the adage, "the pursuit of happiness," rather than enjoying happiness now? The pursuit might not ever produce the utopia to which we feel entitled. But we can choose to be happy now. It truly can happen — it's that easy. A happy life is about the happy journey, not the destination.

Sometimes we believe that when we get a certain job, or the kids are grown and raised, or we have found the ideal partner, or we attain financial security, only then can we relax and be happy. We miss the day that is happening now with our "until then" attitude.

However, this journey we have chosen does not require 24-hour happiness. It requires acceptance of "what is." This is the only time we have to be happy on the planet. We cannot go back into the past and be happy there. We cannot go into the future and be happy there. Only right here and right now can we be happy. Let go of expectations that make your daily peace of mind dependent on what you THINK should happen.

Workbook Questions:

1. This is the only time we have to be enlightened and happy. What sorts of things do you choose right now, regardless of what is happening around you?

2. "Yes, but." "What if?" There are countless ways to cling to reservations about something we might lose or gain. For most of our lives, we sit in our disconnectedness, procrastinate and do nothing. You have made a choice. Are you happy with that choice? Say more.

3. In what ways do you hold back from participating in life with your family, with your neighbors, with your family?

4. In what ways are you too busy to do anything for others, such as civic duties and volunteering?

5. In what ways are you too busy to stop and smell the roses?

6. What do you believe needs to happen in your life for you to be happy? Win the lottery? Find love? Have that car? Put the kids through college? Finally retire? Have good health? List them here.

7. Name five reasons you cannot choose to be happy when things go wrong in your life.

8. You lose your partner; you lose your job; your loved one dies. Beyond the loss and initial grief, what are you still grateful for that can bring a smile to your face? Chocolate? Long walks? Working out? Sex?

9. In what ways can you learn to be happy with things just as they are and not contingent upon certain objects or values?

Harm Reduction

Harm reduction is a universal concept from which everyone can benefit. It is something we can practice when we wish we could slow down and be mindful and more open about eliciting self-change thoughts within ourselves and others.

The idea of harm reduction is to develop both sides of our diametrically opposed feelings about a subject and to slowly develop new strategies and coping mechanisms to make better choices. This, in turn, will cause less suffering and harm to myself and others.

Everything we choose to do in our lives is related. We want to have our cake and eat it, too. That is the conversation we start with. We work toward developing healthy ambivalence.

Harm reduction is the gray area between using and abstaining. Reducing harm creates a world where we have many options besides denial and consumption. If people are going to use drugs or any other substance, we need to address that moving target and minimize risk.

Most people who use something to a harmful degree have no negative effects in their lives and function well in society. These people consume and seemingly have a great life. But we need to be here for them when consequences start innocuously creeping in. We can weave options and choices into the tapestry of their lives.

We are dealing with a well-established system within a system; change comes slowly from both sides. However, any change is good change when people cause less harm to themselves and to others.

We begin where the person is, and find reasons that change is needed right now in their lives. Small, almost unnoticeable changes benefit the community and all of us. Although these changes are almost imperceptible, people are willing to take incremental steps toward more change.

We almost fool ourselves that we are buying into new concepts. Any positive change is good change, no matter how small. Change is the beginning of what happens next. It took a long time for behaviors to manifest. They will not be fixed in a day.

We begin with facilitating change within our hierarchy of needs. We start with what we need right now, today. We create a list of needs based upon what we can do now and what will have to wait until later. We hold our space with patience and diligence for the greater good in the bigger picture. We work with behaviors we still need and use daily, and observe what the risk and harms are. We try to figure out the connection between doing things we enjoy and why it harms us and not others. Then we agree to develop strategies for reducing.

Here are examples of when harm reduction can be used:

- I go shopping to soothe my nerves. I buy things I don't need. Then, I have credit problems connected to my self-soothing. Then, I get depressed about these shopping problems, instead of what I was soothing my nerves about.

- I wish I could have more control over my drinking. Maybe if I could stop after three drinks, I would not have the negative consequences of wrecking my car, or ending up in bed with another stranger.

- I would like to have some control over my anger. When I get emotionally entangled, I undo months of positive action by blowing off steam in a convenient moment on a subject I feel strongly about.

- If I can have safe sex and limit the number of partners I engage with, I am less likely to have serious, life-threatening side effects and diseases I pass on to others. Why don't people understand I need to do things that appear different — but those things make me feel normal?

- I would like to limit the amount of marijuana I use during the day so I can think more clearly and have motivation to do things I care about and need to finish.

- I would like to smoke fewer cigarettes. I know they cause cancer and are addictive, but they make me feel better.

- I like to eat, but I cannot stop once I start. I want to consider healthy choices. I just can't get any control over my diet.

- I get obsessive and compulsive. When I am triggered, I do irrational things that I regret and make people uncomfortable around me.

Workbook Questions:

1. Where would you like to have better boundaries? Eating, smoking, drinking, sex, gambling, anger, thrill-seeking behaviors? Name five you would like to work on.

2. What values do you have that would help you facilitate the change you want in your life? Are you smart? A problem-solver? Rational? Hardworking? Quick on your feet? Name 15 reasons why you can do this.

3. Which communities can you engage with and begin eliciting self-change concepts? What about therapy or a Twelve-Step group? What are your fears about starting? Do you believe you will be vulnerable when you commit to change, and you will lose what you hold so dear with your addictions?

4. In what ways have you been assessed or judged by medical teams, family, co-workers, and friends? Are there some truths to the allegations? What are you willing to do? Would you like help? What would "help" look like that will make you engage and enter into a new paradigm?

5. Are you too young to stop your behaviors? Did you just get started in life and feel ripped off because you cannot have a little fun? Are you still having fun and getting consequences only once in a while? Do you still see value in doing those behaviors? What dangerous behaviors can you slow down?

6. Do you feel judged and stigmatized by your addictions? Do you feel shame and the need to keep everything secretive? Do you wear different masks for different people and believe you can't be honest anymore? Talk about it here.

7. Do you want to change for your family, the judge, or your partner?

8. Do you believe you can get away with your behaviors as long as no one finds out? Explain.

9. Do you believe you would be treated "less than" and looked upon with disdain for what you enjoy doing in secret? Are there healthy ways to do your choices? What are they?

10. Do you wish you could have open dialogue with honest debate as part of your consultation where you would still keep your dignity intact? What would that look like? Let's try a short talk and see how this would go with you as facilitator.

11. What is the real harm and tragic nature of what you are doing with your life? Would you like to find other ways to do your behaviors of choice? What would that look like?

12. Are you judged because of your race, poverty, sexual preferences and/or gender choices? What solutions can you offer for others to better understand who you are, what has happened, and what you are willing to do in a safe environment to change for the better?

13. If you are not yet willing to abstain from your choices, what ways can you implement that are better to make your choices safer for you and others?

14. Why do you believe you are more special and can't be helped with any of these ideals? What makes your story different?

15. How can we position you as being in charge of your recovery, yet have a real voice that is valued and counted upon as part of team resilience?

Healing with Humor

Healing addictions with humor and laughter is the most fun and curative antidote for depression.

Here's a true story. A guy starts telling me all his problems, how he attaches to his belief system, and how he is let down by others. I listen with my Buddha or Jesus, all-knowing-smile-of-charity-and-compassion, I-can-relate countenance. He goes on to tell me about people at work who annoy him and the horrible way that his boss treats him. I keep listening, nodding and saying, "Could you tell me a little bit more?"

So he delves deeper into how his wife berates him and judges him harshly for his poor judgment and lifestyle choices that put their relationship in jeopardy. He tells me how his children won't talk to him and he feels isolated and clumsy as a parent. He wants to be a good parent, but won't accept that being a good parent does not come with bells and whistles. He doesn't want to accept that being a good parent is doing the best you can do and that there are no immediate kudos or laurels.

He then begins a litany of why he does not belong or feel deserving in this life. He says he has been so damaged by his childhood that he wants to die, rather than be fearless and courageous and live boldly.

He continues wanting to find a way to die by suicide and leave all his problems behind. We talk about his excellent physical and mental health, his great job, his car and house, how he comfortably belongs to a great community and all the spiritual work he does, but he dismisses it all as a sort of entitled, privileged state that he has always had.

After two years of regularly hearing his monotonous rambling and trying the 15 recovery disciplines that are not working with him, something happens inside of me. He starts bantering and discharging his suicide club theme song over and over — and I begin to giggle.

We both grinned at each other and then fall into raucous laughter. We did not euphorically complete any mind-blowing spiritual plateau; we did not solve any mysteries about the universe. We surrendered to how hilarious we were in that moment and how we react to and want to defend perceiving life on life's terms.

He states, "I want to kill myself," followed by peals of laughter. "I want a divorce," peals of laughter. "Why won't they listen to me? When will they know my true nature? If they really knew who I was, I would be venerated," followed by snorts and guffaws.

Laughter, giggles, wheezes, coughing. We do this over and over each time he finishes his daily check-in litany. Laughter.

We laugh out loud about the helplessness of our natures and how we gave this dis-ease or discerning pestilence a power source that became hardwired.

It was only when he stopped digesting his negative emoting on a cellular level that he realized he had some control. We become what we think. Only when he stopped using his well-accessorized neural pathway of anger, resentment, fear, and discontentment did he really change.

Six months later, I am struggling with some serious life issues that I will not surrender. I get depressed and don't want to accept life on life's terms. So I call him up and start with a litany of my own. He starts to giggle. I say, "Hey what are you laughing at?" My thin-skinned, unhealed, wounded ego begged for solace but no, he wouldn't let me take my comfort and be depressed.

He said to me, "Just laugh with me once." I unwillingly responded, "Ha ha ha." He said, "Try it again like me — like you laughed with me when I wanted to kill myself and I was hyper-grandiose and didn't want to believe."

So I took a look at how little I was upset. I realized about how I wanted control, and how I was not in acceptance. I started to guffaw like a madman. It became real laughter when I disconnected from my need to be right.

He calls me regularly to give me my fresh, happy laughter.

We did not solve the problems of the world. But he is now living life on life's terms.

The ability to heal with humor, to be able to laugh at the fragility and awkwardness of life's circumstances, to laugh at one's plight and this predicament we are in is a gift. It helps to have a sense of humor because this work is intense and way too serious. Our ideas of laughing at others are epitomized by a person slipping on a banana peel. For some reason, we laugh. When we slip, it's funny in a way, and in another way, it's not. To be able to hold both truths is what we are after.

One way I loosen my burden of serious life is to employ the healing effects of the giggle factor. It is relieving and healing. We develop healthy boundaries with ourselves and, if we can take it easy on ourselves, we will have that much more compassion for others when our tendency is to want to judge them or be harsh. Our lives were meant to be lived joyfully and have experiences we can share to create a oneness of spirit and body.

The Ways that Humor Is Healing
- It's contagious. The abundance of joy and happiness we have is an unending supply; it is our heritage and legacy. Don't worry, be happy.
- It's been proven that laughter is good for our immune systems and lessens the damage of stress to our health.
- We have happiness in abundance that is neverending. Joy dries up only when we do not cultivate our happy gardens. Weeds will grow anywhere. We can always get our misery cheerfully refunded if we stop believing.
- Humor knocks down walls of fear, worry, tension, power, and status. Everyone needs a break from taking themselves or their lives too seriously.
- Laughter distracts stress and relaxes the body's ability to stand back and look objectively at how solemnly we are reacting to a bump in the road. It's just a bump, not the end of the road.
- Laughter releases feel-good chemicals, like serotonin and dopamine, and helps regulate adrenaline. These chemicals reduce stress in our minds and bodies and increases blood flow by unconstricting blood vessels and loosening the body's tension.

Workbook Questions:

1. How can we surrender the egoistic importance of being all we think about when we take life personally and make it about our subjective pain?

2. Name the one thing we all have in abundance.

3. What can we give away freely and unconditionally without losing it?

4. What makes you happy? What makes you laugh? Do you watch homicidal movies or serious plots? How do you feel when you watch a comedy?

5. What did you think was funny as a child? Did you ever use laughter to break the tension when everyone around you was stuck with some unnecessary seriousness, such as over a sports event?

6. Are you able to laugh with another person when your ego is at stake? If not, why not? What do you have to lose if you quit taking yourself so seriously? Why can't you relax?

7. Have you tried looking at yourself in the mirror, smiling and laughing with yourself just because you can?

8. What are your laughing taboos? Are they religious? Something at work? About your art or music? It's okay to be a serious artist and still have a sense of humor.

9. How do laughter and humor have healing qualities? What stops you from accessing this beautiful opportunity?

10. In what ways do happiness, humor and good feelings fight off disease?

11. In what ways does your spirituality want you to be joyous and free-spirited?

Healthy Relationships

Moderation is the key to longevity. Our ability to have relationships with each other is necessary for our need to belong, be part of, feel safe and develop trust.

This requires the vulnerability of communication. The idea of valuing another person's point of view along with your own beliefs seems expansive. How can we agree to disagree? How can we develop healthy discrepancies without denying another person's acceptance?

We all want different things out of our relationships. We also have common things upon which we agree. How can we stay mindful and neutral when we hear something we don't agree with? In what ways can we not shut down with reactive thinking? What can we find of value in the other person? What do we both have in common? Start with anything: two legs, 10 fingers, we are both breathing, we both like ice cream — then we build from that connection. For communication to thrive, we must look for similarities, not just judge the differences.

Remember that our spouses, work partners, colleagues, and children did not wake up today thinking about how to disrupt our lives. Remember also that women typically are expected to perform 90 percent of the emotional labor in a relationship – resolving disagreements, scheduling and preparing for family gatherings, buying gifts for relatives, sending cards, and so forth.

People are not mind readers or magical thinkers. They cannot hear what goes on in the closed system between our ears unless we speak up when something is bothering or distracting us. If we hold it in, we build resentment pressure. Sooner or later, resending those mental images to ourselves will start to be your experience — not the moment we are in right here and now.

Although we react with PTSD from timeless, painful moments in our lives, we need to remind ourselves that a flashback is a memory, not real. We can come back into the room with trust and flash unconditional, positive regard toward the other person.

We should not lash out at simple inquiries from curious loved ones. We should not raise our voices or assume they know how we feel at that moment. We must learn to not react so strongly to others who ask about our well-being. Compassion and empathy do not require another person's participation. Healthy relationships come from the inner work we do to stay neutral, open, willing and flexible. Sometimes what the other does is none of our business. We must take a look at our agenda-thinking. If we do not participate and communicate unconditionally, we will always suffer from the reservations we had when we gave our energies. It doesn't mean we are better — it means we have created a skillful path to communicate with inclusivity and diversity of another's needs.

In healthy relationships we try not to victimize ourselves or others. We try not to personalize or internalize another's experiences. We let them have their feelings. If they spin out of control, we don't get swept up into their experience. We let them spin until they finally come to a stop. Whatever happened is their experience. When we get emotionally enmeshed, we become codependent enablers. If we do not paint a target on ourselves around certain subjects, we are more likely to have rapport. We have a mutually vested interest with another in the value of keeping peace.

Active listening does not require us to respond by helping, fixing, and healing. Sometimes support comes from statements such as, "I really hear this subject is up for you right now," or, "I see how you are feeling about this," or, "I'll take a look at that, I care about what you think." Becoming the Ultimate Observer in our own lives is no longer about our personal station in life. We are able to see the helplessness of another person, and how we all have feelings as a common experience. Another's feelings are not personal toward us. We must learn to not internalize, and to Do No Harm with our response.

Is it really important for us to get emotionally escalated? We can learn to notice when a situation clashes with our morals, ethics, and beliefs. We can pick our battles. One exercise we can use is to notice when our thoughts about a subject are important to us. We can learn to catch ourselves when we believe our truth is more important than another's. Self-righteousness comes at a cost, and it has no healthy place in any conversation. We need to walk a mile in our partner's shoes. Notice how others are willing to listen to us without reactive speaking. We can start giving others the benefit of the doubt — and compromise.

To develop healthy relationships, find things that both parties are interested in that do not require the other to have vested participation. Explore healthy ways to work out, play music, and go to movies with others. Develop your inter-personal and intra-personal skill sets.

To keep friendships fresh, keep a beginner's mind. Do something as a relationship image breaker that makes both parties feel something different, makes you think, and stimulates a different part of your brains. It is possible to keep the honeymoon going with a sense of resolve. Another practice to implement into healthy relationships is to make a gratitude list of all the reasons we enjoy and love to connect with another person. When we are upset or feel off-kilter, we can look at that list and not focus only on the one dark blemish we are letting block out the sun.

By feeling vulnerable and sensitive and processing our own issues about trust, we create equity and give our partners feelings of empowerment and control. We can change only ourselves. We cannot change or expect our partners to change; that is their work. If you do your work, they are more likely to be willing to participate and make their own responsible efforts to change.

Get good sleep, eat well together, and have timed, mindful moments for emotionally escalated topics. Then, let it go. We can also get support and access appropriate people to work with on our issues. Some things are not meant to be worked on with our partners. There could be a conflict of interest or a dual relationship, which is unethical and immoral.

Healthy people exhibit the following behaviors:

- Healthy people make time to listen and honor others' thoughts without judgment. They develop trusting ways that last and keep safety in mind. Good communication keeps everyone on the same track.

- Healthy people talk honestly about things that can be worked on in a relationship without demonizing the partner. They have mutual respect for the safety of the relationship to create fairness and equality.

- Healthy people "drink a big cup of shut the heck up" when they have reactive thinking.

- Healthy people understand that both partners have unique lives — that's what keeps the relationship interesting.

- Healthy people accept others' friends, family, and work colleagues with curiosity and discovery.

- Healthy people encourage others in things they try to explore, even though it sometimes results in someone feeling vulnerable. They give others unconditional support.

- Healthy people compromise and don't make global statements; they leave lots of room for introspection.

- Healthy people keep supporting relationships through good times and bad with an eye on the longer view, rather than immediate gratification or vindication.

- Even when ending a relationship, healthy people keep these tenets as part of healthy closure, so they can continue as friends or constituents on some level.

Workbook Questions:

1. What are your healthiest relationships? Are they with your spiritual group, where you are on your best behavior but hide some of your true self? If so, is that a real, full relationship? Is it healthy?

2. Are you in charge of others? Are you a good leader? Are you accountable for your part? Do you lead by example?

3. Do you treat younger people as responsible beings capable of being taught and trained? Are you patient during their learning curve? Are you understanding of issues they may have? In what ways can you demonstrate a more healthy and trustworthy role in their lives?

4. Do you view others' abundance and happiness as something that is yours also? Are you able to be happy for your friend who got the job or the partner you both had an interest in? What will it take for you to change your thinking?

5. Do you nurture and guide by your example? Are you more of a "Do as I say, not as I do" type of leader? Are you a helper —the "good person"? What happens when you become "just another person" walking side by side with someone, feeling your feelings as another feels theirs? In that capacity, can you give up your role of caregiver? Explain.

6. What would your ideal, healthy partnerships look like in personal, business and intimate relationships?

7. In what ways do you sabotage your relationships?

8. As far as success or failures in your partner's life, what are your limits to celebrating their success or tolerating their failures?

9. Are you a fair-weather partner? Are you around only when things go well? In what ways do you change the relationship to bend to your needs?

10. In what ways do you hold your partner hostage emotionally?

11. Do you judge your partner's family or friends? Do you feel adequate with listening only when your partner wants you to listen, without fixing, helping or finding solutions?

12. Are there hidden things you keep from your partner and the honesty of your relationship? What are they? Are you afraid to talk about the "elephant in the room"? Explain.

13. Are you a jealous partner even when it's not warranted? Explain.

Homelessness

For me, homelessness was a state of mind.

Throughout my life I had places I could go, but I did not feel safe or at home. I felt more at home when I moved around freely.

Although I wanted to feel safe and that I belonged, I was not capable of it. Many people who are homeless live outside the system, instead of accepting a government-provided Single Room Occupancy studio to get them temporarily off the streets. Homeless persons often prefer to live in cars or stay with others in unstable relationships that crash and burn, and then go on the run again.

I lived with others as squatters. Squatters are people who take shelter in abandoned properties such as homes, apartment complexes and warehouses. These people do not own, rent, or have any lawful reason to be there. All over the planet, about one in seven people are squatters. As squatters, many of us felt a oneness and community.

My life of homelessness started with running away. I didn't want to belong to anything that felt like it had the constrictions of my first home or stirred up the Post Traumatic Stress Disorder of my childhood. Our family moved every other year during my youth because my father was in the Air Force.

After running away at 15, I lived in more than 30 places and never felt at home. The only time I felt at home was with a needle in my arm, having sex or drinking alcohol. At the time, it was the first and only lasting love of my life.

Now, I am a person who has a home. But I still live in a world that comes together and falls apart simultaneously. I feel that, even though my wife and I pay a mortgage for our home, we are still paying rent in a way, and if anything else more long-term comes of it, great. During the Great Recession, we had to suspend our belief system about safety, the economy, and our worth, based upon a capitalistic banking system. I am beginning to understand that "home is where the heart is," not where the money is.

Developing community and interpersonal skill sets with others creates a healthy mentality in my life. I realize that having a secure place to call home helps to create safety through community effort. My wife and I watch out for each other, work with community leaders and do service, even though we live in a dangerous neighborhood with suffering people. We nurture the idea of a home that creates shelter, a way for others to pay their bills, a way to get medical help, a way to safely live in a neighborhood without being harmed. And then there is the dignity of having a job to pay for our dwelling. This is what I call the safety of home.

Throughout the years of being homeless, working through my own recovery and helping others to attain theirs, I have observed that we Americans live in a war-ravaged environment where we support prisons and jails as a form of giving people homes. The state of our government and economic choices it made – paying for wars instead of funding education – create an environment that serves and helps no one except for the industry created to guard those prison homes.

We must educate and provide services, not guns. We must provide a safe environment for eliciting self-change thoughts — not prisons. We need to provide food, shelter, clothing and education to develop autonomy and perpetuate a hopeful outcome through our willingness as a society to create methods for people to sustain a living environment.

Today we are disaster workers, cleaning up the carnage after the fact when help could have been administered before. There is a chance for success and survival, if we put money back into communities. However, if we isolate them and let them run amok, it will be on our collective consciousness to be more responsible. We must treat the disease and mental distortions that come from the cycle of unsustainable homelessness. Homelessness leads to drug usage, crime and costly hospitalization as a result of living outdoors in the elements and becoming more health-compromised.

As a country, we could save money by saving lives. Yet we pay, because of our neglect and omission of responsibility. We pay dearly.

People who have been institutionalized begin to think that incarceration is an alternative lifestyle. They know what will happen every day: they get fed, have a place to sleep, and are safe from certain types of danger. Routine creates value. There is a social framework. When released, those former inmates are in a community where they do not have jobs and can't get homes because of the stigma of prison. They are not valued as humans. This cycle continues and reinforces the way we do business in America.

Are you willing to take a longer view and work toward common goals to replace the Third-World America we live in?

As an adult, it took a village to raise me — the entire city of San Francisco. Every single service was a valuable part of my life. Housing, drug rehab, vocational training, mental health, General Assistance, the Internal Revenue Service, Supplemental Security Income – the list of services that were available to help me goes on and on.

I was a marginalized, invisible person for 27 years. Today I am a contributing member of society who gives invaluable service and lives my life as a benefit to others. And still, I am just the beginning of what could be.

As you recover, think about how you can invest in the future of our wonderful country. Think outside of the box of homelessness and helplessness and the fruitless cycle of incarceration. We need new strategies and survival mechanisms to change our gradual decline into disorder.

I am resilient. I am redeemed. I live my life for the service of others. I am forgiven for all the damage I have caused others. When others could not forgive me, I forgave myself. I aspired to live as an amendment for others to believe in and trust that hope is alive.

Workbook Questions:

1. What do you believe homelessness means to those who have not been homeless?

2. After answering the first question, list your organic thoughts and judgments toward those people.

3. During the Recession of 2006-10, about 1.2 million homes were lost to foreclosure. What are your thoughts about that? Normal citizens lost their places of safety, security, futures and stability. Shall we marginalize and diminish their experience?

4. Have you ever been homeless? What was it like? How did you get out of your experience?

5. Have you ever lived on the outside of society — on the marginal boundaries? Have you couch-surfed all day every day and lived a Bohemian existence?

6. As a person in need, did you ever feel helpless, depressed, abused, and violated when you asked for help?

7. Do you treat homeless people as if they carry a disease? Do you cross the street when you see one coming your way? What is your response when they ask for money? Do you think they will only buy drugs and alcohol?

8. In your opinion, what will help these people? How would you implement your strategy with the unstable crowd?

9. What do you think would happen if you lost your home? Would you stay with friends or relatives? Would you feel safe and get back on your feet? In what ways would you recover?

10. What are safe ways that can normal people can interact with and help homeless people in a nurturing way? Volunteer? Serve in a soup kitchen? Give at church? Help the community with spiritual strategies?

11. Do you believe you will be safe and protected within our nation's system when you retire? If so, why? Is there anything you could have done differently? Why are you safe? In what ways do you justify that others will surely suffer? Do others deserve hardship because of their race, the country they come from, or their political beliefs?

12. How does your entitled lottery of birth as an American with privilege keep you from participating in the support of others who have less? It Is time for a "French Revolution" in your thinking?

Internalized Oppression

My oppression came from being brought up with my father's heavy hands of authority and then the law keeping me somewhat in line. That domination led to my becoming a runaway. The homeless lifestyle that ensued eventually turned me into an invisible, marginalized, diminished, bottom-feeder type of person.

I found myself living in the caste system of untouchables of our society that I had previously looked upon with disdain. I was stigmatized as a dope fiend, a junkie, an out-of-control alcoholic, and a rageaholic. I was also a sex fiend with insatiable tastes. I became a mentally challenged, unstable person. I got hepatitis C from shooting dope. Because of my lifestyle choices, many would say I deserved my outcome.

Even being of Polish descent was cause for internalized oppression. The Polish people, my father's father included, suffered terrible things in their society during World War II. One in five people — schooled, intelligent Poles —were murdered. In the U.S., we were called "stupid Polacks." With the last name Kowalski, everywhere I went, I heard the jokes about how stupid we were. Movies such as "A Streetcar Named Desire" further implied the violent nature of being a Kowalski.

When we diminish another's lifestyle, race, choices, culture, age, weight, or gender, we easily reinforce these negative beliefs in others. It is not hard to find others who believe that "we" are righteous and "they" are somehow inferior. We believe "they" are bad, wrong, and deserve the negative proclivities we espouse upon them. Name-calling begins, anger and resentment follows, and a mob mentality forms that does harm as a collective consciousness.

When "they" have no more value, they are easier to kill or harm with our righteous belief systems. People who start wars pit god against god and use that as their justification. By removing themselves and putting a deity in a place of responsibility, they kill for their god. In reality, our brothers and sisters on the planet breathe, walk, eat, sleep, have families and loved ones just like ours. They bleed, pray and love, just like us.

Remember a time when we found ourselves upset with a person or group and wanted to speak up against the madness. We might have used slander, gossip or character assassination through white lies and omission, telling only half of what we knew and "forgetting" the half the listeners need to hear for a full-measured disclosure. Our need to be right creates a need to feel safe, but it also can create a community that takes on the wrath of our righteousness.

Similar to a garden, our negativity grows like weeds. That is why a garden needs to be planted and cultivated. The idea of exploiting others and/or their thoughts creates a dualistic world where someone has to be right or wrong, win or lose, good or bad. As a result, we are left with the illusion that brings immediate, fleeting satisfaction. We perpetuate a fraudulent way of life by continually grasping at self-righteousness. Our main goal is to sustain our way of living no matter how detrimental it is to others. Power is behind oppression.

Moving toward equity-building begins inside my head. For a long time, I accepted scraps under the table of life when there was a chair ready for me at the banquet.

My turn-around thinking included thoughts about doing estimable acts in order to feel esteem. I realized I need to bring everything to this party of life for me to be happy. Others may not be able to give me what I ask for. This idea of abundance means there is enough peace, happiness, justice, and equality for everyone on the planet. I must let go of my dis-eased thinking. I must dump poison in my cup to receive an abundant flow of faith and belief in the unknown. I must take the first steps toward change.

This is an inside job; we begin here. I choose to begin now. The first steps begin the journey. It is not the destination, but the passage that creates evocative self-change thoughts.

The following are tips about healing and overcoming internalized oppression as a moral and ethical duty:

- Sit with persons of other cultures at lunch, business meetings, and social events. Create equitable conversations.

- Transform conflict into healthy opportunities. Rise above, and heal from within.

- Work with healthy communities that vie for changes in your community. There are dozens of nonprofits in my community. That number represents the goodness of people who work together for social change.

- Visit churches, synagogues, and temples. See the similarities of religious opportunities. If you look for goodness, you will find it. If you look for dissension, you will create and evoke it. Your attitude is all in what you think. You have a choice; now use your voice for good.

- Meet your neighbors and create communities of safety. The value of 20 great neighbors can help you to keep in focus the discomfort you feel about a few neighbors who are scary or questionable. See what you can do to help others in a safe and timely manner, and you will make strong allies toward the safety you have created by your fearless integration. Let annoying neighbors become your teachers for compassion and empathy. These qualities do not require the participation of the other party. It is an inside job.

- The greatest thing we can do for ourselves and others is instill hope. When you give hope, you receive it. Hope is the gift that pays back immediately by creating safety and vision for everyone.

- Go to the YMCA and become a mentor or big brother or sister to a young person. Learn how to be of value to your community.

- Go to your library and teach someone how to read, whether they are 10 or 60 years old.

- Become a close friend with someone who has oppression issues. Work with your own discomfort by discussing hot topics that quickly escalate. Keep it safe for both of you. Time these events and agree to disagree as a vehicle for safety.

- People who are oppressed need the values of loving, caring, trustworthy, real friends they can count on. Be there for people for the long haul; it will improve the quality of your life as well.

- Be committed to finding value and worth and helping others to own their belonging, deserving and safety.

- Internalized oppression is a disease of isolation and neglect. We all suffer from it. Make your weakest links in your communities your largest assets by your willingness and commitment to eliciting self-change thoughts in yourself and others.
- Take walks, go to social and political events, and create the diversity you want — not the separation you see.
- Celebrate special days with your community, and find communion with your people. Have healthy pride for your culture's history, progress and identity.
- Support community awareness of your oppression and educate others about your experience.
- Be resilient and heal with humor; this is something we can do together.
- Read books and watch documentaries about others' experiences. Learn, process your own feelings, and take small steps toward connecting with unique communities that pique your interest.
- Learn a new language. Travel to other countries, and learn about diverse cultures.
- Volunteer at a soup kitchen and talk to people. Be the change you want to see in others.
- Find the similarities we all share, and create groups that expound on communication, inherent worth and value. Celebrate the beauty and goodness of all people.
- Move from victimization to taking control of your life and having gratitude for what you have. Don't dwell on real and perceived injustices, but move into solution-focused therapies that can slowly create real change in our society.
- Learn to work with the brokenness of our system, and find ways to thrive. Create success one person at a time.
- Model leadership qualities and integrate others as leaders and trusted peers.

Workbook Questions:

1. What are your limitations to working with others? What do you think about working with homeless people, drug addicts, prison populations, or people of other ethnicities?

2. What internalized oppression do you use as a morality weapon for your cause? How do you do harm to others who are curious and want to explore their part in healing and building change into our society?

3. What are your triggers? How do you process your issues?

4. How do you integrate your work, neighborhood, and spiritual community to create safety and inclusive qualities?

5. What issues do you have about other races, sexual preferences, self-identities, and cultures?

6. What internalized oppression do you have within you that colors the way you communicate with others? In what ways does this stop people from getting close and trusting you?

7. How does your destructive thinking make you harm yourself and your culture with your attachments to your beliefs?

8. How does your pride in celebrating achievements and patriotic fervor make other cultures and communities feel unsafe?

9. How does your culture exclude other people and create oppression? Explain.

10. How does your place of entitlement and privilege make it easy for you to openly deliver answers for another culture? How do you do that without getting your hands dirty in the process?

11. What unfair and belittling things do others do to you?

12. How did you feel when you were attracted to a person of another race or culture? In what ways did you work together to overcome society's judgment? What things worked when dealing with others from another race or culture? What didn't?

Intimacy

Our society defines intimacy in so many ways.

For me, intimacy is a vicarious byproduct of healthy relationships and communication. It does not have any sexual connotation except with my wife.

The idea of moving beyond the safety mechanisms meant to protect us and into trusting relationships is sometimes vulnerable and sensitive territory. How do we move beyond superficial relationships and into intimacy with those with whom we want to connect?

We can create equity with other travelers on this path of life by being genuine and authentic. Healthy, emotional intimacy requires interpersonal relationships where both parties benefit from the opportunity as mature, consenting adults. The idea of groundlessness makes us more vulnerable and sensitive to how others process. Knowing how to gauge that from person to person and situation to situation is the key to longevity and success in relationships. With empathy and compassion, we have processed our own demons and can be responsible guides for others. We realize that this act created equity in all its forms. Life is a "we" thing, not a "me" thing.

Our society suffers from a disease of isolation and mistrust. We have an exaggerated sense of our self-image and the "special place" we worked so hard to inhabit and hold onto. We think we are the only ones; we live in fear of what could happen as a result of our interactions with others and become as sick as our secrets. However, we are meant to share common experiences and to help one another.

The idea of stigmatizing and personalizing our experiences is an egoistic structure that requires much maintenance. Omissions, white lies, half of what someone needs to see, but not the half that would help to heal our common experience. How can we courageously move into transparency with our existence? How can we move beyond this fear-based thinking that separates us?

We can learn to make ourselves trustworthy by creating equity. This happens by moving beyond fear and into our deepest selves and new levels of communication. We must feel vulnerable and sensitive about our disclosure and move beyond the superficial place and into transparent clarity.

We have a lot to gain by the common experience that all sentient beings have. It's not personal, it's not stigmatized, and it's not secretive. It is truth, and it lights the way for real transformation. We must develop mature, consenting adult relationships that are not based on fear and doing harm. We accomplish this by processing our own experience with the safety of others we trust. Start with incremental, day-to-day items of concern, and then develop into more complicated relationships based upon your past work together.

It's sad that this type of closeness gets confused with love and sexuality as a default in our society. We can be close with others without creating jealousy, envy, or hurt pride. It is a gift of abundance to nurture and carefully welcome others with healthy boundaries. Move fearlessly into the bigger picture and value of interpersonal relationships. Are we willing to let go of what others think of us for the greater good of all?

Everyone has intimacy; it's just not appreciated much. People you work with daily and do many tasks together — construction, counseling, sales —all require like mindsets to do the same jobs. We have our experience in common.

This is a form of intimacy, to know all about what you do together in work or play. Building on this base creates a safe haven to move toward other appropriate ways of building intimacy, when it's appropriate or wanted by all. Healthy boundaries are required in relation to the jobs that become available and who should get those jobs. Healthy boundaries also are needed as part of supervision and discipline styles. Skills are required to handle issues with age, body type, race, lifestyle and sexual choices and preferences.

People with close friends are happier. They can say anything without editing and being judged. This reciprocity lends itself to a symbiotic relationship that benefits everyone around them. Making known your thoughts and intentions to a trusted someone clears the air around you. Everyone can stand on solid ground we created by our experiences. This creates a healthy attachment that binds people together.

It is important to be impeccable with our words so we do not get caught up in secrets. Others will feel left out or gossiped about, and that will create a void of doing harm with our intimacy.

Compulsive disclosure to people you do not know is not fair to anyone. Before launching into our stories, we must ask permission for the other to willingly participate. Remember that weeds will grow anywhere, but a beautiful garden is cultivated.

Begin with small, common experiences and develop into complicated scenarios that will challenge and integrate critical thinking and constructive responses by active listening.

Silence is a powerful time for the speaker to reflect and the person listening to process what they heard and how it affects them. Before speaking, ask for permission to respond in kind with safety and trust in mind.

Relationships in which one person benefits, without the awareness of the other person, are an unfair breach of confidence. Be transparent and you will have longer-lasting relationships and walk proudly because of your efforts.

Workbook Questions:

1. What does intimacy look like in your life? What does it mean to you?

2. What kinds of intimacy would you like to develop in your life? With whom? Why?

3. What are you willing to commit to first without the other party's participation? I have said compassion does not require the other person's participation. What are your thoughts about this?

4. What's the worst that can happen if you start sharing healthy ways of intimacy? Is it worth the value of connectedness you will gain?

5. In what ways can you move beyond superficial relationships and into more intimacy with your lives and fellows?

6. In what ways can you develop intimacy, trust, gentleness and forgiveness inside the "mine field" of your own head?

7. In what ways can you courageously move into transparency with your existence?

8. What will help you move beyond fear-based thinking that separates you?

9. Are you willing to let go of what others think of you for the greater good of all? Explain your answer.

10. In what ways do you gossip, slander, and character assassinate with your confidences? What do you get out of that kind of relationship?

11. Why do you think that you are attracted to intimacy with people who are incapable of reciprocity?

12. What do you get out of compulsive disclosure with strangers?

13. Do you work with a person and share intimacy from working together?

14. In what ways can you develop more trust and transparency with your sexual partner? What do you have to lose? List some ideas you think are deal killers in your relationship that you do not pursue for fear your partner will leave you.

15. Were you hurt as a child or youth when others broke confidentiality with intimate details of your life? Were the confidences medical in nature? Were they sexual, physical, racial? In what ways did this experience shut you down from trusting others with intimate details of your life?

Jealousy

We are creatures filled with pride. Our egos want a lot of validation. We believe we must have someone's attention to validate our experience. Others must make us feel complete and whole.

We are overly protective of our family, job and possessions. We are slaves to the value of our lives and create a legacy through our hard work and deeds. We are jealous of others who seem to have the fame, prosperity, happiness and/or sexiness we want out of life. We feel left out and ripped off.

These beliefs do not create intimacy; they create jealousy, codependency and unhealthy boundaries. These basic assumptions create most of the misery on the planet. In reality, if we had what we thought we wanted, we might not be willing to do the hard work it takes to keep it. The illusion that the grass is greener on the other side creates mistrust across the board and devalues everyone's life.

Our anxiety creates fear-based emotions from comparing our lives to "theirs" and assuming they accomplished what they have at no expense or with little work. Our anxiety and jealousy create anger, fear, envy, low self-esteem, hopelessness, and resentment. We act out those feelings and make fools of ourselves.

We may find ourselves in good company with those who believe like we do. Misery loves company.

There are two forms of fear. The first is that someone has something we want, and we are afraid they will not give it to us, whether it is status, fame, respect, love, sex, and/or money. There is a faux anticipation about losing or not getting our needs met that creates a perfect environ for dissatisfaction.

The second form of fear is that we have something, and we are afraid someone is going to try to take it from us. This involves our ability to feel that we have status, fame, love, sex, money, family, and/or stardom.

Dualistic thinking sets off a cascade of emotional acting-out as we anticipate failure and loss of self-worth. This is the place in us where the Seven Deadly Sins — greed, sloth, envy, pride, lust, gluttony and wrath — all wreak havoc.

Jealousy keeps us all in bondage and relational disarray. It is disruptive to envy another's attributes. The truth is, if we had what they have, we would be as hard on ourselves as we are on them. Jealousy is afraid of losing what one wants or has; envy is wanting what we think we want from another's life experience.

Relationship jealousy begins with infidelity. Trust is broken. It can begin with small things, such as our partner talking to someone else. The phone and email become conduits for espionage. Before we know it, we become a sleuth-like character. Instead of healing and rebuilding trust, we create a web of deceit.

Distrust advances to reviewing credit-card statements — and on and on. The need for control over our partner's perceived cheating creates a sense of betrayal that is hard to let go of.

Trust-building and forgiving our partner helps us to have another chance. Letting go of control and trusting the healing process is a courageous character-builder. If we don't try, we will be filled with unfinished business. If we do not empty the poisonous cup, we will carry the poison we wish for another person, but realize later it has soaked into our own flesh, making us sick and toxic.

Forgiveness helps us to trust and love again. If our partners did indeed cheat, at least we gave it our best shot. This will translate into our next relationship as a red-flag question.

Our quest for emotional security is a vulnerable path unto ourselves. It is our acceptance, our trust, and our belief and hope. This is our work. Someone else's actions do not control us. To really heal, sometimes we can arrive at the conclusion that what others think of us is none of our business. We will seek safety and eventually distance ourselves from repetitive-stress injuries, if their behavior does not change.

Sometimes we repeatedly paint ourselves as a target for our loved ones. In reality, our loved ones probably do not wake up in the morning wondering how to make us feel bad. They just want to get on with their lives and their ability to be happy and thrive. They want to feel trusted and valued, honored and recognized for their inherent goodness.

Hope is the greatest attribute we can give to another person. It dies last — but make sure we are not the ones to destroy it. If we want to feel secure, we must foster that feeling of safety and trust. This is our job. Working with jealousy is an inside job. Our partner may have done one thing to betray our trust, but we keep playing that story compulsively over and over again. In a self-fulfilling prophecy of doom, we will eventually erode real trust and create the very thing we were trying to stop.

Ways to move beyond jealousy and stop envy from ruining your life:

1. We adopt many qualities from our companions and our environment. Only you can prevent these incursions. Choose your music, your movies, your friends, and your news sources wisely. Be the change you want to see. You make the difference. If you don't make plans to handle jealousy, others will surely make them for you.

2. Quit watching and buying into media hype. No more movie plots about deceit, for example. Those ideas will begin to digest on a cellular level. You will think you're smart by knowing all about it, but the truth is you were supposed to create other values in a relationship such as trust, fidelity, honor, and equity. You are negatively affecting your spiritual trust by investing in negative emoting.

3. Create art, listen to music, make a scrapbook, play a sport, go running, see a movie with a trusted friend. In other words, keep living your life during your precious time on the planet. Move beyond superficial thought and into genuine authenticity.

4. Sometimes bad things happen to good people. We don't always get everything we want, even though others seem to get things easily and in abundance. Just for today, accept pain and suffering as your teacher, and let go of endless catastrophizing.

5. Make sure you do not get hungry, angry, lonely, tired, fearful, bored or sick. Take care and do extreme self-care.

6. Quit snooping and making assumptions. These behaviors are worse than someone you love having a natural attraction to someone else.

7. Meditate on the good things about your relationship. Aspire toward and intend your life to be full and complete, right here and now. This is the only time you have to feel this way. Poverty is a choice of the mind; quit choosing bad things. Choose to be free from suffering and the root of suffering. That way is no fun and a luxury you can ill afford — it wastes and corrodes our lives away.

8. Heal with humor and laughter. Know that hard times are not personal; they happen to everyone all the time. It's just your turn. Are you going to go down like that? Laughter opens the doors and windows of life. Put curiosity and discovery back into your happiness. If you can predict what is going to happen, you need to quit that job — it's for losers. Approach life as a pleasure and information-gathering session, not a kangaroo court where you are the judge, jury and executioner.

9. Make sure your friends and support groups remain neutral and objective. You don't need any more gasoline and ammunition. And you need to defuse the bomb in your head. You want to agree to disagree. You don't want them siding with you blindly because they don't want you to get hurt. It is not helpful at all if they wish suffering upon the person who is causing you harm.

10. Recover your true self and personal best. Empower yourself. Have nothing to hide. Live life with transparency so you don't get confused and so others are not confused. Keep your message simple and plain. For example: "I aspire to develop a trusting relationship by using openness, willingness, and a beginner's mind."

11. Bring self-security. Actualize estimable acts to create your own esteem. Bring everything you need so no one needs to do anything to make you feel safe. You are safe. You deserve. You belong. Others have gone before you, and you are not alone.

Workbook Questions:

1. Jealousy is an inside job. What are your triggers? Are triggers women, men, jobs, status, wealth, race, social climbing, money, cars, family closeness, trust?

2. What do you do that is mistrustful, sneaky and unfair to your friend, family or partner?

3. What qualities do you envy in others that create jealousy? Why aren't you working on your positive qualities, instead of taking the cheap shot and judging others?

4. What do you do to make people jealous? Are you a showoff? Do you like to make people feel small? Do you exaggerate the truth? How do you make people feel bad because you feel bad about yourself?

5. Which qualities do you believe you do not possess that are important to develop autonomy and trust? Are you fearful, faithless, insecure, distrusting, wrathful, waiting for the ball to drop, looking for something wrong, a non-believer? Do you need to be with someone no matter what happens?

6. How do you wish for bad things to happen to people who are successful? In what ways do you badmouth them if you don't agree with them? Do you try to get reinforcement from friends who think like you?

7. In what ways are you jealous of your partner's friends, gay friends, long-time and cherished friends, spiritual friends, sports friends?

8. How do you dress hot to make others look at you with envy? Why do you drive an expensive car to look good? Why do you need to have more attention than most just to feel normal?

9. What are you willing to do to change your thinking?

10. What can you do differently the next time you are triggered?

11. What can you say when your friends start bad-mouthing a close acquaintance? You know you could be next in line — what could you do and say to create safety for all?

Jobs and Employment

So you need a job, or new employment. Or there are large gaps in your resume that need to be reconciled. You have untold anxiety about even looking for a job. Maybe you believe you are too young and unskilled — or over the hill.

The truth is, no matter how little we think we have, it is more than enough to begin. What we think about first is the beginning of what happens next. We digest our thoughts on a cellular level — we are what we think, and this drives our behavior.

Right here, right now is the only moment we have a choice — to be happy, to be employed, to be enlightened. We cannot go back to the past. We don't know what the future will bring. But we can bring our minds to attention and become as employable as we can — right here and now.

It's best to look for work that fills our souls and satisfies us in some way. We need to make sure we have those skills or start at the bottom and work our way to the job we want. A five-year plan can be an effective way to get where we want to be. We should look for satisfying work where we can use our transferrable skill sets. We are sure to find work with purpose with people who share our enthusiasm and interests.

We strive to be resilient beings, but most of us share a common thread of anxiety about our esteem and being judged during the employment contest. As we go in, it's a good idea to keep the attitude of having space in ourselves for many awkward rejections. "No thanks." "We don't feel you're the best fit." When we don't set our sites too high, we keep our ability to feel safe.

When we come to the table for a job search, it's important to know what they want and what we want. It also helps to know that some jobs are not advertised. We look for and find our niche and then show them why they need our services.

We are selling our services, as well as our opinion of our estimable value. Our personal attitudes and attributes should include the ability to stand on our own, as well as successful social interpersonal skills in relation to others.

Know thy self. What are your strengths and weaknesses? Know your place in the world and your purpose for being here. Show the potential within you. No matter what others think of you, know your value as a person with any job you do and strive for mindful achievements.

To have an authentic interview, watch these key points: Listen completely, and watch your body language. Be genuine and authentic, and create equity by your ability to be vulnerable. Let the interviewer feel safe and remove perceived threats. Show your truth. People want this, and it is in demand.

When interviewing for any job, keep in mind there are commonplace skills that are needed everywhere, no matter what the job description says. Show the interviewer what you've got and what you bring to the table.

Here are a few easy statements to practice and use when appropriate with a potential employer:

- I communicate well and can speak, write and convey my ideas easily to others.

- I am creative and good at problem-solving. I figure out how things work and make sense of them.
- I try to be punctual. When needed, I arrive early and stay late.
- I am dependable and have a healthy attitude, drive, and energy.
- I can analyze and break down problems into easily workable solutions.
- Work is sometimes hectic and unpredictable; I work mindfully to make good decisions, even when a supervisor is not present.
- I am flexible and can adapt. I respond well during a crisis.
- I am trainable, willing, open and flexible to new job opportunities.
- I can work with difficult people. I ask for help when needed.
- I am forward-looking and can foresee where problems will occur, then minimize accidents from happening.
- I am skillful at explaining concepts and patient with the learning curve.
- I develop, teach and mentor others, and strive to have healthy mentors myself.
- I am goal-oriented and solution-focused; I plan ways to achieve.
- I learn quickly from watching others and follow instructions.
- I am able to delegate tasks and let others thrive and be empowered.
- Customers are my priority. I am patient, polite and friendly.
- I am an active listener and really hear requests and/or complaints so I can respond appropriately.

Workbook Questions:

1. What type of work brings meaning to your life?
2. What kinds of work do you like to do? Why? What are your fears about choosing this field?
3. Which anxieties are associated with job search? Age, skills, mental obstacles, ability to get to and from work, money needs, training, education?
4. What are your job strengths? What are your job weaknesses? In what ways do you explain both to an employer? Do you have physical challenges or mental restrictions? What are they?
5. In what ways do you deal with difficult employers, bosses, and/or colleagues? Do you stuff your feelings? Do you rage after work and have seething contempt for everyone involved?
6. What are your fears about someone employing you? Are they real? Who would you be without these fears? In what ways can you change your thinking?
7. Do you go from job to job without thinking about what you want out of life? What will it take for you to realize your potential and move closer to your dream job?
8. What gaps in your resume are you afraid of? Are they caused by addictions? How do you skillfully explain that you benefited from past experience and, as a result, are more trustworthy and employable?
9. Do you enjoy helping others but don't like the salary of social-services jobs? What solutions would work for you?
10. Are you a quiet and shy person who feels unheard? What has worked in the past that helped you feel comfortable and "part of"?
11. If you could choose any job anywhere, what would it be? Are you afraid of doing research in that field? If so, why? Can you volunteer in a related field to discover if you really like it?
12. In what ways do you explain job gaps in your work history? Can you get comfortable with explaining what happened? Will you practice with trusted friends to get that lump out of your voice? If not, why not?
13. What kind of support group(s) do you have that help you to keep your balance and safety with your mental health, while you put out 40 resumes and don't get any replies?
14. In what ways do you intend to wait for the job that will support you and that you will be happy with? List a few ways you will avoid grabbing the first job you are offered that doesn't pay enough.
15. What will you do to be gentle with yourself when you do a great interview, but you're not a good fit for the company? How will you take care of yourself when you hear "no, thanks," over and over?
16. There is a saying that encourages job shoppers to not get depressed until they have heard "no, thanks" 100 times. What are your plans to get through those trying times?

Judgment – Yourself and Others

For all of our lives, we have lived in a world of dualistic values. There is the good one or the bad one, the right one or the wrong one, best or worst, win or lose — always trying our best to fit in with the crowd of our choice while keeping our identity and not rocking the boat.

As a result, we each have a highly-developed critical eye of our own.

If we are so harsh on ourselves and beat ourselves up for nothing, just think how badly we treat others. We try to reach the pinnacle of perfection for seconds at a time, then slide back down as if playing a game of Chutes and Ladders. If we judge ourselves so harshly, how can we be objective about people we don't even know?

Why do we think a good time to pass judgment on others is when our judgment is impaired by our own emotional state of confusion or low-impulsive anger? Yet we are so willing to state our side of the story with a defensive line. We have convenient listening ears. We hear only what we want and disregard the rest.

In what ways can we best recognize our behavior and resist the temptation to act out our anger? How can we recover our senses while we clean up our side of the disaster?

Even during those times when we show good judgment, are we able to hear another's truth? Are we able to let go of attachment to our belief system just for a moment, for the sake of the greater good? For living our lives truly for the benefit of others?

When we respond from an assertion of something we believe in, do we have enough character and self-respect to make amends for our bad judgment? Is there enough to help others feel safe and admit they, too, could have done things differently?

What do we have to lose when we judge others? Self-respect, social status, peace of mind, and our belief system come under fire. It should be all right in our society to make mistakes. There should be a method in place for redeeming our value and judgment. It would be a great way to make life better and a way to make amends with an understanding that the other person may make the next mistake. Meanwhile, we work on forgiving and welcoming them back into the safety of the fold.

This is how we evolve.

If we implement a plan that it is OK to make mistakes, and we create a forum for how we can do it better next time, we can bypass societal brow-beating and shame-based behavior that tells us we are bad people.

When we learn what our mistakes are, we work with solution-focused ideals and strength-based strategies to make accountable, measurable, and observable progress in a healthy direction. We work within a healing model, instead of a disease model.

Self-Judgment

What is the story you tell yourself — and reinforce — every day? Is it any or all of the following?

- I am not loveable.
- I don't deserve to be happy.
- No one will ever love me.
- I'll never get that job.
- Nobody likes me.
- I'm a loser.
- I am a mental health nutcase.
- (Insert anything) … and that's my excuse.

Our self-stories are a safe place to be. Our rut-thinking is well accessorized; everything is in place to keep us from making positive forward movement.

Our stories are comfortable because we don't have to do anything to rock the boat and really work to change our lives. Keeping ourselves down is seductive. We are good at it, and we've convinced everybody around us that we will never move past that bump in the road of life.

Everyone believes in us and knows we can accomplish change, but it's too hard for us to contemplate something different.

Why do we think this is true? Who would we be without that way of thinking? What can we do to turn that thinking around? Why do I believe this is true with others, but not myself? Who would I be without judging others? The next time we find ourselves getting hot and bothered about something everyone else is only observing, we must check ourselves before we wreck ourselves. Why does the situation bother us so much? What do we get out of that dissatisfaction? How do any of those things feed our negative-emoting machine?

Why must we come from a place of diminished returns simply to sit at the table of life? Why do we stay under the table accepting scraps? Let's make the courageous move to sit at the table and participate with all that is going on and available to us.

Is our world created from dissatisfaction with ourselves? Do we judge others with the same depression, anger, fear and anxiety? Then it's time to take a look at how we do our business and change a few things. Let's make a commitment that just for one day, we will try to just accept our day as it unfolds. Everyone gets to live and be free from our torment.

Meanwhile, we will make a commitment to stop, smell the roses and value the precious breath we share with everyone on the planet.

When we feel judgment coming on, we let it pass and get back into the game with a healthy attitude of gratitude. If we can choose to be happy, our thoughts will follow, and then our behinds will fall in line.

Judging is a personal addiction we inflict on ourselves and others. We must notice when we do it and take a look at what is going on inside. HALT: Are we hungry, angry, lonely or tired? We can start mobilizing our mindset to do the next right thing, and then the next right thing. When we feel like a deer in the headlights, we can simply do the next right thing. If we listen to the universe, it will respond in kind.

Are you listening?

Ways You Can Combat Self-Judgment and Judgment of Others

- Look for something kind and gentle you can do for yourself and others.
- Look for the great qualities you or others have.
- Look for the similarities instead of the differences in yourself and others.
- When you compare, you despair. When you compete, sometimes you feel defeat. Be a team player.
- Do something spiritual that doesn't require harsh reflection of you or others.
- Do acts for unconditional reasons and with radical kindness.
- Get out of self. It's not a "me" thing; it's a "we" thing.
- Look at yourself in the mirror and tell yourself how much you love you, and then tell others how much they mean to you.
- Make an affirmation list about yourself and others, and give them a copy.
- Make lists of 20 reasons I love me and 20 reasons I love you, and give them away.
- Pray for the willingness to pray for the willingness to stop all judgment that is not healthy.
- Develop your healthy ambivalence and discernment about issues you are triggered by.
- Active listening means using your ears, mind and body as one unit.
- Don't react after you hear something you disagree with.
- Digest painful thoughts without reactive speaking.

Workbook Questions:

1. How do I benefit from judging others? Does it benefit them that I judge them?

2. How do I hold others emotional hostage with my judgment of them?

3. Why am I so harsh on myself? How much comes from childhood issues or parental qualities gone astray?

4. What are some positive benefits of healthy and sound judgment?

5. How do I judge elders, people of other races, people I work with, my partner, my kids, and my government?

6. How do I reinforce my judging behaviors?

7. Why do I judge myself so harshly when I know it is not healthy for me? Why do I judge my partner?

8. What can I do right now to combat judgment, anxiety, fear, depression, and righteousness?

9. Why do I trust my impaired judgment over and over and feel the repercussions of that choice?

10. What is the next right way of thinking we can impart in our lives so we can live without the burden of judgments?

Keeping an Open Mind

The journey to recovery deals with more than alcoholism and addiction. We got there for many reasons, some which are lodged deep in our souls because of the way we were raised. Sometimes we are receptacles of generations of wrong thinking.

One of the most important traits we need to re-wire is keeping an open mind.

Traits of a closed mind include the following:

- We close down when we hear something we don't agree with.
- We have compromised friendships over small things that don't matter.
- We sabotage work relationships.
- We close down and put up walls to keep others at bay.
- We make mountains out of molehills.
- We polarize politically.
- We classify people and things as beautiful or ugly.
- We have to be right.
- We feel unsafe when we concede to another's truth.
- We can't listen without judgment.

What can we do to "fix" these seemingly insurmountable traits? Let's hike this mountain one step at a time, starting with the basics.

Goal: to not need to fight one against another; to keep safe spaces for another and their thoughts.

When we let go of our perceived outcomes, we are in a groundless space where anything can happen.

We can challenge our own thoughts only when we let go of the attachment to our belief systems. When we no longer need to have control, we can begin to accept life on life's terms. By letting go of intractable thinking, we are truly free to experience something new and different.

We must not believe everything we think. It's OK to allow new ideas to change our perception.

Sometimes, even though we have the capacity to suspend our belief system and consider other truths, we may still believe ours to hold the most truth. There is nothing wrong with that when we have an open mind. Others will see the strength of our open mind and consider the value of doing so in their own lives.

The greatest asset of our strong character is being open, sensitive and vulnerable. We can let down our guard. We remain teachable, willing, open, and flexible with a beginner's mindset. There is true freedom in acknowledging that we don't have all the answers and we don't have to be right. We are able to meet others halfway and join with them as we surrender to each other's beliefs and become collaborative team members.

We make mistakes when we are in hectic situations. We process and work through our opportunity for change. By doing this, we help others to see how to live life. By collaborating, we create a vital and safe place. We go through the gauntlet as a team. Instead of building our case against another, we become solvers and solution-focused assets.

When we have an open mind, we can take all the good and bad things that have happened to us and see how we benefited and learned from the whole experience. It enables us to translate that knowledge to our immediate troubles and experiences with others. We notice that we can find ways to have the inner knowledge that the entire experience is valuable. We need to do it all without compromise to have a full-measured mind.

We trust that our inter-dependence with others creates more empowerment and equity-building for both sides. As the song, "The Glory of Love," says, "You've got to give a little, take a little, and let your poor heart break a little. That's the story of, that's the glory of love."

With a Higher Power's omniscience guiding us, it is like having a diamond with 120 facets cut into the stone and creating our truth. We can see all sides of the gemstone to make ourselves and others shine with the best intentions.

When we believe in the possibility of more truths, we have the powerful benefit and abilities to see beyond our superficial pain-body. We are dealing with the here and now and move into the light of real truth: yours, mine, and the truth. Sounds simple, doesn't it? Keep an open mind until your safety or belief is triggered. This is a counter-intuitive spiritual muscle memory we need to develop.

What follows are ideas that will help us all to do better. We need to keep reminding ourselves that the spiritual moment is when we are distracted, triggered, and want to react. This is when we must stop, recognize our behavior, and practice our lifetime skill. The teacher is always with us no matter how good we get. Something will trigger and undo our finest expressions of openness.

Keep practicing. Hope dies last:

1. If we are triggered and think we are talking too much, we probably are. Listen more than we speak, especially if we are in charge or have control over others' welfare.

2. Keep cultural norms and beliefs as the highest form of recognizing our diversity and inclusivity. Look for the similarities, not differences.

3. Be humanistic. Treat others as if they were your children, elders, or your closest friend. Treat people who are really spinning out and emotionally labile as if they have a terminal disease. Would we yell at someone who was dying?

4. We don't always need to have the answer or know how to fix a problem. But we can always be a trusted listener. Sometimes that is all anyone really wants. We all have answers within us. It is our craft to help others in how to speak their authentic truth and heal themselves.

5. Don't jump to conclusions; there are no quick-fix bandages for the expansive and complicated lives we live. Everyone responds differently according to their needs.

6. Don't assume; it makes an "Ass out of U and Me." Halt the quick and snappy repartees. We might harm someone who thinks differently than us.

7. Even when we are pressured into making quick judgments, we need to take a moment and weigh the outcome. If we can wait longer, we must use that time to mindfully respond. We don't need to spin out with others. Weigh all the facts and realize that we still don't know everything.

8. Someone's crisis does not need us to put out their fire. We can take our time; they have been developing their mindset for longer than the emergency that has happened.

9. Wait at least 30 minutes for all email responses. Don't let your emotions speak first and ruin any chance of future correspondence.

10. If you have a bias or agenda thinking about certain subjects, get trusted support and use that person as part of your wisdom-thinking.

11. Do No Harm. Think about it: Who will be harmed? How this will affect us later down the road when things have changed? Think ahead.

12. If avoidable, we mustn't choose sides. There is no way to be objective or trusted with such a powerful and trusted place in society after our choice is made.

13. Give credit and create an open and trusting environment where there are no such things as stupid questions. Engender creativity and be courteous with all aspirations and intentions with active listening.

14. Be fearless and courageous with limitless thinking in order to tell our truth. Then we must be willing to change and respond with new information when things change. We can be a diplomat. Respect the other's truth.

15. Continually seek new thoughts and information. The only constant about life is that change happens.

16. Don't be brittle and hard-lined. Our attachment to our own thinking and experiences colors our willingness to be open. We need to let go completely.

17. We must always be willing, open, flexible and teachable with a beginner's mind.

18. We need to practice and develop our ability to hold both truths simultaneously. Be the "Devil's Advocate." The "devil" just might be right more than we think.

19. To appropriately process our thoughts, we need to let go of anger, frustration and resentment. Know that we cannot help everyone. When needed, we can delegate an appropriate person to take our place on this delicate subject.

20. We can work with our discernment and ambivalence. Know thy self. Know how we come across to others. Work with our personal quirks and don't give away all your thoughts that are not helpful to the situation.

21. Don't indulge in eternity thinking, or respond from desperate and needy convenience and/or gratification.

22. When we find ourselves having all the answers and needing to be right, sniff around to see what smells wrong. Keep sniffing. It is likely you again. In the words of Ice Cube, "Check yo self before you wreck yo self."

Actions that will keep our minds open:

1. Do art or something new and creative; keep your mind gelling with abstract concepts.

2. Travel and enjoy other cultures, belief systems, customs, and political and spiritual proclivities.

3. Try something new. Educate ourselves about things on our "bucket list" of things we always wanted to do or try. Get out there and do it.

4. We can listen to all styles of music and notice how we feel about it. We can try to understand what others get out of the experience and why we feel so strongly about music.

5. Try out another's religious or spiritual belief. Look at the similarities we all have in common. Be the universal observer in your life.

6. We can watch documentaries, science and technology programs, and history shows. Find out how everything works together. Stimulate your brain with more complex tasks. We don't potentiate full use of our brains during a normal lifetime — we need to use more of ours.

7. Be active and stretch our limits of what we think you can do with an open mind. We can do many more things than we can ever comprehend.

8. Do things we normally wouldn't do. Speak to the people who scare you. You may find out they aren't scary at all. Basically, we need to quit doing nothing. Why not get involved in local politics and work with others on community values?

9. Become part of new communities of interest in your area. Join a stamp club, knitting club, or martial-arts or dance community.

10. Learn non-violent communication. Start having solution-focused difficult conversations. Challenge and stretch your brain's elasticity. Understand that as a species, we are still accepting scraps under the banquet table because of our agenda thinking.

11. To keep an open mind, we must let go of control, conceptions, manipulation, expectations, and not being in acceptance. Surrender completely and forgive completely. Or we can get honest and be genuine about our position — that our minds are stuck and caught up with something in the past.

Workbook Questions:

1. What subjects are easy for you to keep an open mind upon? Name 10: art, work, etc.

2. Where do you draw the line about keeping an open mind? Why? What would happen if you let go of your thoughts and truths? Who would you be? What would you lose? What are you afraid of?

3. Do you have the ability to walk a mile in someone else's shoes? How about their wheelchair? Would you walk in a dangerous neighborhood to smell the roses and watch the moonrise? Do you walk in fear all the time? If so, why?

4. Do you live your life with reservations? Do you live under the umbrella of, "Yes but," "I could," "They should," "We would've," "They didn't," "We wanted to"? In what ways does procrastination keep you from having an open mind? If you are caught up in hesitation and flux, will people trust your truth? Why or why not?

5. Do you easily put down and condemn people of another race? Do you believe persons with mental illness fake their dilemma? Do you believe older people become set in their ways and stop having neural plasticity? Explain your answer.

6. When someone does something you disagree with and you feel threatened or harmed — personally or with social status — do you stop having any contact with those people and cut them out of your life? Explain your answer.

7. When your boss intimidates you and you feel slighted, do you respond to him and the situation with an open mind?

8. Are you a liberal, conservative, Republican, or a Democrat? Do you hold an opinion that another party has less of a moral compass than yours? Why?

9. Are you a good, moral, religious person? Does your denomination have a bias against other religions and beliefs? How do you navigate the murky waters between God and man's interpretation of God's will on this planet?

10. When you see someone do something wrong, do you immediately judge them? Do you know if they were hungry or driven by another human need at the time? Were they driven to their state of mind by the apathy of our society? How can you help them? How do you keep an open forum to listen actively to their request for equity and a fair share of this life?

11. Do you believe in evolution or God's work? In what ways can you hold space for both truths? Can you agree to disagree and hold the paradox of both truths?

12. In what ways do you bring yourself back to a mindful state when you fight with your partner, kids, neighbor, colleagues at work? How do you collaborate with openness?

13. What music do you dislike? Why? Can you think of three reasons someone might really dig that beat that annoys you? Stretch your mind and name three reasons.

14. What happens when you hold two truths as part of a healthy conversation, or just for the sake of conversation? How do you feel about "taking both sides?" Do you feel vulnerable and sensitive? Do you value that kind of equity?

15. In the end, does your unspoken moral compass just quietly walk away from conversations that hold two truths muttering, "Yeah, but…"? Why do you think that happens? Or do you feel authentic and genuine when you are done? Do others get the benefit of the doubt with you? Are you the benefit, and they the doubt? Explain.

16. In what ways do you stretch your mental abilities to keep your mind open? Is it a weak and flabby muscle? In what ways can you strengthen openness and respond mindfully? Where can you get help with that opportunity?

17. What topic triggers get you caught up in a conversation? Let's begin with "child molester." What is your response to reading those words? Are you able to keep an open mind no matter the topic? Try with difficult subjects and pay attention to how your bias, prejudice, racism, entitlement, privilege, and religious or spiritual beliefs keep you stuck. Write about it here.

Medications: Compliance, Side Effects, and Traversing the System

Caveat: These are a few thoughts based upon my experiences. Your own journey needs to be made with help from your medical community. This is your opportunity to create wellness in your life. Find as much as you can about this subject, then experiment and move slowly toward your goals of wellbeing. Every person responds differently to medications. You should rely on your chosen team of medical providers and your own physical and mental responses to any medications as your guideline.

When beginning the journey to recovery using medications for mental health and other medically diagnosed issues, we must be willing to consider every option with an open mind. We can use our ability for analytical thinking and mindfulness.

This is big stuff. It can work in as many ways as our brains can. It's a big move to undertake on the road to recovery, but it is doable with full-measured consideration.

We should be knowledgeable with everything we can learn about medications, side effects and our brain and body's response to them. There are no stupid questions. Anybody should be allowed to talk about concerns, consider how they feel, receive knowledge and reconsider, try new prescriptions with more knowledge, and feel safe and comfortable while doing all of it.

We are dealing with our minds and bodies, and no one knows them better than us. Keep this in mind. Remember, be willing and teachable. We need to completely suspend all our fears and thoughts and let the medications and our bodies adjust. The body is an amazing thing. It will undergo miraculous change if we can weather the first few weeks of adjustment. We can adjust to almost anything. Our bodies are durable and rarely break like a fragile piece of china. We will notice the side effects we experience and learn if we can handle ambivalence.

Some medications will work for somebody, but one medication does not work for everyone. People delude themselves into thinking medications are the cure.

Medications relieve some symptoms and help control your brain chemistry. A smart first step is to begin with lifestyles and cognitive behavioral therapies that will give us tools and mechanisms to change our thinking. When we eventually get off medications, we will revert to our old brain chemistry. So we need to change our brain by doing the therapies.

We do not get a free pass to magical healing. This will be the work of our lifetime — to labor at our abilities to learn and perform new behaviors in place of just feeling our old, conditioned feelings. We now have a choice.

Our lives are a great journey and personal experience. So is the way we relate to life on life's terms. Our bodies are amazing. So is our pharmaceutical culture. We get to decide with our own minds, and we get to have counsel from the pharmaceutical culture, which includes all medical professionals.

I can speak only for myself. Here's how medicine helps me. I started medicating myself with anything that was available when I was very young. In the 1960s, I was part of an experimental culture that tried many drugs and guzzled alcohol and herbal mixtures.

I tried them all and chose to not participate with life on life's terms. For 40 years, I bypassed my own body's chemical process. Then I got scared and decided it was time to clean myself up. I got into recovery and was put on more medication to stabilize me enough to be non-disruptive and of benefit in a program.

At first, I used various medications. I began to have strange feelings and didn't know what to do with my emotions. It took about six different tries with a variety of medications over a period of three weeks, each time waiting to see if my body and mind would adjust — and if I could function on any level. We finally ended up with Lithium and Prozac, which worked pretty well with my brain chemistry. I tried many others.

When we try medications prescribed by a doctor, we have to really pay attention to what is going on with our bodies. Some of us have never done that before. It is a mindful, awakened journey. It takes patience and an open, willing, flexible mind to see what is really going on with our metabolism.

I was told I would be on medications for the rest of my life. I had just stopped using drugs and alcohol to medicate myself over the course of my entire life, and this was not good news for me.

The main thing that happens when we try new medications is coping with side effects. Each medicine may help with mental health, but the seven side effects that the medication produces can be alarming, depending upon chemistry makeup. When more than one medication is on trial, there can be 14 possible side effects. We get easily confused about which is doing what and we feel different things. Some side effects take away the desire to eat, make you eat more than you need, or affect your libido. The side effect list is endless. It affects every part of the body. Read the fine print and advocate about what you are feeling. Find a doctor who will work with you all the way.

My medications calmed me down enough to stay in program and function with others so I was not a liability. It helped me to stay in my seat long enough to learn why I did things. I learned about my brain and how it functions with daily living, processing stress, poverty, homelessness, mental health, sleep, living and coping skills, and survival strategies. I learned about all my triggers that lead me to feel that infinite sadness of bipolar disorder and the whole other array of diagnoses I was given.

For years, I worked with the chemistry of my brain, creating new neural-genesis brain elasticity, and stopped reinforcing old habits which fed that part of my brain. It was a rut with a short runway: my reactions with old, familiar, addictive feelings and the cascade of chemicals brought about by negative emoting. When I interrupted my thinking and suspended my belief system just for a moment, I gained clarity.

Don't believe everything you think, say or do. Look to what is beyond the thought. No matter how far we have fallen, it is more than enough to begin anew. This moment right now is the perfect teacher. We digest our thoughts on a cellular level, and they become what we are — either good feelings or bad. The bad ones turn into stress and then into dis-ease in our bodies. We then become tissue-toxic, so all kinds of depressive, negative emotions lead to openness to contracting diseases such as cancer.

Everyone has the potential for cancers to prosper in their bodies; those bad cells just need a reason to do their job. I have stopped giving my brain bad signals, and I work on positive insight for healthy living.

After four years of being on medications, I wanted to experiment and see what would happen if I stopped. I got my recovery team of therapists and doctors to concede. I demonstrated and advocated for two years to come off medications. It was not easy. When the old familiar, chemistry kicked back into power, I had to take a look at what I was doing mentally with my behaviors. I had to interrupt those behaviors and follow a new strategy.

I mentally worked on every concept in alphabetical order about such things as anger, abuse, abundance, ambivalence, attachments, all the way to Z. I worked with my mind and retro-fitted it with new thinking and new ideals. I fed it positive, re-enforcing menus, options and survival strategies. I worked with every part of my broken mind. I did the Twelve Steps a total of six times to really get a grip on who I am and my place on the planet. I accepted pain and suffering as my teacher until I could find something that finally took its place.

I get a daily reprieve from my suffering based upon my spiritual maintenance. I choose to do this willingly with my every precious breath.

Here's how medications work: They labor with our neural receptors in the brain that give us messages about how we feel. If it's pain, they relax the part of the body that hurts. Pain medicines can relax the hurting tissues and block pain receptors. Mostly, they do the work for our brains so we feel no pain or so we do not feel depressed.

Our bodies have done this work on their own for millions of years of evolution, but suddenly we are physically competing with a pill. We have to adjust to that pill and stop making our own chemistry. We have to marry the pill with our brains and the way our bodies react. When we stop taking medication, we hope we have learned everything about our disease and what triggers our reactions. If it involves physical pain, we learn not to do what hurts anymore.

I replaced my medications by doing therapies such as cognitive behavioral therapy, rational emotive behavior therapy, dialectical behavior therapy, harm reduction, motivational conversations, and non-violent communication. Those all worked with why, how and when I respond to life and how to best enhance my experience in relation to those around me.

Following is a list of some side effects you may momentarily feel as you take medications. Results differ with various metabolisms. Just notice them and don't attach and think that this will be your experience. Most people can handle the meds without many problems or side effects. More often than not, the good benefits outshine the few side effects you may feel. Do not let fear be the only reason you do not engage in this opportunity of a lifetime.

A few side effects for mental medications include:

- Nausea
- Sleep difficulties
- Diarrhea
- Agitation (feeling jittery)
- Rash
- Sexual problems

- Headache
- Loss of appetite
- Insomnia
- Dry mouth
- Constipation
- Weight gain or loss
- Bladder problems
- Blurred vision
- Drowsiness
- Upset stomach
- Dizziness
- Weakness
- Trembling, twitching, or unusual muscle movements

Workbook Questions:

1. Should you take medications, antidepressants, or pain pills? Do you trust your body's amazing abilities to use them and still function normally? How long should you try them? How will you safely stop with the help of your medical team?

2. Will I be living in a chemical straightjacket and have to be on pills and therapies the rest of my life? Why do I think this? What kind of trust-building activities can I engage in to change my thinking?

3. Do you believe your body can naturally produce its own feel-good chemicals? What therapies are you willing to engage in?

4. What physical activities are you willing to try to help your body's ability to produce natural well-being chemicals?

5. What stops you from doing different behaviors to get different emotional results? Do you believe you can do this? How will you start?

6. What will it take for you to be willing to see if any side effects are worth the real and valid peace of mind you might get from taking certain medications? What are you willing to do to handle discomforts until you adjust?

7. Are you expecting your medications to replace your responsibilities of living life on life's terms? What can you do to take more, safe responsibilities? To engage more?

8. In what ways do you think pills magically make you feel better? Why is that a false happiness? What will it take for you to accept good feelings and work with where you are right here and now? This precious moment is all you get to be happy —what is stopping you? Did that ever have anything to do with taking medications?

9. Are you willing to take medications and do the hard work to change your thinking about being balanced and adjusting to life?

10. Are you willing to take medications when you are not feeling well? Do you understand that they need to be in your system and saturate your body with a stable amount in order to do the job correctly? Are you using medications the same way that you used drugs, alcohol, and/or emotions as a vehicle to act outwardly or inwardly?

11. When we get relief from discomfort, we want to grab the steering wheel of life back into our hands and stop taking medications. We think we have life under control again. Are you willing to try your medications for at least a year or two, and slowly learn and adapt, accept what you can, and change behaviors where necessary? Explain how you will do this. How will you stay accountable?

12. Depression and stress actually destroy connections between your nerve cells. We create a well-worn rut in our brains and with our depression have bypassed our body's ability stop skipping the record. Are you willing to take a leap of faith, step into the groundless unknown and move into new frontier? How will you do this? What will it take for you to trust and develop safe ways to engage in your new lifestyle?

13. Why do you take medications? Are you OK and willing to accept your reasons? Do you believe being on medication is a lifetime commitment? Can you stop if you want to? Why or why not?

14. Why do you believe your own body cannot naturally produce the chemicals the medications provide? Do you believe you cannot get support from a group of your constituents to help you cope in place of medications? Explain.

15. What do you like about taking your medications? In what ways do they help you? Your job, spiritual life, partnership, your community?

16. Do you use medications so you do not have to deal with pain, depression, anger, relationships, sex, intimacy, coping, survival, mental health, and physical illnesses that are life-threatening?

Mental-Health System: Navigating the Quagmire

Be prepared to suspend all of your beliefs and take the ride of your lives.

The mental-health system is imperfect and hard to navigate. There is barely help for those who can afford it and little or none for those who cannot. There is no cure or straight path for any mental-health diagnosis.

Each person must become the expert in their own lives and needs. This takes years of patience, practice, and lots of willingness to develop community with like-minded people, counselors, and proper medical diagnostics. There must also be a willingness to try different medications until something works.

Then it's time to start working with the brain to develop an inner dialogue and how to best move forward with what the person believes and what they would like to happen.

I found my own inner journey most helpful in the beginning, with medications to slow me down enough to be able to work slowly and mindfully, and to actively listen and comprehend new ideas.

I advocated for and demonstrated with a healthy support group to get off my medications and trust my new neural elasticity. I began with small but measurable, timely, and observable tasks. As I grew more capable, I took on more complex and abstract concepts, building and learning.

I am now an expert and capable of helping others through the wisdom I have gained. As I write this, it is 15 years later. Getting through the system and using it as the tool it is meant to be is the opportunity of a lifetime — not a quick-fix bandage over an expansive problem.

Suspend your belief systems about diagnoses, disease and cures. Be willing to listen and learn. Without attachment, you are more likely to be a universal observer in your life. It is the opportunity of a lifetime to be patient and keep on track with a longer view. Be willing to listen to multiple truths about various drugs, opinions, and studies. The truth is that everyone responds to drugs with learning curves and has a different brain chemistry.

Know thy self — you have all the answers within. Einstein said we cannot solve today's problems with the same mental environments that created them. He also said without putting energy into the equation, there won't be motion out of our lives. $E=Mc^2$.

With a beginner's mind, we take the leap. Teachable, flexible, open, willing; that is how we trust that the more we know, the less we know, and hold the paradox of both truths.

First we must admit we have a problem and be willing to seek help. Seeking help involves a lot of patience and surrendering what we believed to be true our entire lives. We must surrender that we have something diagnosable in our behavior; we must surrender that the first diagnosis will be made quickly, so medications can be started to get our minds and bodies in a willing and safe state for ourselves and others.

The next step is to figure out what kind of help we will receive. Will we see therapists, psychologists, psychiatrists? Can we afford them? Will we go to AA or NA meetings or whatever meetings are appropriate for us?

There are many free communities that support each other. Hope is not lost. Will we go to a recovery facility, stay in-house or use their day-treatment programs to best work our program? We must decide whether we can keep our jobs and what the stigma of recovery is at our workplace. There may be too much stigma attached, and then there's the risk of losing our jobs if they found out we have drug or alcohol problems. We may have loved ones or family members who will be conflicted and worried about the stigma and their own place in the community.

All along this path, we come to terms with the fact that we no longer have complete control over our lives. We temporarily commit to being in a fluid state of mind. We will be called many things that we are not completely in agreement with.

We have the ability to hold many truths at once. We realize there is no harm in learning about the hundred things that could improve our lives and give us more freedom than we have ever had by illuminating our minds with new possibilities. It will feel strange to have a group of people who know our issues and will call us on our stuff when we are being willful and stubborn. We may be in denial about our diagnoses and get to demonstrate and advocate for our recovery, showing our new skills and weaknesses.

All of this is a moving target that we learn to manage. We will keep learning more and making daily adjustments. Soon we will walk over the burning coals of our lives without getting burned.

If you are a poor person with no funds, you still have rights. However, you must be willing to really go after your recovery and make extraordinary efforts to keep the opportunity going. You must do anything and everything to put your recovery first. Everything else will fall into line. For example, you may have to prove that, although you have made money and taken care of yourself in the past, you need Supplemental Security Income (SSI) during your recovery.

I was a person under the radar of society. I had to prove I was still alive and prove my identity. I had to prove that, although I had serious mental-health issues, medical problems and drug addictions, I had no paper trail with their system. I had always worked under the radar with no proof of my work. I was a John Doe who had to prove my issues to get help.

For a homeless person, it is a daunting task. I had to get a state ID. I also had to get my birth certificate from another state. I had to prove my identity to hospital officials, and I had to get an SSI card re-issued to prove I was me. How do you do all that with no money and no resources?

Once you get into the system, you must start your journey to prove why you, of all the homeless people in the city, should receive help. Why should they take a chance on a flight risk who may disappear back into the abyss?

After being on SSI for four years, I then had to demonstrate my functionality for two years to get off my medications. I also had to prove I could hold the job I had landed at Goodwill. Finally, I had to start accepting that, by working and getting off SSI, I would make about the same amount of money. But I also gained self-respect, autonomy, and the start of the long, hard journey toward being a thriving member of society.

Workbook Questions:

1. How will you get set up to see a therapist? How will you pay for your visit?

2. Will you use an emergency room or suicide hotline to get immediate help?

3. How will you get into a program that helps those with drug addiction, alcoholism, and mental-health issues?

4. What paper trail do you have from past mental-health breakdowns?

5. What is the purpose of getting a diagnosis? What will you do with it when you get one? How will you learn to use the diagnosis as a strength?

6. Do you need to get on SSI? Why? What is the benefit?

7. Do you have insurance to cover medical bills? How do you process the stigma at work about having a mental illness? Do you feel vulnerable working in a business that helps people with mental illness? What conflict do you feel between what you need and where you work?

8. How have anger and violence in your past affected your mental health? What consequences have you endured – imprisonment, fines, courts? How can you become willing to work on these issues and make them a priority, so your support group and medical professionals do not suffer because of your "unfinished business" with anger?

9. What are your thoughts about taking medications? What experience have you had in the past? How did they help you maneuver through your situation?

10. How did you self-medicate with acting-out behaviors, drugs, and/or alcohol? How did these help you? Explain.

11. Do you trust doctors and the medical profession? What are your feelings? Do you think they have all the answers for your life? What are you willing to do to help?

12. What will it take for you to connect with others who have the same diagnosis as you? What would be the benefit of having combined knowledge from your peers? How could you use it? What would it take for you to trust their experience to help you with your diagnosis?

13. How can you become willing to hear what a medical team thinks of you, when they judge you with a diagnosis? Are you willing to process this frustration without ending up like you have a mental-health straightjacket that follows you?

14. What are your plans for the future to live as normal and prosperous as you can? How will you demonstrate and advocate for your right to that prosperous life?

15. What lengths are you willing to go to in order to get your head squared on your shoulders, get a job, get a home, and feel as normal as you can?

16. Are you willing to go to Alcoholics Anonymous meetings, or Debtors Anonymous, or Sex and Love Addicts Anonymous, if any of them are appropriate? There are support groups for almost everything we do as a culture. Are you ready to get help as a safety measure?

17. Will you consider being full-measured and demonstrating and advocating to get help within the system? When you become healthy, will you take time to be responsible with your gift of sobriety and get into a maintenance mode of safety for all caregivers and loved ones?

Mindfulness: An Awakened Mind Can Access Emotional Intelligence

Your future is spotless, unwritten, unscathed. The slate is clean. Write what you want, and it becomes real. Things happen; life shows up. Disasters are coming, and crises will arise. It's what you do with those challenges and opportunities that makes the difference.

You ultimately fill your future through your choices. We attract most of what happens to us in life by the way we react when things happen. We want to learn how to dance with life, rather than be defensive and react. Reaction is a muscle memory that involves the reptile part of our brain used for fighting, feeding, sleeping, and making babies. We overreact to compensate for not wanting to feel what is happening. We try to protect ourselves from having to process anything that requires us to do critical thinking and accept what is happening.

Most people live in a world of diminished returns, where they react to events. It creates "the sky is falling" thinking. Then something else goes wrong to reinforce that mentality. It feels like the world is in collusion or conspiracy against us.

Mindfulness is all about the space between our thoughts – that nano-second before we react, or about a second and a half between our thought and our action. That's how long it takes before we make a wrong move or say something we regret.

We want to make that space before we react neutral for as long as we can, until we develop how to use our wisdom. We learn how to think things completely through while, getting help from our support groups and responding with emotional intelligence.

It starts with our breath. We practice becoming aligned with our thoughts and breaths, working together to calm our spirits and brains. I will suggest some ideas, and you may find your own way of doing what you need for self-care with a community that supports your needs.

So we get into a comfortable position, in a place where we can bring our minds to attention. We observe our breathing and how we feel in our bodies. We observe but don't react to our thoughts. Breathe in and slowly breathe out, over and over.

At first, we simply try to notice breathing in and out. As we do this, we notice our thoughts moving fast, wanting to keep us distracted. Notice them, and let them go. Try not to attach. Our thoughts are like clouds, and they will move past us. It is our attachment to our thoughts that causes us suffering. We hold onto them, ruminate and create tape loops of resentments.

We observe how we feel in our bodies, where we are holding tension, and let go of that as much as we can. We try slowing down our thoughts by sitting in a meditative position on the floor or in a chair. There are as many ways to meditate as there are people. Explore and find what works.

Ways to Access Mindful, Emotional Intelligence

How we respond to life on life's terms improves when we access our emotional intelligence. Let's take a look at our lives and how strong the familial bonds and work relationships are. Accessing this intention and aspiration is a testament of skills.

We attract negative consequences as a result of trying to persuade people that life is against us. But life happens — that's all. We start right here and now to make better choices based upon this precious moment and focus on what can happen with solution-focused therapies.

Accessing mindful, emotional intelligence is all about how we relate and respond with our experiences. Be genuine, authentic, approachable and trustworthy with "diametrically opposed feelings" in ourselves and others.

- Identify what triggers the threat toward stability and mental health. Notice the feelings as an observer, not a person reacting. Differentiate the two states of being.

- Use skillful means to seek emotional safety for all parties. Always be a responsible agent of peaceful change as you evoke self-change thoughts in others.

- Understand the true nature of feelings and emotions, and move into solution-focused coping mechanisms for change.

- Take accountability and use healthy boundaries to keep everyone on their sides of the street.

- Relieve stress and create equity by effective communication skills. See beyond problems and personal insults, and look for truth through active listening. Make it about the speaker, not you.

- Empathize and have compassion without emotional enmeshing or selective hearing.

- Be preventative in nature. Restore order and take the heat out of emotionally escalating moments.

- Always take the "longer view." Tomorrow is another opportunity to gently repeat and make clear our reasons and views. Pick your battles, and don't fight at all, if it can be helped.

- Know thy self, and others will know you more clearly. Be transparent and live with courageous, fearless, and limitless thinking.

- Be able to laugh at any situation and begin healing with humor. Keep everything in perspective. "This is just a bump in the road, not the end of the road."

- Speak in a way that others can hear you to better get your needs met.

- Invest and value relationships with long-lasting tenets of mutually satisfying, happy and healthy emotional outcomes.

- Be forgiving and let go of the reasons for conflict that do not apply to the present moment. By forgiving, the negative messages that cloud thoughts are set free, and poison is released to create a clear and present state of abilities.

- Be an expert on reasons that create and contribute to anger, and teach others how to activate those life-saving principles.

- Recognize stress and immediately prepare the mind and body to navigate skillfully through crises and/or disasters.

- Develop resilience to muscle memory impulses. Visualize yourself being safe and protected. You deserve, belong and have a right to happiness. Visualize that as abundance you can freely give to others. There is enough love, patience, trust and willingness for everyone.

- Be culturally appropriate with social cues. Understand stigma and cultural competency. Be fluid in diverse populations and inclusive of everyone's emotions and thoughts. Develop a sense of safety and belonging.

- Be a complete person taking mindful care of your biological, social, physical, monetary and spiritual needs.

- Do extreme self-care when dealing with emotionally disturbing situations. Stay in the moment, and deal with what you can to create new opportunities at that time.

- Be willing to agree to disagree. The war is over in your mind, if you are willing to let go. We all make mistakes and need to be forgiven to start again with fresh, clean intentions and peaceful resolutions. Forgive yourself, and forgive others.

- Know your race or class distortions, and work on your weakness in those areas.

- Lastly, don't come with a lot of ammo to a confrontation. Sit back, and let others spin out of control, if they must, so you can be the sane party. Your partner can come back into the room with safety and understanding, instead of blame and righteousness.

Workbook Questions:

1. How do you bring your ideas to the table and accept what others hold as truth without personalizing or feeling judged?

2. In what ways do you facilitate empowering others at work as they go through the learning curve and develop their personal ambivalence about new challenges and thought-provoking self-change thoughts?

3. In what ways do you do personal work to take care of yourself spiritually, physically, mentally, and biologically?

4. What are your triggers? What makes you feel like an exposed nerve? What takes you into a timeless, hopeless feeling? What do you do when you notice that vulnerable feeling?

5. Do people look to you for collaborative team-building ideas that benefit your work team?

6. Are you comfortable working and collaborating with other cultures or people with disabilities?

7. How does anger influence what your response will be with others who are also angry?

8. In your opinion, what is unforgiveable? Why? What would it take to create a new way of looking at your brittle thoughts?

9. How do you make more space between your thoughts before you impulsively blurt out something you will regret for a long time?

10. How do you respond to others when you are stressed and in fatal peril? How do you make space and seek safety for both parties?

11. How do you meditate, pray, exercise, or use humor in staying approachable about emotionally escalating events?

12. Why are you a safe negotiator? Can people trust that you will hold their confidence and thoughts in a safe place?

13. How do you hold your loved ones, work colleagues and families as "emotional hostages?"

Neutrality: Staying in the Middle

We attach to things that create safety – or sometimes to things that compromise our safety. Our attachments cause us to resist listening to another's experience.

We fear we will have safety taken away and that our way of life will not be validated. Sometimes after having something for so long, we may feel we deserve more. We feel we are entitled to our privilege at the expense of others' beliefs, races, causes, etc., even when it is unfair. Even when we are spiraling with this out-of-control thinking, we believe we are righteous in our cause.

Tolerance without bias creates safety, patience, compassion and empathy for others. Sometimes when we allow ourselves to say the craziest things in our minds, we are surprised to learn that we do not believe everything we think. It helps to be around safe people we trust who can handle that phenomenon. This unrefined chaos is where much change occurs. It creates our moral compass. Our truth is always changing as we learn and adapt, co-create and advocate for our new beliefs born from past truths.

If we stay non-biased in our opinions, we can be trusted servants for others. People who distrust will judge us for our neutral stance, and they will judge others for their beliefs and opinions. It is our choice not to defend or spin out with concretized thinking. If we hold that hallowed, groundless space, there is safety for all.

People can get emotionally escalated. They can also realize when they have chosen the mob mentality. They can come back from the far left or right and be grateful for their journey to and from the edge of extreme beliefs. It is healthy for others to make this journey, and they will have more compassion for those who need to take escalating choices on subjects close to their hearts.

We can simply observe life's ups and downs and attach to neither the good or bad; just hold the middle ground and be the universal observer. As observers, we listen and get stimulated and swayed by arguments for and against. We hold the space between and create a safe place for everyone. As we feel our mind getting pushed to and fro, we suspend attachment and let go. By these actions, we are able to feel groundless without attachment, to become comfortable with uncertainty, to hold the paradox of both truths, and create safe space for everyone to contemplate their truths.

By living with discernment and ambivalence, we hold a healthy tension of diametrically opposed truths. We are in the master's course when we work with others and their process of dismantling attachments and old truths that do not work or fit into their lifestyles. We get to watch as they change. We do not change others but create a safe place for change to occur. It's a choice.

Being a peacekeeper requires the ability to have your own truth and not defend it. Keeping an open forum for change to occur, we agree to disagree. That is one of our options. If everyone thought the same way, we would have no diversity. When people believe they are unheard and suffering, they sometimes they come across as unskillful and tactless. They might be loud and have a direct, aggressive agenda.

The other-sided belief system will respond in kind, if they feel their safety is challenged. We can learn to communicate in a way that others can hear us. This is our craft; we empower others because we are defenders of multiple truths and contradictory views. We are not weak, even though it appears we have no attachment to either agenda. We become freedom advocates in the truest sense. This is real democracy.

Workbook Questions:

1. Explain how you watch news and what happens when you hear something that goes against the grain of your belief system.
2. Do you believe it is your duty to actively advocate for others who suffer from the inequities in our society?
3. What can you be neutral about? The weather? Sports?
4. Does your partner feel safe talking to you about bills, food, driving, and/or sex? If not, why not?
5. When do you find yourself getting righteous and finding fault with others' thinking processes?
6. How do you feel about Republicans and Democrats?
7. How do you feel about Palestinians losing their homes to Israel?
8. How do you feel about abortion?
9. What religious views do you hold that make others feel "less than" and sense the wrath of your deity's decrees?
10. What do you know about non-violent communication?
11. Are you a safe person for others to have difficult conversations with about escalated topics?
12. Do you feel as if you lead two lives with your belief system? Do you feel fraudulent with your identity?
13. In your life's experience, how do you hold two truths? Which subjects come to mind?
14. Do you believe in feminism? Do you believe in it if it means giving up the entitled-male system?
15. What are your triggers that keep you feeling stuck and untrustworthy?
16. What issues do you hold onto for the safety of your race or culture?
17. What core belief systems keep you from hearing another's truth?
18. Do you believe if we educated poor people, they would be a problem to society? Would they get "too smart"?
19. Explain how you are tolerant of others lifestyles. What is your opinion about kids wearing pants sagging below their waist, or clothing that may be different than yours?
20. Why is it important to you to find solutions, fix people's problems and give them strategies to live? How does that stop them from coming to their own conclusions about which way to go and what to choose for their own lives?

Objectifying Others and Being Objectified

To objectify someone is to take away their humanity and treat them as if they are an object.

We generally do not treat objects as if they have feelings.

Government officials, prison guards, womanizers, employers, killers, soldiers — all have to find that place in them that objectifies others to keep and maintain their feelings. They live inside their idea of law and order and the ability to minimize damages done to another.

Racists call persons of color dehumanizing names and segregate them to live in separate areas. Racists say, "They are different from us." Then racists distance themselves from the people they objectify and blame them for creating misery. Once we start name-calling, it's easy to tolerate or join a mob mentality – or to imprison a whole population of, for example, young men of color in California. One in 27 black males will be incarcerated before reaching age 21.

Depersonalizing another human makes them into something easily ignored or disposable. In wartime, it makes other populations easier to kill. When we objectify and dehumanize Muslims, it makes it easier for us to kill them.

Suddenly, parents and children of another culture are killed, leading others to make self-righteous assumptions that they are somehow connected to the beliefs of less than 1 percent of any culture. This is called objectifying.

Consider this: Humans who have empathy for each other care about what happens to others and have their best interests in mind. When they see that another is hurting, they are capable of feeling a similar experience.

In comedy routines, people are objectified, and vulgarity is used to desensitize us as people are dehumanized. Unfairness is put into a sometimes humorous platform at the expense of the party being ridiculed.

It's easy to find things "wrong" with different people and cultures. That makes it easier to dismiss shame-based ideals and values that we do not feel obliged to contribute to the other party's well-being. If we look for something wrong, we are bound to find it in excess. If we look for something similar to other cultures, we are also likely to find that.

When we are in a crowd of our peers, we can openly dislike, vilify, chastise, and be unkind as a group. We create a vigilante-type justice where we openly become moral judges and juries and execute our beliefs on another. Think of it like our political process: We supposedly send our best people to represent our beliefs, but listen to them brow-beat and bash each other and watch them play dirty tricks and fling slanderous accusations to win the vote. It is a precarious way for a democracy to function.

Once we objectify people based on race, it is easier to objectify others as well – seniors, persons with disabilities, persons without homes, persons with addictions, persons of other genders or sexual preferences — the list can be endless.

For example, let's look at a homeless person who stands on a corner at a busy intersection.

We are in the safety of our car, annoyed that we had to stop at all. Our windows are rolled up and the air conditioner is blasting. We see a dirty, disheveled person holding a sign, coming close to our window. What thoughts flash through our minds?

Most likely, we feel discomfort that the person wants something from us. We don't like them that close. They are probably on drugs, we presume. We consider the possibility that they are going to hurt us. We don't want to give them money — how dare they ask? They will probably buy alcohol and drugs. We wish the light would turn green so we could just go.

That scenario is an objectification we do daily.

We can replace the person or situation and recreate the scene with anybody — peers, co-workers, church people, sales people, people who serve our food, our spouses, our children. The possibilities are endless.

Let's talk about the guilt of not helping and how that sickness permeates our society of immediacy.

The entire idea behind objectifying is to put our needs above someone else's. We prioritize our hierarchy of needs and can't be bothered to be concerned about what or who is not in our tunnel vision. As a result, our station in life is improved at the expense of another.

Military service members are a good example of treating people as if they are a tool or weapon of our mentality. Another is to deny the decision-making process for people who are elderly and can't advocate for themselves. Then there is the slave mentality that states we own someone and can do what we like with them.

Dehumanizing someone and then being able to exterminate them based upon a perceived difference of moral values is another example. Even treating people as if they are disposable financial assets, such as professional athletes or tech workers, is objectification.

If you have been objectified as a woman or a person of color, you are likely familiar with the emotions that surface such as loss of dignity, anger, fear, resentment, retaliation, and the anxiety that you will be oppressed again. You lose self-esteem and worth and might even have a victim mentality from enduring it for so long.

We all inadvertently make choices that appear to hold sway over others' lives and welfare. We become the perpetrator of change in their lives. We try to elicit self-change thoughts and sometimes we unskillfully drop the ball. This is a natural part of change.

If you are the perpetrator, here are some things you can do:

- Treat others as equals; create a sense of fairness and justice for all.
- Develop your empathetic skills and know what it is like to walk a mile in someone's shoes.
- Learn to care for what you don't value. When you care, it hurts you to hurt them.
- Learn to feel vulnerable and sensitive. Know what your triggers are. That will create empathy.
- Make alliances with people with whom you are not comfortable and learn why you have those issues. Make it about you and your learning curve.

- Don't create isolation for people who struggle with identity, cultural inclusivity and diversity.
- Work slowly and mindfully. Objectification is a concept that has gone on for generations, and it will take some real thought and time to stop it.
- If you are being objectified, here are some survival strategies:
- Hang with and get support from people who value your worth.
- Stay in situations where you get back what you invest.
- Do estimable acts to create healthy esteem.
- Create your own value and worth. Remember that what others think of us is none of our business. When we start thinking about them, we stop being authentic about ourselves.
- Find others in another culture that you get along with. Or find safe people to be with. Or develop relations with healthy people, and don't hang out with hurtful people.
- Don't bring a can of gasoline to speak with someone who is making a bonfire with your emotions. Do not consider these types of thinkers as a great investment of your valuable time on the planet.
- Don't get used to mistreatment or accept it from any institution.
- Help others who suffer like you, and you will help yourself.
- Treat bosses as if they, too, have to tie their shoes and put on their pants just like you do. Sometimes they make mistakes and have bad days too.
- Speak out when you hear things that are wrong. Become a freedom creator.
- Process your feelings about inadequacy and "less than" tendencies, and know thy self.
- Notice when you compare yourself to others and objectify yourself. Then be more forgiving of others, now that you know how much you do it.
- Don't be like a moth to a flame, trying to receive comfort from the source of your pain.

Workbook Questions:

1. What long-term loss of personal security is developed by objectifying another culture? Look at the prison system, our veterans — come up with a few more.

2. What happens when your mental system of sacrificing another's worth and value comes down upon you and you feel as if you must live in a gated community? Do you feel like the one behind bars because of the society you created or perpetuated?

3. In what ways do you minimize your behaviors toward homeless people, other races or cultures, other sexes? How do you treat your elders? Name some other ways that you objectify.

4. Which countries do you think less of? Name some nations you feel are inferior to yours. Why do you think the way you do?

5. Are there sports teams other than your favorite that you objectify and down talk to at games? How do you respond to their fans? Do you get emotional enough to shout, "Booo!" Do you want to get into a fight at a game after drinking?

6. Do you believe prisoners are "less than" people and deserve what they've got coming? Do you believe they deserve the way they were brought up and made to live in poverty? Do you believe they deserve whatever happens to them once they are in the prison system? In your mind, how much do they really deserve?

7. Do you feel strongly about abortion? Should religions be able to monitor personal choice? Explain your answer.

8. When you get pulled over by a law enforcement officer, do you feel unjustly picked out? Are all police officers unjust? Does your belief have to do with your trust issues? Explain.

9. When you see a sexy person and visualize what you would like to do with her or him, do you become a misogynist, a womanizer? What if that person was your friend or daughter — does that change how you would respond? Why or why not?

10. Do you minimize the experience of a person in a wheelchair? Do you ever speak with people with disabilities? If not, why not? Are you objectifying their existence?

11. When you see older people driving and get mad because they are driving so slowly, do you have a reaction that is like objectification? Tell me more.

12. Do you have strong feelings about cultures coming over our borders? Do you want them all to be sent back to where they came from? Explain your answers.

13. In what ways do you objectify yourself in comparison with others and their worth, status, value, and social standing? Do you treat yourself badly and feel depressed by the comparison? Tell me more.

Oppressor and Perpetrator: Healing from Causing Harm to Others

I learned from the pain and suffering I experienced as a child that if an oppressor held all the power, then I wanted to associate with the oppressor. I became what I hated most. I became what happened to me. I became the oppressor and perpetrator.

That was my position of safety, value, power, control and comfort. So I was the victim *and* the violator.

For many years I blamed others for my unhappiness, and it worked. I got a lot of comfort and sympathy — and then I got retribution and payback when I changed roles.

This happens to many children who respond to what happens to them as innocent survivors. They learn to perpetrate those behaviors on others, whether it is mental, physical or sexual. Doing so creates a sense of safety, empowerment, and control, along with societal intent passed on from generation to generation.

Ongoing violation also creates an entire group of survivors with their endless quests for being whole again and getting justice from their violators. In the case of death, the family gets retribution.

In fact, generational recidivism keeps that fraudulent way of life, hurting people who hurt people who hurt people. With the "an eye for an eye" attitude, the world could easily become blind on many levels of unfinished healing.

It doesn't matter if we were victims as children first and then learned that behavior. Our innocence was taken. We learned to violate victims whose own innocence was taken by us and now they became perpetrators of unhealthy, judicious laws that create more suffering and violent behavior behind prison walls.

Some inmates get out of prison, violate their parole, then return to prison and take it up a heinous notch with more violent ways of demeaning justice.

When will this stop? Who will admit that the system has flaws that need attention?

Education will help the most. Admitting that the part we play as a society reinforces the "eye for an eye" system that keeps both parties participating in the furious malaise of our times is a step in the right direction. Otherwise, everyone remains in fear and pain, and we keep mutual suffering in place.

There is hope in the form of working with your part in what has happened.

When we learn everything about the ways we are participants and know our part in the dualistic participation — whether willingly or surreptitiously — we are responsible for practicing extreme self-care and coming to acceptance with life on life's terms.

Disasters happen, crises happen, unfair things happen; life is not fair or just. All forms of control become corrupt; absolute control corrupts absolutely.

After years of my part in what I contributed and attracted to myself, I learned that forgiving myself for being innocent and violated was OK. I learned that instant gratification was the reward for becoming the one with the power who controlled through taking, violating, oppressing, being a predator, and perpetrating. But that quickly dissolved into me suffering as my victim suffered, and I relived that suffering for my entire life.

When I forgave the people who violated me, I cleared my psychic sack of poison and reservations I had about being completely free. I was able to accept that good and bad things will happen, but I can't live my life in a bubble. I was not going to be gagged and tied by the thoughts that plagued me, trapped inside a prison of my own making. When I realized my perpetrator responded from his own experience and upbringing and just transferred what he was taught onto me, it became easier to forgive myself.

When I began with forgiveness for my predators, I at first had to ask God to love him 'cause I couldn't. I asked my Higher Power to do the heavy lifting of forgiveness, 'cause I couldn't. Then I learned how to pray for the willingness to pray for the willingness to forgive that other suffering person, and to pray for understanding and doing the next right thing with service toward others suffering the way that person did.

I learned that if I made the aspirations that they be free of suffering and the root cause of their suffering and need to harm, then with happiness and insight they might be less likely to harm me or others in the future. I also made a living amends for my part in whatever transpired with the person who violated me.

We all have a part in everything that happens to all of us. We have a collective responsibility to move beyond our personal suffering and think about society as a whole and what we can do together to create more healing, forgiveness and education, for all of us.

As I became more skillful at forgiveness, I prayed for suffering people all over the planet who suffered as I did. I learned to aspire and intend that all beings could be free of pain and suffering along with the root of their suffering, which was usually their own thinking. At that point I learned about the master's course in forgiveness. I learned to wish that people like Hitler could be free of pain and suffering. If they were healed and healthy, they would be less likely to make others feel the pain and suffering that they themselves felt. I wished that others could have the happiness I wanted in life, so I could give my greatest contribution and share my purist abundance.

Do you want to be righteous, or do you want to strive for happiness? Do you want to be righteous, or do you want to pursue happiness and peace?

I have forgiven myself for becoming a taker of life, a subjugator of others' inherent worth, a judge, jury and executor of my painful experience who projected it onto everyone else. I forgave myself for expecting others to take care of the justice and keep meting out sympathy for my victimhood.

I do this work and service to others as my vocation. I choose to live right here in the middle — groundless, vulnerable, and empowered with grace and abundance.

Workbook Questions:

1. In what ways have you oppressed family, friends, and positions of power?

2. In what ways have you perpetrated suffering onto others? Were they of another race, ethnicity, age, ability or gender than you?

3. Were you caught and persecuted for your crimes? Did the social impact of your act equal the response you were given as punishment? Explain.

4. Have you moved on from this type of behavior? If not, why not? What types of things do you do now that are different?

5. Have you made amends and asked for forgiveness from your victims? If not, why not? If so, what was their response? If you haven't tried, what are you afraid of?

6. Do you still cling to victimhood and all the benefits you receive from playing that role? What behaviors still work? Are you still angry, unresolved, unhealed, too damaged, resentful and angry? Which punishments would you deliver to your oppressor? Do you feel righteous? Explain.

7. In what ways does your spirituality come into play with oppressing others of another faith? In what ways do you perpetrate fraudulent, unfairness – bargaining deity against deity? Belief against belief? What similarities do you find with other religions and spiritual beliefs?

8. Were you violated as a child? Was your innocence taken away? If so, in what ways does that affect your thinking today? Do you still suffer from an act done many years ago? If yes, then what will it take for you to feel better? Do you believe that if the person was caught that their punishment should be the same as what they did to you? Do you believe that they are capable of change and becoming a trustworthy person of value in the community? What are your thoughts and fears about that?

9. What has worked for you to heal from your transgressions done to others?

10. Do you have any service you do for others to help make up the damage you inflicted on society?

11. Is the following statement true for you? "I would rather work with someone who knows himself and admits he does these acts than ramble on with someone who is blaming another for his malaise." Explain your answer.

Original Diagnosis

However you have been labeled or diagnosed, whether you were taken into custody when you were out of control or something less severe, use that as a starting point toward recovering your best self. People are not their diagnoses. Labels are a way to clarify where to begin toward healthy ideals.

Don't let people treat your behavior as psychologically abnormal or unhealthy. Don't do that to yourself. You are a complicated person living in a hectic and unpredictable world. You are a survivor who made it with what you knew how to do in the past. We honor that it worked for you so far. Now is the opportunity to make healthier choices based upon what you are learning about your dis-ease.

A diagnosis is a beginning to get you started on the journey of a lifetime. It's like playing "Whack-a-Mole." New character defects arise, and old ones come back to visit from time to time. It's a milestone. Mark it to start your accountable, measurable and observable journey of discovery. I lived undiagnosed until I was 42 years old. I had diagnosed myself as "double-psychotic, paranoid and schizophrenic." Then I was diagnosed by professionals as "bi-polar manic depressive with psychotic features." I was amazed at how on target they were with their diagnostic tools.

The official diagnosis was my beginning. I learned many other ways to do things. I was dysfunctional, and at first, my efforts seemed utterly hopeless and futile. That is a common experience for most of us. We want to figure out the fastest ways to get better; cut corners on how to excel, and catch up on as much lost time as we can so we can finally be normal and balanced people.

The truth is, we can be only here and now in this moment. If we truly feel what we are feeling, it will pass if we let go of our attachments and trust the process of healing. Healing has its own time and way of working out what's best for us.

Once we have worked through all the components of our original diagnosis, we notice there is a tractor-trailer load of character defects that lead us to our mental health and other related addictions. That is what this book is all about. If you do the work, you will unravel all those behaviors and engender newer, healthier ways to cope and be skillful.

Keep your eyes on the prize; take the longer view; be willing to work on getting better for the rest of your life. If you make a five-year plan, you are more likely to finish everything you started out to achieve. Persistence and stick-to-it-iveness are more common paths to wisdom and success than a high IQ.

You may start out by being an angry, violent person, or a drunk, or a drug addict, or a sex addict. It doesn't matter where you begin. Know that others have gone before you; you are not alone. You are safe and protected. There is a path to follow.

I am now a healed person in recovery. But I still have the propensity for my past dis-ease. I know that if I do the work to keep my world intact, I am more likely to make it through the occasional hardships of living life on life's terms.

Workbook Questions:

1. If you haven't been diagnosed yet, what is your best thinking about what your diagnosis is? Explain in detail how this affects you in social circles, societal expressions, jobs, and spiritual opportunities.

2. What stigma do you have from your diagnosis that makes you feel like you are wearing a badge of shame?

3. In what ways do you use your diagnosis to take it easy and not participate because you have "such-and-such diagnosis," and this is used as a life sentence, instead of an opportunity to change your life?

4. How does your culture view your dis-ease? Does it seem like there is an epidemic of "Flavor of the Month" diagnoses going on? How does this frustrate you?

5. How do you hide evidence of your diagnosis but have selective places where you choose to reveal what is truly going on with your life?

6. What diagnosis have you overcome? Broken bones, cancer, liver problems, colds, mental-health issues? Explain. How can you use what you learned from those experiences? Include them with your diagnosis.

7. How can you use your inner wisdom to come from a healthy place with abilities and strength-based thinking toward your betterment with your diagnosis?

8. Do you think it's glamorous to have a manic-depressive (bipolar) diagnosis because so many famous and creative people have endured the same diagnosis?

9. What can you do today to work in a positive way toward making your life different and move above and beyond your present circumstances?

10. Who does your support group consist of? Is there a therapist? Name the people who help you in the professional arena.

11. Do you hang around successful people who made peace with their diagnosis and seemed to have moved beyond their former way of life? How did they do it? What positive aspects do you get from these people?

12. In what ways can you help others who struggle with the same problems that you have had in the past? What stops you from helping yourself by giving service to others?

Overwhelming Debt and Spiritual Ecology

Are you in psychic debt? Do you draw more from your brain in worry, pain and blame than you do in healthy choices and fulfillment? Do you worry more about what could happen but almost never does?

We spend so much time resisting what is that we forget to use the opportunity as a stepping stone to a bright future of overcoming all obstacles. We invest all of our energy in the perceived wrong we believe was done to us. It happens to everyone on the planet, sometimes daily. Why do we choose to suffer? It is like we speak into a narcissistic mirror that parrots our perceived wrongs back to us. We focus on the perceived wrongs, instead of seeking resolution and healing.

Spiritual debt and financial debt have much in common. Financially speaking, if you do not have credit, you know how hard it is to establish yourself in this society. If you've lost your credit, you know the shame and humiliation that goes with it. If you are in extreme debt, you know that credit won't help you, because high interest rates would exponentially increase any debt you have.

The final obstacles I faced in my recovery were failure to thrive, fear of success, and fear of abundance. Even if you suddenly become rich, money does not fix all of your problems. Let's say a young athlete signs a contract paying millions of dollars per year. Society wonders how this person could spend it all and end up broke years later. Many people were never educated about how to handle finances and successfully play the game of capitalism.

I come from a hard-working family that sometimes barely got by. I felt guilty for resting. Once I grew up, I thought I had to outwork everyone and make them feel like they were not enough. I believed if they lived in fear that I would take their job next, then I was doing things right. The truth is, I always looked like I was doing something, even though not much was getting done. I came up with a few sayings, such as, "Can't you see I've been working by the mess I've made?"

Being a workaholic and a speed addict, I would work for days without resting, compromising my mental and physical health and creating a psychotic nightmare for employers and friends. I was too busy to take care of things like rent and bills. Instead, I would spend that money on sex, drugs, and rock and roll.

I would never take vacations or time off, so I would be so frazzled that I would eventually pass out from exhaustion or be too drunk to make it to work on Mondays. I felt like I deserved these times off because I never rested properly. I was an entitled and privileged American and thought that I deserved well-being without doing anything in particular to achieve it. I would work, no matter how physically bad I felt with a cold or injury. As a workaholic, I based my very worth as a human solely upon my ability to work. Besides, I was living beyond my means, paycheck to paycheck, so I couldn't afford to stop working.

I was raised with the illusion that credit was something you initially worked hard for, so you could then proceed to spend beyond your means until you max out your debt load. This was how I believed people achieved that capitalist lure of "having it all." That, in turn, creates the pressure of owing payments and being hounded by credit companies. Inevitably, I stopped answering my phone to avoid collection agencies calling hourly. I also did not listen to my parents' warnings about the IRS, who also were hunting me down. This creates a psychic PTSD of struggling behaviors, and it seems insurmountable.

Even when people face bankruptcy, they sometimes claw their way out, only to get back into debt again. This is when debt becomes a bona fide addiction. It is what all consumerism is about. We are conditioned to buy things to make ourselves feel better. We see ads about expensive items, and we become conditioned like Pavlov's dogs. These ads tell us we are entitled to have these things. Better yet, we should buy the car for our partners or children – *they* deserve it. The message then becomes that we are failing if we don't provide it to them. The ads say, "You deserve this for all your hard work. Reward yourself now. Just buy this product, and you will feel better instantly." They make it so easy to fall into the money trap.

Whether poor or rich, many people fall into this cycle of taking their debt to the maximum. The consequences are stress, pressure and depression. If you follow this cycle, then no matter how much money you attain, you will always increase your debt accordingly and need more. But don't worry, you still will have our capitalist culture selling you the delusion that debt is wealth. The message comes straight from the top. As I write this in 2020, our president reportedly has hundreds of millions of dollars of debt. He refuses to disclose his financial records, and he so far has not had to answer to anyone. If our leader is doing this, how long until others rebel? The old adage should read, "The rich get richer and deeper in debt and the poor get poorer and will be born into capitalist servitude."

The U.S. comprises about 4 percent of the world population, but we use roughly 24 percent of all the resources and energy on the planet. Others suffer and live with less, and we believe we deserve more and can never be satisfied. More, more, more. Just like with addiction, "One is too many, and a thousand is never enough."

Our capitalist nation was built upon the idea of taking all you can and leaving scraps for the future generations. Our country has robbed developing countries of their wealth by hanging the golden carrot of support and resources in the form of loans and business that seemingly will improve their way of life. Then, when they inevitably cannot pay us back, we take their water and mineral rights. We then install international corporations that support the International Monetary Fund. In cases like Nestle, based in Switzerland, and our own diversified ownership of Coca-Cola, we own and use the resources of impoverished peoples, only to deepen their hardship. In one community in Mexico, Coca-Cola takes most of their water, forcing the impoverished residents to buy either expensive bottled water or much cheaper Coca-Cola, leading to skyrocketing rates of deadly diabetes.

So, how does one person stop this self-destructive cycle? How do you create something out of nothing? First, stop all debt. Traditionally, this is done by filing for a formal bankruptcy, but you can also stop acquiring any new debt right now. Let everyone know what you are doing, and wait the seven years it takes to establish credit again. Start living by new rules. If you can't afford it, don't buy it. Buy only essentials that will sustain you through the challenging times. Buy only things you need, if you cannot repair what you already have.

When I started crawling out of my financial wreckage, I could not afford to order food during fellowship gatherings after Twelve Step meetings. I would see people order food and leave half of it to be taken away, because they were full and just ordering food to be social. In the beginning, I ordered only water and sat with everyone to share the social experience. Act as if you are where you want to be. Dress for social success, and courageously show you are worthy of communing with peers. Being broke is a travesty, and feeling poor goes deep in your psyche. It starts with the mindset of poverty, which you digest on a cellular level, so not only do you feel hungry, you are mentally setting yourself up for continued failure with your negative mindset. I would splurge once a week and buy myself coffee at these social gatherings, and the server would keep me topped off when she came around to serve the paying guests. I also drank a lot of water. It's good for you and fills you up with necessary fluids for your body to flourish.

To start rebuilding credit, get a debit card with a company you do not carry debt with, or sometimes even one that you do. Use this new debit card as your measurable starting point. By using your debit card and paying your bill, you create equity with the banking system, showing that you are able to save a few dollars every month consistently. This adds up with time, and you are more willing to invest in yourself. Once you keep building this new muscle memory, you may eventually be able to open a retirement account, such as a Roth IRA. Sometimes your employer provides matching funds, so you can invest even more for your future.

I spent the first few years of my financial recovery just getting used to basic survival. I got married at 50 and started investing at the highest allowable levels. My wife and I read a book called "Smart Couples Finish Rich." There are many books that provide similar information. I started investing more and more money, realizing that I was investing in the later years of my life, which were coming up quickly. As I stopped making frivolous purchases or upgrading items that perfectly met my needs, I was able to invest even more in my retirement fund. This may sound crazy, but you can do amazing things if you stop being influenced by ads telling you that you should have the latest, greatest and newest. You don't really need new products. Instead, your essential goals should begin with the ability to eat and stay housed if times get rough.

To build your housing stability, or if you need to move, start the process by getting in where you can and being responsible. You are on a seven-year plan to recapture your life. From this moment forward, you will live within your means, using government assistance when you can for supplemental income and food assistance. Use employment offices to find feasible work. Spend money for food, shelter, utilities, transportation to work (including gas and insurance, if you use a car). Find the programs that provide free or low-cost health care for people without money or health insurance.

These are just a few suggestions. There are many relatively simple books by credit experts with good financial advice. Read or borrow them for free at the public library.

In what ways are you spiritually or mentally bankrupt? With your family? With your job? Do you feel you just take, take, take? Are you the kind of person who drinks caffeine in the morning and then keeps trying to get more out of the caffeine without letting your body rest?

Everybody seems to be in a rush to get somewhere. We feel the need to get more than enough. What if we run out? As a society of takers, we often justify our means by citing our entitled and privileged society. Those who live on the bottom of the food chain are sometimes forced into crime to survive. Sometimes, almost everyone seems to be on the take. Our culture is a perpetrator of fraud, honoring only those with money or scholastic degrees. Most others are discarded as throwaways in the bigger picture of the Haves and the Have Nots. It's a fraudulent system that discards our moral compass. The people committing the biggest crimes will never be caught, because they are the corporation reps that make our stockholders win-win-win.

How can we find a place of peace from within and – person by person, one at a time – start to do the next right thing ... and then after that, the *next* right thing?

We can use time management to focus on financial and emotional abundance. We can use the same methods to spend less and less time and energy on worry, fear and procrastination. Some of us truly do have to use every moment to survive, but honestly ask yourself: When you tell someone, "I'd love to help, but I just don't have the time," is that always true? What happened to the idea that abundance is abundance for all, including you and me? American culture is ego-based. We're encouraged to focus on I, me, mine. If we all were this selfish, what would the U.S. look like? Oh, yeah – take a look at the news. It's all around us.

When I was a kid, I thought I had to steal to keep up with others. They had and I needed, so I took. I was a taker. I had poverty of the mind, and nothing can quell that hunger, when you're blinded by entitlement of this poverty thinking. You take, but you can't see that you already have the keys to the kingdom through simple willingness to use your energy wisely. Most of us are judging, comparing, negatively emoting, and creating a time loss of procrastination. Think of all the things you could get done by getting your ass in gear and letting your mind follow. Or get your mind in gear, and your ass will follow. Get going.

When you have poverty of the mind, you are spiritually bankrupt. You come from a place of less-than and accept scraps under the table, never realizing there was a banquet on top of the table and a place with your name on it, waiting for you. It was your thinking and belief in what you were told that kept you locked in this prison. I am telling you right now, you are free – free to enjoy all the little pleasures and small, virtuous moments you earn through a life of service. You can benefit from the vicarious byproducts of serendipity by having a healthy relationship with life on life's terms.

I was in a prison of my own making, bound and gagged by the mistaken beliefs that plagued me. I always felt the world owed me a living, and when I received scraps, it was not enough. I begrudgingly took them and complained the whole time of my injustice. Then, I slowly realized it was all in my head. I learned early in life to work off the books and stay outside the system. I learned to avoid the IRS, and then I got in tax trouble and had to clean up the messes I created in my life. I would have declared bankruptcy, if I owned anything of value.

Our society is based upon an idea of "good" credit. This system lets you spend money you do not have and gives you the false sense that living beyond your means is sustainable. In most cases, people become indentured to the system. It looks and performs like a system of servitude, except you are a servant to advertising, commodities, your car, your housing, your job, your education, your children's education, and to all the things you believe you will "need" next. By agreeing to the idea of almighty money as the only currency of value, you are letting go of many reasons to be loving, kind, generous, forgiving, accepting, and tolerant. This is what creates servitude into the future of debt that is unsustainable. It's a short-lived pleasure at the expense of the future of the planet.

Living within your means and being happy right here, right now, is the ultimate quest. Anything else is unreliable and will eventually let you down. Refusing to be satisfied with the here and now is the cause of all our problems. "When I get so-and-so, I will be happy." When I finally retire. When my kids are out of college. When I get that job. When the partner I want loves me. When I win the lottery. Instead of always waiting for the "when," choose to be happy now. This moment right here is the only time we can choose to be happy, no matter what irritates us or feels unfair. It is our attachment to this negative emoting that tricks and deceives our brains into projecting and transferring our unfinished experiences upon people we care about.

Which of These Behaviors Are Yours?

- Time debt
- Poverty of the mind
- Bankruptcy
- IRS debt
- Mental-health debt
- Angry and negative-emoting debt
- Spiritual debt
- Sex-seeking debt
- Food and overeating debt
- Overworking and underearning debt
- Alcohol or drug-addiction debt
- Credit debt
- Spending beyond your means
- Compulsive buying
- Low-impulse spending because it's on sale
- Buying objects to keep up with the Unsustainable Joneses
- Hoarding and clutter
- Eating out too much
- Buying coffee at Starbucks
- Buying new things when the old things "ain't broke"
- Losing your home
- Credit-card balances rising while your income is decreasing
- Paying the minimum amounts required (or less) on your accounts
- Juggling debt, such as applying for a new credit card and using cash advances from that to pay an existing card
- Having more credit cards than a winning gambler has poker chips
- Dancing near the edge of the credit limit on one or more credit cards
- Consistently charging more each month than you make in payments
- Working overtime to keep up with your credit debt
- Uncertainty about how much you owe and not much interest in finding out
- Receiving notifications about delinquent payments
- Using credit cards to buy necessities like food or gasoline

- Dipping into savings to pay monthly bills
- Hiding the true cost of purchases from others
- Signing up for every credit card that sends you an unsolicited offer
- Keeping your shameful debtor's-prison mentality a secret from everyone

Restoring Financial Sanity to Your Life

1. Determine precisely how much total debt you have. Make a list of all debtors, and begin seeking the best strategy to pay them off.

2. Debt reconciliation is an effective strategy to pay off your debt load. You may have to pay back only about 20 percent to 75 percent of your outstanding debt. Enrolling in a debt-reconciliation program may also help you lower your monthly payment. Also, the debt consultant may offer various strategies to help you reduce or eliminate creditor harassment.

3. Make sure you know all the facts about debt reconciliation before you sign up. This will help ensure that you don't get ripped off. Get everything in writing, such as monthly payments, estimated duration of the program, and approximate savings.

4. Remember that debt elimination has a temporary negative result on your credit. Seek a debt-reconciliation company that offers free credit repair. Also, they should provide free attorney consultation in case one of your creditors threatens to sue you.

5. The moment you decide to pay off your balances, your creditors will be strict in regard to your debt-elimination program. They will prohibit you from charging any more. The idea is to ensure that you won't add debt before paying them back.

6. Remember, this is just the start. Don't rest on your laurels; keep a sense of urgency.

7. Go to Workaholics Anonymous or Underearners Anonymous. They are virtually free and help people deal with the realities of getting out of debt and overcoming all the mind-sets that keep us prisoner.

Workbook Questions:

1. In what ways do you spend money and credit for things foolishly like there's no tomorrow? How do you minimize the risk while you are buying and "forget" that you have no means to pay it back? What are the tactics you use to be irresponsible instead of being mindful and thinking ahead?

2. How do you feel overpowered by advertising telling you that you need the latest, greatest gadget, when yours is working perfectly fine? Do you just keep the old product lying around? Where do you think all this garbage ends up?

3. How do you justify buying things you can't afford? Do you buy them for a loved one with immediate needs, instead of taking time to explain why this behavior may be unhealthy, codependent, or a Band-Aid over an expansive problem that took a long time developing?

4. Why do you think that driving recklessly is dangerous, but putting yourself into the nonstop stress and anxiety of credit servitude is safe and acceptable?

5. In what ways do you think white-collar crime is OK? In what ways are you willing to justify breaking the law?

6. How do you put your future, your health, and your family at risk by going into debt that you cannot pay?

7. Do you have a sick loved one (human or other), and you feel compelled to spend beyond your means for treatments that you cannot afford under any circumstances? What makes this behavior OK? How does it amplify the problem and make the sick loved one complicit with your inability to have healthy boundaries about financial solvency?

8. Name five things you can do today to start your life going in the right direction. Name five splurges you are willing to stop – for example, buying Starbucks coffee and pastries every day, going out to lunch four times a week, buying unhealthy fast food instead of preparing cheaper, healthier meals at home.

9. How can you become willing to work this hard and consistently for your own mental health and the safety of your monetary well-being? Are you willing to get help from people suffering like you via online resources or with Workaholics Anonymous, Underearners Anonymous, or other self-help groups?

Person-Oriented Recovery: Client-Centered Approach

What do you want from your recovery?

Caregivers, sponsors and counselors take what they know about you, your wants and needs right now — that is where we start, and where we review your history, past trauma and your cultural proclivities. We assess your strengths and get to the work at hand. We use your comprehension about what is going on in your life, and develop your diametrically opposed feelings of change.

This recovery machine is all about you. You are in charge – your focus, your goals, and your direction. Our job as a society is to help you stay out of what was destroying your chances of success and doing harm to yourself and others. If we can help you achieve autonomy, society will no longer support a dysfunctional approach to helping others through a welfare system instead of an empowerment model for living.

When we approach this kind of problem/opportunity as if somehow we are good and you are the one in need of help, we remove our ability and goodness gained from collaboration and empowering others. We know all people have answers within them; it is our craft to put the responsibility of eliciting self-change thoughts back into their capable hands. This move appreciates the original diagnosis but moves away from diagnosing, education and experts as the "end-all" way of helping those less capable.

Own your recovery. I have a manual — let's take a look and see what works for you. What would growth be for you today? In what ways can you achieve your personal best, and what does the path to that look like? I will walk beside you and enjoy the blossoming of your life. Hopefully you will choose to help others with the "each one teach one" mentality, and I will have worked myself out of a job. In theory.

So where would you like to start? What would you like to accomplish first? Do we begin with the ability to talk about and have a harm-reduction conversation with whatever mental-health problems or diagnosis you have? That also creates equity in our conversation.

You will use your transferrable skills of determination, resilience and person-driven direction to help us discover your independent best guess on how to move forward in your life.

The journey of a lifetime begins with one step. On a scale of 1 to 10, how do you feel about a certain subject? Let's make a pros-and-cons list to hone in on what would be helpful and most beneficial for you. What are negative impacts and barriers? What do you want to do next? Our collaboration is being led by you, unless you are in a facility and have an agenda. Then we work with both needs as part of the collaboration.

What do you bring as your individual strengths to the party of life? How can we use your powers to help you, instead of focusing only on what's wrong with you? We need to fix that mentality. We use your empowerment to move beyond uncomfortable stigmas that feel debilitating. With your abilities for recognizing your own self-change language, you become the biggest asset in your life. When you start from a place of having abilities to change, we can access those qualities more easily and not get stuck on shame or fear-based idioms. Using strength-based ability, we will examine your most favorable outcome and process your limitations with addictions and mental capacities. We can have a framework of someone capable of small, progressive successes that lead to a more skillful outcome. We will have a holistic view based upon your ability to participate.

Following are some strengths we can count on with your person-centered approach:

- Your biggest strength is that you are a survivor of all that happened to you. You still show up every day to learn how to better do life on life's terms.

- Your ability to surrender. You understand this is not personal and surrender to your spiritual support group or clergy. You are learning your limitations and developing survival skills and coping mechanisms. You have intimate knowledge about your disease of addiction and mental-health issues. You work diligently with your physical health. You recognize the importance of working with your job or community to give back and how that affects your mental health. You have a support system of friends, family, colleagues, and mental and medical assistance — and know how to best use them. You have interests and hobbies, musical and artistic talents, and/or writing competencies to keep you lively. You are developing autonomy and working with your ambivalence to change and accept who you are right now at this moment.

- Words to think about are: collaboration, partnering, teamwork, interpersonal and intrapersonal skill sets. You have the ability to create agendas, move beyond your limitations and keep moving toward new abilities until they become your comfort zones, then assess and move beyond those in a safe and wholesome manner.

- Your ability to move out of the closed system of me, me, me, and my, my, my, and I, I, I, and into, "We can do this together; it takes a whole village to raise us and we are willing to work with our village." That way of thinking is based upon the idea of resilience. We don't claim to have all the answers. We know we cannot see beyond right now. We also know that if we follow what we are doing now, we will have something new to do later. Our ability to do the next right thing after the next right thing becomes a mark of our persistence and character — which can become wisdom and genius. The connection that things will change and be hectic and unpredictable is our craft of getting comfortable with uncertainty and helps us to succeed.

Workbook Questions:

1. How do you work with your spiritual community and stay honest and clean about who you are and what you want out of the relationship? What are your fears about engaging more intimately?

2. In what ways do you count on and rely upon your addiction community, sponsorship, calls to others, service at meetings?

3. Once you have begun your personal insight toward evoking self-change thoughts, what would help you the most to achieve your goals?

4. What goals would you like to accomplish in the next few months? How would you move toward your achievements?

5. How do you work with your physical body challenges? How do you keep a good healthy mindset toward the future?

6. How do you use your mental-health facilitators and your medications toward achieving your lifetime goals?

7. Name five recovery strengths you have that are powerful motivators of change in your life.

8. How do you handle assessment and move through the contemplating stages of change? Are you immobile? Are you in acceptance? Do you use this as a guide or roadblock for your growth?

9. In what ways do you partner with your environment? How do you benefit by having that healthy relationship?

10. How can you use what you know about your diagnosis and turn each of those warning signs into evocative self-change thoughts?

11. What cultural roadblocks are before you to engage more fully in your personal recovery?

12. What bias or disbeliefs do you have about your abilities that you would like to change?

13. What do you want out of life?

14. What would you like to accomplish?

15. What are the roadblocks to your success?

16. What are the deal killers for you to continue, and how can we move into action statements and improve our thoughts about giving up?

Personalizing and Internalizing

Me, me, me, me. I, I, I, I. They did this to me. They don't understand me. When will my true worth be revealed and venerated? If only they knew who I was — I would be treated differently. Who do they think I am? How dare you do that to me? Why is it always about you?

How can anyone get their needs met when you make their story all about you?

Now that we're done talking about you, how do you *really* feel about you, you, and you?

I can't get a word in edgewise when you make everything about you. You're so busy thinking about yourself — you're all you ever think about. Do you wake up in the morning and paint a target on yourself? Does everyone seem to hit the bull's eye all day long? Does focusing on yourself lead to you playing the victim? Is your self-talk negative? Do you demote your skills and values?

Do you have hyper-grandiose, narcissistic tendencies, learned helplessness, or act as if you're OK until you break down and go ballistic?

Our mind goes where our thoughts go. If we keep acting like Velcro for bad stuff that comes into our lives and filter all we see through a negative light, we are bound to have heartache and challenges that seem personal.

The best way to get out of ourselves is to get into making life about others. When we actively listen, we will learn that there are others who suffer, are having a bad day or traversing a difficult experience.

If you are the kind of person that has unhealthy boundaries, you need to make sure you don't emotionally enmesh with others and live your life vicariously through their experiences.

A great way to learn to listen involves hearing what is going on with our friends, hearing their requests, asking permission to give advice, and offering our willingness to have healthy boundaries and not make the issues about us. Understand that their issue is their experience, and when we make it about ourselves, it takes away our ability to hold a neutral space for them to cathart about what they feel angry or confused about.

There are people who deal with conflict by looking at the situation as if it was about something they did wrong. Rather, they should listen to the other person's experience. Doing so will help them see that there is a right and proportionate amount that is their responsibility, and they can own what is theirs. Then they can work toward solutions about how to make the other person feel better, while taking care of their responsibility for their own feelings and knowing that the rest is not theirs to personalize.

Dealing with conflict feels personal, especially when it is with someone we love. We want them to feel good; we want to be the helper; we want to save them from suffering, and we want to fix them so we don't have to deal with the problem anymore.

So we take on a proportionate amount of blame, and then we respond from a blame stance and shame-based idiom, instead of hearing someone's needs and helping them to best take care of themselves with a menu of options available. When we are good listeners, we can parrot, mirror, and repeat back what the other person said, and they can hear the inside of their head through your ears. This helps them to redefine their thoughts and requests. If we make the issue about ourselves, we actually distract their thought process and derail their self-introspection.

When someone makes requests, we get to consider that they may be in a bad mood, and those requests may change. If they are mean-spirited and blaming, we can hand back what they tried to make our problem and put the burden of change into their capable hands.

When we take on what is not our emotional burden, we get into trouble. Firstly, it's not our job. Someone else's issue is not our responsibility; it takes up a lot of bandwidth that is distracting during the day. After unloading, they may move on with their day, but we are stuck in a personalizing feedback loop and making their problems all about us.

As children we were taught about good and bad. We took and personalized bad things from the messages our parents, teachers, coaches, and clergy gave to us. We were told that something was wrong with us, and we needed to make it right, feel bad about it, and not ever do it again. We were made to expect and accept punishment for our wrongs. We personalized our guilt and shame and interpreted them as something wrong with our deepest being. We believed we were broken somehow. We lost self-esteem.

All of those stifled, harmful emotions create the stressful belief that we are unredeemable. As we grow into adults, we still have that mindset, with conflict forming our critical-thinking mind.

We must have healthy boundaries. We must feel our own safety and esteem and be able to "let it fly if it does not apply." This is the price of living life on life's terms. We learned pessimism as a way of making life's issues about us doing something wrong.

Now is the perfect time for us to learn optimism. We take what we hear and know that emotions and trouble are impermanent and will pass with time; the situation at that moment is not a life sentence. We need to start living our lives as an inspiration and aspire for positive experiences to come into our being every day. If we choose to live this way and write gratitude lists of what we are happy for over our lifetimes, we will balance out and rise above the negative trend of our lives.

Life is not after us personally. Yet because our thoughts repeat old messages, we actually attract almost everything that comes to us. We need to surrender the idea that we are "that important." We must quit admiring ourselves in such a negative manner. It only manifests pain and suffering.

A phenomenon happens when people communicate their wants and needs to each other. The relationship of listening and processing and acquiring more information projects our experiences onto the other person. This is transference. Then we add the projection of our own subjective thoughts, which creates counter-transference. When this really gets going, we can wind up with four different narratives playing at once. The real me is playing "the movie inside my head" on you, and the real you is projecting "the movie inside your head" on me. This is where most of the confusion happens. What's real, and what's transference? We personalize the experience, even when it has nothing to do with us.

It helps to just sit and listen as a universal observer and not personalize or bite on anything we hear. We want to mindfully respond to the others' thinking and requests, not blurt anything out in defense. We must remember that the issue at hand is their problem and process; we are there only to help them understand how to help themselves better.

If we do have a part in the situation, we must have healthy boundaries and create equity by owning our part. We don't have to disagree just because we hear something we don't like. We can let it pass. The issue is about them, not us.

Make a five-minute rule for people who have emotionally draining problems they want to suck us into. After five minutes, we can remove ourselves from the problem. Call a friend, take a walk, do something to get our balance and esteem back. We must not write a novel in our heads about what our friend was talking about. Doing so reinforces their negative thinking. We become consumed in a chemical cascade in both of our brains.

When we are distracted from our safety rules, we are no longer living our lives autonomously as our genuine selves; we are emotionally enmeshed into the other person's problem. Feeling their anger, anxiety and stress creates a domino effect.

Solutions for Change:

1. Recognize when you are getting neurotic, and notice when you feel toxic with taking on others' lives and problems. Resist the temptation to get sucked in. Walk away. Recover yourself as best you can by doing estimable acts and practicing optimistic thought patterns.

2. When you compare yourself with others, you will feel despair. When you compete with others, at times you will feel defeat. Stop participating in a dualistic world of good/bad, right/wrong, win/lose. Hold the middle ground, and be gentle with yourself. Get used to groundlessness; get comfortable with uncertainty.

3. Take what is yours and stop there. Process a tidbit and keep it right-sized. Do not let the other person outshine the sun with the rest of their problems — you can ill-afford them. It takes a lot of energy to process both your experience and theirs. Make that precious time about them.

4. Be able to have a laugh at how absurd you feel when you get caught up in a negative feedback loop. Heal with humor. Then you will have great reason to laugh in the future because life will come up with opportunities many times a day. Choose optimism and happiness — it's your choice.

5. Stop trying to be a people-pleaser. What others think of us is none of our business. If we just keep doing the next right thing and then the next right thing, and we will do well.

6. Forgive ourselves and others for everything, one and all. We are the ones who keep carrying bags of poison around our necks. Let them go, and we will be free.

7. Let others take care of their own problems, especially if we are the cause of them and yet we are doing nothing wrong. Some people are not nice, and some are mentally ill.

8. Have a support group that knows all about us and does not respond to our bias toward a subject. We need to have objective, neutral support with people who will lovingly call us on our stuff, and show us how to do it better next time.

9. Observe ourselves feeling our stuff, and then we can get to work on estimable acts. Keep it to a five-minute time limit for the emotional woo-woo-woo, then stop – or the wave action will keep building until we have an emotional breakdown. It's our choice. We cannot afford the luxury to be depressed any longer; it is not fair to our co-workers, friends or family.

10. Do service and help others. It is the quickest solution to get out of self. Make our lives about generating hope in others. Then we will acquire hope in our own lives.

Workbook Questions:

1. In what ways can doing service for others get you out of yourself and making everything about your experience?

2. In what ways do you recognize that you are a people-pleaser? How do those things compromise your happiness and well-being? Do you need another person to be happy in order for you to be happy?

3. What are three signs that you can recognize when you are making an issue all about you again?

4. How much time do you give emotionally draining people? How about family or loved ones?

5. What learned optimism can you think of that will make your life move forward?

6. What happens when you let go of the responsibility of another's happiness? Do you feel awkward, "less than," guilty — like you could have done more?

7. How do you still internally respond to messages you were given as a child about how certain issues are your responsibility? What can you do to seek safety?

8. What kind of support group do you have? Do they commiserate with you and agree? Do they say, "Oh that's too bad"? What do you get out of this sort of non-challenging feedback?

9. What are healthy boundaries that you will consider when you are feeling triggered by another's experience?

10. How can you become a more active listener? In what ways can you really listen without taking things personally or becoming a fixer who has solutions? What would happen if you helped others to come up with the answers themselves?

Pleasure and Information-Gathering

"Wow!" and "ah-ha!" moments are made of insight and discovery. Attaching to what you like creates a strong desire to know and learn something. When we want to learn more about a certain subject, we come to it with pleasure and start the information-gathering process. We are less likely to have hang-ups about doing what we learned and more willing to accomplish new feats that meet our needs.

When we are in information-gathering mode, we have not yet attached all of our needs to attaining insight, facts and the truth. When we are in discovery mode, we become inquisitive. Our learning is heightened, and we are willing to take chances while exploring with abandon this new wonder. Our craving for awed admiration or respect is driven, and our thirst is unquenchable. We are willing to do any work to attain a new state of bliss. The bliss we feel is our brains rewarding us with chemical messages that this is good and healthy. The particular subject may not bring exact achievement, but we realize it's the journey and not the destination we enjoy.

As a caveat, remember that we try to get addiction-like pleasure out of anything that makes our brain chemistry light up like a Christmas tree. We must be careful not to have our curiosity turn into our next "flavor of the month"— a fix-all solution for all of our problems.

Think about what you want out of your life. Let's write those things down and put our energy toward them, but in a new way, instead of wanting, needing and feeling desperate to get them. Don't judge others who already have what we desire. We can examine our list in a way that explores our needs and desires. Let's look for the similarities in our lives associated with what we are after. We already have most of what we need to attain anything we want. We need to be diligent and persist in our endeavors and make them our life's aspiration. Inspirations come and go, but aspirations for our lives last long after the thrill of reaching any goal is gone.

To be healthy and well-balanced, we maintain curiosity about our surroundings so we do not get bored and complacent. We enjoy learning about our environment, what makes it tick and what we can do better to make it a more fulfilling journey. This uncertainty drives our desire to find out about unknown factors. We take a chance to improve our lot to make our lives more complete. If we are unsatisfied, we will go to any length to find something different, bigger or better to make us feel that satisfaction. The gray area we live in is the balance between the states of Needing and Wanting.

After we have taken care of our normal survival needs of shelter, food, sex, job security and the like, our brains still love to keep us alert and awake to new things; to keep alive our interest in life, liberty and the pursuit of happiness, fun, art, music, and learning. Our brains awaken our arousal system which stimulates our neurotransmitters to be alert and ready for action. We stay aroused and keep an optimal balance between performance, curiosity and discovery about our surroundings so we do not get unsatisfied and complacent. We learn and practice and then become proficient and skillful. Then, we move onto the next right thing, which keeps a healthy tension and balance of our worlds.

Our mesolimbic reward pathway interprets stimulations in our brains as good. We fulfill the wants and needs of our lives and maintain vigilance on what our moral compass thinks is good for us. Once we confuse our brains' chemical-feel-good wash with unhealthy desires that cannot be sustained, we constantly repeat much confusion, and sadness is created.

Most of the attention in our brains comes from what we are interested in. What we are interested in gets the most attention of our brains. This is also a source of the most addictive qualities in humans. Our interest starts out innocent, then becomes a thrill-seeking hunt day after day — hobbies, adrenaline-producing sports, sex, music, drugs, dangerous behaviors, driving fast, making money all fall into this category. Our brains reward us with chemicals for positive and negative wants and needs. We have nurtured those conditioned habitual responses and reinforced them time after time. We need to be careful of what we wish for. We can have almost anything — so we should make sure it is what we want. Moderation is the key to longevity.

Workbook Questions:

1. What is your motivation to move into a healthier lifestyle? What rewards do you feel in your body?

2. What questions would you come up with for a job you were interested in? How would you stay curious? Who would you ask if there are openings at a job site?

3. People will tell you almost anything if the topic is about themselves. What questions do you want answered about a certain subject? How do you best ask what you would like to know?

4. What topics are you interested in? Sports, sciences, arts, crafts, spirituality? Make a list of 10 things.

5. How can you approach your subjects of interest without getting emotionally challenged? How can you keep your search safe?

6. What unhealthy things do you do that your brain rewards you for? Anger, righteousness, overworking, sleeping, eating habits, sex addictions, crime behaviors, depression, ego-grasping?

7. What is the benefit for you to stay detached as you learn about something new? Why do you think that "flavor-of-the-month healing" is the saving technique that will change your life?

8. What does being curious look like to you? Think of a person you want to meet. What would you say to them that is appropriate and yet creates a connection for further opportunities? Are there others who have information about a subject you seek? Are you willing to be patient and not shut down after getting a few bad responses? If not, why not? What's the worst that could happen?

9. What physical activity makes you feel better after doing it? Running, music, art, sex? Name some things to see the correlation. There are no wrong answers — our brains reward us chemically for anything. We can be better monitors in our lives and get healthy rewards from our oneness of person and our realities.

10. What are the "ah-ha!" moments in your life you would like to learn more about?

11. How does desperate wanting and needing ruin your experience with others and your connections in your life? How does your low self-esteem create distance in the first minutes you meet someone?

12. What do you believe you are missing out on or were cheated out of in this life? What small steps can you take toward your dreams and goals to achieve that missing piece?

13. What qualities and similarities do you already have that will be transferrable skill sets for your new aspirations in life?

14. Do you easily get bored after starting something or coming to a roadblock? What stops you from persisting until you get what you were after?

Posifying Your Resistance

Resistance to change is a healthy part of our evolution.

Despite our resistance, some innovations create time-saving ways to get more done. Sometimes it is counter-productive when we analyze and rationalize why, where, when and how to accomplish myriad things.

In the past, our efforts were used to survive. Now we no longer need to worry as if we are in danger and our lives are in peril; we know if something is good and healthy. Yet when change is for healthy reasons, we are in danger of wasting precious time. The critic, judge and perfectionist in our minds often get in the way of following through with wholesome discipline.

We can learn to use our natural reactions, transfer the useable part of those skill sets, and move into action while incorporating new concepts of thinking and doing.

Learning bad habits was much more fun and less hassle. We enjoyed the immediacy, convenience and instant pleasure. Once we got used to feeling good quickly—whether it was eating, drinking, drugs, sex, gambling, and/or thrill-seeking—we found it hard to be normal and go through the daily humdrum of a regular life.

The trick to enjoyable change is to bring all that former excitement toward healthy goals that have the same direct and instant involvement. We replace old ideas and functionality with longer-lasting things that are more mentally sustainable.

It's normal to have adverse reactions about safety and predictability; it can produce inner turmoil and nervous responses. However, we can break patterns and think about ways we can move toward change despite feeling fear. We need to get used to being comfortable with uncertainty and to empower ourselves with groundlessness.

The universe wants us to grow, blossom, and thrive. We must develop faith beyond what we can see. Then, we must move into actions that will perpetuate change. Self-talk is a preview of what will happen. We are what we think. Make the best of every situation and enthusiastically support what you think. Everything happens in its own time—not in our time. This is where surrender and persistence make or break our commitment. We are moving into reality and away from immediacy and convenience.

If it is hard for you to consider change, just think how difficult it is for others. One way to deal with resistance is to welcome it as a teacher. Find out what fears and insights worry you and make a pros-and-cons list. If the pros win, move in small, almost imperceptible but steady steps toward the fruition of your goals. Adapting to new ideas and learning special knowledge or new, difficult, physical movement is hard won by using the learning curve of trial and error.

When using our ambivalence and pre-contemplation about eliciting self-change thoughts, we can use reasons that will benefit our lives as a motivation for change.

Look for long-lasting advantages and cost-effectiveness. Look for health benefits. Look for time-saving qualities that change will bring. Look at the spiritual peace of mind attained. Look at the social benefits of streamlining clumsy and emotionally draining behaviors. Look at the services rendered to others.

When beginning something new, create a fearless and limitless-thinking attitude and a "can-do" spirit, and know that you will make mistakes and fail in some aspects. Keep your eyes on the prize and work toward progress, not perfection.

Change is the opportunity of a lifetime, but we must be mindful to keep it simple and doable. Make sure it is easily repeated in little steps, so you can learn in bite-size increments. Make small, measurable goals. Look at the benefits of more time, happiness, peace, functionality and money—and streamline your life.

Ways to work with and effect change in your life:

Find ways to develop trust; work with those principles and build upon what works.

- Accept that innovations are part of a normal and healthy life.
- Stay flexible, honest, open, willing and teachable with a beginner's mind.
- Clarify your concerns about a certain change. Be clear about your fears.
- Work with your diametrically opposed feelings for and against reasons for change. This is your work and your responsibility. Be pro-active with a sense of urgency.
- Make sure everyone concerned is consulted about proposed changes and has a fair chance to respond with a proper amount of time to process their thoughts.
- Be willing to actively and assertively listen with an open mind, suspending your judgments for the sake of equity-building. Everyone believes what they believe—until they don't.
- Remain curious and full of discovery while listening.
- Develop strategies and coping mechanisms out of the group's decision for the greater good of the whole, and make final decisions workable.
- Accept losses and look toward rewards and benefits of teamwork and collaborative efforts.
- If something is wrong or unhealthy for you, accept this as a fact and consider self-change thoughts.
- Be willing to work for the long haul, not just for the immediate convenience of the moment. Think ahead.
- Use parts of existing work ethics and beliefs, and show how the change will manifest more benefits than cost.
- Make changes workable, timed, measurable and observable with the ability to adapt. "We are building this plane while it is flying."
- Show up as a team and agree to disagree, but own the transition and work together to make the best effort. This is where we comply and become workers toward one goal that was agreed upon. We surrender to concepts and join in to what was agreed by all.
- Stop complaining about not getting your way. You can work toward change or choose to work somewhere else. Don't let the whole group go down in your unskillful, intractable positions about what transpired. Don't become the problem—stay in the solution.

- Work respectfully toward change thoughts and leave negative emoting and biased thinking at home. Don't undermine every effort everyone has made in order to satisfy your selfish, unhappy motives.

- Work toward developing trust. Be a change agent of connective ways of healthy maneuvering toward the benefit of all.

- Be proud and say it loud—own it, be it, believe it. Change happens.

- Be a non-dualistic, trusted servant and help others who suffer from their positions, thoughts, and/or the results of change. Be understanding and work toward solution-focused ways where they can thrive and be in abundance.

- Use healthy peer pressure to make more things work toward the desired goals and aspirations of others.

- After accepting these changes in your life, dress for the change you want in life, and act as if this has already happened. Even though it may feel inauthentic, "fake it 'til you make it" until your new life becomes real. Perseverance is part of wisdom and genius—but you have to use it.

Workbook Questions:

1. In what ways do you resist changes in your life? What's behind you not accepting change that is healthy?

2. In what ways do you procrastinate from doing new and healthy behaviors that will benefit you and your loved ones? What have you done in the past that has worked? How can you use these same techniques and benefit?

3. In what ways do you take the "devil's advocate" position, disagreeing, fighting and haggling over positions on subjects? Why do you always have to be louder or right about aspects of your beliefs?

4. In what ways do you trust and love people but are unable to love and trust their decision-making processes? In what little ways can you transition to equity-building and autonomy, built upon the trust you already have for your loved ones?

5. Why are you afraid of change and doing new things? What do you have to lose? Do money, trust, business position, losing face and/or social status hold you back?

6. What bias, prejudice, or fears make you less likely to work toward change on emotional topics? What qualities would make you feel safe enough to speak your mind and listen to others?

7. How are you resistant to stopping addictions such as drinking, gambling, smoking, eating, and thrill-seeking behaviors? On your best days, what do you do to curb the flow of emotional cascades in your brain? What are you willing to consider today as change-talk about these subjects?

8. When working with others in a group, how do you feel unheard, small, and/or invisible? How can you rise above the noise and feel safe, heard and equal?

9. In what way are you a predator in a safe environment and believe that using others' weak positions is part of power and control? How do you benefit from this abuse?

10. When working with others, why do you always have to win and be right, or else you will believe you lost and others are against you? What is it about your personality that needs to create resistance with others who are having a nice day of critical thinking? Why do you feel disrespected?

11. Why are you resistant and impatient when it comes to listening to your family about issues you believe are none of their business? Why do you make it personal? In what ways can you come from a place of safety for everyone and look at how behaviors affect all? "It's a we thing, not a me thing."

12. How do you have problems with being one of a crowd and having one voice among many? What are problems you believe keep you from participating on an honest level? What would help you to feel more respected, loved, appreciated, valued, acknowledged and heard?

13. How do you come to an argument with gasoline to throw on a fire, instead of arriving with a menu of workable options and maneuvering techniques? What can you do to be a team player?

14. Are you a fighter for freedom and the underdog? Do you always have to point out the inequities of your beliefs but are unable to sit at a table and listen—without an agenda—to others' points of view? What solutions can you bring?

Positive Affirmations and Gratitude Lists

We can honor, empower, and acknowledge ourselves and our environments by timeless, mindful declarations of known truths. Look for similarities in what you desire, not differences that keep you from acquiring happiness.

To do something we are not doing now and want to have in our lives, we must take a leap of faith. By belief in the unseen, we are willing to surrender what we have now and walk gracefully over the burning coals of our lives. We aspire and desire to be our experience in this life. We make it our intention to move toward truth, no matter what our lot in life is right now.

We become extraordinary people by living within our means and doing the extra it takes to get out of our superficial thinking.

In some circles, this attitude is called, "Dress for the job you want, not the job you have." "Fake it till you make it." "Act as if." By doing those acts, we surrender our core beliefs and move into a groundless space — feeling vulnerable, yet making inroads toward our goals.

When we honor ourselves for our inherent worth and value on the planet, we do not need all the ways in which people seemingly have power over us. A good rule of thumb for autonomy is, "What others think of us is none of our business." We lead empowered lives by doing the next right thing, doing the work for work itself and not based upon the reward system that requires others to make us feel worth.

Instead of reinforcing a system of why we cannot be, have or acquire, we move into a positive owning of a position of choice and clarity.

We move beyond, "I didn't do well enough" to a sense of wealth that includes, "I deserve," "I belong," and "I have arrived." We are in a new place for the longer view of the greater good in our lives. We still must process the same old neurosis of stress, but now it is positive stress. We have made a choice to choose and accept this "poverty of our minds." We are still doing the same amount of work but have surrendered our egoistic, unsatisfied nature of not being enough.

When we affirm our new position in life over and over again, our attitude serves and reinforces our ability to accept "what is." We realize what we have no control over. We move into what *can be* in all its glory with our inherent worth as a sentient being.

I like to write my positive affirmations and gratitude lists into the future of what I truly want my experience to be. I will start off with, "I am so happy and truly grateful now that _____ has happened and my life is fulfilled." I name 20 things I am working on in my life and write them down as being done and accepting that I already have them. This positions me to work out little details I can do daily to make these things happen.

When we write a gratitude and positive affirmation list each day, we are investing in a spiritual equity bank. By our consistent perseverance, we have abundance that we can withdraw from when our spirituality is weak. There are no upper limits of this goodness.

It has been said, "You are what you want and you become what you think." It's our choices that bring unhappiness. When we are happy right here and now with what we have, we can more easily move toward our aspired goals. So we begin with gratitude for what we have. No matter how little it is, what we have now is more than enough to begin.

If we state right from the start that we are happy and love and accept ourselves exactly as we are, right now and here in this moment unconditionally, we have a pivotal moment of holding the paradox of this truth. We know we are ideally suffering in this moment, and yet we claim our happiness. This is where change begins.

Trust, surrender, acceptance and grace help create our leap of faith. We affirm what is important to us. We bring our minds to attention and work from a fulfilled space toward timed, measurable, and observable increments of change. The difference is that we are already happy and in acceptance of our station in life.

How we make the person we are and our reality blend into one being is a slow and deliberate process of aspiring and intending our life's goals, not an immediate gratification that was inspired. Inspirations come and go, but aspirations last a lifetime.

Keep your gratitude positive. Claim your inherent worth as a human being, don't start from a derogatory place. An example is, "I have money and safety," rather than, "I am no longer poor and vulnerable." Reinforce and own your thoughts of wealth in a healthy way.

Everything that we experience is viewed from what we believe. In a way, our self-talk becomes our reality. If we reinforce negative self-talk, we project our harmful view and thoughts and imprint the world with it. When we judge and compare ourselves with others, we feel despair at the inequity. When we are always competing as a way of life, we can never relax and enjoy, for fear that we will lose what we have won.

Following is an example of an affirmation list:

I am good. I am at peace. I have abundance. I choose to be happy. I am healthy. I am patient. I have enough money. I have the power to change my life. I am driven to move beyond my circumstances. I trust myself. I have inner wisdom to change. I slowly breathe and calm my racing thoughts.

Aside from your affirmation list, I would like you to consider not believing everything you think. Your best thinking has brought you into some demoralizing positions. Let's move beyond your superficial pain-body.

Workbook Questions:

1. Name five things you have always wanted but believe you do not deserve. Claim them now as if you own the mental and physical aspects of that desire.

2. Do you have issues with the nature of positivity and need to hold onto your views? If you believe that positivity is fake, what are your reasons? How does this type of thinking serve your needs and thoughts?

3. What transformations would you like to bring about in your life? What are the deserving positive affirmations you can start focusing on to get you in the mood and then act as if those things are who you really are, have always been, and that you're just starting to access this person? What qualities do you have that will help you to attain that way of life?

4. What values are you willing to put in motion to attain your intentions?

5. What does your negative self-talk look like?

6. Imagine how good you could feel if you started affirming your own life. What do you think will happen if you started positively affirming the lives of your loved ones?

7. How many days are you willing to commit to your new way of life? You have done your old behaviors your entire life — which thoughts are you willing to elicit self-change?

8. How do you work with your own resistance to change? Resistance is healthy and was created to keep you safe. In what ways does this way of thinking sabotage you from achieving your goals?

9. What things happened in your childhood that still have power over your thoughts, keep you stuck in the past, and keep you from fully participating with what you would like to achieve now?

10. In the past, what made you feel good and safe?

11. Do you use your religious experience to have a feeling of goodness? Is your happiness dependent upon your deity?

12. How does your spiritual experience incorporate wellness, aspirations and features of gratitude?

13. How do you use negative self-talk to keep yourself in a defeatist attitude and a diminished return on your investment?

Post-Traumatic Stress Disorder (PTSD)

As humans, good and bad things happen to us. We seem to be able let the good things slide off us like we're coated with Teflon, but we focus on the one bad thing or circumstance that did not go our way. Those bad things stick to us like Velcro.

Bad things happen to good people. Without the ups and downs of life, we would not have any emotional diversity. We wouldn't know to be aware of and stay away from bad things. We would also not be able to know when things are good and to be grateful for the blessings of impermanent good times.

News and other media outlets make money and get ratings based upon our emotional connection to bad things that happen to others. Sensationalism sells. We are inundated with more and more bad things so that "normal bad things" are just ordinary. Sensational news sources can be a repetitive-stress injury. It is like having an injury that we keep poking the stick into to see if there is still a wound without going through the process of healing. "Ouch, that still hurts! Please turn off that wound channel!"

We have recurring thoughts in our minds when we are triggered by something, and they cascade into disturbing flashbacks. We have dreams or attach to others' pain and suffering, which can be triggers. We seemingly repeat old wounds with our memory.

This anxiety disorder corrodes our wellbeing. We respond to life with a fear-based, pensive approach, instead of with curiosity and discovery. Sometimes we have a kind of amnesia and avoid anything related to our experiences. We can't be free and live authentically with pervasive fear of having stressors that may send us back into that mentality.

No matter what has happened, it is healthy to process grief and violated experiences and to take the time to really understand. We have the choice to heal and realize our experiences have happened to hundreds of thousands of people on the planet — it is not personal to us. It is our attachment to our thinking that keeps us stuck in fear-based thinking. We are afraid lightning will strike again and again in our lives. By our thinking, we can stop being a lightning rod for attracting bad things. We can heal into a safer, more predictable place of peace.

By attaching to what went wrong in the past and trying to avoid repeating it, we actually send a wounded signal out to the universe, in a way. In our best efforts to stop our pain-body from returning, we can attract the trauma to return like a boomerang. You cannot heal your disease with the same ingredients that created it.

The problem that repeats itself over and over again is seldom the source of the trauma. The amygdala in our brain, which serves to protect us from past harms, will misfire repeatedly, putting us in a constant state of fight or flight. Then, our mesolimbic-reward pathway, used for our short-term memory, gets hijacked. We reward ourselves with blame for our past trauma as the reason for our present suffering.

This takeover of our brain by the reptile part of our thinking process is commandeered by our fear that whatever happened before will happen again. Your disease becomes the No. 1 thing you focus on. It overtakes your normal functions of eating, sleeping, procreating and defecating. It keeps you on high alert. Your body starts in the autonomous nervous system, which consists of the parasympathetic system of "rest and digest," and moves into the sympathetic system of "fight or flight," which keeps you in a limbo state of fatal peril.

This creates the PTSD feeling that the sky is falling and your paranoia that trauma will happen again. You block your own ability to relax. This constant state of hyper-vigilance cannot be maintained by the body's natural ability. This makes you like the feeder fish at the bottom of an aquarium, waiting for the ominous, big fish to eat you. You cannot find a way out of the aquarium of your mind.

When you are in this constant state of diminished returns from past trauma, you create a failure-to-thrive attitude. This is the entry point into mental and physical maladies that occur when the body is continually traumatized and held emotional hostage. The body makes stress hormones, and these create tension in your nervous system. Your body partially shuts down from this tissue-toxic way you have tried to protect yourself from what went wrong in the past.

By attaching to old suffering that is no longer happening, you continually renew your suffering mentally and physically. When you shut down your digestive system in this fatal peril, you shut down 150 million neurons in your stomach that create 95 percent of your serotonin, which is used to make you feel well. Your digestion system contains 4½ pounds of bio-mass that is reliant on you to keep your mental systems going. These all work together for homeostasis or wellness in the body.

You now have a mental and physical shutdown of sorts. Do you really have the luxury to focus on something that might recur with as much likelihood as being struck by lightning twice? How many times will you strike yourself with your own mental lightning? Are you the rod attracting it?

I would like to focus on healing techniques for all of us when we are triggered by anything that happened in our past. We respond from PTSD from both positive and negative stressors.

We attach to getting good things, such as jobs, safety, relations, family, houses, cars, boats, financial security, physical well-being and safety, and healing from an illness. These are positive stressors that we need to process. Because we have been violated in some way, we are always waiting for the other shoe to drop. We fear that we will lose what we have gained, and that our health, mental well-being and safety will be taken away.

Healing and Moving Beyond Traumatic Events

1. Be willing to seek help with medical communities and others who have suffered as you are. They did it, gained closure, and got back into the game of life — you can, too. Find community with survivors who have created a safe place for processing. Connect with like-minded people who have suffered, found a solution and care about you doing the same.

2. Avoid self-medicating with alcohol and drugs, or other compulsive behaviors that momentarily self-soothe. Some of these portents of distraction may include acting out with anger, eating, shopping, gambling, isolating, etc. If it feels as if you are obsessing with something else to stay distracted from your PTSD, you probably are. Those methods bring brief and momentary bliss, but misery is always cheerfully refunded after the convenience is gone.

3. Write down a list of all the bad things that have happened to you, along with your fears and mental and physical violations. You cannot know fear until you can hold it in your hand. Look at your fears as an observer; realize that those events are not happening right now. Close your eyes and breathe; slow your heartbeat. There is nothing dangerous happening right now. You can be at peace. Thank your brain for calming down, and put all those thoughts on a shelf where you can get to them later. You can make an imaginary shelf in your room and put them there. They do not have to rent space in your head and write novels about what happened over and over again. Slowly, day by day, you will work with one piece at a time, and give it the healing it deserves. You will use recall only when you are in danger. Those mental images do not get to keep you emotional hostage. They have a safe place on a shelf outside of your head.

4. Be willing to put a joyful exertion into your well-being and healing. The sooner you seek help, the quicker you can tackle and address your triggers that send you into these downward spirals of recall. Those tragedies of your life are not weaknesses, but a path toward empowerment, compassion and empathy for yourself and others who suffer as you do.

5. Be full-measured in your willingness to cut all of the traumatic triggers out of your life. If you had cancer, would you cut just a little out and let the rest fester and kill you? Avoidance only creates an exhaustive feedback loop by your omission to accurately process it. With family, friends and loved ones, you come off as a wounded, unhealed person who cannot fully participate on a genuine, authentic level, because you have chosen those things to be the reason you checked out on life. Until you address those issues, they will surreptitiously run your life. Everyone around you will suffer as you project those experiences onto people around you.

6. When you keep negative, fear-based emotions on alert all the time by the feedback loop you have created, you are in a heightened adrenaline state. Your body cannot cope. You will continuously break down and reinforce negative thoughts. You digest your thoughts on a cellular level; you are what you think. Eventually you will become tissue-toxic from all the tension and stress created by your choice. That is where physical and mental calamities take seed and thrive. Eventually you will stop having faith and stop surrendering. You will build walls that keep poison alive and prominent. You will pull away from your life, your loved ones, and people at work. You will start to hang out with people who reinforce and enable your diseased thinking so that you feel safe and heard.

7. You get used to recalling and processing in a more timely and accurate manner, keeping space for life on life's terms. Process what is happening right now, because you have done the work to process what happened in the past. You will have more self-esteem, feel empowered, know how to appropriately vent past trauma and restore your wellbeing in a timely manner. You will have more control of your life and be willing to surrender what you are powerless over. It no longer has power over you.

8. Through your fearless process you can help others who suffer as we did, and heal one person at a time. Your family will learn a new way to willingly move forward with those fears you imprinted on them. You will stop the negative cycle of fear-based recidivism. You can be part of healthy communities that are healing.

9. You get to access and use your medical opportunities for healing. You might consider taking some helpful medications for a time while you process your experience. Then you

can consider restoring your brain's chemistry to its healthy former state without medication.

10. Name and claim what your strengths are. Acknowledge them and use those, instead of the fear-based ease of contentment.

11. Find ways to relax and meditate, in nature or a safe room, yard, or spiritual group.

12. Be gentle, loving and forgiving of yourself. You have probably been doing these behaviors in some way for a long time. Take some time to heal. This is the journey of a lifetime.

Workbook Questions:

1. What traumatic, re-occurring events play over and over in your head and stop you from enjoying work, family, and going out in public?

2. What has brought you comfort in the past? Was it momentarily or long-lasting? What stops you from engaging in these behaviors now?

3. Did your event happen when you were an innocent child? Does anyone know? What is the stigma attached to getting help and processing this dilemma?

4. Were you the perpetrator of harm to others? Have you processed your part in this? Have you really forgiven yourself? Do you do service to help others? Explain.

5. In what ways do you calm down and relax, come back into the room after you have been triggered? Do you take a walk, meditate, call someone, or act out in anger? Explain in detail a few ways you cope.

6. Do you have a repeating tape loop of old, bad stories that are played over and over again to anyone willing to listen? Does that bring you momentary safety? What would happen if you stopped that cycle? Would you feel unheard or less than? Explain.

7. Do you watch the news and read about trauma in the paper? What benefits do you get from hearing those bad things over and over? Are you compelled to hear only violent tragedies? What do you do to balance the horror you read and see?

8. Do you believe your pain is personal? Are there others who have suffered as you have? When you hear another's story, are you thinking of one of yours that is worse?

9. What healthy things do you do to keep your mind in balance? Do you work out? Do you go to happy events that are social or spiritual? Take walks in nature? Explain.

10. Do you believe you will never heal from PTSD? What will happen if you surrender that belief and feel groundless and curious about the uncertainty?

11. Do your loved ones suffer with you and your experiences? Do you hold them emotional hostage for what happened to you in the past? Explain.

12. What healthy things do you think you would like to try to move away from your fear-based idiom?

13 Steps for Managing Flashbacks

Written by Pete Walker, M.A., MFT – Reprinted with Permission

1. **Say to yourself: "I am having a flashback."** Flashbacks take us into a timeless part of the psyche that feels as helpless, hopeless and surrounded by danger as we were in childhood. The feelings and sensations you are experiencing are past memories that cannot hurt you now.

2. **Remind yourself: "I feel afraid but I am not in danger! I am safe now, here in the present."** Remember you are now in the safety of the present, far from the danger of the past.

3. **Own your right/need to have boundaries.** Remind yourself that you do not have to allow anyone to mistreat you; you are free to leave dangerous situations and protest unfair behavior.

4. **Speak reassuringly to the Inner Child.** The child needs to know that you love her unconditionally- that she can come to you for comfort and protection when she feels lost and scared.

5. **Deconstruct eternity thinking:** in childhood, fear and abandonment felt endless - a safer future was unimaginable. Remember the flashback will pass as it has many times before.

6. **Remind yourself that you are in an adult body** with allies, skills and resources to protect you that you never had as a child. [Feeling small and little is a sure sign of a flashback]

7. **Ease back into your body.** Fear launches us into 'heady' worrying, or numbing and spacing out.
   [a] **Gently ask your body to Relax:** feel each of your major muscle groups and softly encourage them to relax. (Tightened musculature sends unnecessary danger signals to the brain)
   [b] **Breathe** deeply and slowly. (Holding the breath also signals danger).
   [c] **Slow down:** rushing presses the psyche's panic button.
   [d] **Find a safe place** to unwind and soothe yourself: wrap yourself in a blanket, hold a stuffed animal, lie down in a closet or a bath, take a nap.
   [e] **Feel the fear in your body without reacting to it.** Fear is just an energy in your body that cannot hurt you if you do not run from it or react self-destructively to it.

8. **Resist the Inner Critic's Drasticizing and Catastrophizing:** [a] **Use thought-stopping** to halt its endless exaggeration of danger and constant planning to control the uncontrollable. Refuse to shame, hate or abandon yourself. Channel the anger of self-attack into saying NO to unfair self-criticism. [b] **Use thought-substitution** to replace negative thinking with a memorized list of your qualities and accomplishments

9. **Allow yourself to grieve.** Flashbacks are opportunities to release old, unexpressed feelings of fear, hurt, and abandonment, and to validate - and then soothe - the child's past experience of helplessness and hopelessness. Healthy grieving can turn our tears into self-compassion and our anger into self-protection.

10. **Cultivate safe relationships and seek support.** Take time alone when you need it, but don't let shame isolate you. Feeling shame doesn't mean you are shameful. Educate your intimates about flashbacks and ask them to help you talk and feel your way through them.

11. **Learn to identify the types of triggers that lead to flashbacks.** Avoid unsafe people, places, activities and triggering mental processes. Practice preventive maintenance with these steps when triggering situations are unavoidable.

12. **Figure out what you are flashing back to.** Flashbacks are opportunities to discover, validate and heal our wounds from past abuse and abandonment. They also point to our still unmet developmental needs and can provide motivation to get them met.

13. **Be patient with a slow recovery process:** it takes time in the present to become un-adrenalized, and considerable time in the future to gradually decrease the intensity, duration and frequency of flashbacks. Real recovery is a gradually progressive process [often two steps forward, one step back], not an attained salvation fantasy. Don't beat yourself up for having a flashback.

Copyright © Pete Walker, M.A., MFT. "13 Steps for Managing Flashbacks." (925-283-4575)

Powerlessness and Unmanageability

We all want to feel power and freedom from our circumstances and stations in life. Many of us have the grass-is-greener syndrome when, in reality, the grass is green if you *look* for green, one way or another.

If our picker for empowerment is broken and we keep running into a wall, when the doorway is only a foot to the left, we can choose to take that corrective step.

We live in a world of indecision, economic downturns, and countries spiraling out of control. We gain power and balance by accepting what is and getting comfortable with uncertainty. Our ability to value both sides of what can happen leads us to feel less stress about one vs. the other. It is only when we attach to our wants and needs and look at the reasons we want this or that for immediate gratification and convenience that we see the faults in our thinking – and then the path to redemption.

Redemption is one result of the ability to accept life on life's terms. "No" does not always mean no forever; it may also mean "not right now." We are a culture of fast food and fast cars. We live so fast that we forget the value of stopping and smelling the roses. Only then can we see that what we thought were roses were simply thorns without a flower. Slow down, breathe, pray for willingness to pray for willingness to accept life on life's terms, just as it is.

In what ways does this attitude affect our lives by the inability to act or respond to people, places or things? For example, our children are doing something of which we don't approve. Remember when we did many, many things that scared our parents? Look for the similarities and not simply fear-based differences. The idea that we are special and make life all about us and our experiences is what brings us the most discomfort.

When we treat power struggles as a loss of power, we want one outcome over what may actually happen. This attitude is the cause of our suffering. We are not ready for what really happens. We have been in fantasy and wishful thinking for our outcome. If we look at the reasons for unhappiness, we will find it is usually aligned with wanting things to go our way so we can feel fulfillment and safety. Our ego, which is never satisfied, feels momentary bliss.

Instead of drained feelings and other uneasy responses, let's get comfortable with uncertainty and go with it, follow it, and explore all we can do with what we have, instead of attaching to a negative outcome. We usually follow our thoughts. Therefore, if our thoughts are negative, we will arrive at a place that corresponds to our feelings.

What does lack of control look like? Is it manifested in overeating, anger, loss of control, feelings of ostracism? Our responses to situations tell everyone what our agenda-thinking is, what our shortfalls are and how to take our power away. Most of us give our power away, not realizing its value. We learn to live without our power, in pain and unnecessary suffering.

Similar to gambling, our opponents look for signs of weakness when we give away the cards we have and lose our power to wager. And like gambling, your brain still rewards you, whether you win or lose.

How do we reveal what we are thinking? Are we able to manage when annoying traffic on the way to work backs up and makes us late, and there is yet another accident right in front of us? Management of our emotions is an aspiration of cognitive behaviors that work together to make us have a more streamlined world with less confusion.

Does our management style make others' lives unmanageable? We can learn to be more conscious of the way we conduct our business. It's all in how we look at things. Our perception tells us that a person walking by outside is dangerous, but it may be a person simply walking by outside. It is our bias that leads us astray. If the person in question does not look like us, and we associate that person with misperceptions taught to us in the past, we have judgment. When we associate fear with our perception, it is less likely that we will be able to come back to a calm disposition until we have somehow made peace in our minds.

When we don't like someone, and they walk up and ask a simple question, do we catch ourselves when we respond with an untrusting, mean-spirited disposition? We must keep an open mind about whatever happens to us and not attach to one side over the other. We need to stay curious about our choices and process our mental scenarios of "What's the worst that could happen?" We want to be able to process joyful exertion when things turn out differently. The outcome is a surprise, not a death sentence.

Let's take a longer view for our happiness — let's say, a five-year plan. With that timeline in mind, we have a lot of room for navigation and path-finding to develop discernment toward our attachment to one thing happening over another.

When our sense of power is based on our personality or ego, life is tough. We are likely to meet struggle, pain and hardship. There is another option. Our spirit is immense and magnificent. We can call on it at any time.

When we become a team player with life, we cooperate with what is. Try going without a computer for a few days, or the phone for a week. At first we think we need it and can't live without it. But after a while, we will wonder why we became so attached. The peace we feel is so rich and full. We have so many devices that are supposed to make our lives simpler; yet, they take up all the bandwidth of our brains just learning to use them.

The Way to a More Powerful You:

1. Help empower others overcoming fears and disappointments as you empower yourself and realize that life is not personal — it just is.

2. Take a look at why you believe your thinking is true. Develop the turnaround solutions you would offer to a friend. Be courageous to try them in your own life.

3. Be gentle with yourself as you explore other options that used to scare you.

4. Surrender everything you think, say, and do, just for today. What is the worst that could really happen while you sit in peace and acceptance? Usually not much.

5. Let go of your first thought of reactive thinking.

6. Accept yourself with all of your defects and warts.

7. Work toward common, mutual developments and cooperate with others. Don't fight for selfish needs.

8. Forgiveness is complete and absolute. Forgiveness halfway is feeding resentment.

9. Live your life as a joyful and curious adventure, with ups and downs being part of the natural experience.

10. Keep willingness as a permanent address to your soul. It is inexhaustible.

11. Make a positive affirmation list of what you have. Write your wants and needs into the future. Such as: "I am so happy and grateful now that I have _____ in my life."

12. Know your limits, and don't make promises you can't keep. Take a look at why you have limits.

13. Choose happiness, and get back on the horse when you fall. Rewards will come for the effort you made.

14. There is no permanent perfection we can reach. Don't expect perfection.

15. Stop giving away your precious power; it is your life source. Say no. Say yes. Say something. If you do not make plans for yourself, someone will surely make plans for you.

16. Trust the process of life, and transcend your daily struggles as bumps in the road, not the end of the road.

17. Name 10 things you have power over. Examples: brushing your teeth, waking up on time, eating what you like, taking a different route to work, etc.

Workbook Questions:

1. Can you verbalize the incomprehensible demoralization of your soul? Can you describe the terror of the feedback loop in the closed system between your ears, where no one can see, hear or get in to help you? Give some examples.
2. What are you angry about the most?
3. Why do you feel hopeless and want to give up?
4. What are you passive about, but appear aggressive and annoyed?
5. By your omission or lack of participation, what are you most afraid of someone knowing? Why does shame and stigma have so much power over you?
6. Have you always responded with limited control when you broke up with someone, lost your job, or had financial stress?
7. When a doctor speaks to you, do you feel as if you have no control over your diagnosis? Do you have misconceptions about what you are in charge of and how much power you have in decision-making?
8. Do you feel supported by loved ones when the going gets tough?
9. Which support groups with people of like mind are you willing to participate in?
10. What realistic hopes do you have about what has worked for you in the past? What will it take for you to engage in self-change thoughts?
11. Play the whole situation out. What's the worst that could happen? Can you live with that the result? If not, why not?
12. Name four relevant things you are powerless over with any situation. Name four powers you *do* have over the state of affairs.
13. What does unmanageability mean to you?
14. In what ways do you act out and make everyone around you feel unsafe and vulnerable about what you will do next?
15. How do you benefit from destructive behavior? How will you feel without it? Will you think you are a coward, a fake, a fraud, a phony? Why do you believe that behavior is real and genuine?
16. What is the real cause of your unhappiness? Does your happiness cause unhappiness? Why do you choose one over the other?
17. In what ways are you a predator in a safe environment? Do you pick on people because they are vulnerable?
18. Did the above types of behaviors happen to you when you were younger, and now you are doing them because it's all you know? If so, explain.
19. What has worked for you in the past that has helped and is a proven method for change?
20. Do you believe you can be helped?

Rage Disorders – Intermittent Explosive Outbursts

See also: Anger Management; Abuse; Control Issues; Fatal Peril and Fight-or-Flight Syndrome; and Oppressor and Predator.

Do you walk around the planet like a loaded gun, just waiting for any excuse to explode with furious discontent?

Do you have road rage and want to kill someone because of the way they drive? Do you lose control when someone of authority asks you to perform a simple task? If a police officer pulls you over, do you create more trouble than the stop was for? Do you walk on eggshells and break all the eggs in your basket over and over again? Are you supposedly the "good one," the breadwinner, the "trusted one"? Are you holding your loved ones emotional hostage with your unhappiness?

Repeated, low-impulse outbursts create a formula for domestic cycles of violence. Outbursts can include breaking things or being full of rage when we don't get our way or our needs don't get met. Outbursts occur when we are incapable of taking care of whatever it is by ourselves.

After acting out, we can see the trail of destruction from our tantrum — sometimes injuring others on purpose or accidentally, or focusing our energy on destroying ourselves mentally and physically.

It takes only a moment for this negative emoting, but it sets up a lifetime of perpetuating, self-fulfilling prophecies of doom. During the calm after the storm, the predator feels worse. We experience helpless feelings of remorse, embarrassment and regret. This is the honeymoon period. It disappears after a few weeks, and then disappointment and frustration come back into our lives with tension and acrimonious case-building against others, with our reasons for dissatisfaction. This results in another explosion.

Whether it is us or somebody else with a high-powered hose, this kind of poison is spread as an equal-opportunity destroyer of safety and peace for all. We are predators in a safe environment. Remember, it took a lifetime to acquire this disorder. It will take daily commitment to build the skills to combat this behavior.

Usually it is a learned behavior, either imprinted on us by family members or by getting away with acting out until it gradually grew to our present uncontrolled state.

Warning signs include a racing mind; adrenaline rushes; irritability; easily triggered, reactionary thoughts, and tension-building.

To prevent these kinds of behavior, it is important that we not get hungry, angry, lonely or tired (HALT).

If we have the tendency to indulge in explosive outbursts, we can help ourselves by following a few of these examples:

- Get support from others who are angry, and learn what your own triggers are.

- Write a gratitude list every day. Start focusing on what is going good in your life.
- Eat, sleep and rest well.
- Time your involvement with stressful situations. Make sure that after five minutes, you remove yourself from the triggering environment.
- Take walks, meditate, and seek appropriate medical help and medications.
- Find out what your triggers are, and know the warning signs.
- Spend more time with people who are also working on controlling their anger issues.
- Quit hanging out with angry people who are OK with your anger and even encourage it.
- Try finding groups you want to join. Use the impetus to be on your best behavior.
- Recognize your behavior, and resist the temptation to act out. Recover your senses, and move away from the trigger. Don't bring a can of gasoline to the fire.
- Get a sponsor who can handle your particular outbursts and who doesn't get bothered by people like you.
- Go to Anger Management classes four or five times. Make it a five-year plan to get a grip on your disease.
- Help and sponsor other people like yourself. There is no quicker way to realize that this disorder is not personal, but an experience you can learn to manage better.
- Commit to Do No Harm to yourself and others.

Workbook Questions:

1. How many times have you taken Anger Management classes? Will you consider taking one a few more times to save your life, your loved ones, and people who have to be in contact with you?

2. What are your triggers?

3. How do people know to be safe around you and not emotional hostages?

4. Why do people fear you and your outbursts of anger?

5. Name five reasons you feel justified getting angry.

6. How do you enjoy having power over others? Explain a situation when this has occurred.

7. How do you take advantage of power and control over others? What will you lose if you stop acting that way?

8. Control is questionable when the person exhibiting the behavior has control issues with others. What are your control and safety issues? Have you been hurt in the past?

9. In what ways have you moved beyond your anger in the past? Explain your process. What stops you from engaging daily with a hopeful, healthy place to strive for?

10. Were you brought up around an explosive outburst disorder? Does it run in the family? What have others in your family done to cope? Why not you?

11. Name five things you can do when you feel like turning into the Hulk.

12. What are some reasons you want to change? Loved ones, jobs, social status, being deemed trustworthy?

13. Should you wear a T-shirt that says, "Doesn't Play Well with Others"? Or, "Stand Back 10,000 Feet"? In what ways are you a thin-skinned target, and everyone seems to hit your bull's eye, no matter their intentions?

14. Are there some people with issues you know who have overcome them? Would they be willing to help you?

15. Can you get serious and humble enough to make forward movement with these ideals?

16. Have you been jailed for being a danger to yourself or others? Have you been admitted to a hospital observation ward as a 51/50? Explain.

17. Have you had homicidal or suicidal periods and didn't feel heard? What did you do?

Relapse

For many years, we addicts have been conditioned by our upbringing and communities to do what we do.

We have survived and come out onto the other side of the abyss, able to maintain and support our lives. However, as we choose to move into self-change thoughts, we sometimes fight our DNA and a lifetime's worth of conditioning.

We swim upstream into new ways of living. We have been practicing addictive behaviors for many years — how many doesn't matter. What matters is that we know that change is a process. We take two steps forward and one step backward.

Sometimes we work for months on doing well and getting our new life. Then in an instant, we mess up six months of hard work.

What do we do?

Too many times, we are hard on ourselves. We have unrealistic views based upon expectations and perfectionism. In recovery, we take our lives "one day at a time." There are 24 little hours, good days and uncomfortable days. As we develop awareness of our warning signs and triggers, we move into actions and changes in a resilient search for freedom from painful suffering.

One tool for success is making sure you are with a support group that is patient and works with you while you develop skillful means of long-lasting change. Have friends and colleagues who will call you on your stuff and speak out when you are in danger.

Book-end with people you trust – meaning, speak with them before and after a potentially triggering event. Book-end when you are going to job interviews or emotionally escalating family events, breaking up with a partner, or going through a frightening experience. Call them and say what you are about to do and what your best outcome might look like, and tell them you will call afterward. Ask if they would be available to process your feelings with you. Know your triggers. Get into actions that will prevent you from feeling so vulnerable.

Our brain chemistry is being re-wired one action at a time. If we relapse, we notice every underlying reason. We make direct changes in our environment, attitudes, and lifestyles when we feel that our path is slippery and unsafe. We look deeper at the reasons we get triggered. One situation at a time, we use our newfound wisdom to move just a little further into safe actions.

Recovery is like learning to walk. We almost fall into each step, and regain our balance. We look around to see where we are going and then fall into the next step. Then we repeat the process.

As addicts, we do not get to rest on our laurels. We do the hard work at hand and get results. At first, results are almost imperceptible. But we keep going with our leaps of faith, trust, belief and surrender. One day at a time, we get a reprieve based upon our spiritual maintenance.

We did our addictions 24/7. Our thinking supported our actions. Now that we are trying to change everything we think, say and do — all of our thoughts, words and deeds — we must fill the emptiness that was our addiction with hundreds of recovery options. We stay healthy and recovered by having no "dead time." We choose to do the next right thing and then, after that, the next right thing, until 24 hours of recovery has passed. Then, we repeat this mindset.

The inside of our brains is like a thousand mouse traps. At first, everything triggers us. When one mouse trap goes off, it sets off a thousand other little traps, triggering a confusing cascade of chemicals in our brain. We go haywire with all the unsettled feelings.

We have been doing our addictive behaviors and making our actions seem OK for such a long time. Now that we are trying to change, our addiction is stronger than a gorilla doing push-ups. We get a few kernels of truth and recovery, and then our stinking-thinking mind starts taking over with analyzing and rationalizing. Suddenly, we are in fatal peril. Fight-or-flight impulses bewilder us and keep us in a state of flux. Only by suspending our beliefs, surrendering our thinking, and turning our will over to a higher power or recovery community can we come safely back into a reasonable state of mind.

We use cognitive reasoning and develop tools that help us to recognize, resist, and recover ourselves. We have a sense of urgency for doing the next right thing and then looking for the next right thing after that. We become calm. We listen, slowing down our brain to rise above the noise in our heads and the cacophony around us. We listen assertively, actively, and mindfully for our next safe and healthy choice.

Some of our addictions require us to be in relapse mode all day. We are so used to reacting from a gut feeling or muscle memory that we get angry, mentally unstable, or rageful. Then we turn our emotions inward and harm ourselves. One moment at a time we Do No Harm to ourselves or others.

Other issues with high risk of relapse include sex addictions. We sexualize our stress and our words; objectify people we meet, and fall into relapse. It's tricky to recognize our part in this.

With food issues, we are at risk of relapse every time we look at, shop for or eat food. We also can get triggered by looking at options for eating or watching commercials. We are conditioned to react to all of those societal norms. For most people, it's no problem. They are able to emotionally regulate themselves. We are learning how to do it better. This is called recovery. It is the process of a lifetime.

The following is a partial list of relapse triggers. You may suddenly realize you are triggered by almost everything.

- Abuse
- Addictions
- ADD/ADHD
- Anxiety
- Bipolar Disorder
- Death and dying
- Depression
- Eating disorders
- Grief and loss
- Mental-health disorders

- PTSD and trauma
- Stress
- Exercise
- Relationships
- Work and jobs
- Social events
- Sleep
- Family issues
- Retirement problems

No matter what the relapse is, feelings of helplessness, hopelessness, and delusional thinking take over. We are burned out and can't cope anymore. This is relapse.

In recovery, we try to stay focused in those moments. Once we realize we are triggered, we have a choice to get into healthy alternatives. We realize what we are thinking, right here and now, is the beginning of our brain's ability to choose actions over chemicals going astray. We try to use our wisdom and make space to notice, "Oh, yeah, my brain is working overtime. It's worried, being hyper-vigilant, and micro-managing my emotions."

If we can put space between acting out on those emotions or "chemical cascades" in the brain, we can move back into healthy choices. This space between our thoughts is what we call mindfulness. All of our recovery is about making this space before we react longer and longer, until we learn to make space one day at a time.

In the beginning, we do it one second at a time, then one minute at a time. We keep working with our recovery community and medical helpers to make more space in our day, along with choices in our minds.

Let's say that we have relapsed. We've made a dumb choice. We feel guilt, shame and remorse. After five minutes of wallowing in our hypnotic, infinite sadness while watching our waves of emotion get bigger and bigger, we have a choice to stop the tide.

Sometimes the cure is that we have to simply shrug our shoulders and admit we are powerless over those feelings. We recognize our behaviors, we resist the temptation to act out, and we recover our ability to make the next right choice. We forgive ourselves, and move forward into healthy actions.

When we experience relapse with our emotions or anger, we momentarily act out, and the chemicals in our brains are overstimulated. We stop. We use all of our recovery tools, and come back to our healthier choices.

That moment is the beginning of what happens next. What will we choose? Anger? We know where that will lead. So we call someone, we go to a meeting, we go somewhere safe, we stop and try to figure out what caused the trigger to trip, and work toward making healthy choices.

We remember that recovery is a slow process. We mustn't give up on ourselves before the miracle of change can take place. We are planting seedlings that are sprouting up all around us. If we give up, we crush the sprouting, healthy choices.

By walking carefully around our brains, the more space we put between our thoughts, the longer it will be before we act out and cause harm to ourselves and others.

Recovery begins with a thought. There is a brief pre-contemplation about what might happen if we do not act out addictive behaviors. After that, recovery is about having more thoughts and choices about how to make space between one thought and another and to slow down. We give ourselves choices.

What will you choose today? You have all your power; you have all the answers within you.

Workbook Questions:

1. What do you believe you relapse with — is it a behavior? Are you sorry all the time? Angry? Entitled? Sad, depressed, passive-aggressive?
2. If you relapse with food, how does it begin? What are your warning signs? What are your social and environmental cues? What types of food do you relapse with? Candy, desserts, ice cream, fatty foods, too much salt?
3. When you spend money to relieve stress and make yourself feel better, what triggers your expensive coping behavior? Are you a shopaholic? Do you relieve stress through retail therapy?
4. When having sex or asking for it, how do you honestly convey your needs? In what ways do you care about your partner's needs? Explain how you try to stop behaviors such as using sex to relieve stress, instead of having healthy relations with your partner.
5. What part do you play in blaming other people for your unhappiness? Do you then "take your comfort" and act out in unhealthy ways? In what ways do you act out?
6. In what ways are you a secret, rageaholic driver? How do you act out and relapse with your behavior?
7. What are your triggers? What happens that makes you unstable to yourself and others? How long does it take for you to really see what happened? A minute? A few days?
8. How long does it take for you to move into recovery ideals that require forgiveness, surrender, and action?
9. In what ways does your support group call you on your stuff when you feel triggered? Do you have strong recovery peers who've got your back?
10. In what ways do you relapse while parenting?
11. If you have grief-and-loss issues, how do you stop from sinking into depression and infinite sadness from poor choices in the past? Do you consider that an emotional relapse?
12. How do you move beyond money you owe the government without giving up? Do you owe child support? Taxes? Reparations? Do you feel like a failure because you cannot pay the money back? Is that a thriving relapse?
13. What gives you hope? What gives you faith? What develops your trust and belief in the longer view, so you can last in the bigger picture of life?
14. In what ways do you use exercise as a tool to keep you on the up-and-up? What do you know about the healthful effects of working out? What does exercise do for your muscles and brain chemistry?
15. How do healthy eating choices stop you from making bad decisions? Do you believe that eating right could be one way to stop relapse behavior? What are your thoughts?
16. How do spirituality, faith, trust, belief, and surrender play a healthy role in stopping you from relapsing?
17. In social settings, how do you get along with others? Do you need to be in control? Have expectations of others? Are you not in acceptance of the way your life is right now, causing you to hold others emotional hostage? In what ways would you say you are in relapse mode with your predatory behavior?

Relaxing

In recovery, more than ever, we need to build ways to recharge and invigorate ourselves.

Our lives are filled with deadlines, commitments, familial responsibilities, medical needs and everything else we do to keep treading water and to stay afloat.

Sometimes we go through failures with our jobs or other areas of our lives. If we do not back off to rest and recuperate, we cannot rebound and succeed. Time off lets the body and brain rest and develop willingness toward healthy intentions in everything we do. During resting times, we sift through what our personal talents are and enjoy the preciousness of personal relations. Without the stress and tension of everyday life, we have hope and can face life with dignity. We stop seeing things as all-messed up and instead look into a globalized view and find out what's really going on. We respond, instead of reacting to seemingly perilous issues.

We are able to notice other responsibilities of living when we relax, such as playfulness. We also notice others as individuals and look for similarities rather than differences.

By taking time off, we assess what feels good for us and notice how precious down-time is and what a difference a comfortable environment makes in our lives. We take walks, play music, watch media, notice our partners, children and animals, and honor their presence. We dress casually and wear comfortable apparel that makes us feel safe. During that state of peace we are able to listen intently yet assertively for cues to get the most out of requests others make of us. We can calmly state our position and offer opportunities of what we can and cannot do at that moment.

Taking a little time off also gives people and difficult issues a break. It's amazing to realize that the world will keep spinning with and without us. It's our choice and responsibility to be alert and to reorganize our focus about what inspires us to go back to the grind of our daily jobs. We stop multi-tasking and mindfully choose to do one task at a time, so we don't feel overloaded and get stressed out.

When we take time for solace after grief and loss, we reflect on what a great contribution that person's life was. We acknowledge how valuable the person we lost was, and what impact he had on our lives. We can truly let go of what is lost and missing by giving the powerful moment the respect it deserves. The act of relaxing or letting go empties the space, attachments, and beliefs that went along with them. We make space for new things to come, and there is a willingness and energy to be vulnerable as we tread into new directions.

When we slow down cacaphony and commonplace distractions, we rise above disturbances and can mindfully maneuver over what was a painful interruption. By being calm and at peace, we can finally share ourselves intimately with friends. A change in our behaviors and spiritual connections helps us to stop using self-defeating behaviors as coping mechanisms and to face our troubles. By doing the act of self-care, we can encourage others to take time to work on their own problems and stop enabling themselves with quick fixes that do neither party any good.

By taking a break, we can welcome new ideas, ways to exercise, and work on our food plan. During our lifetime, we will experiment with new ways to cope and communicate, to practice self-care and rebound.

We are resilient creatures; we can be happy if we choose. We are not gilded birds in a cage, but we must let ourselves out once in a while, or we feel trapped.

The perception of excitement takes on new meaning when we enjoy vacations. We rest at the beach; we go on journeys of discovery. We listen and are curious about the world around us. We experiment with our sexuality without stress or feeling hurried. We get massages and take long, luxurious baths; we do things we really want to do.

Practicing self-care creates space for reflection. We can analyze what is wrong, figure out how to manage it, own our part and come up with solutions that create compromise on difficult issues for both parties. We can honestly ask for help and be still enough to listen to what our higher self can do in response.

Workbook Questions:

1. Name five things you do to relax.

2. When you relax, are you doing things that are healthy for you?

3. Do you use sex, drugs, or alcohol to relax?

4. Do you use adrenalin-pumping excitement to relax? What do you get out of that powerful action?

5. In what ways do you relax your mind? Do you meditate? Do you pray? Do you take a bath? Name all the ways you relax your mind and turn the world off.

6. In what ways do you relax your body? Do you work out? Do you bike, swim, walk, dance?

7. What thrill-seeking behaviors do you pursue when relaxing? Does your everyday work keep you sitting all day? In what ways do you not relax while you are sitting? How do you keep busy while being in one position all day?

8. In what ways do you relax in community? How do you handle the noise of family and friends at a party where you are trying to chill out?

9. In what creative ways can you relax and take a break? Music, art, dance, poetry, media, mobile devices?

10. How do you let go of what you cannot control? In what ways do you surrender and take a break?

11. In what ways do you ask for help, so your mind stops churning out manic dis-ease? How do you make the world stop for a minute?

12. Are you able to listen better when you stop racing thoughts? Can you mindfully move into the next right thing to do? Do you access your higher power to help carry the weight of the world or to love those who are hard to love?

13. Name ways you got successful down time in the past and recharged your batteries.

14. How do you "skip the record" of your life and mix things up, so the mundane, everyday responsibilities and chores have breathing room? Name ways you break out of the monotony of your daily grind.

Resilience

With all the things you need to fight, what does it take for you to come back swinging? What are ways you fight, collaborate, fit in, take your place, be quiet, surrender yourself, and quit painting the target on your spirit? You have what it takes to get back into the game of life.

We all have expansive, challenging experiences that put us on the edge of our comfort zones. They seem to all happen at the same time and make us feel invisible, small, and unheard. We perceive these times as personal slights against our essence of living.

Feeling those emotions so intensely is what we want to bounce back from. We need to have a reserve of spiritual energy for those times. Most people live their lives unaware that they need practical, holistic, preventive measures to bounce back from life on life's terms. When our egos make what happens to us seem personal, we suffer. Bad things will happen in life and pain will occur, but the time we spend suffering is optional.

It's great to be self-sufficient and confident in our skills. It's also nice to have options to surrender and let go to a power greater than ourselves. This concept includes the deities of all religions, but it also includes anything greater than us. This could be community, the universe, and the like. When things get to be too much, it's nice to let it go. We are not meant to hold the weight of all life on our shoulders. Smart people have options. They know hard times are not personally seeking to destroy the fabric of their lives and belief systems.

There are good days and bad days. Think of them like dark clouds going by with rain and thunder. They are impermanent. If we do not catastrophize, they will pass and we will see a different experience in the "skies of your life." When we attach and personalize life and let one dark cloud outshine the sun, we experience destructive, intense emotions. The whole sky could be blue, but we focus on that one small, dark spot and make that the reason for our unhappiness.

Let go and surrender all attachment. Surrendering does not mean losing — it means joining together, being one with others. Even if surrender is death, acceptance is the answer to all our questions. We live with expectations, wanting control, not being in acceptance, having an agenda, and wanting to manipulate time and space so everything will go our way. This is impractical and egoistic. The world does not revolve around our wants and needs. It keeps spinning with or without us, even when we are sick and cannot participate. Our experience here is valuable and important, but it is not all; we are part of a bigger truth.

Transcending pain and suffering is our craft. We turn poison into medicine. We have developed skillful means to accept and understand what is. Life is temporary; nothing stays the same. Life is only change. We need an inner strength to keep our heads above its cacophony. Each of us has different strengths for different adversities.

The key to resilience is to stay open, willing, flexible and teachable. We learn to bend and that our threshold of pain is much more than we can fathom. We learn to heal from whatever life throws our way. This is all impermanent. We learn to get comfort from uncertainty.

Ways to Have Resilience in Our Lives:

- We must be impeccable in word and deed. Let's get together with people who have what we want and would love to share the abundance with us. Find and stick with people who will sit with us and be with us and our experiences, keeping us on track and in balance so we can rebound more easily.

- Visualize that life is temporary, and it is not about us. We are about life. It's our choice to accept pain and suffering as our teacher — just for today.

- We do this life thing one day at a time. We surrender the future and the past. We have control only of our happiness in this moment. What do we choose? It's our choice. The feeling will pass, but our attachment wants to hold on and make it all about us.

- When we make life personal and about us, when our thoughts ruminate out of control, notice and pray for the willingness to pray for the willingness to release that negative contract. We are making life on life's terms.

- Realize the impermanence of our experiences. We need to find ways to be grateful for every breath and to do service for others. By helping another, we can let go of our thoughts about suffering. We develop empathy and compassion for all suffering, sentient beings.

- Be preventive and holistic in our thinking. Remember the saying we have used in this book: "We want to *be* ready, so we don't have to *get* ready." We must have in our treasure chest resilient ways in which we respond to life. Know thy self, our triggers, our mental health, and our physical health. Study what happened to other family members in the past. Be situationally aware of all that is going on, so you can respond to life. Be prepared; no one gets out of here alive.

- Have a form of meditation or prayer that lets us hold in silence the paradox that both truths happen at once. We are not sure of the answer, but we are mindful enough to not react and to sit with the discomfort. We can be the observer in our lives. We can sit and watch as we spin out of control. Let ourselves stop, and then remind ourselves that we are safe. Our inner child needs to be re-parented with a safe environment for our spirits to dwell in. If there is chaos around ourselves, just sit with it. If we are not in danger, just observe that we do not have to waste any precious energy. If we can do something, by all means do it safely.

- Accurately process what is happening with ourselves and others. Make a pro-and-con list; a list from one to 10 of how strongly we feel; a fear list, and a gratitude list. We can share these with others who will not judge, but let us develop our inner wisdom for our best experience possible. We have all the answers within us. This is our journey.

- We must have healthy internal and external boundaries. We need to know when to own our thoughts. When they are toxic, use a trash-removal system for yourself and what others bring. It's up to us to keep ourselves safe.

- It is important to have timed limits of three to five minutes with emotionally escalating people. With ourselves, notice when we are ruminating. See when waves fall over us and get larger and larger, and when depression knocks at the door. After five minutes of feeling anything with anyone, we have the choice to stop. We ultimately know where suffering will lead to. The war is over if we believe it is. What do you believe?

- If healthy things are happening and we feel left out, we can choose to go with the flow, join in, rejoice, let go of our egos, "don't worry; be happy." One of the most difficult ideas to imprint is being happy for others when they have what we want. If there are sad or bad things happening, we must process our situational awareness and respond to ourselves first with extreme self-care. And then, if we can, do service and help others. Only then can we transcend what is happening.

- The greatest thing we can give ourselves and others is hope. Live our lives as an inspiration of hope with the intention of spreading it around. Hope dies last. Make sure it does not flicker out. Be well. Do well. Thrive.

Workbook Questions:

1. What adversity have you bounced back from with grace? How can you use the skills you learned with a new problem/opportunity?

2. Whom do you use as a sounding board to get out of stress and overwhelm? Do they actively listen or try to fix your problems for you? What do you need? Be willing to say what you need and accept the help you are given.

3. In what ways do you evolve with self-efficacy? How do you move beyond personalizing and start working with others? "It's a we thing, not a me thing."

4. In what ways are you able to empathize with yourself without that old voice telling you what you did wrong? How do you create self-esteem? What acts do you engage in to move beyond the pain body and fear-based thinking that paralyze your life?

5. How do you use your emotional intelligence and mindfully maneuver past "blaming"? In what ways do you move into being a courageous person, learning and responding to life on life's terms?

6. How do you invest in developing rarely used spiritual muscles so you have the capacity for weathering a hardship storm in your life? If you put nothing into your spiritual bank, you will be spiritually and morally bankrupt. You will suffer. What can you do to be prepared and ready for life?

7. In what ways do doing service and helping others create self-esteem? How does resilience help you to handle your own problems?

8. In what ways do you develop strategies and possibilities for creating a safer way out of bad things that happen? How do you perceive possibilities and stop sitting in the problem?

9. In what ways do you move beyond victimhood and into solution-focused therapies?

10. In what ways do you stay hopeful and pro-active? Remember, "We want to *be* ready so we don't have to *get* ready."

11. At what point do you seek professional advice? What does it take? What are you willing to consider as help? Are you able to sit with your pain without doing anything about it? What's it going to take to make a leap of faith and share your painful experiences? What will help you see and trust that others are resilient enough to help you make changes in your life?

Sanity

The Sanity Clause. What keeps you safe and sane as you journey from here to there?

It doesn't matter where "there" is. The idea is to be able to travel anywhere, physically or in your head, with a cool, smooth disposition, and handle anything that comes your way.

People are not the sum of their diagnoses. People are complicated, living in a hectic and unpredictable world. The more skills we have to successfully navigate the quagmire, the better chance there is for peace of mind along the way.

As a society, we can reach a ceiling of comfort, look forward, and challenge the old, entrenched ways of thinking. We can skillfully engage in adjustments as we notice where we are vulnerable and let go of all assumptions. Our convenient truths bring instant gratification but leave us void of healthy ways to move forward with integrity in our lives.

Your sanity does not require the participation of others. You can be alone in a crowd that emotionally escalates into mob mentality and be the one who can bring calm, because you have surrendered what others think of you and their consensual validation.

We strive to become fearless and courageous, without limited thinking. We choose to do the next right thing. We take emotional care of ourselves, so we are clear and clean of counter-transferring our experiences onto others. We are objectionable, trustworthy and called upon because we are transparent and people know we will not quickly pick sides.

As our discriminating wisdom keeps us flexible and responsive, we learn the many truths we choose stem from our choice for that moment, but might be another truth later. We accept that in real critical thinking, we are often apt to be wrong or "off," and accept that as part of impermanent truths capable of change.

The only constant is that things will change. Change is a phenomenon that occurs when people, thoughts, and values collide. Then we must choose, for the greater good, what will best make our society work for that moment.

If we work within a closed system that does not value our experiences, we lose the ability to feel safe and to belong. Our sanity is tested, abused and devalued. How can we hold our space and activate our powers with abusive counterparts, while our main goal is to do no harm?

We often we bring gasoline to those moments and side with others to get our viewpoint honored. We can still hold our space while honoring others' viewpoints. Skillful ways of doing this include the attitude of, "I honor your truth. I see how you feel about this subject, and I know that it took a lot of courage for you to be this honest with me." This does not mean you do not have your own views and that they are unimportant. By siding with someone else's truth, more space is created for your truth to thrive congruently. There are three forms of "reality": yours, mine, and the truth. They exist simultaneously.

One thing to keep in mind is that just because everyone is doing "it" does not make "it" right. Vices, habits, errors in thinking and doing, political dogmas and the like are not sane. They are conditioned responses. We just get used to them. The idea is to know in your heart what you are doing and recognize your behavior without getting paralyzed. Move into eliciting change talk for yourself and others. Do this together as a collective consciousness. It starts with one heart that is set on change. Is this your heart of hearts?

Sanity is being comfortable with change.

Sanity is being still when you hear news or learn a new way of doing things. You don't have to get on the emotional roller coaster and end up somewhere unsafe.

Sanity is keeping mindful and alert with a healthy sense of urgency to pay attention. You want to *be* ready for what may come next.

Sanity is detachment and choosing not to get hooked with the next emotional/chemical cascade in your brain. You understand that the emotional barrage is only chemicals creating feelings. Your distractions will change; your feelings will change, and the chemicals in your brain will calm down.

Sanity is the ability to stay in the present moment and realize it is the only moment you can do anything about with what happens in your life. You can't change the past; you can't predict the future. You can only respond to what is happening right here and now.

Sanity is trustworthy, stable, healthy, constant, resilient and ready for whatever comes before you, even when it's dressed as a wolf.

Sanity is the interpersonal way you connect with your environment and keep all as safe and trustworthy as they are capable of being.

Sanity is knowing you don't have all the answers. You can suspend your thinking and ask for help without losing status, yet still feel safe and secure within yourself.

Workbook Questions:

1. Name five ways you keep cool, calm and collected while others are in disarray.

2. How do you handle yourself when you are at a peace rally that changes into violence? Or you see it on TV, but cannot do anything about it? What is your mental process?

3. How is your sanity tested by what others do?

4. Why is your sanity dependent upon what others do?

5. What can you do to make yourself autonomous yet still engage in the human process of "quid pro quo"?

6. How can you build your sanity muscles? Name the values you have. Do you have the same sanity abilities you expect of others? Are you willing to exercise them when it seems unfair and there is no trust?

7. How does sanity give or take your ability to feel peace, freedom and fulfillment?

8. If the idea of insanity is doing the same thing over and over, expecting different results, what might the idea of sanity look like? Create a metaphor.

9. In what ways does abstention or procrastination keep you from being heard and having peace of mind?

10. What are pro-active ways to keep sane?

11. Do you know of ways to better address wrongs committed by others, but you feel powerless in implementing change? Are you afraid you will be judged by the unskillful mob?

12. In what ways do you keep your sanity?

13. How do you calm down your excited and disturbed mind?

14. What "sane thoughts" do you remember when things around you escalate?

15. What does this mean to you: "The more I seem to learn, the less I seem to know."

Secrets and Self-Disclosure

As clinicians, we are responsible to warn our clients not to tell us anything about abuse that we are required to report. We are trusted helpers, shadows, and guides. As Sherpas, we guide people who want to receive redemption and/or recover from what life has done to them. We are keepers of secrets, although we are required to disclose some suicidal behaviors and abusive crimes.

To move a person beyond what has happened to them in this life, we need to know details, so we can address the behaviors, not the person.

Following are some of the ways in which we all have common threads with secrets and self-disclosure.

Secrets are powerful. They elicit responses of trust or betrayal. They put others at risk of having knowledge of powerful events. Secrets can be tricks to deceit. There is a saying: "We're only as sick as our secrets." We need to reveal as much as we can mentally and spiritually, except when doing so will seriously injure ourselves or others. Do No Harm.

Trust is something we earn by incremental steps built one upon the other, with increasing amounts of responsibility given to us as we prove we have what it takes to responsibly care for more information. We become trusted servants of our fellow beings. When someone shares personal and vulnerable positions with us, we are always the responsible party. Our actions create changes in people's lives. Sometimes, as in times of war, "Loose lips sink ships."

Our quest as sturdy, balanced people is to be open books, confident and comfortable with ourselves and able to respond well when others break our trust. We learn to address the behaviors of others and let our experience be a reason for change. How we deal with compromising instances and still stay open and willing to collaborate is our quest.

We learn to create equity by our self-disclosure in a manner that is safe for all. That is the mark of our skillfulness and craft as trustworthy servants. We become transparent with our environment. People can see our truth clearly and understand that our trust has been hard won through honesty. When we make mistakes, we take ownership and make amends.

As we change, we may find that when talking amongst people we are comfortable with, we are relaxed and relate to each other while still holding onto our partial perspectives and bias — especially where frustration and loss were involved. We try to tell our story and have others champion our cause. Sometimes our righteousness comes out looking like gossip, character assassination and slander of any other party involved. In those cases, we get to look at what motivated us to compromise the other's integrity.

Those whom we have hurt in the past fear we will repeat what happened. With that fear comes the reality that we typically do attract what happened; it is a cycle, and we are afraid or unwilling to trust again. We keep secrets that actually perpetuate our belief system of mistrust. Everyone can see what's going on except us. By withholding, we become the ones who are not trusted, and we suffer for that as well.

Some families are private and do not allow divulging family secrets because of shame-based, religious and/or moral obligations. Culturally we all want to fit in and not be ostracized for our beliefs — so we live by omission; we don't say why we do "that," we simply don't say anything. We all want to look normal — or appear better than other families.

Intimacy is a way for us to develop more than a superficial existence with each other. But it requires that we be healthy, mature, and consenting adults as we move closer together. We learn to not send mixed signals that cross safety boundaries. We know how to honor our trust and value each other's truth. We know the sacred bond of not disclosing unnecessary information to curious, inquiring minds. We are trustworthy with many people on a variety of issues, and yet able to speak our truth in a safe way for everyone to understand.

Common things people tend to keep secret are basic, such as money and credit issues, family and marital issues, mental-health issues, and disease diagnoses. Other family secrets include criminal records, mistakes made as youths, Internet interests such as porn or gambling, retail shopping and the like. Our common experiences and sharing leads us to discover that we are all basically garden-variety people with similar problems. Stigma and shame stops us from connecting with others and finding solutions and options. Sadly, at times it is more comfortable to stay stuck in secrets than to move forward with workable solutions.

It is important to have healthy boundaries and develop trust and alignment of values through equitable introspection. We need the ability for critical thinking for both parties to stay objective without bias toward delicate issues. We must agree to disagree and accept the other, while holding the paradox of our own beliefs.

There is some shame associated with medical diagnoses and mental-health issues. Anyone's knowledge of those could compromise your job and social status. How we move beyond secretive and shame-based idioms is the mark of our craft as sentient beings who share many like-minded experiences.

If we look at the similarities of people and their experiences, we are likely to keep a broader mindset when it comes to critical thinking and objectivity.

Those from different cultures believe that they must keep their experiences under a veil of secrets for fear that they will be misunderstood, singled out as a culture, and then racially profiled.

Honesty in a relationship is valuable. Trust is earned. We must realize that sometimes our truth can hurt loved ones and friends. We need to value and learn healthy boundaries but not walk on eggshells and live in fear of stepping on relationship landmines.

People with weight or body issues may eat secretly so they don't get judged by others about their choices of foods and eating styles.

Isn't it interesting that we are most likely to "tell all" when we are with strangers in an elevator or a cab ride? We easily talk to a stranger we know we will never see again. Plane rides are great for that kind of release. We can really tell all and let go of the consequences. This kind of cathartic release is healthy. It is a fact that when asked about our family, jobs or life in general, we are more comfortable telling another our problems.

The same effect is created in support groups where there are confidentiality rules. People can tell their truth in safety. Sometimes just the act of saying troubles out loud creates the first time they can hear how serious they feel about something. They can also see how unreal their words sound and that they don't really mean what they thought they believed. It is so important to move beyond feelings of fear and living in secretive worlds. We all have common experiences; we can learn from each other the ways to better adapt and move forward.

Something many of us do is keeping feelings close to our chests after hearing traumatic news. People will ask how we are doing, and we say, "Fine." We minimize the opportunity to share our fresh pain with another. We believe it is our personal pain and forget that we are all equal-opportunity seekers for joy as well as pain. It is worth the time to take a look at why we think our pain is personal and must remain silent.

With the ease and various content with Internet porn, many lead dual lives that keep them from living authentically with another person. We can move into getting our needs met in a relationship by addressing all of the ways in which we use fantasy, isolation, magical thinking, and mind reading to guess our partner's wishes, or experience what we share as a connection.

These are great examples of our sick secrets and inner cries for unmet love. We try to find harmony with oneness and that person's reality.

Workbook Questions:

1. What secrets will go with you to the grave? What could happen if you trust someone and processed your deeply held value with them?

2. What cultural values keep you from being honest with others? What's the worst that could happen? Lose face, a job, your status in the workplace or community?

3. Is addiction part of your shame and fear of disclosing? What are your addictions? Gambling, porn, drugs, alcohol, shopping, and/or compulsive issues? Name as many as you can here.

4. Have you accidentally disclosed secrets or personal business and were embarrassed? Have you ever been in trouble for breaking someone's trust or anonymity? What happened? What did you learn?

5. Are you a trustworthy person who is capable of keeping confidential information? What are your limits?

6. Do you feel comfortable telling things to strangers you will never see again? Why do you think that is so?

7. Do you know how to use support groups and medical professionals to work on secrets and disclosing your deepest truths?

8. Do you keep the secrets that you or another family member have had thoughts of suicide? Hatred of or disgust with another family member? How do you feel this separates the family from having real intimacy with so many secrets flowing around?

9. When an issue becomes personal with someone, mudslinging is going on and your reputation is on the line, do you break confidentiality just because the other did? Do you go down the immoral road of character assassination just because the other party did? Do you have a moral compass that helps you to move away from that behavior?

10. Are you comfortable with your vision of yourself, your self-esteem, your valued place in the community? Do you know how to shake off broken trust like water off a duck's back? What do you have that is so invested that you begin to negatively emote and create a cycle of recidivism?

11. Do you have the willingness to learn more about healthy disclosure? What are you willing to do?

Self-Care

What you do to take care of yourself has the most influence on the way you relate to the rest of the world.

When you work on your mind and body to keep them physically, psychologically, socially and spiritually sound and fit, your world will embody a full and healthy life.

Healthy foods are more easily digested. Our mood improves when we exercise. Our brains are stimulated to produce "feel-good chemicals" through these daily movements. You move muscles, which creates a better self-image and relates to how you are seen by others. The chemicals released also decrease stress hormones. All from that burst of energy you receive from exercising.

Another great way to relieve tension and improve your mental attitude and social skills is by doing service for those who suffer. By volunteering to help others, your self-esteem is raised. You get outside of the "closed system" between your ears. Give energy to what interests you and makes you come alive. Find community with like-minded individuals. Seek out those who practice art, music, sports and reading. Learn all about what you love, and cherish your precious gifts.

When your mind and body are at peak performance, you will be at your healthiest state and can combat diseases, reduce stress, and keep your metabolism ready for what comes next. Fuel and exercise create energy to manage bodily functions. More blood and oxygen will go to the brain, helping you to think better. You will sleep soundly at night from supporting all these aspects of your health.

Moderation is the key to longevity. Persistence is key to developing your personal experience with wisdom. The choices you must make will become clear as the tinkling of a bell.

Start with the basics. The way you go to sleep is the way you will wake up. If you rejuvenate that miraculous machine you are in charge of, it will run well. The way you choose to go to sleep will affect how you sleep. The quality you put into your sleep affects your health, emotional balance and energy levels.

It's smart to take a look at how you overdraw from your sleeping equity accounts. You might come in too late, party too hard, work on a project into the wee hours, or just spend time on your computer or watching TV. You might also worry about things that may happen and dwell on them, causing yourself stress about something you can do nothing about and have no control over. It all adds up to not being prepared for the day ahead and the opportunities coming your way.

After you wake up, how you start your day is generally how the day will play out. When you wake up late, reaching for and running toward the day in a diminished and rushed state, you will always be trying to catch up. This will keep you in peril. You will wonder when the jig is up and when the other shoe will drop. This is no way to keep balanced. The choice is yours.

When you wake up mindfully, aware of yourself and your surroundings, you will move with skill and determination to follow your intentions and aspirations for your day. You awaken with gratitude and move toward your life goals with joyful exertion. You will pause and think about what will happen that day. You will begin your self-care routine and eat mindfully. You will make sure you have everything you need for the day ahead.

Another primal component of self-care is eating. You truly are what you eat. If you choose healthy foods, chances are with some exercise, you will do well. Learn about healthy foods and know what works best with your body. It's your choice to put in good foods, so your body can create healthy energy.

Have spiritual aspirations, such as a morning reading or a website that sends a daily quote or healthy thoughts. Take a few moments for mindful repose. Create a way to have a working, walking, eating, sleeping type of mindful approach. Fill your day with 24 hours of goodness. When you have tension, keep it right-sized and appropriate, and don't let one dark cloud outshine the sun in your day.

Self-Care Techniques You Can Try

A healthy person knows how and when it is time to assert themselves and their ideas. He or she will know when to speak out against the madness of unfairness. Holding negative emoting inside creates sickness, disease, tension and unhappiness. Speak up and be heard. You deserve to be here. Take your place, collaborate, and thrive with good intentions and abilities.

Relax and stop your world for a few moments. This helps with energy management. How you turn off and check out of the furious disorder of your life is important. Close your eyes and relax for a few moments wherever you are, if it is safe. Watch something funny or distracting to get your mind off what you are working on. Stop working and make a conscious choice to relax. The challenge will still be here when you return. Go to the gym, take a walk, meditate, go for a bike ride, and enjoy some shopping. Relax; the world will keep turning without you for a few minutes. New ideas will come into fruition by walking away from a stressful situation. While you sleep, your mind comes up with all kinds of ideas and practices that evolve from simply taking a break.

Be here and now in the present. Be mindful about what you can do and what will have to wait. Be the universal observer in your life and notice — without judgment — how your mind is driven to distraction. Come back to the moment and realize that feelings and energy levels are like clouds blowing to and fro on the wind. They will come and go, but you can remain calm as you watch and gently navigate turbulent times.

Notice your attachment to your thinking, and let go. You are not meant to hold onto poisonous thoughts and suffering. As you breathe in, notice what is up for you. On your exhale, invite empathy, compassion, trust, faith, and belief — whatever you need. Give this gift of mindful abundance to yourself and to others. Once you access this energy, you will know it is limitless, fearless and courageous. You do the deed for the act itself — not for rewards or immediate gratification.

Write down what you hope to get done in one day and journal about what stressors you encountered. By this act, you can work toward healthy ambivalence and solutions.

We are given only a certain amount of time in one day. We make choices that create our reality. We cannot do all things or be all places at once. We have to choose the best next right thing to do and garner the greater good from all of our hard work. Prioritize these precious moments, and make healthy choices with your own 24 hours.

Don't eat a meal right before you sleep. Your body will digest the food during slumber and might cause discomfort and unsettling dreams.

You can also choose not to work on all of the problems of that day. Put them on a shelf. They do not get to rent space in your head all night long, distract you and cause distress. Give emotionally escalating events and stressful people five or 10 minutes at a time, then put them back on the shelf until you can work on a solution later.

Do not let others' bad planning and disasters demand an immediate response from you. Mindfully navigate their dilemma and come from a place of offering solution-focused skills. Only they have the choice to stop putting bandages on expansive problems and make choices about what they choose to do in the future.

Reduce stress in your life, and live as drama-free as you can. Use healthy boundaries and show people where they end and you begin. Make sure they know you are not an enabler with codependent tendencies.

Use gardening as a relaxing tool. Till the soil; plant; rejuvenate; encourage sprouting, watering, and caring for the Earth.

Use your spiritual tools, such as meditating, breathing, prayer, yoga, surrendering and accepting. Experience joyful exertion for your life's ideals, aspirations and intentions toward living to cause no more stress and do no more harm to others.

Mentally challenge yourself with critical thinking and conflict resolution. Use motivational speaking and non-violent communication.

Take time to sit and notice what is going on with your brain activity. Notice it and also what is going on inside your body. Pay attention and relax any tension.

Remove noises and distractions, and be heard above the clamor in your life. You are in charge of what happens. Take ownership.

Just like in an airplane, put the oxygen mask on yourself before you help others. Take care of your needs, and make sure you are safe and can process your experience. Then if you have the energy, help others in a timed and measurable way. Then, go back to extreme self-care in processing your experience.

In small, daily increments, we have just enough time to do things for ourselves. What is it that you do for yourself in between the things you have to do?

Our self-care at work includes training, workshops, human resources, team-building meetings, and fun, community- and strength-building parties.

By doing service to help others, we use a counter-intuitive ability to thrive and get outside of ourselves. It is by this precious act that we realize life is not about us. Life is a "we" thing. We are all responsible for making our world a better place, one person at a time.

Who can you help today?

Self-Care Practices – Make Them Your Own
- Do at least five of these every week.
- Treat yourself or your partner to flowers, dinner, a show or movie. L-I-V-E.

- Play in the rain, sun, or snow.
- Go to the beach, and feel the power of the wind, surf and sand.
- Meditate and breathe; relax and let hope live inside your heart.
- Go to a chiropractor; get acupuncture, or try something new for your body.
- Hold hands or snuggle with your partner; it relieves tension and stress.
- Write, journal, speak your mind with written words, and listen to what you say.
- Turn off the computer, cell phone and TV for 24 hours.
- Go on a spiritual retreat; feel the healing love of others on your path.
- Take a sick day from work, and use it as a healing, mental-health day.
- Keep your daily to-do list to four items or less.
- Go to a playground, and act like a kid.
- Try healing with humor; laugh at what usually makes you mad. Use the giggle factor.
- Take pictures of what you love to look at.
- Look; notice the beauty in all that surrounds you.
- Stand up and speak about something you truly believe in, in a non-violent way.
- Treat yourself as deserving; consider giving to yourself unconditionally.
- Dress for fun, success, and/or comfort— you decide.
- Do image-breakers that stop you from acting only one way; break out of monotony.
- Look for a job you would love doing, and start making inroads toward it.
- Clean house, and give away or re-purpose what you love to another who will cherish it.
- Hire someone to clean your house. Hire someone to mow your lawn.
- Be generous; use the power and abundance of your smile to heal others.
- Forgive yourself and others completely.
- Make a Bucket List, and do one thing on it to break monotony.
- Eat, drink and be merry without self-criticism or guilt.
- Watch comedy, cartoons, and children's movies, if they comfort you; don't judge yourself.
- Smile at strangers without being scared. Besides, they won't know what you're thinking.
- Practice radical kindness to strangers and unconditional regard toward everyone.
- Go through your contact list, and call people just to say hello.
- Enjoy water sports such as rowing, riding or driving a speedboat, skiing, sailing and canoeing.
- Plan a comedy night with YouTube or Netflix, or go to a club.
- Use spirituality when the mud is hitting the fan; change yourself.

- Listen to your body, and do restful things before sleep.
- Play music; make art, and dance under the stars.
- Clean your house, but hire someone to do the things you hate to do.
- Go on small power walks during your breaks at work.
- Be mindful about what and when you eat.
- Practice deep breathing; let your thoughts pass by like the clouds in the sky. Let go.
- Go somewhere beautiful outdoors; sit in the sunshine and get your Vitamin D.
- Put your music on shuffle, and let serendipity do the rest.
- Enjoy the animals around you. They are waiting for you to notice them.
- Exercise hard, then relax and stretch. Feel the power of your precious body.
- Write an "I'm so happy and grateful now that…" list and own what you want right now.
- Soak your feet, paint your nails—or get a manicure and or pedicure. Buy clothes that fit your body. Buy comfy clothes to relax in.
- Buy tickets to a play, sports game or a concert—go do something!

Workbook Questions:

1. Are you miserly with your self-care? Is it something you leave to do last? What will it take for you to put your self-care on top of the "to-do" list?

2. Name five ways you do self-care during the day. Why so little? What will it take for you to do self-care in all your activities? Can you be this mindful?

3. Do you just accept that your job is stressful? Are your personal experiences and feelings not valuable when it comes to making money?

4. When you have engagements or interactions with your family, partner, kids, and/or boss, do you make sure you take care of yourself first? What do you have of value to offer others?

5. How is it unfair to others when you give without healthy boundaries? If you do not make plans for self-care, someone will make other plans for you. How will you speak up and value your life and worth?

6. How do you value and take care of yourself when you are tired? When you are overworked? When you are sick? What are you afraid will happen if you take personal time off? Getting fired? What?

7. Can you develop better eating and sleeping habits? Do you operate in a diminished capacity and accept it as normal?

8. Do you party in excess? Do you drink when you're happy? Sad? Angry? Do you have a problem with drugs?

9. How do you do self-care during emotionally escalating episodes? What could you do better?

10. Do you give anger and depression more power than healthy ideals? How do you keep your mental balance?

Self-Empowerment

Our personal power looks and acts different in various areas of our lives.

We are often caught up in flux and stasis, and we procrastinate instead of engaging our capacities. Procrastination often takes up all of our valuable lives with remorseful thoughts. It also erodes our resilience. Let's take healthy steps and move beyond our superficial pain-body.

Responsibility over our lives begins in four areas: mental, spiritual, physical and emotional. We practice responsibility in our personal life, at work, on a team, with a group, at church, and with others in all facets of our lives.

Most of us roll along haphazardly and get what we can. We disproportionally strive to get more of what we are good at and therefore create imbalance. We usually confuse abundance as having plenty of what we don't need. In what ways can we hone our abilities to have energy and power like a balanced and well-honed steel instrument — strong, yet flexible and supple?

Spiritual Self-Empowerment

What is your spiritual or religious belief system? What kind of god do you believe in? Is your faith based upon your own strengths or does it focus on your weakness and sins? Does your belief give power to you or take it away? Do you believe you deserve to be well-balanced and belong on the planet?

As we navigate toward our higher selves, we all want to evolve toward it with resilience and an improved ability to solve our problems. We want to feel good about our ability to make choices and decisions that lead us to feel renewed and hopeful. We want to feel empowered in our healing and unification with our higher selves.

Self-awareness about our place in the universe raises our status as beings of worth. It creates self-confidence in our ability to have faith in what is and move beyond our fear-based existence. We align ourselves with yearned-for positive qualities to complete our unfinished selves. We evolve one day at a time through surrendering hardships and through our ability to suspend our empirical thinking. We learn that we don't have to go anywhere to find our life teachers; whatever goes wrong, creates tension and connects us to our pain-body becomes a spiritual teacher. The idea of getting power from what goes wrong in our lives is counter-intuitive to always wanting to win and do good.

Sometimes life just is, that's all. With our free will we have a choice to evolve or stay the same — the choice is almost always ours. We must become willing participants and awaken our willingness to listen to the universe calling us. Are we listening?

Emotional Self-Empowerment

We relate to our environment using what we have around us. We empower the wholesome way that we are inclusive and support others around us. We use our communication talents to position and influence the behaviors of other people. We are empathetic and trusted; our rapport helps others, which in turn helps us. By empowering others with service and altruistic intentions, we utilize our emotional intelligence. We are self-empowered. Our acknowledgment is measured by the way others move our positions, thoughts, and requests into an equitable, functioning society.

Empowering Our Emotions

How do bad thoughts translate into what we're drawing into our lives? We come in "tore up from the floor up." How do we become willing to do things differently? What kind of trust do we need? What kind of hope would instill faith for us to take a chance and try something else? Do others have control of your emotions? If we are in control and holding everyone else emotional hostage, what kind of world does that make? If we make others feel insignificant and useless, how long will it be before we feel our own wrath?

Inspirations come and go; hopes and wishes come and go, and being lucky comes and goes. If we choose to live our lives as an aspiration, we wake up every day willing to do the deed at hand. We have willingly chosen our way of life, and we know that even though we do not have it all today, by the end of our lives, we will have more than we have right now.

What if this moment were the only moment we had to be happy on the planet? What would we choose? Happy or mean? Unhappy? Non-believing? What do we need to be believers, and what do we want from the world? What are we afraid of asking the world for that we don't believe we will be given? How do we stop bad things from happening to us right now and, in the future, slow them down? How do others do it? How do normal people do it?

We have a transferrable skill set in our arsenal. As much as we believe in the safety of negative emoting ("Why bother? Who cares? Give up! Huh-uh"), we can turn that negative power into our most positive asset. We turn poison into medicine. Once we release the negative stress that we put on our bodies a shift happens. All of the negative is turned into a positive healing force of good toward our minds and bodies. We start with a leap of faith and belief in the unknown that something is available out there, that others are accessing a better and safer life, so "why not me?"

We trust the process of doing small, yet measurable, observable acts, and build upon our mindful, small successes. It's a daily process we do with regimentation. The more we put into our self-empowerment, the more we get out of it. It is a spiritual bank of well-being of which there is no upper limit.

What does your internal belief system look like? Are you a bad person who has sinned, will never be any good, can never be redeemed? Do you believe in a shame-based faith where you have an angry god who punishes and doesn't forgive? Maybe we could let go of this angry-god concept and find a loving, forgiving, nurturing and empowering belief system.

Physical Empowerment

There are many ways to increase our activities that give us greater health and improve our time on the planet. We need only think ahead and do those activities now, so we are ready when times are tough.

Ways to increase our physical attributes will also make us feel emotionally, spiritually, and mentally fit. Physical activities done for an hour a day kick off our body's ability to create feel-good hormones and reset our brain chemistry. After a workout, we feel better and can have a great experience with our minds and bodies for the rest of the day. Exercise also gives us emotional resilence and helps our bodies increase the ability to fight disease by pulling all resources to hand, available and on call.

We can start with simple things such as walking in our neighborhoods or in nature for a few minutes; taking the stairs instead of using an elevator; parking farther away so we get a small walk in. We can use house-cleaning; washing clothes, windows or dishes; vacuuming; gardening; dog-walking, and mowing the lawn as exercise credit. Not only will this activity make us feel good physically but chores get done, too!

We might choose physical workouts with others or at home on television. With the choices of yoga, Pilates, cardio kickboxing, gyms and more, ways to work out are endless. But we must do something. We are putting equity into our physical bodies. If we do not put anything into ourselves, we won't get anything out.

We also have to feed our machines. Our bodies crave to be fed; it's up to us to feed them the right foods that will sustain and help us to endure whatever lies ahead. If we don't invest in our eating habits, the lack of care will catch up with us sooner or later. The combination of not eating and not working out can have catastrophic effects on our health.

Mental Empowerment

What we do to increase brain activity is as important as the physical work we do with our bodies. In a way, the brain is its own body and wants to be entertained with abstract and complex, problem-solving opportunities. Unfortunately, most people use very little of the brain. We have a Ferrari under our skull cap; yet, we never take it out for a spin to see what it can do on the roadmap of our lives.

After doing physical workouts for an hour, the brain is available with its chemistry in harmony for task-oriented skills. Think of it as a "use it or lose it" machine. It will do only what the server commands of it. This genie in the bottle will give us all the wishes we can handle. New job, hobbies, computer skills, education, new languages, learning how to live and feel better about ourselves — the list is endless.

Once our brain is at attention, we can start our neurogenesis by doing small tasks in our choice of skills, such as learning something on a computer. We start by turning it on, working on orientation skills, moving into more extensive skill-building, and eventually we are professionals at what we do, if we put the time in. We will create new neural pathways and proceed toward learning other skills. We build skill upon skill and become masters of our own mental empowerment.

If our track record is based upon our childhoods and what transpired with our early adult lives, it is not a life sentence. We can start the change in our lives right now. Let's begin. Honor that this is the first step in the first day of the rest of our lives. We start with incremental skills that build upon our diligence, persistence and perseverance. What can you do today to start your empowered, autonomous existence?

The following are ways to start your day differently:
- Wake up earlier and have a mindful session where you meditate on your day and your breath. Notice where your body and mind are out of balance, and adjust your focus to release tension there.

- Eat noticeably healthier foods that give you energy, not make you sleepy. Some grain, some fruit, some protein. Challenge yourself to eat better. Eating better will make you feel, think and sleep better.

- Make a list of what you would like to accomplish. Schedule it out roughly, and be happy with whatever you get done. Challenge yourself with simple skills at first, and then work toward more complex tasks until you get proficient. This is most important.

- Stay task-oriented; be mindful, and do one thing at a time. Finish, and move on to the next task.

- When you feel your old defeatist attitude creeping in and making you feel "less than," angry, confused, and defensive, recognize your behavior, resist the temptation to act out and then recover your life by doing the next right thing, and after that the next right thing.

- Dress for success. Dress for the job you want, not the job you have. Act as if you are where you want to be. Visualize your future; don't dwell on your past.

- When you feel small, invisible, and unskillful, let yourself have five minutes with it. Choosing to do that for a set time makes it your choice to continue down that path. That is where change begins. Get out of your normal routine, and do the next right thing. Your only real job in life is to do the next right thing.

- Have accountability partners that you book-end your plans with. Let them know what you got done that day. This is a sure-fire way to stay accountable.

- Be impeccable with your words and your inner dialogue. Be gentle with good and bad things that happen. Stay in the gray area, and notice your reactions without acting upon them.

- Forgive yourself for anything that happens you aren't happy about, and try to do better next time. That attitude holds a lifetime of actions, aspirations and intentions. Inspiration is temporary and fleeting, but aspirations are a committed way of living.

We will know fear when we can hold it in our hands and see it for what it is. We will know our power when we do not let others take it. If we do not make plans, others will make plans for us. We must learn in incremental steps to trust our inner wisdom. By doing service and helping others, we feel better. We find ways to help others with what we know how to do. By our giving, we are receiving. We get esteem and empowerment by doing estimable acts.

It is naturally counter-intuitive that we would give while we feel so bad and have so little ourselves. But as we do the work of helping others while we suffer, we transcend into our own self-empowerment. To get through that feeling, we have to meet it head on, face to face.

Think about what empowerment means to you. Is it a new job? Being in charge of your life? Paying your bills and taxes? Having a great relationship with yourself and a partner? Move toward your goals.

Workbook Questions:

1. How does your spiritual belief system make you feel safe, complete, whole and empowered to move through life with health and balance? Do you have a punishing god? How do you spiritually get your power?

2. What or who has the power over you? Who or what siphons and drains your power away emotionally, physically, spiritually, and/or mentally?

3. How do you give your power away by being silent, shy, invisible? What have you done to take back your power, get a voice, take your rightful place, and be seen?

4. What physical activities do you practice every day to make sure your body gets action? Name five activities you would like to do. What will it take for you to get going?

5. In what ways do you challenge your mental capacity? How do you emotionally stabilize your mental and emotional self to work together as a team?

6. Would you be able to do more if you were emotionally stable? Name ways you can improve your resilience and take charge of your life.

7. Name some ways in which you feed your body to empower your mental, physical, and emotional being. What will make you have better decision-making food choices? Why would you finally eat better?

8. How does procrastination keep you from achieving goals? What is the list you would like to accomplish? What will be the first step toward achieving your goals? Keep it simple.

9. How do your spiritual or religious beliefs give you empowerment? How do your beliefs center on having power and righteousness over others who are "less than" because of their own beliefs? How do you keep your balance with discord in your life? Do you have a loving, teaching, giving, spiritual path? Or does your judging and harsh god like to keep you in a diminished state? Does this belief keep you hostage to a higher power that does not acknowledge your well-being?

10. Why do you need to have power over others? Why do you feel unsafe with creating equity with people of color or of a culture different from yours? What fears do you have of others getting educated and empowered? Why?

11. What would happen if you had the power you needed to do everything you wanted and got the life you deserved? Would you want others to have what you have? Would you share? Why or why not? Explain your belief about empowered abundance for all.

Self-Esteem and Negative Self-Evaluation

Self-esteem is realized by your actions with others.

This interpersonal reflection of our deeds and our community create how we feel about ourselves. Self-esteem should not be confused with narcissism, hyper-grandiosity, or ego-clinging.

The idea of healthy self-esteem requires us to let go of attachments and expectations, and just do the next right things because they are healthy and good to do. Our esteem is built by doing healthy, estimable acts. Life shows up, and situation by situation, we deal with it using our wisdom and discernment.

We are mindful and measured, with the abilities and goodness we bring to our environment. We strive to create equity, safety and forward movement toward communities with abilities to change and maneuver in these trying times. The saying, "What other people think of us is none of our business," means that sometimes we have to courageously do what we believe is right. We are not going to blow smoke up people's jumpers to get our needs met or be placating people-pleasers. We are strong, dedicated, service-minded people who live our lives for the benefit of others. We develop and create healthy relationships.

Usually when we are feeling good, we don't notice how healthy and happy our lives are. When things go wrong and people judge us, we tend to feel low self-esteem. Someone has let the air out of our balloon, and it "harshes our mellow."

By the continued act of harming others by belittling, judging, objectifying, and name-calling, we eventually self-fulfill our prophecy of low self-esteem. We get used to "the way it is." We forget to access the long and well-worn road of our past accomplishments, and we let one dark cloud outshine the sun.

Well, no more, my friends. We are in control of our thoughts. What we think becomes what we believe about ourselves. No more name-calling or belittling ourselves. We must be impeccable with our word. Don't judge others, lest we be judged ourselves. Be willing to access the benefit of the doubt, and move into empowering others as a way of making healthier communities. We are what we think we are. In a way, others are what we think they are, too.

Ways to Develop Esteem

- Be mindful about what you are doing. Put some thought into how, where, when and why you are doing whatever it is.

- Know thy self. Do not self-deprecate. Stop putting yourself down. Look for kernels of truth about the goodness and intention of what you are doing and why that is valuable.

- Do the next right thing with kind acts toward loved ones, colleagues, and strangers. Practice radical kindness and unconditional, positive regard toward others. Each day, love yourself by saying affirmations out loud, looking into the mirror and facing your fears. Move beyond static and flux and into motion. Just for today, say, "What others think of me is none of my business." Say it over and over when you are frozen in fear and can't do your job well.

- Start accepting groundlessness and uncertainty as a safe, neutral harbor.

- Catch negative self-talk. Calm that part of your brain with soothing and affirmative replacement sayings such as, "I am safe." "I belong here." "I deserve to get this promotion."

- Act as if you own what you want in your mind. Dress for the status and place you want. Fake it till you make what you want out of your life.

- Use joyful exertion with your life force, with a sense of urgency that this is a timed event.

- Hope dies last. If you give yourself hope, you can give it to others. If you can give it to others, you can be patient with yourself and your struggle. Hope requires participation, faith, belief, patience, surrender, grace, acceptance and exertion toward your desired goals. Faith without working toward your goals is just procrastination.

- Stop medicating yourself with alcohol and drugs. They just don't help a whole lot.

- Be gentle with yourself. Understand that mistakes are like clouds going by in the sky. They happen; they come and go. It is our attachment and brutalizing of ourselves and others that creates a lot of damage in the world. Stop participating in that way of living, and start forgiving yourself and others.

- Live fully, without regrets and reservations. No more could've, should've, would've, yes-but and if-only. Those words create void and diminished self-esteem.

- State the positive aspects of doing. "I have good intentions." "I made great effort." "I came close to my goals." "I feel satisfied, hopeful and willing to try again." "I made some mistakes, and I am improving day by day."

- People see what they want to see. If you are looking for something good and hopeful, you are apt to find it. If you are looking for something wrong, bad or unskillful, you can easily find that, too, along with fault with almost anyone or anything. Put on a new set of Goodness Glasses, and see the world in a hopeful light.

- Think of all the possibilities and choices that can be made. Work with your ambivalence, and trust yourself. Start with imperceptible items at first, and then move toward complex situations. Trust is earned, not given.

- You have a right to feel your feelings. But after five minutes it's your choice to keep the waves of distrust, anger, and fear growing and rolling in, or to choose to shrug them off, get off the beach. Realize that whatever happened is a bump in the road, not the end of the road. Get back in the driver's seat of trust.

- Do estimable acts toward others as a way to build self-esteem. Do it with healthy boundaries, so you do not build up resentment toward those you help. When you help others, let go of the outcome and the reward system. Do it because it is the right thing to do.

- Let people be wrong.

- Don't personalize what happens to you with global statements such as, "I deserve this." "Now I feel like a total failure." "This always happens to me." "Now they really know who I am." "I have been found out — I am a fake and fraudulent person."

- Don't paint a target on yourself that others can aim for and hit. Stop playing the victim, no matter what happened. You deserve to be seen, feel safe, feel honored and acknowledged and deserving of egalitarian virtues. Only you can give them to yourself.

- When something goes wrong, instead of putting yourself down, think of all the good intentions, effort, and exertion you put into that project. Give yourself credit for what you do. Name five good things about your effort. Put it all in balance, so the one unfortunate instance is right-sized and appropriate.

- Detach with love to others' negative ideas and talk. Do not slander or gossip — it is poison that harms everyone concerned.

- Be assertive with what you know to be truth. Stand by your words; be impeccable with your speech. Believe in something, then learn to trust what you believe. You might have to stand alone for a bit. Tell yourself it's OK.

- Trust that there are three truths: yours, mine, and our combined truth. None of these require putting down another's belief. People who choose to honor the complexity of multiple truths can feel good about themselves, as well as having a different experience with another.

- When someone else gets the job, the partner, the raise, the car, or the object of your desire, try being happy for them and work on their happiness becoming your happiness. If they have the happiness you desire in the world, they are less likely to do harm to another. If you are able to be happy for them, you are more likely to move toward that ideal. If we foster a bad feeling toward someone receiving abundance, we foster that same kind of delusion for our own abundance. This is a law of abundance — that there are enough resources for all. We just need to work on the system of equal redistribution. That is the real task.

Workbook Questions:

1. Do you have a difficult time with growth and change? Do you fear your ability to handle challenges you will face? Explain.

2. How does being afraid of doing something, and worried about what others think of you, stop you from living your life and realizing your true potential?

3. Do you believe your self-perception? Do you believe "the way you think about yourself in relation to others" can be changed? What is the perception you want others to believe about you? What small changes can you put into place to make that happen?

4. Do you put yourself down simply so you will feel safer and won't have to participate in life on a level playing field? In what ways do you use excuses to stay stuck? What will happen if you move beyond excuses and showed up ready to make mistakes toward changing your life?

5. What happens when you affirm things about your abilities? What will happen if you tried to stay positive for an entire day? Who would you be?

6. As a child, were you put down and violated because of your skills? Were you told you were stupid, or discouraged from singing because you didn't sound good, or told you're not good at something because of your gender or ethnicity? How can you heal your inner child and make powerful affirmations of your worth today to change that old story into healing?

7. Do you live in fear and feel compelled to be a people-pleaser and butt-kisser? How does that erode your self-esteem? What is the worst thing that will happen if you are honest with others? What small acts can you do to make inroads toward a realistic situation?

8. What are your thoughts about what others think about you? Why does it bother you so much? What are you doing that makes you feel ashamed? What's the worst that can happen if you let go of all that worry?

9. What successes have made you feel empowered in the past? Can you use those experiences to help you to make better choices about self-image?

10. Do you have reservations about what you can achieve? Are those excuses based upon self-deprecation? Are they based upon what others think you can do? What will the turnaround thinking look like?

11. What are your low self-esteem triggers? Are they comfortable and familiar?

12. Are you cocky and arrogant about how well you do something? Why do you feel the need to overcompensate for your skills? Why do you have to be the best? What happens when you are just one of the crowd?

13. What are your short-term goals for the next month? What are four things you want to get done this year? By goal-setting, you get to work toward something of value. When you have that value, it radiates into all areas of your ability — skillfulness, happiness and worth. This is called self-esteem.

Self-Monitoring and Self-Regulation

Are you easily distracted? Do you resist anything but temptation?

First of all, most of us live in fear of starting new things or learning new ways of living our lives. We judge what will happen in the future by our experiences of the past. We see the world through our own life's lenses, jaded by negative things that have happened.

Maybe we begin things and get the ball rolling. But whatever we expect doesn't happen fast enough. We get bored and distracted and find ourselves on a working mission creep. We get discombobulated and are all over the place. We are driven to distraction. "Can't you tell I've been working by the mess I've made?"

Sometimes we want to have new adventures and trophies of our worth and value, so others will know who we are. We want them to value and venerate us from having to feel the discomfort of life.

In all of these distractions, we are not really showing up for the job at hand. We have an agenda and pre-conceived expectations. We exhibit a form of control and manipulation so things will go our way. We like to look good in front of others. We want to be "the good one" in others' eyes.

Our egos spin out of control with immediate wants and needs. We lose track of what our life is really about. We need to do certain things to keep on track with our "mission statement" for our lives.

We desire to stay on track with all the aspects of our lives. We don't want to be unbalanced and good at only one or two things.

So we need mechanisms in place.

When we bring our mind and body to attention, we are capable of learning new concepts. Those new ideas lend themselves to our becoming skillful on many levels. We learn to manage and organize our thoughts. We need supervision to keep us on track, keep us balanced and accountable, and measure our worth through the short moments we have on the planet.

You've heard the saying, "Don't become your own doctor." This simply means you cannot always be objective when it is you who needs things that your mind may not be willing to do or accept. We need others to learn and integrate our own experiences. Otherwise, we are in a closed system between our ears—nothing gets in and nothing gets out. This is not healthy.

Learning to be pro-active has a preventive quality that leads us to authentically live our lives, not to simply react to whatever bad things resulted when we neglected responsible positions in life.

By interaction with others, we get to be part of the direction-driven process and accomplish our dreams and goals in the interpersonal panacea.

We can piss and moan that others have what we want, and flow with the negative emoting and reinforcing behaviors it creates, or we can choose to stick with winners. We find out how they learn and thrive. We find a community that resonates with our new wants and desires, and we integrate what they do. We stay accountable.

Once you have done the work to problem-solve the questions below, you will have a plan to do anything in your life. Follow these sage cross-examinations, and hold yourself accountable to a community of peers who work in tandem.

Become a self-regulated learner, able to handle anything, including the distractions life has to offer. The key to foster lasting success is persistence.

Workbook Questions:

1. What are you failing to learn or grasp in the content of your life?

2. What negative attitudes do you harbor about successful people living your desired dream?

3. What negative self-talk do you repeat so that you're not engaging in successful learning opportunities?

4. Which mentors are you willing to find or study under?

5. What free resources are available in your community? Can you access them to gain new accountability in your life?

6. Where are you willing to volunteer to get more information about your new interests?

7. What would a pleasure-and-information-gathering session look like for you? What questions would you ask? How would you address your fears of moving your intentions in this direction?

8. What behaviors would you like to target for regulating in your life? Name 10.

9. How willing are you to work on character defects that keep you from obtaining your goals and wishes intended for your life? What are the defects? Do defects include procrastination; entitlement; sloth; lack of belief in yourself; low self-esteem; arrogance?

10. How do you plan to break the cycle of failing to monitor and evaluate your learning? What calculated and organized method do you think will work for your life? What has worked in the past?

11. What method do you have in place to handle frustrations, failures and setbacks? How will you grow and learn to "get back on the horse"?

12. What is your wish list of goals and accomplishments that you want to regulate and sustain? Write everything down and sort it out later.

13. Picture yourself having your first success. How will your status, job or relationship be different?

14. What can you do as an "image-breaker" to move out of your comfort and safety zones?

15. Are you able to be mentored? How well do you take instruction from others?

16. Can you surrender your ego; everything you think, say, and do, and all your thoughts, words, and deeds, just for today?

Service to Ourselves and Our Community

"Service to others is the rent you pay for your room here on Earth." Muhammad Ali

Service is an act of love. Service keeps us sober and living our lives for the benefit of others. It keeps our experiences real and validates our aspirations and intentions for life.

To paraphrase the Beatles, in the end, the love you take is equal to the love you give. Service as a vocation is a way of securing your wellness on the journey of life.

In recovery, A helps B, and A gets better. Through this act of service, we can connect with others' suffering and get out of our own suffering. By this work, we know our experience is not unique. Invoking self-change thoughts in others gives us relief from our own demons, self-obsession, and egoistic clinging. It gives connection to our empty God hole. It fills this space of our lives with belonging, participating, social value, and esteem.

"We make a living by what we get. We make a life by what we give." Winston Churchill

When I live my life with service as vocation, I get myself out of the idea of me and mine—away from I, I, I, I, and me, me, me, me. I'm so busy thinking about me, I'm all I ever think about. Now that we're done talking about me, what do you think about me?

Ego-massaging creates an untenable and unsustainable "me" machine. The massaged ego always wants more—more perfection, more abundance. It is a self-fulfilling prophecy of doom that will never stop until we have a nervous breakdown and become willing to learn about less, less, less.

When I first came into recovery, I did not like other people. They irritated me. They annoyed me. They asked questions that were personal. They had agendas, and they wanted something from me.

As for me, I was judgmental, critical, abusive, passive-aggressive, vulnerable, sensitive, cowardly, a fake, a fraud, a phony, and a liar. Would you want service from someone like that? Would you want to receive help from someone that disturbed?

My first attempts at giving service were feeble, similar to someone offering a box of chocolates, but some were gone, some half-eaten, and your favorite ones, which I promised you, were not in the box.

This is how service starts—with big mistakes. You will keep making mistakes until, by the grace of your persistence, you actually help someone, and they say, "Thanks." It's a learning curve of persistence and intention.

When I was younger, I made conditional agreements with God. I said I would give a great amount of money to helping others if only He helped me. Alas, through my own selfish downfall, I never made it to my lofty ideal because I put "me" before "we."

Service is not just doing something because everything is going your way and you feel good about giving. The great thing is that anyone can start service at any time with nothing but the abundance of unending charity, compassion, hope and small acts. This choice to give abundance when you feel as if there is nothing left in your heart is when the spiritual moment actually happens. Through daily commitment, you build equity with the universe.

When you smile at someone and say hello, you reverberate throughout the universe. When you ask a person in a wheelchair how he is and include him in the conversation instead of pretending you don't see him, you are giving service. When you speak with an older person about death and dying, you help her to process what she is about to go through. You help them prepare for their journey, and they won't feel so alone on their path. Give service at your level of comfort and then begin doing more, as you realize you are filling your 24 hours with the best intentions and aspirations anyone could have. Fulfill yourself one day at a time.

There are benefits from giving service. You meet people you would never know who appreciate you and value what you do. You get outside of yourself and into "we." You volunteer, and this precious spiritual tithing develops your goodness and well-being. You are investing in your spiritual bank of well-being that has no upper limits.

Some of us live empty, spiritually bankrupt lives because we do not stretch and maintain our "giving service" muscles. We don't have the equity to rely on when we feel weak and depressed. To feel self-esteem, you must do estimable acts. This is how you achieve self-worth. Vitality and well-being, health and happiness all contribute to a long life well-lived, with a feeling of completeness and fulfillment.

Consider making a mission statement for your life. Use meaningful quotes and adopt the ideals of those who made service a part of their lives' vocation, such as St. Francis.

For myself, I pray to live my life for the benefit of others and to fight depression in the world. So I achieve two goals at once. I work on my own demons through helping others with their work with depression. When I am engaged with my reason for living, I do not focus on negative thoughts. I am a useful and helpful person. As a result, I create that identity and claim that gratuity for myself.

If you work with a population mired in trouble and calamity, you will develop compassion and turn that poisoned thinking into healing. You now can authentically work with others because you did your personal growth. You work alongside your bias, resistance or racism, and process your own demons while helping others.

However, there are requirements for self-care. When you help others, always help yourself first. Perform extreme self-care by putting the oxygen mask on your own face first so you can help others, just like on an airplane. Move slowly and do small tasks daily that build upon each other. Find a support group where you can process the emotions that come up.

It's easy to do too much and lose your own life in the process. You can get emotionally enmeshed in others — living their lives vicariously, their ups and downs, wins and losses — and forget about your most precious asset, which is your mental health and well-being. Have healthy boundaries, and know your limits. "Know thy self." If you don't make plans for your well-being, someone else will do it for you.

You can pull back and regroup at any time. Say, "I'm too busy," and take a break. You need to be in top shape to do the work at hand. Others are not mind readers. You need to say what's real for you and what is manageable. By this act, you learn and define your own healthy boundaries as you teach others about them.

Where I live, there are dozens of nonprofit agencies. Find your passion. Has someone in your family suffered from something in particular? Is there something you want to learn about? Is there something that could boost your career? Whatever you choose, get value from what you do on as many levels as you can. It will be satisfying on multiple levels. Look to your spiritual community, your civic community, your medical community, and impoverished neighborhoods to do service.

Rules of Thumb:

- Volunteer at the National Alliance on Mental Illness (NAMI).

- Help out at meetings of Alcoholics Anonymous, Narcotics Anonymous, Sex and Love Addicts Anonymous, Underearners Anonymous, or any other appropriate Twelve Steps group. Do service at Smart Recovery or Life Ring meetings or at your house of worship. Help them to get in touch with today's needs.

- Give what you can give.

- Get your neighbors to clean out stuff they no longer use. Gather it up to donate it to a secondhand store, or call a social-services agency for pickup.

- Gather all building materials your neighbors bought for projects they decided not to do. Donate them to places such as Habitat for Humanity.

- Volunteer at the library to help people looking for jobs on the Internet. Teach someone to read. Help children with what they need.

- Help at soup kitchens.

- Find your niche and develop it. The contagion will spread—others will want the incredible feeling, too, when they see the change in your life.

Workbook Questions:

1. In what ways in your daily life do you give service for others? In what ways would you like to give service but are afraid you will not be safe? What do you fear?

2. In what ways is your life completely self-serving? In what ways does this leave you with time you can use for service? No matter how little you have, this moment is the perfect teacher.

3. What can you give of yourself to help others? Money? Time? Knowledge? Passion? Experience?

4. How will you benefit from service? A new job? Kudos from your community or church?

5. What problems do you experience when working with others? What behavioral traits are you willing to change for someone else's benefit?

6. In what ways do you feel racist or unsafe with other cultures? Do you believe life is "us against them" in some ways?

7. Have you experienced the pleasure of someone simply saying "thank you" after getting your help? How did this make you feel?

8. What are ways you do extreme self-care?

9. What do healthy boundaries look like to you? Are you able to set healthy boundaries to avoid over-commitment?

10. In what ways will service affect your status in your community? Are you willing to sacrifice what others think of you in order to do the next right thing?

11. What people in the community have wonderful lives that you want for yourself? How will you attain this abundance?

12. In what ways do you believe you have nothing to give, and your life is too much of a disaster to be of service to others? In what small ways can you help? Think about serving by setting up chairs, making coffee, cleaning up, taking out the trash, thanking the speakers at recovery meetings, and welcoming newcomers.

Shame

From the moment of birth, children begin to learn the meaning of shame. Feeling bad about ourselves is nurtured into our psyches, and we are ignorant of the origins of our shame.

The child is judged as behaving badly for crying or needing food, attention, a diaper change. She can't move and is held hostage right from her first unmet need.

As a child grows from 1 to 4 years old, unskillful parents teach what is good, what is bad, what is right and what is wrong. But those "rules" change with the weather. There is no stable way to regulate mood swings to correlate with requests from the child's parents.

As a result, the child learns to get their needs met whether or not there is resistance and accept the process as part of life. As they age, they have difficulty belonging when most children find acceptance and connection. So the child starts doing things that they don't necessarily really believe—just what they learned as survival techniques.

When the child is older and has control of their life and the thinking behind it, they are willing to have a teachable, willing and open beginner's mind and to work toward communion with their peers as part of living life on its terms.

Dishonoring their country, family or community and/or embarrassing them bring them feelings of disgrace and humiliation. This is assigned to the child by others. They may not acknowledge that it exists, so those emotions are primarily felt only by the child who believes in the construct created by that micro-societal norm.

For those who believe in giving shame, be mindful that shame has power, abuse and control and comes with an agenda. For those who receive shame and believe they are compelled by it, be aware that it is a negative and destructive moment. Your emotions are affected. Shame creates confusion with whatever place you thought you had in the community. Trust is broken. You ask yourself, "How long will it take for forgiveness? How do I repent?"

When you have bought into your community's values and ideas of worth and made a personal decision to move your moral compass away from that group, you will be alone, humiliated, cast out. Your inner critic will run rampant with your emotional lability. You will be judged by others, you will judge yourself, and then you become a judge of others based upon their behaviors.

The community becomes entangled in a negative-emoting, shame-based faith. No one wins. All suffer from creating an unconscious, demeaning position. It is a perpetual-motion machine where both parties choose to participate.

This cycle can end. The war is over when you believe the war is over.

Leaving will create another type of dysfunction that escalates with fear-mongering. As others are dehumanized, leaders are more capable and more likely to make easier choices and decisions to harm or remove the non-believer. Where there is blame, there is shame.

Shame is part of Post-Traumatic Stress Disorder (PTSD). Shame is a repetitive-stress injury, like a carpenter hammering nails the same way for years.

With any of the previously mentioned scenarios, it is important as a recovery community to keep the learning curve open and mindful for the change process to take hold. With grief and loss, survivors have the emotions of denial, anger, bargaining, depression and acceptance to wade through. The stages of change are pre-contemplation, contemplation, preparation, action, and relapse. These are all part of myriad opportunities to grasp and act on.

This is a lot of information to deal with as a client who is learning. It is also quite a large undertaking for the community and skillful practitioners who guide clients through this quandary.

The skillfulness with which we execute our craft is the measure unto which we are viewed as a society concerned with progress made on these issues.

Ten actions to rise above the shame concept:

1. Notice when you are triggered by events. Make sure you are with trustworthy people.

2. Make a list of all of your shame-based thoughts. Notice how they repeat. It's manageable once you can see it on paper and stop them from going around the feedback cycle in your head.

3. State out loud: I am safe and protected. I have all my power. Many have gone before me, and I am not alone. This is a disease of isolation.

4. You cannot heal shame by using what brought you shame. Try new things; learn from others who do not think like you do. Join communities of hope and redemption.

5. Go back into your childhood and find the crux of your shame-based thinking. Heal from within. Go back and re-parent your inner child. Teach your inner self to recognize when you are having a flashback, and remind yourself that you are safe.

6. Trust in the plasticity of your brain's ability to re-wire itself with new cognitive thoughts. Aspire to these new tenets of belief with your life.

7. Surround yourself with community and clubs who believe in you and your abilities. Begin to trust them and believe in yourself.

8. When you feel a shame flashback, remind yourself that you are in the here and now; you are safe and no one will harm you.

9. To feel esteem, you must do estimable acts. Do service for others when you are suffering. Doing so will get you out of your own head, and you can see that the suffering is not personal.

10. Completely forgive everyone with radical kindness. Stop the resentment cycle of your own making that holds you prisoner. Be free. Be the change you want to see in your life.

Workbook Questions:

1. Why do you believe you are flawed, broken, and unable to accept that others will love you until you learn to love yourself?

2. If depression is how you process shame, do you feel stuck between anger and grief? What can you do to get free without lashing out and blaming others for your unhappiness?

3. How do you hold loved ones emotional hostage? Explain why you feel bad and why your pain and suffering is so real and pervasive. Why is it more important than others around you?

4. What will it take for you to feel safe and start feeling worthy of love and belonging?

5. Name five ways in which you feel defective with your surroundings and community.

6. What ways does being a perfectionist keep you from enjoying your life here and now?

7. How would you describe your inner critic? Does it work for you or against you? Why do you listen? What do you get out of not trusting your best self? What will it take for you to replace those feelings with something that brings a different state of being?

8. Guilt creates the idea that you did something irreparable. Shame is the glue that makes you believe you are bad or different. What would your life look life without those feelings?

9. Instead of learning 1,000 strategies for coping and survival, why not just stop believing in debilitating processes?

10. Name five things you can do to improve your self-esteem, such as service, honor, confidence, abilities, belonging, feeling part of community, spiritually accepted, virtuous, honored, redeemed and the like.

11. If your cycle of shame is generational oppression and family dysfunction, how will you be the first to stop the cycle? How can you stop being the observer as others in your family choose to hold on to those beliefs? Are you afraid of not belonging even to them? Explain.

12. What are your internalized, shame-based idioms? In what ways do you perpetuate this onto others and keep the disease going with friends, colleagues, and loved ones? How can you let go of this debilitating power?

13. In what risk-taking ways can you begin to have intimacy with people around you and safely process your feelings?

14. If you have internalized shame, in what ways are you rigid and controlling with your peers? Does anyone escape your inner critic's judge, jury and executioner's blade?

15. If you did not have the shame game, would you have any game at all? How can you use this groundlessness and vulnerability to create a feeling of equity with others who suffer from perpetuating that fraudulent way of life?

Situational Awareness

A conscious choice we make to stay mindful consists of three attitudes: knowing where we are and what we are doing; being in charge of our experience, and being versatile enough to handle most anything life throws at us. Change is always happening, and we have no control over most of our fate. However, we do have control over how we respond to life. When we live in shame, fear, and regret, we will always meet life with a diminished return before we even begin.

Perceiving Life Accurately

The gist of awareness is being cognizant of what's going on around you at any given time. You still participate, contribute and look at all the aspects of good and bad things that may occur. The key is to remain flexible, see opportunities and thrive, despite challenges in a hectic and unpredictable world.

No matter where you go, there you are. If your profession is paramedic, firefighter, police officer, or emergency-room doctor, you have to be able to survey the situation in an instant; look at contributing factors, and assess which features are important for your best estimate about what to do.

Awareness is like a sixth sense—you must choose to engage this part of your brain. You can monitor normal activities, and be ready to respond when change emerges. The craft of this work is to make a chaotic situation look as if it is under control. When people respond from a fear-based place, a situation can easily get out of control. They respond from everyone who is projecting their experiences of pain, suffering, and confusion, and transferring those panicked emotions onto others. Nothing gets done in this furious-paced situation with a lack of understanding and uncertainty.

Another part of skilled work is to recognize clues and early warning signals that things could go wrong. Most people live in a place of responding to life. I encourage you to look ahead for clues and ominous signposts. Live with a healthy "sense of urgency," looking forward with preventative and holistic ideals.

Here's an example: Native Americans looked seven generations ahead. They knew how to manage and maintain the resources of the land. In two years, the westward-spreading white colonists killed and decimated millions of buffalo that had roamed the land for eons. The white hunters and settlers took the main food source of the native peoples, leaving them to face suffering and starvation.

Another part of situational awareness concludes that the "problem that repeats itself over and over again" is seldom the true problem.

While you are distracted and working on what appeared to be the cause of the trouble in your life, you miss the real nemesis, which creeps into the problem and inflames like an unstoppable virus. Be omniscient in your view of what has caused your problem and get as much information as you can from all involved parties, no matter how unskillful and crazy their input sounds. Look for kernels of truth that resonate.

Know your own personal bias toward yourself and your community's prejudice or favoritism. You may blame others when you would be better off creating a solution with inner work. Watch for paranoid and delusional thinking in yourself, which precludes quick answers that blame others. Do the work to clear and clean up what you can. Afterward, work with others on solutions, goals, focused collaboration, and thriving systems.

Your growing awareness of yourself, your surroundings and situations will save your life, prevent harm to others, and give you healthy boundaries. You will learn how to speak up through your mistakes and uncomfortable attempts. This is part of the learning curve. As you progress, you will stop being like Chicken Little, who constantly cried, "The sky is falling!" You will become more skillful and use complex abilities to maneuver any obstacles. You will also become a trusted and valued servant because of your ability for critical thinking. As you learn and conquer, teach your skills to as many people as you can.

Workbook Questions:

1. Do you believe you are usually the last to know when big things happen —like climate change?

2. How do you respond when an emergency happens? What would you do if you were at an emergency scene and there was no one coming to help?

3. Do you attract a lot of the things that happen to you through your own actions or inactions? What happens when you sit passively and don't act? Do you have complacent negativity?

4. Do you watch the news on television and think, "This is just the way it is. Some things will never change"? What will it take to get you on the proactive side of life? Instead of focusing on what's wrong, think instead how your thoughts can move toward what you can do and what you can control.

5. For example: Think about what's happening in your life right now. Analyze your family, your job, and the political climate. What is your view? Where do you stand? Does anything seem hopeless? What is *one* thing you can do that will improve a situation and cause no harm to others?

6. In what ways are you proactive with your friends? Do you have healthy boundaries? Do you seem to fall from one disaster to another? If so, what's your part in this? What can you do differently?

7. Are you a person who was hurt in the past and have to keep up a hyper-vigilance of monitoring your life even when everything is OK? What can you do to self-soothe and tell your brain that life is a good place now and you don't need to worry?

8. Do you experience paranoid and delusional thinking that others are always going to harm you? Are you afraid of people from another culture? Do you breed and contribute to a racist culture of fear by portraying a whole race of people in a negative light with your mistrustful thoughts?

9. Notice what is going on around you right now. Think about sounds, smells, your sensations of warmth or a cool breeze. Is the heater on? Can you hear birds? Or are you still and quiet? Can you hear your heartbeat and blood coursing through your veins?

10. When you are with kids at a playground or walking along a dark street, what are your thoughts about safety and survival? What happens when your kids fall down or a stranger walks up to you? How do you react? How do you feel when you find out that they only wanted the time of day, and you acted cold and impersonal? Do you believe you are drawing bad things into your life from fear-based thinking?

11. How do you respond to getting a medical diagnosis—a cold, a broken arm, cancer? What about when a family member is diagnosed with something?

12. What happens to you when someone in your family dies, and everyone falls apart and is unskillful with communication? Are you able to stay neutral and facilitate progress without blaming others and falling apart?

13. When you are called into the boss' office, what is your awareness level? Are you casual or expecting the worst outcome? How does your negative response reinforce fear-based thinking?

14. When you are looking for a job, do you hunt as a person who is employable? Or do you hope, wish and need some luck beyond your skills? What can you do to improve your self-esteem in order to meet your future employer as an equal person of value?

Social and Sexual Anorexia

Sometimes the need to be right separates you from connecting with others and sabotages your relationships. You can feel that your thinking is valid and real, and space around you is created. This space keeps you from openly participating in life and conversations. Your self-righteousness, zeal about religions, politics, your disease or perceived maladies, your attitude of social entitlement and privilege all create a small playground for you on the planet.

Others dodge the human experience in their community by total avoidance, keeping to the shadows, being the wallflower, looking spiritually inward and not sharing their own human experience with anyone.

As we age, we are separated from participating with others and become less inclined to interact with our peers. As they die off one by one, we find ourselves isolated and alone.

Does your sexual experience include embracing the Internet, where you have gratuitous sex with fantasy cyber beings? They are fantasy; there is intrigue, and the experience may even include dangerous and thrill-seeking behaviors where you enjoy the most intense orgasms caused by words, celluloid or cyber-space. In real life, you find no contact with a human with a pulse. This is a form of social anorexia.

Are you the type of person who always gives of themselves by helping, fixing things and doing service? Are you perceived as a "good one" but can never experience blessings for yourself because of lack of trust and an inner belief that you are unworthy? This is another form of anorexia and comes from "reverse pride." It is the same sound an egomaniac makes, only in reverse. It sucks the life force out of everyone and outshines the sun.

When you are stuck in a closed system, you will become locked in a prison of self-fulfilling prophecies. Your life becomes hyper-grandiose, when everything is all about you and how you feel and respond. Now that we're done talking about you— or avoiding you—what do *you* think about you? This type of thinking turns into a narcissistic-like structure.

Our experiences as children are imprinted in our psyches. If we were taught bad habits and were violated emotionally, mentally, and physically, we respond to our world from that damage. We need to heal whatever happened in our childhood to participate and process those violations. We can then live in the here and now, with tools and skills to participate with safe, loving people we can trust. We can process the normal parts of relationships the same way others do.

When we are hurt in a relationship — when we feel totally damaged and violated — and we do not heal from those intense wounds, we make an unspoken contract with ourselves to never put ourselves in harm's way by having close, vulnerable, sensitive contact with another. We may become controlling and have a litany of unreachable goals that no one can live up to. They always end up failing us, so we move on to our next victim.

We treat each relationship as the last one, never growing past the point of pain and suffering. We replay that same outcome over and over. We may choose to never be in any vulnerable position with men or women, and project our experiences upon our social, work and spiritual communities.

As parents, we protect and shelter, but project and transfer our imprint of distrust to our children. Our bias becomes a judgment and prejudice for all who look and act like such-and-such.

Or we can be the painfully quiet person who holds a room hostage. Everyone feels our uneasiness. We are the white elephant in the room but act as if everything is OK. We come early to avoid social contact and leave early so no one notices our existence. We have many shallow, predictable acquaintances, or we mesh with a few and become part of the "two broken people trying to make a whole person" syndrome. We begin to judge others with whom we disagree.

My form of personal anorexia was that I emotionally entangled in another's life, problems, ups and downs, wins and losses. But I avoided responsibly taking care of my own life and problems. Another form of emotional enmeshment was my passion about being superficial in everyone's business. I flitted around like a social butterfly but had a locked door to any intimacy into my own, miserable life.

As we begin to process the incapacitation of our shyness and work to create real intimacy, we will discover that it is an inside job. We need to pick up that "10,000-pound phone" and call someone. Or we need to get into a group that allows for our tendencies toward shyness.

When we move beyond superficial existence, we will become genuine and authentic in all areas of our life. We create equity with our environment and learn how to trust again. We need to have the attitude that the worst that could happen already did, and how we move beyond suffering and pain is the mark of our character and courage and faith in action.

Being a man who had multiple relationships at once, I never had to commit to any form of comfort in a relationship. I could give love and make someone physically happy and fulfilled, but I could not receive that happiness in return.

Until you hold fear in your hands and see it from outside of your experience, you will never know what it is and what it can do. We can create freedom from fear by little acts of courageous, fearless, and limitless thinking. Build upon each small act, and develop thicker skin. Stop painting a target on ourselves that makes everyone an expert at hitting our soft spot. Turn all our reasons for *not* participating into reasons to live day by day. Start being vulnerable enough to take on life on its terms. Process your fears as we move into the sunlight of being.

It is an inside job within a closed system that we have built to keep others out. We have constructed a personal, private, gated community of one. Let's tear down those walls, and empty our diseased cup. Let's replace it with the work at hand. Start small and build upon little acts that become more complex. You will have powerful, spiritual-muscle memory that can protect you, act, and move inside of any crowd. You are the only one who can change you. But if you change yourself, the ripple effect on others will be like a chain letter of love you hand out into the universe.

Do things that are an "image breaker" for you. Join Toastmasters, be the secretary of a Twelve-Step group, volunteer at work for something that moves you beyond your superficial, safe self and into service as a vocation. Turn poison into medicine. Be a metaphysical alchemist of these times. Be the change within, and you will affect the world around you.

Actions to Change the Dynamic Disorder of Your Life

Be social. Get outside your comfort zone and be vulnerable. Go to a movie, a rally, a walk, or a picnic. Go bowling, to a concert, or out to lunch. Whomever you're with, be with them completely, as if that person is the last person on Earth.

Pick someone you have always liked. Go up to them and let them know how much you appreciate their existence in your life. Honor them—and your fear.

Release tension. Work out in a gym or run outside for a few blocks.

If you find yourself alone and muttering, or talking to your cat or an imaginary person who did something wrong to you last week, use this as a great opportunity to speak to someone who has a pulse and a heartbeat. Through your vulnerable exchange, you will create equity with yourself and another.

Go with curiosity and discovery. Explore something new and unusual. Look at the micro and macro of being here now.

Go with pleasure and information-gathering for new insights about certain things that trigger you. Pretend you are doing research for a special friend. No one need know the special friend is you.

At your place of work, participate with the knowledge you have gained, to help with any project. You already have loads of intuitive ideas that used to hold you hostage. Now you can free your colleagues from the prison of your making.

Go out with people of all genders, ages, sizes, and ethnicities to discover how to relate your experiences and to share the similarities we all have in common.

When you begin to feel invisible, small, puny and unnecessary, start doing services that benefit others. You will acquire self-esteem by doing estimable acts.

When you feel exhausted by simply being around people, it is a good time to help people who have mental challenges. Take it easy on yourself and them. Become a big brother or sister for someone.

When you feel like "being seen" is unbearable, shrug your shoulders and surrender. Laugh at yourself and the absurdity of your situation. Tell yourself what a hot piece of property you are, what a catch you are. Act "as if." Fake it 'til you make it. Dress for the job you want, not for the job you have.

Take a walk and get vitamin D from the sunshine at no cost. Your feel-good chemicals are released by taking a walk, and that alone can put a smile on your face. A walk in the sunshine will do good for your muscles and mind. Dopamine and serotonin are released throughout your body. Once you begin, this chemical cascade means the sky is the limit for your abundance and mental health.

Workbook Questions:

1. Do you live in a fantasy world, waiting for a special person to notice you? Do you wait for years in vain for connection?

2. In what ways do you take risks with others when you feel vulnerable?

3. Are you able to have sexual relations but not authentic heart-to-heart connections? Explain.

4. Are you able to have heart-to-heart relations but not sexual intimacy? Why? What would it take to get there? What are you afraid of someone finding out?

5. What self-image thoughts keep you from engaging with others?

6. Do you have shame and/or fear about wanting to have a sexual connection with someone of the same sex?

7. Are you having sexual relations with yourself and don't need anyone else to fulfill your needs? When you are with someone, are you unsatisfied that they cannot magically know how to meet your needs and please you? Do you repeat this cycle with new people and believe you will never be satisfied?

8. What are your deepest fears that you hide from others? Do you know of others who speak openly about them? Are your fears about body image, mental disorders, family secrets, and/or medical problems?

9. What is the difference between shyness and being paralyzed with fear at social events?

10. What intense feelings of connection happen when you bond with others? Do you get tense? Hold your breath? Feel engulfed by ominous fear? Does your heart feel like it is stopping or missing a beat? Explain.

11. What do you think will happen if you release these suppressed feelings? What's the worst thing that could happen? Are you deathly afraid of losing someone and being alone forever?

12. How have others made fun of you in the past? Did they target your looks, your thoughts, the way you work, or how you have sex? How does this affect the way you approach these people, places and things?

13. What fears do you have about engaging with someone new? How would you feel if someone left you?

14. How were you abused as a child or young adult? In what ways are you traumatized from these old wounds with new partners? What new communities are you willing to join to talk through and heal from this trauma?

15. Would you consider going to Sex and Love Addicts Anonymous meetings to learn about your relationships, sex and love opportunities?

16. How do you take care of all self-intimacy needs before you go out with someone? For example, do you smoke, drink, have sex, etc., so when you are with them, your needs are

already met and won't be projected onto your date? Do others bore you to tears because you're blinded by your own attitude?

17. How do you push others away so you do not have to be intimate? Are you sarcastic? Do you just say yes to everything and try to be a people pleaser? Do you have deep conflict within yourself and go with someone, even though your inner wisdom screams "NO"?

18. When we were younger and often abused, we learned to repeat those attracting behaviors with new people. Now it seems like we are in "Groundhog Day" when it comes to relationships. In what ways do you keep attracting the same abusive lovers and friends?

19. How do you slander and gossip with people just to fit in? Does that behavior feel like trust and intimacy to you? Is it fair to the people whom you are talking about? Do you believe others are doing this to you? Why? How can you break away from this?

20. Why do you settle for less and deprive yourself of vulnerable, nurturing experiences? How are you obsessive and compulsive in your thinking? Why have you made your thoughts real? Who would you be without a safety net?

21. Do you live in two worlds – one of fantasy, thinking about what someone else *should* be thinking and talking about with you? Do you think they are mind readers and should intuitively know how to speak to and approach you?

22. In what ways do you sabotage intimacy and protect yourself from relationships?

23. Do you deprive yourself from happiness and thriving by self-destructive inner voices that keep you in a deprived state?

24. In what ways were you emotionally neglected as a child?

The Spiritual Moment Is Now

What are spiritual qualities to strive for and understand?

Love and kindness toward ourselves and others are a healthy and safe way to get to know and develop our intentions with each other. We can start with acceptance of others and creating equity within our environment – to be one spirit with each other and the planet, to commune together. We work first with ourselves and then develop empathy and compassion for others. We learn to appreciate that all beings have similar good intentions and well-being within them.

How do we help them access this generosity? As we grow in spirituality we are able to hold multiple truths, understanding that we all have ambivalent truths competing for realization. We develop healthy discernment and let go of egoistic clinging to be right, win, and/or make our point. We become humble and naked before our fears, and walk over the hot coals of our lives with integrity. What's the worst thing that could happen? We become intimate with all aspects and derive wisdom from perseverance and the consistency of living our truth through the qualities listed above.

My spiritual moment is when the solid waste hits the fan and I feel attached to my belief system, appalled, indignant, retributive and righteous in fear with no faith or trust. It happens when trust is lost, and I feel sensitive and vulnerable. When I get angry, ugly, and say unspeakable things, that's the time for my spiritual moment.

Another time is when I make "foxhole prayers" to a random god when my life is in danger. When people are in war and getting bombed from above and can't run away, they start to believe in a higher power — that is a foxhole prayer.

Many people use one hour per week with a religious or spiritual community to consecrate a spiritually fulfilled moment, then get back to the grind of living and forgetting. How can we make more of our time a 24-hour journey toward spirituality? I have heard it said that people who are afraid of going to hell get religious. I have also heard that people who have been to hell and don't want to go back get spiritual. This is what happened to me.

One of my favorite examples to explain the idea of being spiritual is using St. Francis of Assisi's prayer as part of my awakening, mindful expression in this life:

Prayer of St. Francis

Lord, make me a channel of thy peace, that where there is hatred, I may bring love;

that where there is wrong, I may bring the spirit of forgiveness;

that where there is discord, I may bring harmony; that where there is error, I may bring truth; that where there is doubt, I may bring faith; that where there is despair, I may bring hope; that where there are shadows, I may bring light; that where there is sadness, I may bring joy.

Lord, grant that I may seek to comfort rather than to be comforted; to understand, than to be understood; to love than to be loved. For it is by self-forgetting that one finds.
It is by forgiving that one is forgiven.

It is by dying that one awakens to Eternal Life.

The idea of this prayer is that we bring everything we need to this party of life. When things are down, we bring the game changer. We do not require others to do or be anything. We are autonomous. This does not mean we are separate—it means we can get life back on track by acceptance and doing the next right thing. We can change this prayer to our own needs by replacing whatever we lack with a positive and hopeful expression. We can own what we want in our minds and then work toward those goals without lack of having this kind of life and reinforcing lack, or desperation and neediness. We claim our inherent right to happiness, freedom, and prosperity.

Whatever you write down, you can become. By sharing your intention with a group of like-minded people and writing down your thoughts, you will move out of static nothingness into a hopeful and intended future.

Your future is spotless. There is nothing written on the chalkboard in the sky about your life. You write your own destiny. Quit writing about all of your reservations and procrastination that keeps you from arriving at your new destination. Take all the reasons why you cannot do something — words like "and," "if," or "but," — out of the excuses why you do not, cannot, will not, have not, and move your thoughts into "I can," "I will," "I want," "I pray for," "I aspire for," "I will for it to come into my life."

There is a Tibetan meditation technique called Tonglen, which means "giving and taking" (or sending and receiving). You breathe in others' suffering and pain and accept it as real. I like to add that you don't have to swallow those emotions whole, just understand the person's predicament and hold space for this truth. Then you breathe out trust, belief, hope, faith, charity, empathy, and compassion. It is a meditative breathing practice that aspires and intends for anything you set your mind to do. It is a practice to understand your pain and suffering, disease, happiness— basically anything you feel is not personal and about you and your experience.

Life happens; crises happen; disasters happen. It is what we do with our will and energy that makes the difference in how we survive.

We will use pain and suffering as our example. Begin stating out loud, "May I be free of pain and suffering and the root of suffering," then work on people you love and value and intend them to be free of suffering and the root of suffering. As you mature in compassion and empathy, you include people who give you a hard time and make you feel unsafe. By aspiring for them to be free of pain and suffering, the chances are that they may have a different life experience and be able to have others enjoy precious freedom and choose not to harm others with their projected pain and suffering. Another take on this subject is, "Just for today, I accept pain and suffering as my teacher." This is finite and doable, one day at a time. With all things in recovery, we work toward a lifetime of healing consistency. Play the long game.

Another way I access my spiritual connection is with gratitude lists. My favorite way to do this is that I write into the future and claim that it is now done. I write my own future based upon my intentions and aspirations for my life. This is how I change the disorder of my life, by living as an inspiration toward these goals. I intend for those things to happen. I look toward a future where I claim that I have those ideals.

Then I thank myself in advance for the goodness inherently coming my way as a deserving person working hard toward my goals. I have arrived at my destination of abundance or acceptance, and I deserve goodness happening to me. I belong with healthy feelings. I am happy now. I accept and have willingness to make these goals a long-term plan worthy of investment.

It looks like this:

Gratitude List

I am so happy and grateful now that my rent is paid and my job is secure.

I am so happy and grateful now that my parent is using a walker after their knee replacement.

I am so happy and grateful now that I took my car to the shop and got the transmission fixed.

I am so happy and grateful now that I spoke with my boss and received a raise for my job.

I am so happy and grateful now that I got my mortgage refinanced and live more securely.

I am so happy and grateful now that my child understands what I say and responds in a timely manner.

I am so happy and grateful now that my chemotherapy is done and the cancer is gone.

I am so happy and grateful now that my hurt back is healed and I can work again.

I am so happy and grateful now that I communicate effectively with my wife and we keep respect and safety as our reality.

Another experience that rocked my world is that I could basically ask for anything if I asked in a way that was of service for the benefit of others. I still held on to my old, diseased way of thinking as I became more ambivalent and discerning with what I wanted. I was able to be spiritually right in any moment.

I found that spirituality is trying to do less harm to others. When you live your life for the benefit of others, it may start out as selfish and egoistic, but as you do the work and grasp the concept, you will slowly create a wellness for yourself. It starts out with you thinking you are helping others; that you have been given a gift; that you are the good one, and that you have special ideas about helping others. You begin with this novice, egoistic approach and grow into a place where you can wish that others have the abundance you have. You can aspire that all suffering people have happiness, freedom, and abundance — not based upon your need for it.

When you do service for others you will often find that you are the one who benefits. By your act of selfless giving, you create a pay-it-forward policy of spiritual equity. You surrender and become groundless. You find that grasping for worldly objects and possessions is something that had "branded" you. Like a Pavlovian dog, you were conditioned with ideas of wanting the latest phone, car, trophy partner, well-behaved children, a nice house, a safe neighborhood, an ideal job, money. You were told that these things would bring you closer to an ideal of feeling better and being the "good one," closer to happiness and wellness.

You begin to believe that the place of entitlement and privilege came as a byproduct of living in a time when birth and the lottery of life had goodness coming to you. Others? Well, I guess they deserve what they have coming. Reinforcing this thinking causes all suffering on the planet.

So, getting things you want in the name of asking for them by doing service for others is a safer direction. If others benefit, you move away from being a taker of life and resources and become a benevolent benefactor by aspiring for others' goodness.

The most important part of a spiritually fulfilled life comes from accepting where you are right here and now and trusting the process. The idea that happiness can be accessed at any other time is not real. This moment right here, right now is the only time we have that we can truly be happy and in acceptance. We cannot go back to the past. We cannot predict the future. Only here with our precious "present" can we turn our lives around. The spiritual moment is now.

Workbook Questions:

1. What does spirituality look like in your life? Do you believe you must have a religious connection to feel spiritual?

2. Is it hard to have faith when you feel violated, hurt, and/or in danger? How do you protect yourself without letting others have your spiritual powers of trust, kindness, love, empathy and compassion?

3. Is it hard to wish another person happiness when they are going for the same job you want, and they get it? What stops you from being spiritual at that time?

4. In what ways do you have "selective spirituality" based upon getting what you want and feeling good before you are spiritual? Is it about you being the "good one" who is here to help others because of your status and grace? What will it take for you to humble yourself and become an equity-building servant who empowers others? Do you believe others have answers within themselves?

5. Why do you believe you are entitled to good things? Is it because you have invested in good?

6. Why is it hard to explain to others why you do service to help people out of the goodness in your heart?

7. In what ways are you ashamed of what others think about your spiritual choices? Do they make you feel ashamed for believing in your choice of higher power? What is your ego trying to protect you from? What's the worst that could happen—an inquisition?

8. Do you need to believe you are going to Heaven if you are "good" on Earth right now? Just for a minute, think of how you would feel about doing the next right thing because it is the "right thing to do." Why do you believe you have to get paid later for being "good" now?

9. In a world with so much suffering, how can you safely go where danger is and bring goodness and education about another way of life?

10. When doing spiritual work with others, how do you put yourself first, have healthy boundaries, create a timed event to help others, and then surrender and let go of the outcome? Where do you have difficulty with that statement?

11. Are you able to access your spirituality during times of disaster or crisis? Do those times find you facing them with no power and surrender? How can you ascertain your power base, consider with caution, and exercise your strengths?

12. Do you have a spiritual practice of giving with no conditions? What does your conditional gift consist of? What does "unconditional positive regard" mean in your life?

13. What do you have an abundance of? Is it happiness, because you have chosen to be happy? Is smiling with your face and body an act of giving to others? How can you use all of the abundance you have to instill hope in others?

Stress – Negative and Positive

Only you can manage your emotions, problems and opportunities. Make time for everything you do, and then take extreme care of yourself during the downtimes.

If you do not take care of Number One, you will regret it. It's on you to take responsibility and know your limits and healthy boundaries. You are in control of what happens in your life. You cannot be a thriving workaholic. It soon will have only diminished returns, and your hard work won't be worth much.

Tension is a healthy part of your spring-like reflexes, but too much tension and you will be ready to snap. Not enough, and you will have no drive or control. We need to keep healthy stressors and learn to respond to the happiness of good *and* bad things that happen in our lives. Positive stress is that good things happen; it is the opposite of negative stress. But you need to be good at processing both, or your life can be at peril.

Take a look at your life, and pinpoint your stressors. Is it your personality, your job, your environment? When you've identified them, start the process of management. Get rid of things that do you no good. Work on personality traits that are not reliable in the long run. We live in a fast-paced, fear-based world. Throughout most of our lives, we are paralyzed and live in the flux of procrastination. We are frozen in a state of non-movement with fear that we will do something wrong or make a bad choice. When we live this way we have no peace.

We only have today to do what needs to be done, so let's live for today, pick what we can manage, and make longer plans for more difficult tasks. Maybe a five-year plan is a good one. Put the rest of your baggage on the shelf. Do not let those items rent space in your head; you are writing novels about things that don't matter. Do you really have the luxury of storing so much tension that gives so little relief?

What is the cause of your stress? Name it, write it down, look at it for what it is, and find a way to let go. Your mind cannot relieve stress by re-sending mental images about whatever it is that ails you in a tape loop inside your head. You cannot solve a problem by focusing on the problem. You must think in a solution-focused strategy. Once you name your stress, find out if it is inter-personal or intra-personal.

When your stress is inter-personal – or related to dealing with people, places and things – you internalize that stress. You have the choice of blaming circumstances or others for your unhappiness and all of your problems. The way out of that stress ultimately comes from your inner work and acknowledgement that you have no control over what others do. You can be responsible only for how you respond to life on its terms. Acceptance is the answer to all your questions.

Complete forgiveness of all that has happened is a mechanism to let go of attachment, even to your hierarchy of needs and your thoughts about safety and what you think will bring you peace.

If your stress is intra-personal, ultimately you are responsible. The work is an inside job. You must deal with your inner conversation about how you judge yourself and your skills. If your thinking is judgmental and rigid, you will cause yourself harm. If you are always trying to be a perfectionist and cannot accept that what you do is good enough, you will never be satisfied. You will always chase the ambiguous and not be happy in any moment.

This moment, right here and right now, is the only moment in which you can ever be happy. It's your choice to let go of all reservations and excuses.

Here's how to start living, processing stress, and letting go of the rest:
- Be in the moment. Write about things you are happy with and focus on them. Don't worry, be happy now.
- Stick with others who are happy and well-adjusted. Ask them how they do it, then listen and do what they do.
- Make a daily list of what makes you feel stressed. Let it go. You are most likely safe.
- Close your eyes. What do you see? Is the stress really there, or is it your self-talk that loves to hear its voice obsessing and being compulsive? Forgive yourself and let go.
- Make a list of five things you will try to accomplish today. Be happy with the three you got done.
- Think about what feels out of control. Observe and watch yourself spin out, but do not participate. Just observe, "Oh there I go again." "Oh I feel it coming on." Be the universal observer in your life.
- Re-parent your inner child. Make a safe and healthy environment. Be gentle, loving, and understanding of yourself.
- Make sure you rest. Do three things that make you happy. Forgive yourself for anything that happens that you don't like. You will do better next time.
- Make a list of goals for the next five years. And quit beating yourself up daily—this is a lifetime process. Do not spin out. Rather, watch and the world will keep spinning fine without you. Trust.
- Do an image-breaker of things that keep you emotionally rigid. Let go of your serious and protective demeanor when it is not needed. Be playful where you feel most serious.
- Think about the job you have, the relationship you're in, the place you live, the city where you dwell, your community where you have social contact, and your service to your community. Where do you have the most stressful contacts? Make sure whatever you do is worth the stress and hassle you process daily. You were meant to have a happy life, and that takes balance.

Here are some ideas to "stress-arrest" your life:
- Change your self-talk into a soothing and supportive language of acceptance of your hard work, and that it is enough.
- Quit awfulizing, catastrophizing, and globalizing. Be impeccable with your words. If you can't find something supportive and positive, don't reinforce your negative thoughts. They do no good.
- Quit being a perfectionist with yourself and others. Blur your eyes a little for real happiness. Let go. Do you want to be right all the time or sometimes just be happy and full of grace?

- Have some form of physically working out to get your body chemistry and brain chemistry firing. This will release helpful de-stressors and happy brain chemicals for peace of mind.

- Find something you like to do: a hobby, caring for an animal, spending time where you feel good about what you are doing. This is one instance when life is really all about you for a moment! This is your time; spend it well. Get away from electronics.

- Know thyself. Know when to take on responsibilities and when to sit with the discomfort of saying no with healthy boundaries.

- Eat healthy foods that create healthy body functions and healthy mindsets. Your food and thoughts are digested on a cellular level, so only feed yourself healthy foods and thoughts.

- Stop drinking, smoking, and watching violence on TV. These do not soothe your spirit.

- Sleep well. Have some form of meditation or restful inspirations for your life, so the language of your life is in tune with your intentions.

- Heal with humor when life gets too serious. Find ways to gently smile and have peals of laughter with yourself and with others who are doing this work. Laughter relieves stress and releases feel-good chemicals in your brain. You will think more clearly and with more possibilities.

Workbook Questions:

1. Name five external stressors such as work, taxes, etc. Name five internal stressors, such as self-esteem, your love life, mental health, etc. You will possibly have these around for the rest of your life, so what can you work on?

2. Make a five-year plan, and be hopeful that your diligent work will bring peace and insight. What do you do to unload and relax? Is it another form of work? Is your "relaxer" still on the computer where you work all day? What can you do to get away from this kind of relaxing for a few hours?

3. What foods do you eat that promote healthy chemicals in your brain to give you an edge on stress-free living? What little changes can you make for a happier you? Which things will you never give up?

4. How do you sexualize your stress? How do you use anger as a release of your frustration? What can you do to change this way of thinking?

5. What outdoor activities can you engage in where you live? Are there woods around? Parks or pools?

6. What ways do you daily stop moving and practice breathing with some form of meditative qualities? What would you like to try? Why? Why not?

7. How much sleep do you get every night? Do you feel tired during the day? Do you nap or take 15 minutes off, just sitting with your eyes closed? Are you afraid of doing this? What can you gain from taking more breaks?

8. What unhealthy habits do you make OK? Drinking, smoking, thrill-seeking behaviors, anger, road rage? List some others. Explain how this releases stress for you. Is it fair to your fellow workers, teammates, family, partner, and spiritual community when you have outbursts?

9. How are you addicted to drama? How do you get energy from high-octane activities just to feel normal? Name a few ways you do this with unhealthy people. Do you get a free, chemical high?

10. Are you a perfectionist who is never happy with your outcomes and always second-guessing your work, so you never find peace with the great work you have done?

11. What mental-health diagnosis have you been given that contribute to your stressed-out life? Obsessive-compulsive, hyper-grandiose, narcissist tendency, authoritative-combative syndrome? Name some you think could be on your list.

12. How do you plan to say no to peers, bosses, etc., when they keep adding things for you to do that are not on your job description? How do you let people know when you are doing too much?

13. How do you start on a task, distract yourself, and get on a "mission creep" so you never get much work done? Can you resist anything but temptation? What can you do to stop these behaviors?

14. What soothing gestures and inner dialogue do you use daily to be gentle with yourself and promote your mental health? Are you enough just as you are? Or do you constantly have to prove yourself to others? Is this from low self-esteem? What can you do?

Survival Strategies

Survival strategies are what you do to safely navigate through the hardships and challenges you face in life.

When you feel vulnerable and hopeless like an endangered child, it's time to kick your extreme self-care into gear and start recovering your life.

Disasters happen; change happens. We have to fluidly maneuver whatever comes our way. Accepting life on its terms and thriving is where we want to end up. Acceptance is the answer to all of our problems. After acceptance, we can rebuild, recover, and make the best of what is left. We do not live in fear, yet we use all of our empirical knowledge to access our best wisdom for any given situation.

Challenges show up in life that are hard to navigate without losing your step. It's good to have a backup plan that you know will keep you safe and empowered as you make bold new moves to accept life on its terms.

The spiritual moment is what happens when things don't appear to go your way. Are you prepared? What's your plan? When something goes terribly wrong in our lives we are like Chicken Little who runs around yelling, "The sky is falling, the sky is falling"?

Preventive strategies are essential. There are disaster plans for earthquakes, fires, floods and blizzards, but we think so little about our own lives and preparedness when disaster is personal and strikes near home. Categories may differ, but our plans can generally cover all problems:

1. Recognize and gauge the event. Honor that it is real and happening now.

2. Assess the damage without catastrophizing.

3. Consult your support group, spiritual connections, mentors, medical professionals, and trusted friends and confidants.

4. Work out ideas, thoughts, strategies, and coping mechanisms to survive and adapt to your environment.

5. Begin experimenting with what works for you and your circumstance. Make lots of mistakes and consider it part of the bigger picture for your personal learning curve.

6. Once you find out what works for you and are comfortable and willing to stick to it, keep this maintenance phase going with a sense of urgency and diligence.

7. Accept this moment in your life and come to terms that it is your reality. Take the longer view.

8. Be willing to realize that whatever has happened is not personal and about you. Others all over the planet are suffering the same way that you are. Move into the service of helping others to keep your happiness and develop your amazing self-esteem.

9. Realize that you are constantly triggered by people, places and things that give you temporary flashbacks to traumatic experiences, which make you think and feel as if you are in an unsafe place. This is Post Traumatic Stress Disorder (PTSD). Realize what is happening, and use your tools to go back into a place of safety, belonging and deserving of all that others have.

Below are triggers that make us all feel unsafe. We need a plan and a way to handle anything that comes our way:

- Legal issues
- Internal Revenue Service problems
- Sex
- Sickness
- Psychological/mental health
- Temporary or permanent loss of physical ability
- Social anorexia vs. social butterflies
- Spirituality and religious issues
- Returning from combat
- Job
- Money
- Coping mechanisms
- Thriving ideals
- Death and dying
- Getting fired
- Auto accident
- Survivor guilt
- PTSD
- Divorce or breakup of a loved one or family
- Drunken-driving issues or driving under the influence of drugs
- Criminal lifestyle
- Anger issues
- Loud, vulgar people
- Domestic violence
- Crime
- Relationships
- Environment of depression
- Sudden loud noises
- Politics
- Stressful news reports

Workbook Questions:

1. What do you do when you are triggered and feel unsafe? In what ways can you come back into your body and what is really happening?

2. What preventive measures can you take when things become untenable, instead of having to get ready after something goes wrong?

3. How can you stop attracting hectic and unpredictable moments? What is your plan, who do you call, what groups will you attend?

4. In what ways do you assert your boundaries and stop others from causing harm or mistreating you? In what ways do you remove yourself from the dangerous situation or emotional escalation?

5. In what ways do you recover your mindful world and realize that the danger has passed and now you are safe and moving toward healthy choices, no matter what has transpired?

6. Imagine a safer future, where you are back in charge of your life. What does that look like? What will you do to attain that safety?

7. What skills and resources are available to you? How can you access them? What's holding you back?

8. How do you meditate or slow down your breathing and relax your body? When you close your eyes and hold still, can you see that nothing is happening right here in this moment? When you relax your muscles and back tension, can you feel the healthful aspects of this?

9. How do you stop your fear-based inner critic and release the panic button? How can you stop catastrophizing and get back to ways of reason?

10. What solution-focused tools can you access? What strategies have worked in the past with similar situations?

11. With death, dying, grief and loss, there is a process that is personal and unique to each person. Are you listening to your deepest self? Are you comforting and self-soothing these feelings with your community?

Survivor Guilt

How many of you have outlived others?

How many family members have died inadvertently through your hands by neglect or association?

When we are the living, we are left to deal with these issues.

Why them and not me? Did your loved ones die before you had the chance to be there and tell them how much you care? Did you miss the boat for being a son, daughter or parent, or lose your grandparents, partner or loving friends in tragic circumstances?

Are you still dealing with the perpetrators who killed your loved ones and the effects of justice in our society?

When we get into recovery, we realize a few new things because we have the opportunity to process them. By grace, awakening, and daily doing our spiritual effort, we get a daily reprieve from our dysfunction and madness.

Then we get to process our experience. We received the chance for recovery, when others did not. Sometimes we feel alone and have to process positive stress the same way we would with our incomprehensible old selves, except now we know we have a choice. This is the real work of recovery.

What do you feel you have lost? Write it down so you can know this fear for the first time and meet it face to face. This is the turn-around thinking we need to keep in mind. Not what we did or what happened before — but what we can do now.

What we can do now are things such as praying for the other; forgiving the other; letting go and letting your higher power do the heavy lifting with "triggery" people. But forgiving ourselves for still being here is sometimes the hardest thing of all to do. Forgiving others who committed an act out of a fierce belief — well, this is hard stuff.

Another technique to use is completely forgiving ourselves and stopping negative attachments that keep us in a resentful tape-loop and feedback cycle. Once we stop that and do the next right, healthy behavior, we are released from our infinite sadness. We honor and celebrate the lives of those lost on the way. We are the courageous few who have made it this far. Words such as "fair" and "just" are not helpful toward getting closure through forgiveness. Anyone we have hurt or destroyed is gone. This is the only moment we have right here and now to do something different. No more destroying lives, being incarcerated in our heads and in society's systems of retribution. The only real justice is to stop the recidivism of these behaviors.

When we live with guilt and negative attractions to others when they die, suddenly all our wasted energy has turned more intense. We could have had a more intimate, authentic and genuine experience with those individuals. Also, when someone has caused harm, and we vengefully want to do similar harm to them, we're really not that far apart. Why are they so much worse than we are? What is the breaking point of acceptance and forgiveness for this experience we all share? If we keep perpetuating shame, fear, guilt, and biased thinking, how can the cycle stop?

To be a complete human, we must regain what we have lost: our trust, generosity, beliefs, and confidence in others. We need to regain these to continue living full and abundant lives without reservations that hold us hostage emotionally.

If we have inexplicably lost loved ones, I am certain they would want us to go on and live our lives to the fullest. They would want us free from trauma and the drama that we could not control from the past.

Things to remember when you feel guilty about surviving:

This is a feeling, and it will pass. All of our lives are fleeting moments, full of change. Those who are left need you in a healthy, resilient state so they can move on together with you toward what comes next. There are many who love and appreciate you. What you feel is normal, but it is also a disease of isolation and separateness that need not be. Begin loving all those around you. What is left in your precious life needs your attention.

Make a gratitude list of what you have left. Living is for the courageous, not the timid and weak. Be strong and thrive. Watch how others process great loss and learn from them. Terrible things will happen to us during our lifetime and cause pain. Sometimes the way we suffer is optional and can be done with a benefit for the living, instead of infinite grief and loss for our loved ones. Your loved ones would not want you to keep suffering. They would want you to be happy and fearless and move on with your life.

You were left here for a reason, and it was not for unnecessary suffering. We have no control over fate, luck, or hope, so accept what is and do the next right thing. It's time to end worthless ways of self-deprecation and move on toward instilling hope and aspiring for your life to be different. Recognize what happened, resist the temptation for fear and shame-based guilt, and recover your most resilient self.

It's OK to be sad, and it's really OK to process and be happy. Reassess your life and values and determine what you believe in. Live your life to the fullest with joyful exertion in all you do.

If you have done harm in the past and are looking for closure because you no longer live that way, be it as a soldier, a criminal, a firefighter, police officer, nurse, caregiver or anyone else on this journey, the most important thing you can do for all involved is to "Do No Harm" to yourself and others as you learn about your part in what transpired. Then move on with therapy, clergy and maybe even the legal system if appropriate. This is a long process and you want to be careful and mindful about your journey.

All of us – in this process of living to get our needs met – have either willingly or unconsciously caused harm to another. We live in a dualistic world of right and wrong, good and bad, win or lose. Unfortunately, in that system, someone also lives and dies. If we try to hold a neutral place and learn about the gray area between our ears, there is a lot of potential at our disposal.

Death, dying, grief and loss is the one area we can have more acceptance with learning to process and get closure. Getting closure requires a community to process our feelings of guilt, loss, and tragedy; being the victim or the perpetrator, or being someone who could have done more with the responsibility and knowledge at our disposal. How do we turn this negative impact into a positive, life re-enforcing gift? Find others who have a similar experience and ask safe questions that keep all parties able to participate.

Talk about feelings we all have when similar things happen in our lives. Learn why you want to change your thinking and gain closure with the living-amends process. In some instances, you may not be able to make amends because it will cause you more harm and hurt others. Get as much information as you can, and be informed in your decision-making process. Do not senselessly self-punish without doing all the groundwork to know thyself and your situation.

Aim to live your live so others in the future may benefit from the way you conduct your business. Live your life for the service of others who have suffered like you and who have caused suffering. Forgiveness and complete acceptance of yourself is suggested.

Forgiveness and complete acceptance is also suggested if you were perpetrated against. We tend to carry a sack of poison around for the person who caused harm, but we are being poisoned by our own thinking. Make amends the best you can. Do not live the lifestyle that caused harm.

Be more mindful of others around you. Quit personalizing your experience. Things happen to all of us around the planet. Learn about being a victim, the victimized and a victimizer, and teach others how to live with this profound knowledge.

Workbook Questions:

1. What have you survived that you feel guilt or shame about? Were you innocent or complicit?

2. What have you done in the past that has worked when similar situations have occurred?

3. What has shame-based guilt, self-hatred and deprecation done for your life? Say more.

4. How do you forgive yourself for simple things? Why not do the same for bigger-ticket items? Why do you feel this is personal? Why do you continue to cause suffering to yourself and others?

5. What holds you back from forgiving someone who has done wrong? Why can't you forgive? What stops you from accepting this situation?

6. If you are in a caregiving, responsible situation where others lives are in your hands, how do you perform extreme self-care so you do not burn out in your profession?

7. Name five things you can help someone with who is going through this situation. Why can't you do those things when they happen to you? Why the disconnect?

8. Do you feel you are not worthy of forgiveness? Do you feel responsible beyond what happened? Do you feel like you are carrying a burden beyond the grave and harming yourself and your loved ones in the process?

9. In what ways do you isolate yourself from being part of living and think you're different? In what ways does your ego hold you back from forgiveness?

10. What activities are you resilient with? Can you use some of these models and skills while letting go of your unmanageable guilt?

11. How does negative attachment to loss and suffering complicate your healing process?

12. Does your guilt have religious or spiritual intonations that cause your conflict? Would a new, forgiving and accepting way of life give you peace? What stops you from letting go of shame-based faith?

Thrill-Seeking Behaviors

Some people can resist anything but temptation.

What activities are great adrenaline rushes for you that also might be hazardous to your health? Do you practice careless dating (online or otherwise)? Do you buy fast cars and then think you need to drive fast? Do you have road rage? Do you skydive or jump off bridges from great heights? Do you shoot drugs without knowing what's really in them? Do you drink to excess and forget what you did the night before? Do you go out with strangers, do drugs and have unprotected sex that might give you diseases? Do you talk back to people of authority, taking the issue to the edge of serious misconduct?

Just to feel normal, I need three times more attention than most people. I just don't get enough from life, so I take what I need.

Before I was in recovery, I needed lots of drama and trauma. I was a high-maintenance drama queen. I had to have the most excitement, whether it was positive or negative. If someone seemed normal, I dismissed their wonderful qualities, called them "boring" and had nothing to do with them. I played music on stage and needed all of the stardom. Then I'd *need* the death-defying feats to maintain my stardom. It didn't matter to me if people spoke good or ill of me, as long as they kept talking.

People who are addicted to thrill-seeking behavior use their five senses to pull out all the stops. They want to see more color and more images. They're always on the hunt, looking with hungry eyes for the next exciting hit, be it sex, a nice car, a violent movie, or glorious, scenic nature.

We listen for stimulating information about technology, nature, science, music – we need more, and we need it louder. We love to touch bodies. We long to work with our hands, using all kinds of tools, art, musical instruments, food. We love to mix and match our senses. Experiencing these things at normal levels is not enough. Without thrills, boredom seeps in and dulls the effect. Nothing has a kick to it. It all feels predictable.

As we grow older, we use substances such as alcohol and drugs to maintain the high or low that stimulates us to the edge of our consciousness. We party heavily and use people in the same way we use stimulants, then discard them after our initial thrill has waned. We use our emotional roller coaster to maintain high highs and low lows.

My unregulated ups and downs turned into manic depression. Today's immediate and convenient thrills are tomorrow's lows. People hooked on adrenaline don't even need drugs. They get their high from the adrenaline rush that goes with thrill-seeking. Their bodies are the ultimate chemical producer that gives them the highest of highs, as long as they keep doing the adrenalized behavior.

Sensation-seeking is the ultimate way to get high. But just like with all chemical dependency, we need more and more to give us what used to be a great time. Sometimes thrill-seeking behavior turns into the ultimate self-destruction. Anti-social manifestations such as anger, aggression and hostility all lead to wanting to be seen and remembered. Thrill-seeking behavior is sometimes at the root of events, such as school or workplace shootings. When all else fails, the ultimate thrill is being someone who takes our own lives or entices the police to do what we don't have the courage to do – end it all.

Here are 10 tips for thrill-seekers who want to find a better way:

1. Know thy self. Get to know your ups and downs, ins and outs, why you do what you do. Learn to accept yourself exactly as you are, right here and now.

2. Be mindful about doing no harm to yourself and others. Check out motivating factors that keep you different and isolated from others in your social group. Take a look at how you can collaborate with others who practice less dangerous forms of thrill-seeking.

3. Know your genetic makeup and find the middle ground between your chemistry and your needs for a thrill. Take the longer view.

4. Find healthy ways to have fun and get your needs met. Keep safety in mind and challenge yourself in safe ways to go to the next level. Make a lifetime journey of exciting opportunities that stay age-appropriate, so your body can manage the challenges at hand.

5. Find healthy counterparts for unhealthy habits and dangerous risks. Create new habits that are safer for you, your friends and loved ones.

6. If you are into fast cars, fast sex, weapons, drugs, alcohol, anger and/or ego, trade those in and get the help you need to kick those habits. Get help. You're worth it.

7. Weigh the pros and cons of what you're doing with a social group that calls you on your stuff. Really listen to the concerns of family and loved ones, and let them weigh in with equity in your decision-making.

8. Whatever you're comfortable with, explore the other side. If you're shy, force yourself to do something exciting. If you're outgoing, look inward for adventure. Find balance with yourself and others, and you will feel more like you belong.

9. Use your abilities and areas of achievement to do things that you are less confident in. Slowly build upon your skill sets in those new areas.

10. In what areas do you freeze up and lose control? Notice why you do not feel confident. Stick with it and make a five-year plan to strengthen your new ways of living.

Workbook Questions:

1. If it all comes down to genetic pre-disposition, how can we balance the good in what we have and learn to be happy with the results?

2. How can we use this practice to do service helping others who suffer as we have?

3. Name five healthy ways you can get an adrenaline rush without harming yourselves or others.

4. What social activities can you pursue that are healthy and inclusive?

5. Would you want your teens or your parents doing those activities? Why or why not? Why is it OK for you but not for them?

6. How much of your thrill-seeking behavior is to feed your ego? Can you ever get enough to satisfy your need? What's your exit plan to grow old gracefully?

7. How can you alter your brain chemicals to enable your enjoyment of the simpler things in life such as a sunset, a walk in the woods, and/or doing service to help others?

8. How can you learn to be satisfied with sometimes coming in last? Can you do the deed for itself and nothing more?

9. What are healthy ways to have fun? What groups can you join? Where I live, there are dozens of nonprofits for which you can volunteer. They need all kinds of help with every kind of activity. What's stopping you from being a real hero?

10. What are negative health effects from your thrill-seeking? Are there ill effects such as prison, debt, job loss, inability to play well with others, loss of partner and/or family?

Transferrable Skill Sets

It doesn't matter what we used to do in our addictions. It only matters what we do next.

We can take what we know and transfer that energy into something useful.

In every profession, there is a need for people with transferrable skills. We go through our lives doing the best we can, working and educating ourselves to be the best version of us. Then, the best version of us needs to change to keep up with the times.

No matter how far we have fallen, wherever we are, we have more than enough to begin. This moment right now is the perfect teacher. Everything we have done before was preparation for what is about to happen. We have all the insights and answers within ourselves and need only to access our own hierarchy of needs. We must be fearless and check what is appropriate for ourselves, no matter what we did before.

Let's use being a drug dealer as an example. Dealers had to develop a trusting clientele who will not rip them off or turn them in to the authorities. They need a source they take care of and get their product from. They have to watch quality control. They have to make sure some of their clients are not doing too many drugs, and they have to do extreme self-care to survive in their jungle setting.

Look at the following Transferrable Skills Checklist. What skills does a drug dealer need to succeed? As you can see, almost half of the boxes could be checked. This goes for whatever anyone has done with their own lives, from educated to "veg-ucated."

Applying our existing skills to the work of self-change, we can move beyond that stuck place. It is important when looking at our skills to be open and willing to use critical thinking. Think outside the box. We have built a whole world of values, and now they are going to help us thrive and survive in a different way.

We are hot pieces of real estate that people will want. We have only to realize that. Our employer has needs we can satisfy with all of our inherent knowledge, waiting to be accessed. We've already gone way past Square One in the real-time game of life. The first step is to show employers how our experience can benefit them.

The hard part is recognizing what we want to do with our lives. We can use personal reflection and evaluation to know what we can physically and mentally offer. With an open mind, let's pick something that excites us. Think of the skills we offer. We can try what we're interested in by volunteering, to see if that work is a good fit.

Transferrable skill sets work in every part of our lives. Disconnectedness from ourselves and our realities causes dysfunction and holds us back. We can use the same formula for all of our needs – biological, spiritual, psychological and social. Try it, and enjoy living your life to the fullest. The good news: Everyone is capable of attaining most of the skills on the following list.

Workbook Questions:

1. What transferrable skills do you possess? Go through the checklist.
2. After looking at the checklist, what would you like to explore for your life to improve?
3. What is your dream job? What's holding you back? Can you volunteer to get started?
4. In what ways can you learn with curiosity and discovery and find your own skill serendipity in this life?
5. What skills do you downplay?
6. Why are you afraid to make the move with your skills? How can you turn that around?
7. What resources do you have available that can help you reveal your best self? School, church, community centers, hospitals, recovery facilities?
8. How can you turn your life around simply by changing your thinking?
9. What would your ideal life look like from morning until evening? What would you be doing?
10. What angry thoughts do you have about the system holding you back and not letting you participate? How can you turn those thoughts around so you do not give away your power?
11. List 10 jobs you have done. Now list 10 jobs that are similar.
12. List 10 jobs that interest you but you believe that you could never pull off in real life. Why not?
13. Are you good with children or senior citizens?
14. What is your ideal job? What are the steps to get there? List five things you can do to position yourself for that job.

TRANSFERRABLE SKILLS CHECKLIST

This example of a Transferrable Skills Checklist appears in numerous places on the Internet. Do your own Web searches to find one that suits you best.

☐ Key Transferrable Skills Meet deadlines	☐ Classify data	☐ Research
☐ Ability to delegate	☐ Compare, inspect, or record facts	☐ Create new ideas
☐ Ability to plan	☐ Count, observe, compile	☐ Design
☐ Results oriented	☐ Research	☐ Speak in public
☐ Customer Service oriented	☐ Detail-oriented	☐ Edit
☐ Supervise others	☐ Take inventory	☐ Write clearly
☐ Increase sales or efficiency	☐ Working with People	☐ Prefer details
☐ Accept responsibility	☐ Patient	☐ Understand the big picture
☐ Instruct others	☐ Care for	☐ Leadership
☐ Desire to learn & improve	☐ Persuasive	☐ Arrange social functions
☐ Good time management	☐ Confront others	☐ Motivate people
☐ Solve problems	☐ Pleasant	☐ Negotiate agreements
☐ Manage money/ budgets	☐ Counsel people	☐ Decisive
☐ Manage people	☐ Sensitive	☐ Plan
☐ Meet the public	☐ Demonstrate something	☐ Delegate
☐ Organize people	☐ Supportive	☐ Run meetings
☐ Organize/ manage projects	☐ diplomatic	☐ Direct others
☐ Team player	☐ Supervise	☐ Explain things to others
☐ Written communications	☐ Speak in public	☐ Self-motivated
☐ Work independently	☐ Help others	☐ Get results
☐ Computer Skills	☐ Tactful	☐ Share leadership
☐ Other Transferrable Skills (Dealing with things)	☐ Insightful	☐ Think of others
	☐ Insightful	☐ Direct projects
☐ Use my hands	☐ Teach	☐ Team builder
☐ Assemble or make things	☐ Interview others	☐ Solve problems
☐ Safety conscious	☐ Anticipate needs	☐ Mediate problems
☐ Build, observe, inspect things	☐ High energy	☐ Take risks
☐ Construct or repair	☐ Open minded	☐ Empowering others

☐ Off-bearing or feeding machinery	☐ Kind	☐ Creative, Artistic
☐ Follow instructions	☐ Take orders	☐ Artistic
☐ Operate tools and machinery	☐ Listen	☐ Music appreciation
☐ Drive or operate vehicles	☐ Serving	☐ Dance, body movement
☐ Repair things	☐ Trust	☐ Perform, act
☐ Good with my hands	☐ Working with others	☐ Draw, sketch, render
☐ Use complex equipment	☐ Negotiate	☐ Present artistic ideas
☐ Use equipment	☐ Understand	☐ Play instruments
☐ Dealing with Data	☐ Adaptable	☐ Expressive
☐ Analyze data or facts	☐ Outgoing	☐ Add any other Transferrable Skills that you think are important
☐ Investigate	☐ Using Words, Ideas	
☐ Audit records	☐ Articulate	
☐ Keep financial records	☐ Innovative	
☐ Locate answers or information	☐ Communicate verbally	
☐ Balance Money	☐ Logical	
☐ Calculate, compute	☐ Remember information	
☐ Manage money	☐ Accurate	

Trust

We've got to give a little to get a little. When we trust others, they begin to trust us. And vice versa.

Trust starts to develop before we reach age 1. Either we get our nurturing needs met, or we cry unattended. The response either way colors what we experience throughout our lives about trust. When we cried, did we get hugged or hit? Who was there for us when we needed them?

If a child's emotional needs are met, the child is able to develop trust. If a child grows up in an unstable environment, he develops attachment disorders or feels an attraction to unhealthy people.

Our relationship with trust shows us how we respond to life. Do we feel slighted, burned, hurt, ripped off or violated by an incident others are fine with? Do we react distrustfully and not know what we are reacting to? Or are we gullible, believing almost anyone and anything? Or do we have contempt prior to investigation?

If we show up at this party of life without the trust we need to fully participate, we are unprepared for human interactions. If we are savvy in our people skills and have a grip on what should happen in an interaction, we are more likely to get our needs met. But if we are easily offended, we should look at why we are so thin-skinned and ready to react negatively. If it feels like I have a target painted on me and everyone seems to hit a bull's-eye, I need to take the target off and work to build my interpersonal skills.

Key elements of trust include the willingness to be open, flexible, honest, and teachable – to have a beginner's mind. We must think of our own internal resistance as a positive force and as an accepted, normal stage in a time of change. We should also honor each other's inquisitive minds as others work to understand themselves.

We need to develop a moral and ethical compass that is not based on getting one over on anyone or making a fast buck in an unsustainable agreement. We should be forthcoming with helpful reminders to others, while avoiding half-truths or convenient omissions.

Our trust should begin and end with us, no matter how the other person responds. When we experience a conflict, we need to take a look at another's truth and have compassion for them. Trust is a process that is built upon little acts that lead us to gradually take bigger steps. It is only by acts of improper taking that trust is broken – taking advantage, taking for granted, taking what is not part of the deal. Life is never perfectly equal. Sometimes we will get more out of it than others. But if we hold onto the idea that abundance does not mean fear or scarcity, there is always enough if we also bring gratitude to the table – for ourselves and others.

It is important for us to move beyond another's inability to trust and to keep an open place for them. We must hold our ground and keep doing what we believe, with or without them. Let us provide a safe and stable platform for them to lean upon as they build their trust. We can be safe sponsors of new, trusting behaviors that may not reflect our exact truth. We need to leave room for others' truth, too. We must do no harm. We practice our trust skills because it's the right thing to do, and we receive joy from doing that.

We also must be forthright as another person gives trust her best shot. We can make decisions that prompt a symbiotic connection to create intimacy, especially if we don't currently get everything we want out of this relationship.

We have our own beliefs and rules that connect us and our society's ideas that govern our practices. To really develop trust, we must be willing and patient enough to bear witness to mistakes and interpretive nuances that create conflict. We can go beyond superficial impatience and buy into a longer view of what could develop when everyone ends their childish games and fear-based thinking.

One practice I employ is stating, "May I feel trust and peace. May my friends feel trust and peace. May my enemies feel trust and peace. Let there be trust on Earth, and let it begin with me, because I am a bad-ass peacekeeper."

What's needed most in the world is to let the people around us know we will make room for them to grow in a safe environment. Even though they feel they must advocate and demonstrate for their own position, welcome them to the fold. The circle of trust between humans is the greatest emblem of hope. If we do this for others, they will value trust more, as well as the society that enables them to regain it.

Workbook Questions:

1. In what ways can you build trust with others? What are you willing to offer in good faith as an asset?

2. In what ways do you require more from others because you do not trust? Do you have reservations about making a commitment without everything up front, where we take no chances?

3. What are your cultural beliefs about trust? Are they coming from a place of entitlement and privilege?

4. How might you distrust someone who comes from a different culture than yours?

5. What are you not willing to trust about your life partner, co-workers, or business associates?

6. How was your ability to trust broken when you were a child? In adolescence? In adulthood?

7. Do you believe everything you want to hear, even though you know you will be harmed? Are you like a gullible deer in the headlights? Do you set up the love in your life to fail? If so, why?

8. Provide three examples of where you currently see trust in your life.

9. What qualities can others always trust in their relationships with you?

10. In what ways do we feel slighted, burned, hurt, ripped off or violated by an incident that others are fine with?

11. How do we react distrustfully and not know what we are reacting to, stopping any connection of goodness from something that happened in the past? Or reacting from something that happened long ago?

12. With people in power or prestige, are we gullible, believing almost anyone and anything? Or how do we fight the other side, no matter what, because they are of another political party, financial system, or form of government, such as communism vs. democracy?

13. How do you come to most situations with gasoline and ammo, cocked and loaded with contempt prior to investigation?

Turn-Around Thinking

Sometimes we are quick to answer, and we assume we are right. We have contempt prior to investigation. We polarize our thoughts so our way works out, and others – oh, well, they have to suffer.

Through years of attaching to this mindset, we now believe what we have hardwired into our brains.

Consider this: What if there are simultaneous truths around us, and we need to up our game to fit in and be social? What will it take for you to consider your beliefs with a beginner's mind again, where you do not have to be right or defend your position? Our beliefs give us safety and comfort from the delusion that we have some control. We block other choices to eliminate confusion. While this is good for some issues, it has limits.

There is a human tendency to want to be right. Some of us believe that being wrong means we have lost power; that we will be harmed or violated, that we are stupid, or we will have to surrender to other truths. All of those areas are vulnerable and sensitive territory. We can be groundless and open and still have power while we honor the thoughts of another. Agree to disagree. Realize there are three sides: yours, mine, and the truth. Value and recognize that multiple truths can exist simultaneously.

If we make room for another person's truth that bears no resemblance to our own, what's the worst that could happen? We lose our position. We lose a relationship. We lose our job or our family's trust.

In what ways do we bring gasoline to the fire? The worst that could happen is we stay stuck and immobile in our thinking. We have the keys to our freedom. All that is required to unlock the door is to have a beginner's mind; stay open to suggestions; have a willingness to consider change, and remain teachable.

Why do we defend our truth?

Sometimes, I look like a hard and brittle-minded person who is not open to diversity and change. This can hurt me in my community. When we find ourselves able to have the last word on the weather, forecast the news, or solve a dilemma, we might start smelling that something just isn't right. Keep sniffing – it's bound to be us.

How can we keep safety in mind with another's views on religion, race, age, gender, society, guns? It's a big list to stay open about, but there is value in doing so.

We create the opportunity for discussion and a forum for change. By keeping ourselves open, we can observe without being the enemy. It's interesting to take a look at the new powers we have when we listen to others. They will say anything; all we have to do is ask. If we create a safe place, people will tell their truth. We have not given our thoughts to muddy the waters. We are active listeners, and by gentle mirroring, we can reflect others' thoughts back and let them — maybe for the first time — hear their own voices and thoughts. They can self-reflect on why they hold their ideas.

With our goal of keeping an open mind and noticing when we are getting triggered, we can turn poison into medicine and stop the downward spiral of our thoughts.

If we are negative-emoting, then judging the acts or beliefs of others is our comfort zone. It's easy and fun to look at what's wrong with something. Those who are good at it apply this skill in all areas of their lives. They are like Velcro for the bad things that happen to them and like Teflon for the good.

Does that describe you? Turn that thinking around. Notice when you do what you've always done. Recognize it for what it is worth and how it diminishes your position. Recover as a person of value, seeking positive solutions, goals and strategies. You may come up with a solution for climate change and save the planet!

When we globalize our words – "you always" or "you never" – we force the other person into a defensive mode that is most likely not accurate. Instead, use words with positive and hopeful intonation such as, "When you do this, I feel vulnerable." Notice how this emphasizes that we are the one having the feeling. This way, we're not coming from a place of blame for the way we feel inside. The inside stuff is our responsibility.

Act as if we are already where we want to be. Act as if the other person is already acting the way we want him to act. Stretch our brains into elastic openness. If we believe the war is over in our own minds, then the war is over. Others can feel their feelings, and we do not have to give our power away. Act "as if." Dress for the job you want, not the job you have. Fake it till you make it. Be the change you want to see.

When we are able to be the observers and detach with love, we can for the first time watch the others spin out of control and choose not to join them. This was our old behavior. With two people spiraling out of control, there is little hope for redemption.

We must be impeccable with our words, thoughts and deeds in everything we think, say and do, and be willing to make amends if we have done harm to another. We can write an Affirmation List that focuses on the healthy and hopeful ways something could turn out.

For practice, before you write down your first negative thought, begin with this: "I am so happy and grateful now that I feel safe and did not cause my loved ones any harm." Take your old behavior and turn it on its side. Start with your easily accessible sneers and passive-aggressive remarks, and turn the phrase into something positive.

Life is only as we see it. Most people are as happy as they choose to be. Life is a fragile and brief period we spend on the planet. Take each mindful breath, and Do No Harm.

Workbook Questions:

1. In what ways can you apply turn-around thinking in your life?

2. What thoughts do you believe that will never be able to be turned around? Why? Do you tire of carrying this burden around your neck and feeling deep thoughts while the other party has moved on, forgiven themselves and forgotten about you? Can you afford the luxury of carrying those heavy weights around?

3. If you are willing to try turn-around thinking first, do you think others might be willing to try it with you?

4. How would turn-around thinking help with your depression or anxiety?

5. In what ways can you turn your life around and be successful?

6. What old ways of thinking were you able to turn around in the past?

7. What would you like to happen in your life? What would it take to make that happen?

8. How does negative emoting keep you in a state of flux and inability?

9. Explain how you are sick and tired of accepting scraps from others.

Victims and Survivors

If you are a survivor of physical or emotional violence, abuse or harm, take all the time you need to practice extreme self-care, and get all the resources available to heal and recover. This is a lifetime journey, and every moment is precious. I encourage you to learn to create a healthy state of willingness to live in the sunlight of the spirit.

The language of violence and abuse has long been a problem. If someone harms or injures me, some might call me a "victim." But that implies that I'm powerless to overcome what was done to me. It defines me by the harmful actions of someone else. I much prefer the word "survivor," which tells me and the world that I may have been permanently changed by what happened to me, but I am much more than that one experience. As a survivor, I take back my power to choose who I will be and what I will do with my one and only life.

At times, being a "victim" instead of a "survivor" has been seductive for me. I was violated, so I deserved sympathy, didn't I? Morally, that feels attractive. At the beginning of my journey of recovery, my thoughts sometimes sounded like this: "Entitled, privileged, righteous! I was wronged. I was violated. It was personal! Can't you see the pain I'm in? If only you knew who I was, I would be treated differently! When will these injustices validate me and my suffering?"

But that way of thinking is its own prison. As the old saying goes, do you want to be "right," or do you want to be happy? These beliefs are sometimes ego-based attachment to what went wrong in one finite moment of our lives.

While you help yourself heal by practicing extreme self-care on a daily basis, you may become ready at some point to think about the person who harmed you. Understanding why the person harmed you sometimes can free you from anger, blame, hatred, resentment and other emotions that – when allowed to rage on and on unchecked – do nothing but burn your own energy.

So what about our perpetrators? Why do they hurt us? Did someone harm them first? If we eventually can find compassion for them, that may heal some of the dark energy inside us. Having been both the predator and the prey at different times of my life, I have learned to dance the thin, gossamer thread in between.

As a child, I learned to accept abusive treatment. My safety was taken away through abusive consequences for things I did. I was harmed and lived under the constant threat of punishment. This happened to me because it happened to my parent before me. We both are survivors of generational abuse.

Once I learned to accept abuse as a consequence for my choices, I grew older and began to confusedly apply this to other areas of my life. I began to overcompensate and expect bad things to happen. I even attracted negative consequences. We are sometimes responsible for things we attract in our lives by the way we internalize our experience. Think about these scenarios: persons who keep getting jobs where they are disrespected, over and over again. Persons who constantly attract abusive partners, because that is all they know how to attract. Persons who sabotage their own new opportunities by repeating the same behaviors. It becomes a lifestyle of hypochondria as we digest these negative thoughts and believe our own delusions.

I was beaten and sexually violated in my youth. At that age, I had no idea what it meant to do the work of healing as a resilient human. I did not know I was capable of great change. So I carried all that damage into every relationship. I had a tractor-trailer-load of ways I needed others to act so that I could feel safe. In my best efforts to create a healthy new relationship with a partner, friend or employer, I would keep others always on guard as my emotional hostages. I was never able to overcome my need for them to wrap their lives around my "wound channel." I was always vigilant, watching for their perceived wrongs, so I could point them out to protect myself. This was how, unbeknownst to me, I used my own learned helplessness to constantly build a community around me of family, co-workers and lovers who were enablers in my codependent quagmire.

Some people are "triple-diagnosed," as I was when I got into recovery. That means in addition to having mental-health and addiction issues, I also had chronic physical-health problems – hepatitis C and cirrhosis. This was a common outcome of years of living homeless with drug, alcohol and sex addictions as my only coping mechanisms.

With this combination of issues and no tools to handle them, I felt like I was being sucked into the La Brea Tar Pits, trying to move out of this infinite sadness with only my head sticking out, gasping for air and attention. I was pleading for help, but I never knew how to accept help when it actually arrived.

As a person with a big thermal signature on the planet, I used the resources available to an unhoused addict with untreated mental illness – although many of these resources are cogs in the recidivistic system that perpetuates the disease model.

I used hospital emergency rooms; behavioral-modification facilities; therapists; countless drug counselors; nutrition counselors; psychologists; psychiatrists, and doctors for tuberculosis and hepatitis C. I helped at least five dental students graduate by rebuilding my teeth during a 12-year period. Pro-bono lawyers resolved my tax mess with the IRS. I took five years out of the lives of both the IRS and the lawyers. Just think of all the government agencies that worked with me in this time period. A pro-bono lawyer helped me receive Supplemental Security Income. Getting SSI took four years; getting back off of it took another two years. Goodwill and the California Department of Rehabilitation trained me to be employable. I used all the Twelve Step programs, going to thousands of meetings of Alcoholics Anonymous, Narcotics Anonymous, Sex and Love Addicts Anonymous, and Underearners Anonymous. Countless sponsors are part of my journey to become who I am today.

Our work is to learn new ways to take responsibility for what happens to us. We can let go of these attachments to our DIS-EASE and allow true healing to take place.

In the United States, we are told we have the right to freedom and the pursuit of happiness. We sometimes seem to believe this entitles us to constant, uninterrupted happiness. It does not. "Happiness," however you define it, is something that comes and goes. Our culture looks at pain as a disease to be cured, rather than as a naturally occurring part of the human experience.

It doesn't help that we live in a culture of entitlement and privilege gone astray. We lay all of our personal damage against a broader belief system with high expectations of total control and a refusal to accept what is. At the same time, the bully mentality of "canceling," or casting out, public figures for their questionable choices gets a lot more attention than the unglamorous daily work of wholesome discipline, self-care, amends and redemption.

So many people really need help and cannot access it because of the racist, classist barriers of our culture. Applying a thin layer of nonprofit organizations and volunteers over the top of that gutted infrastructure doesn't help. I'm not talking about doing some perceived kind act once a month to make you feel better about yourself. I'm talking educating ourselves about the realities of our system and then demanding real justice and democracy for those who deserve it. We have to be able to have these difficult conversations and develop dialogue and critical thinking with non-violent language that creates equity.

We have to be willing, as survivor and predator, to realize the flaws of our dualistic system. The idea of one person being virtuous and another being a demon perpetuates this fraudulent way of life.

What do you have to lose by letting go of the victim mentality? Can you stop being "judge, jury and self-appointed executioner" under the guise of being a victim? What are you willing to do? What would happen if you dropped your weapons? Who would you be without this fear-based thinking?

As I live my life with these tenets, I am a vulnerable and sensitive person who knows who, what and where I am in this three-dimensional chessboard of life. Just for today, you can hold onto the short-term pleasure you receive from eliciting sympathy against perceived injustices and demonizing others. Or, you can let it go and accept life on life's terms. All people have the capacity to change their thinking.

When you start to be drawn one way or another about emotionally draining subjects, and you feel something is not quite right, start sniffing around. This is the opportunity for change.

In this quest, we are moving from helplessness to hopefulness, from passivity to a pro-active stance, from pessimism to optimism, from negative emoting to positive visualization, from shame and guilt to doing estimable acts for healthy self-esteem. We are striving to move from self-blame to positive self-image by acts of radical kindness and unconditional positive regard for ourselves and others.

When you live your life for the benefit of others, only then are you heading toward a safer future for all. Both sides have a lot of work to do. But this is the path we can take.

Workbook Questions:

1. How are you sometimes stubborn with a brittle viewpoint? Why do you dismiss possible solutions? Can you implement self-change thoughts that require you to accept constructive criticism from those who care enough to give a damn about you? Take ownership of your thoughts. Be responsible, and process your grief and loss. It's OK to feel the way you feel, but you do not have to keep this thinking forever, if it stops working for you.

2. When you begin negative emoting, is it hard to quit defending a broken-down lifespan of woes and mistrust? If we focus only on the bad things, then we are re-enforcing and attracting bad things to us. This thinking creates your self-fulfilling prophecies. What have you done in the past to interrupt this tendency? Can you write a list of positive qualities to equalize the bad thoughts about the person, place or thing? Can you imagine, for a moment, what it might be like to experience the other's lifestyle and the choices they made, and why they would make those choices to survive? Why or why not?

3. Can you create mindful, solution-focused alternatives; healthy choices; coping mechanisms, and survival strategies to create equity and safety for yourself and others in the future? Can you process this terrible thing and move forward with forgiveness? Do you understand the reasons both for and against it?

4. How can you move beyond personalizing, globalizing, awfulizing and demonizing the other party? What is the gray area we can all inhabit in between?

5. What can you do to claim your power that does not require blaming or punishing someone else? Can you consider the possibility that the perpetrator needed help before they committed the crime they are serving time for? Why or why not? Which came first, the chicken or the egg?

6. What lifestyle choices can you develop to help you move beyond keeping yourself down and being helpless, or living in fear of something happening again?

7. How can you become curious about experimenting with new, fearless actions that might lead you into that job you want, the peace of mind you need, or that relationship that requires you to act and think differently?

8. Even if you live in a system that violates the tenets of socio-economic opportunities, what longer view can you take? Can you create a five-year plan that gives you time to build small habits that develop into more complex practices, which in turn lead to longevity with peace of mind and acceptance of what is?

9. How can we let go of this learned, internalized oppression and blame and focus instead on praise and gratitude for the things we do have?

10. What are you willing to do to be morally responsible without judging others? How can you use your good sense to achieve your own happiness, peace of mind, and safety?

11. How can we stop painting a target on ourselves and taking blows that are really not ours to take?

12. In Tai chi, you bend and move your mind and body, so people's energy and momentum flow by you like the wind through a willow tree and do no harm. It creates the need for the perpetrator to make a change so they do not lose their balance, keeping the burden of change in the hands of the emotionally escalated person. How would this help you?

13. In Taekwondo, you turn your energy in and around and walk with the other person's energy. You are taking a walk with them, side by side, instead of trying to stop their energy. When you are walking together with a person's energy, it is easier to say, "My, you have a lot of stuff going on here. What would you like to do to take care of yourself, instead of making it all about me?" How would this help you?

Warning Signs

It's Valentine's Day. You want sugar, but you're diabetic.

It's New Year's Eve, and everybody is drinking to celebrate. Why can't I?

Someone upsets me, and I choose to get angry. The chemical cascade of emotions in my brain wants retribution and payback.

Warning signs, triggers, things we deem unforgiveable, personal slights, feeling unheard. Ominous frustration, holding others emotional hostage. Horny, hungry, angry, lonely, tired. Burnout.

We thought once we started our road to recovery, the world should pay attention and cut us more slack, because it's hard for us to change.

We need to have a sense of urgency to recognize, resist and recover ourselves, but we feel weak, threatened and/or vulnerable.

We may have recovered from our drug of choice, but we are still vulnerable to all the reasons that led us to use. We are sensitive and don't have great coping mechanisms. Some of us still have targets painted on our backs, and people seem to hit a bulls-eye on our emotions every time.

If we do not want to relapse, we need to see all the ways living life on life's terms makes us act out emotionally and feel vulnerable. We want to understand how threats exist in our lives.

There are times that when it looks like we might make it, we end up relapsing into old ways. We may not use or drink again, but we might as well be a "dry drunk," because we are doing everything except drink.

When we are lonely, instead of making an effort to meet people the old-fashioned way, we try to circumvent. We try a dating service. We are still unhealed but expect that everyone will accept us exactly as we said we are on our dating profile. We offer people a box of chocolates, but we're not honest about what is in the box.

We need to be hyper-vigilant with our fragile recovery and emotional changes. Our support groups and families have given us so much — let's really do this thing right.

The reason we stay close to our recovery community is because they can call us on our stuff when we act out. We trust their hard-won advice.

When we got loaded in the past, we received immediate gratification for our convenient effort. All of our troubles were gone for a few hours. Now we have a lifetime of repairing all of that damage. Yes, it's our choice, but here is where many give up and relapse.

Take the longer view — the five-year plan — before giving up.

If you hang around with crappy people, you start feeling crappy. We don't need to visit old friends and think we have to be sexual. If the issue is food, we need to make a thousand choices each time we eat; it's hard to do the right thing when we're alone, so we eat with people we trust.

The reason we try to do our recovery 24/7 is because we need to do positive things to replace the years of making bad choices 24/7. The truth is that not everyone makes it. If we want to be one who does, we'd better do our recovery like we did our addiction — 24/7.

There are big warnings. Look at this roadmap as an example of what to look for:

You saw your old girlfriend or buddy lately, and they are looking good. They're happy and miss you. They look as if they are fine with their casual using, but you know you can't casually use. You go by that place, or other places, and can't help but reminisce about the years you spent having fun there. You know if you stop and go in, you're going to get loaded.

Or, something happens to knock you off track, and you lose your composure. Then you get frustrated and want to act out in your old ways, which include self-medicating the way you know will work. It's attractive and immediate gratification, but it leads you back into incomprehensible demoralization when you come down.

So watch out for people, places and things that are triggers waiting to be pulled.

When we stop going to meetings and stop calling our colleagues daily to check in, we are in dangerous waters. When we stop doing self-care, miss therapy appointments, and make our depression more important than our need to recover, we are in dangerous territory.

Take an inventory right here and now: Are you a dry drunk or "dry drug-of-choice" person? Are you doing all the same ol' behaviors but without using? Are you getting triggered by life on life's terms? Do you exhibit no coping skills; act out miserable behaviors, and stress out your loved ones and colleagues with negative emoting?

We start thinking this stage is all recovery is, but alas — it's just the first step. If we stop growing here, we are in trouble. Recovery is a daily commitment, one day at a time, 24/7. We try to replace our 24 hours with recovery ideals. When we were swimming in our addictions, we committed a considerable amount of time to our behaviors. Let's do the same with our recovery time right now, and swim in a new pool.

Another warning sign is that you see someone from the old crowd, and they are so happy to see you. They miss you dearly and catch you up on all the high-maintenance drama going on with all your old friends. It's provocative and alluring. You feel you can resist anything but this temptation. As a result, you start to romanticize about the "good 'ol daze."

Stop! Save your ass! Call someone, get to a meeting and tattle on yourself. This is how we stop recidivism — we stay hooked up to our new network and book-end with our sponsor. We tell somebody our next moves, and stay accountable.

The biggest sign of relapse is when we start to think, "Yeah, I've got this thing licked. I will take control of my life again. I don't need all these trappings to stay sober." Slowly, we stop calling people; start missing appointments; make excuses for not going to meetings, and start slipping back into the well-accessorized rut we know and can defend so well. Hell, we've spent most of our lives defending this way of life; it's what we know best. We start abandoning our new lives and new-found recovery ideals, making excuses for why we don't need to do recovery. We stop hanging with our recovery posse, because we're not like those people after all.

If you are starting to reconnect with old friends, longing and feeling romantic about the old days, thinking you can do your addiction safely now that you have some tools, and start to grab the steering wheel of your old life again, WATCH OUT.

Complicated and mixed emotions follow. You start stressing out and feeling lonely and depressed. People start letting you down again, and you will return to a fatalistic way of thinking. Before you know it, you will be back in the "good 'ol daze," ready for the perfect storm and relapse. You'd better call somebody!

Workbook Questions:

1. Name your warning signs, the ones you know are your signs of danger.

2. What are neighborhoods you need to stay out of? Which friends do you need to stay away from?

3. What triggers you emotionally, stresses you out, and makes you want to crawl into a hole and die?

4. Do you fight with your loved ones or feel unsafe? If yes, in what ways?

5. Do you have issues at work that seem insurmountable? What are they?

6. In what ways are you like a "dry drunk" — you're not using, but your behavior is not fun to be around?

7. In what ways do you know you are in danger? What do you do to save yourself? Whom do you call? Where do you go?

8. When you miss your regular group meeting, what do you discuss with your sponsor?

9. In what ways can you handle "constructive criticism" and use your emotional intelligence to move beyond the struggle to return to your old life? How do you get back into feeling safe and trusting your emotions again?

10. In what positive ways do you do preventive measures to create longevity in your recovery?

11. In what ways do you grab the steering wheel of your life and forget to surrender and be in acceptance of what is?

12. In what ways do you use your support groups or spiritual groups and stay transparent with your need for accountability?

Wholesome Discipline

Wholesomeness comes from a moving target of choices.

What are healthy choices we can make today? What is on the menu of options?

Options can change things we know how to do, or things we are willing to try as we get more established and trust that doing the next right thing is valuable. Given options, we are more likely to proceed.

If we work with the collective good in mind, we can ask for anything we want. This is wholesome: common good, awareness of others, sharing openly. When we live our life with those values, we give worth to moral wellness, ethical ideals, sound and virtuous being. If more people lived with those sorts of ideals, there would be more advantageous nourishment in both mind and body.

Try to do one good thing, instead of focusing our lives on what we do that is not healthy, such as overeating, gambling, sex addictions, anger, violence, drug and alcohol addiction, shopping, and obsessive-compulsive disorders. We can do a simple task that is headed toward eliciting self-change thinking.

Self-change thinking doesn't come about by obsessing constantly about what we are doing wrong. The internalized shame that comes with it becomes the mark of our character. Self-change happens when the "value that we do have to give, no matter how small," is measured as being worth more than all the gold in the world.

The path to healing is paved with small act after small act — doing the next right thing and then the next right thing. That is how we effect permanent, positive change in our lives and in our world.

If we begin now, that is the greatest gift we can give ourselves: self-worth and self-dignity.

Workbook Questions:

1. What can you do that is good for you and does not hurt another?
2. In what ways do you nurture your community?
3. How do you feel about the kind of healthy discipline that is a choice?
4. Name some of your wholesome disciplines.
5. How can you find community where you fit in? In what ways can you thrive with them?
6. What are some consistent, healthy ways you take care of yourself?
7. How do you fill your 24 hours every day with healthy choices? In what positive ways do they affect the people around you?
8. What bad habits do you have that can benefit from your transferrable skill sets and put ideal values into motion?
9. What helpful ideas do you have about wholesome disciplines and how they have brought value into your life?
10. If you knew someone who was stuck with your former ways of thinking, how would you help them to see how fortunate the effect would be on everyone around them if only they gave it a try?

Epilogue

"Treasure Chest of Wellness" was the result of years of writing my experiences and sharing them with clients and groups in the Chemical Dependency-Intensive Outpatient program I ran in California. It was the culmination of my own recovery journey, begun more than 20 years ago in a detox in San Francisco.

Recently, I moved from the San Francisco Bay Area to Northern Michigan. I've been thinking a lot about how some Americans know states like Michigan only as places they see from airplanes while flying from coast to coast. My wife and I have moved from the urban Bay Area to a rural part of a "Flyover State" … from a "blue" part of the U.S. to a "red" part.

This move has inspired me to write a book for Americans based upon the separations caused by our belief systems. I am excited to tackle these issues, such as race and political propaganda, that divide our nation. The new book will deal with all the reasons we don't communicate skillfully about emotionally charged subjects. I will strive to share a menu of options, choices and survival strategies to start the conversation on an individual level and keep it going.

Don't sink the relationships in your life. This is the precious time we have left to change our collective consciousness and become brothers and sisters taking our precious breaths on this planet. We deserve to honor each other and work together on our collective legacy of empowerment. No one gets out of here alive. We will all suffer from things that happen to us, but it's our choice to learn how to suffer less by surrendering the impulses that we can control.

Needless to say, we people in the "Flyover States" have needs and thoughts like everyone else. We need representation that is just and fair to build equity and worth. My working title for the book is "Flyover States of Mind." It will deal with many frustrating and irritating issues caused by the dualism of our country. I have chosen about 60 subjects that separate us as a country – and healing actions we can take. We all deserve to believe in each other, be proud of each other and honor the best we can all aspects of our diversity. We are the biggest melting pot of diverse cultures on the planet, and all of us (except the Native Americans we displaced) arrived here from somewhere else.

See you soon with the blessings of the future!

Acknowledgements

Our expressions in this life are a reflection of everything we have been exposed to, good or bad. I would like to honor all the people from the streets where I was homeless for many years. They had street smarts and survival skills. They made hard choices to live or die, and that takes a lot of moxie and courage. Many of them lost hope and died unrequited. This book was written to help people find their own resilience and overcome all obstacles in their lives.

Thanks to the incredible Kathryn Sterbenc and Heidi Wallenborn, who helped edit my scribbles into intellectual property of value. Thanks to Dariah Lacey for formatting this into a beautiful manuscript.

I would like to thank the clients with whom I worked for 10 years. They helped me to dial in and create this client-centered, person-centered book, with worksheets that anyone can do for themselves, and anyone can understand. This book is now also a tool that anyone can use to support another suffering person, thanks to my hard-working clients.

This book would not be possible without the skills and creative talent of a number of people who created a multitude of Evidence-Based Practices, including Harm Reduction, Motivational Conversations, Cognitive Behavioral Techniques, Rational Emotive Therapies, Mindfulness Practices, Dialectical Behavioral Techniques, and the Buddhist practice of conscious endeavors to overcome all obstacles and be in accordance with acceptance, if nothing can be done. Non-violent communication, anger management, parenting, relapse prevention and all the therapies used for all diagnostic predictors help empower our clients to be inherent beings of worth and value who give back to our society.

I would like to thank Pema Chödrön, my spiritual teacher and the inspiration to change my whole life and ways of thinking, communicating and creating wellness with any community, because of the openness and skilled demeanors she espouses. I would like to thank my Soka Gakkai Buddhist community for always helping me to be the most useful and service-minded citizen of the world, in touch with all aspects of well-being and aspirations to happiness and abundance for all.

Through the support and guidance from my team at Fremont Hospital in Fremont, Calif., I was encouraged to explore and create new strategies that worked for the clients, not just rote, one-trick repetitions of a single paradigm. Our mental-health and addiction clients are the real teachers, guiding us to what would help them to overcome their own dilemmas. Each one of us has all the answers to all of our own problems, if we use our challenges as opportunities to evoke self-change.

The information in this book is available only because of the hard work and research of many people working in the industry, as well as the tried-and-true success of people who have overcome all obstacles in their lives with addiction and mental-health diagnoses.

Thank you for the nurturing help and support of so many individuals at Fremont Hospital in Fremont, Calif., including Mary Jennings, PsyD; Krysta Crames, MPA; Dr. Thanh Nguyen; Marlon Rollins, PhD, and Bethany Nance, MFT. Thank you to the skilled healers who helped save my life during my early recovery, and whom I am now proud to consider friends and esteemed colleagues, including Wayne Garcia and Tamara Tucker of the former Walden House (now Health-

RIGHT 360); and Mena Zaminsky, Dee-Dee Stout and Tandy Iles, all of whom taught me at City College of San Francisco. Thank you to the medical professionals who worked to rid my body of hepatitis C and also helped me survive the treatment and its side effects, particularly Kimberly Cusato, M.D., of Kaiser Permanente and Diana Sylvestre, M.D., of Oasis Clinic in Oakland, Calif. And sincere thanks to Pete Walker, M.A., MFT, for allowing me to include his powerful "13 Steps for Managing Flashbacks" in this book.

Finally, I would like to thank the friends, family and neighbors who trusted me to impart my thoughts during our mutual dilemmas and create a safe place to live together. Thanks, Dino Santamaria, Dwight Ost, Linda Ost, James Anderson, Simon Michael, David Kriozere, C.J. Hayden, Ed Sterbenc and Cathy Fitzgerald.

This book could not have been written without the love of my beautiful wife, Kathryn Sterbenc, and my loving and supportive family, especially my parents, Lester and Alice Kowalski; my sister, Kathryn Kowalski; and the loving memory of my deceased brother, Mark Kowalski, who helped me to understand that simply being a brother is more important than being an addiction counselor. I was finally able to be his loving brother, with no expectations or agenda. Thank you, brother.

Made in the USA
Middletown, DE
05 September 2022